NATIVE AMERICAN LANDMARKS AND FESTIVALS

A Traveler's Guide to Indigenous United States and Canada

ABOUT THE AUTHORS

Yvonne Wakim Dennis is an award-winning author of non-fiction books for children and adults, many coauthored with Arlene Hirschfelder, including Visible Ink Press' *Native American Almanac*. An avid multiculturalist, Dennis interweaves environmental justice into all she writes. Although most of her publications have been about Indigenous peoples of the United States, she has also penned books about the diverse cultures of America. She serves as the Education Director for the Children's Cultural Center of Native America and is a board director of Nitchen, Inc., an advocacy organization for Indigenous families in the New York City metropolitan area. She is a multicultural consultant for businesses, schools, and publishers and is a columnist for *Native Hoop Magazine*. In 2014, Dennis received the National Arab American Museum's Best Children's Book of the Year Honor (for *A Kid's Guide to Arab American History*), a Sanaka Award, and the David Chow Humanitarian Award.

Arlene Hirschfelder is the author or editor of over 25 books about Native peoples, including the *Native American Almanac, Native Americans: A History in Pictures* and *The Extraordinary Book of Native American Lists*. She and Yvonne Dennis have authored five books together, including the award-winning *Children of Native America Today* and *A Kid's Guide to Native American History*. She worked at the Association on American Indian Affairs (a civil rights organization), for over 20 years and has years of experience consulting with publishers, museums, schools, and universities. In addition to being an author, Hirschfelder has co-curated exhibits at the Sequoyah National Research Center in Little Rock, Arkansas, and the Mitchell Museum of the American Indian in Evanston, Illinois.

NATIVE AMERICAN LANDMARKS and FESTIVALS

A Traveler's Guide to
Indigenous United States and Canada

Yvonne Wakim Dennis and Arlene Hirschfelder

VISIBLE INK PRESS

Detroit

Visible Ink Press®
43311 Joy Rd., #414
Canton, MI 48187-2075

Visible Ink Press is a registered trademark of Visible Ink Press LLC.

Most Visible Ink Press books are available at special quantity discounts when purchased in bulk by corporations, organizations, or groups. Customized printings, special imprints, messages, and excerpts can be produced to meet your needs. For more information, contact Special Markets Director, Visible Ink Press, www.visibleink.com, or 734-667-3211.

Managing Editor: Kevin S. Hile
Art Director: Mary Claire Krzewinski
Typesetting: Marco DiVita
Proofreaders: Larry Baker and Shoshana Hurwitz
Indexer: Larry Baker

Front cover image: Bears Ears National Monument (Shutterstock).

Back cover images: Cerni Museum (Ekke [Wikicommons]), Trail of Tears sign (Yam Nahar), Dartmouth Powwow (Šarūnas Burdulis).

Cataloging-in-Publication Data is on file at the Library of Congress.

10 9 8 7 6 5 4 3 2 1

Printed in the United States of America.

CONTENTS

Contents

CANADA

PHOTO SOURCES

Aesopposea (Wikicommons): p. 120.

Ah-Tah-Thi-Ki Museum: p. 49.

Allen4names (Wikicommons): p. 305.

Americasroof (Wikicommons): p. 29.

Ammodramus (Wikicommons): p. 139.

Joe and Janette Archie: p. 279 (top).

Lee. D. Baker, Duke University: p. 17.

John D. Barbry: p. 65.

Michael Barera: p. 265.

Jennifer Billie: p. 42.

Bill Reid Gallery of Northwest Coast Art: p. 389 (top).

Andreas F. Borchert: p. 190.

Boyd's Cove Beothuk Interpretation Centre: p. 333.

Joel Bradshaw: p. 322.

James Brooks: p. 276.

Jeff Brunton: p. 208.

Sarunas Burdulis: p. 19.

Canadian2006: pp. 372, 273.

Carptrash (Wikicommons): p. 41.

Cculber007 (Wikicommons): p. 57.

Jeff Clemmons: p. 61.

Steve Colwill: p. 348.

Csmith/dbb1 (Wikicommons): p. 58.

Daderot (Wikicommons): pp. 14, 389 (bottom).

Kenneth Darland: p. 94.

Yvonne Wakim Davis: pp. 88, 342.

Jeffrey M. Dean: p. 131.

Roger Dennis: p. 341.

Ebyabe (Wikicommons): p. 50.

Ekke (Flickr): p. 326.

Chris English: pp. 172, 219.

Ian Freeman: p. 380.

Jean Gagnon: pp. 357, 358.

Gillfoto (Wikicommons): p. 283.

Gooseterrain (Wikicommons): p. 141.

Government & Heritage Library, State Library of North Carolina: p. 75.

Susan Guice: p. 66.

Gutworth (Wikicommons): p. 106.

Hakkun (Wikicommons): p. 92.

Jim Hammer: p. 96.

Hans-Jürgen Hübner: pp. 383, 387.

Rhonda Humphreys: p. 89.

Jamestown-Yorktown Foundation: p. 86.

Ethan Jarrett: p. 46.

JustSomePics (Wikicommons): p. 340.

Doug Kerr: p. 34.

Ketchikanadian (Wikicommons): p. 279 (bottom).

Khayman (Wikicommons): p. 356.

Jan Kronsell: p. 74.

Kwanlin Dün Cultural Centre: p. 381.

Library of Congress: pp. 168, 263.

Lordkinbote (Wikicommons): p. 281.

Lumbee Homecoming: p. 78.

Ken Lund: p. 250.

Joe Mabel: p. 64.

Thomas R Machnitzki: p. 48.

Martin1971 (Wikicommons): p. 192.

Barb Mathers: p. 179.

McGhiever (Wikicommons): p. 111.

Dan McIsaac: p. 337.

Mobilis in Mobili (Wikicommons): p. 86.

Monti 102 (Wikicommons): p. 327.
Moondigger (Wikicommons): p. 201.
Museum of Ojibwe Culture: p. 105.
Yam Nahar: p. 43.
National Gallery of Canada: p. 344.
Niagara66 (Wikicommons): p. 115.
Nk'Mip Desert Cultural Centre: 386.
NovaScotia.com: p. 336.
W. Nowicki: p. 323.
Nowosielski (Wikicommons): p. 379.
Olekinderhook (Wikicommons): p. 51.
Andrew Otto: p. 274.
Owen (Wikicommons): p. 385.
P199 (Wikicommons): p. 351.
Panoramique (Wikicommons): p. 320.
Mike Peel: p. 194.
Penobscot Museum Nation: p. 10.
John Phelan: p. 37.
Pjposullivan: p. 347.
Pjsham (Wikicommons): p. 122.
Qias (Wikicommons): p. 339.
Thomas Quine: p. 25.
Daniel Ramirez: p. 316.
Dustin M. Ramsey: p. 9.
Jeffry Reed: p. 45.
RicegoneWILD (Wikicommons): p. 306.
Graham Richard: p. 277.
D. Gordon E. Robertson: p. 352.
Herb Roe: pp. 71, 82.
Bernt Rostad: p. 271.
Royalbroil (Wikicommons): pp. 102, 174.
Bob Rulz (Wikicommons): p. 366.
Runner1928 (Wikicommons): p. 110.
Benjamin Schleifman: p. 270.
Elliot Schwartz for StudioEIS: p. 5.
SeanMD80 (Wikicommons): p. 195
Shutterstock: pp. 1, 12, 16, 22, 26, 101, 176, 183, 184, 199, 205, 206, 209, 214, 216, 222, 223, 224, 227, 230, 232, 233, 234, 236, 239, 241, 243, 245, 247, 252, 255, 258, 261, 268, 289, 294, 299, 300, 301, 312, 313, 318, 321, 325, 329, 350, 354, 361, 362, 365, 369.
Eileen Soler: p. 42
Bernard Spragg: p. 324.
David Stanley: p. 384.
Brian Stansberry: pp. 83, 84, 85.
Steelyken (Wikicommons): p. 54.
St. Nin (Wikicommons): p. 59.
Rob Stutz: 178.
Tom W. Sulcer: p. 21.
Sulfur (Wikicommons): p. 130.
Matthias Süszen: p. 367.
Mykola Swarnyk: p. 346.
Thivierr (Wikicommons): p. 363.
Ken Thomas: p. 364.
Thomas200 (Wikicommons): p. 55.
Toohool (Wikicommons): p. 293.
Thomas Tunsch: p. 315.
U.S. Department of Agriculture: p. 6.
U.S. Forest Service: p. 185.
U.S. Mint: p. 99.
U.S. National Park Service: pp. 15, 108, 112, 137, 188.
Veilenser (Wikicommons): p. 13.
Zachary Williams: p. 77.
WinterCity296 (Wikicommons): p. 377.
Woodland Cultural Center: p. 343
Don Woods: p. 11.
Catherine Wright and A Wandering Wombat: p. 73.
Ymblanter (Wikicommons): p. 181.
Zeph77 (Wikicommons): p. 38.
Public domain: pp. 39, 69, 114, 119, 308, 370, 382, 390.

ACKNOWLEDGMENTS

Wado to all the folks who were so kind and helpful with research, inter-views, guided tours, photos and lots of support: Eddie LaGuerre, Laura Buckley, Derek Bryson, Jennifer Billie, Eileen Soler, Anna Mullican, Cindy Lavallee, Janet H. Wiley, Deanna Wampler, Danisse Neashit, Rhonda Bathurst, Sandra McDonald, Bonnie-Lou Ferris, John D. Barbry, Carrie Dilley, Carla Hilde-brand, Helene Scivoli, Susan Guice, Bank Street Writers Lab, and many oth-ers. Wanishi to Docs Levine and Ament, Dawi Winston for the healing. Gracias to my sister-friend, Arlene Hirschfelder, my adored coauthor. Danke to Roger Jänecke and Kevin Hile for working with us again! Shukran to Roger Dennis, my wonderful, helpful husband. I thank you all in several languages! I ask forgiveness for any mistakes I may have made.

—Yvonne Wakim Dennis

Special thanks to my co-author, Yvonne Wakim Dennis, who is a pleasure to work with; Beverly Singer for sharing her knowledge about landmarks in the Southwest and Pacific Coast states; and Bill Hanson and Kate Troll for shar-ing their extensive knowledge about Alaska landmarks. I am indebted to dozens of people at museums, cultural centers, and other sites who patiently answered my questions. Thanks to our publisher, Roger Janecke, and editor, Kevin Hile, for their commitment to publishing *Native American Landmarks and Festivals*. Finally, thanks to Dennis Hirschfelder (again) for his boundless support.

—Arlene Hirschfelder

ALSO FROM VISIBLE INK PRESS

African American Almanac: 400 Years of Triumph, Courage and Excellence
by Lean'tin Bracks, Ph.D.
ISBN: 978-1-57859-323-1

Black Firsts: 4,000 Ground-Breaking and Pioneering Events, 3rd edition
by Jessie Carney Smith
ISBN: 978-1-57859-369-9

Black Heroes
by Jessie Carney Smith
ISBN: 978-1-57859-136-7

Freedom Facts and Firsts: 400 Years of the African American Civil Rights Experience
by Jessie Carney Smith and Linda T Wynn
ISBN: 978-1-57859-192-3

The Handy African American History Answer Book
by Jessie Carney Smith
ISBN: 978-1-57859-452-8

The Handy American History Answer Book
by David L Hudson, Jr.
ISBN: 978-1-57859-471-9

The Handy History Answer Book, 3rd edition
by David L Hudson, Jr.
ISBN: 978-1-57859-372-9

The Handy Islam Answer Book
by John Renard, Ph.D.
ISBN: 978-1-57859-510-5

Native American Almanac: More Than 50,000 Years of the Cultures and Histories of Indigenous Peoples
By Yvonne Wakim Dennis, Arlene Hirschfelder, and Shannon Rothenberger Flynn
ISBN: 978-1-57859-608-9

Please visit us at www.visibleinkpress.com.

INTRODUCTION

Indigenous peoples have been involved with tourism since they first hosted guests through exploratory and early colonial encounters, yet Indigenous ownership and control of such venues is a relatively new phenomenon worldwide. Indigenous tourism encompasses a wide range of experiences, including cultural tourism, ecotourism, adventure tourism, gaming, resorts, and other related services.... Beyond a purely economic analysis, tourism can be a catalyst for cultural perpetuation, the protection of natural resources, and an instrument of community pride and building bridges between peoples.

—Alexis Celeste Bunten, PhD (Aleut/Yup'ik)

Federal governments in Canada and the United States have both passed laws supporting cultural tourism in Native communities as a viable method to improve the economy for Indigenous peoples. The plan is for Native communities, tribal entities, to present their cultures in a way that is appropriate, respectful, and accurate while earning income. Some call it ecotourism; others refer to it as cultural tourism; and still others call it experiential tourism. Across the two countries, visitors can choose from a vast array of adventures associated with Indigenous cultures: dog sledding; camping in a tipi; hunting and fishing expeditions; exploring museums, ancient buildings and rock art; researching Indigenous history with the people descended from that history; creating art; herbal walks; building and sailing in canoes; hiking along ancient routes; festivals; powwows; and preparing and eating Native foods. In addition, tourists can experience activities at Native-owned vineyards, hotels, water parks, sports complexes, rodeos, campsites, casinos and resorts that feature fine dining, and an incredible variety of entertainment. Indigenous points of view are voiced in state and federal parks, federal and international heritage sites, public and private museums, and non-Native events that include Indigenous collaboration. Wherever possible, we have cited contemporary events like film festivals, book fests, and award ceremonies.

We have included sites that welcome visitors. Some Native landmarks are holy lands, where ceremonies have been observed at the same sacred place for thousands of years. Rituals practiced by Hindus, Jews, Muslims, and others can be observed any place in the world. Because of federal policies, today many Indigenous ceremonial grounds are located in public parks or buried under manmade lakes created by the U.S. Army Corps of Engineers in spite of protests from Native nations. When traveling to ancient sites, keep in mind that you may happen upon a ritual; take care not to disturb participants or treat the sacred rite as a tourist attraction. And always leave the place as pristine as you can.

Out of respect for First Peoples, we did not feature many "tourist attractions" like battlegrounds or sacred burial sites. Eurocentric language, which is most accepted in popular culture, usually defines a battle as a "victory" if Anglos won and a "massacre" if Indigenous people won. And in most "battles" Native people were trying to defend their homelands and families. Defense of homelands is central to American patriotism and often used to rationalize battles on foreign soil, but history has not given Native people that same consideration. For these reasons, you will only find selected iconic battlefields described in this book. The book is organized by country, region, state, and province or territory, and alphabetically by town, city, or other locale where the landmark, festival, or event is located. Each region begins with an overview. Under each town are entries of the places to visit in the area. Each entry ends with an "Info" section with addresses, phone numbers, and websites whenever available. Some sites are so remote that there are no addresses listed, so it is important to check the websites before embarking on a journey to America Samoa or the Far North!

In the back of the book, you will find further resources, as well as a helpful description of powwow etiquette for those unfamiliar with these ceremonies. For making your visit as complete as possible, contact individual nations for events, historic sites, and proper etiquette when visiting. For Native visitors, customs change from nation to nation, so it's important to give a last-minute check when traveling to a new place.

The United States has territories populated by Indigenous people that are now under the administration of the U.S. The state of Hawaii has a strong Indigenous presence as do the U.S. territories of American Samoa, Guam, the Commonwealth of the Northern Mariana Islands (CNMI) and other Pacific Islands. Like Alaska Natives and American Indians, they have a special political and legal relationship with the federal government because of their status as Indigenous peoples who once exercised full sovereignty in areas that are now part of the United States. Puerto Rico is also a U.S. territory; the island abounds with Taino history, sites, and culture.

North America includes twenty-three countries and nine dependent territories; this book only focuses on Canada and the United States. We apologize. Hopefully, someday there will be a landmarks book, volume two, so the Indigenous sites of the rest of North America will be honored. There are a few listings of events organized by Americans who descend from Indigenous communities in other parts of the Americas. More information about these groups is described in *Native American Almanac: More Than 50,000 Years of the Cultures and Histories of Indigenous Peoples* (Visible Ink Press), which would be a perfect companion book for this guide. The borders that mark the United States and Canada are fairly recent in the long history of Native peoples and historically had nothing to do with first communities and territories. Celebrations like Día de Muertos observed in many American communities can be traced to a centuries-old Aztec festival. People now labeled Americans or Canadians or Mexicans are often members of Indigenous groups that traveled freely among the three countries plus many other nations that mark today's maps.

Many Americans and Canadians are familiar with casinos on Indian lands but know little about the enduring and vibrant heritage of their Native hosts. Whether it's the annual All Indian Rodeo in Las Vegas, Nevada, or a dog-sledding trek in Arctic Bay, Nunavut, or a rough ride to the ancient Kaunolu Village Site on Lanai, Hawaii, there is lots to experience in the Indigenous world right around the corner!

I think tourism is a good vein to take. It is the new buffalo for the tribe. It's renewable, it's sellable, and it can create jobs and opportunities.

—Strater Crowfoot, past chief of the Siksika Nation, 2006

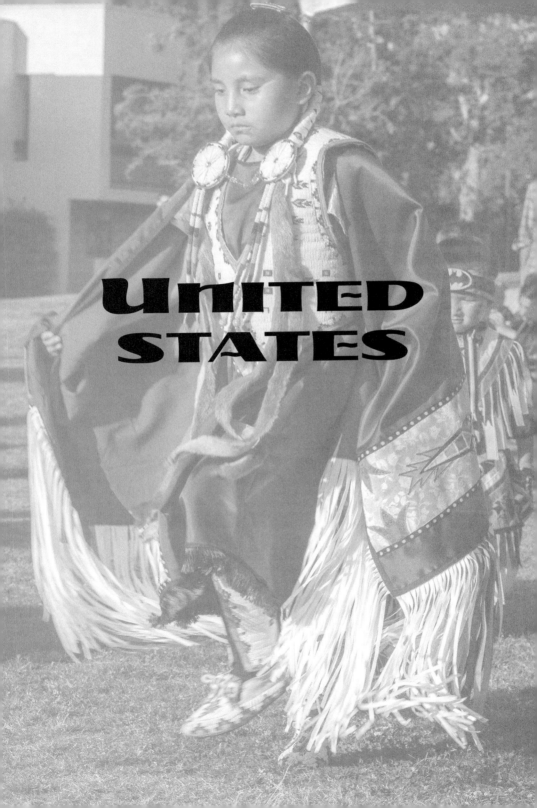

UNITED STATES

UNITED STATES
OF AMERICA

Reclaiming our language is one means of repairing the broken circle of cultural loss and pain. To be able to understand and speak our language means to see the world as our families did for centuries. This is but one path which keeps us connected to our people, the earth, and the philosophies and truths given to us by the Creator.

—jessie "little doe" baird, Wampanoag Language Project Founder

The Northeast region is picture-postcard perfect from its verdant Catskill and Green Mountains, part of the Appalachian Range, to the sparkling bays and storied islands of the Atlantic Ocean to its iconic Finger Lakes to its legendary Hudson River to its tenacious, old-growth forests to its pulsating canyons created by towering skyscrapers in New York City. Warm-to-hot and humid summers and cold, snowy winters sandwich the lovely, too-short springs and glowing, colorful autumns. The Haudenosaunee and Wabanaki realms have been sliced by Canadian/U.S. borders; the Wampanoag, Shinnecock, and Narragansett homelands are checkerboarded with summer playgrounds for the dominant culture's rich and famous. The Cornplanter Seneca Reservation in Pennsylvania has been turned into a dam, its residents evicted. Pennsylvania, like a dozen other states, refuses to recognize tribal governments, so bands of Lenape who still live there are no longer legal entities. In spite of the greatest challenges, Northeast First Peoples are intrepid and survive.

Long before Europeans arrived, Northeast Native nations had long histories filled with traditions of diplomacy, democracy, and successful governing. In fact, the Haudenosaunee constitution was an inspiration for the founding fathers of the United States, although they missed a lot of the finer points like women's equality and the right for everyone to have a vote. Colonial powers so admired the great nations they encountered that the English, French, and American patriots vied for their attention and assistance.

As in other parts of North America, most major roads in the Northeast follow the same routes laid out by Indigenous peoples. New York's famous Broadway itself was a major trading highway for Lenape traders and their customers. The economic systems of the region were splendidly sustainable and a blueprint for resolving contemporary issues of managing resources.

Today's Northeastern Native peoples determinedly struggle to regain lands, reestablish a strong presence, have their civil rights respected, and become economically stable. Some have been successful with return of lands and self-governing status, and several have developed vacation and resort enterprises as well as educational and cultural opportunities for tourists. From Carson Waterman's (Seneca) stunning murals in the Seneca Allegany Resort and Casino, Salamanca, New York, to the Aquinnah rainbow-colored cliffs of Martha's Vineyard, Massachusetts, homelands of the Wampanoag, the Native Northeast has much to see and do. The region is a tourist's delight.

CONNECTICUT

Connecticut's Native citizens number around 37,700, and the state contains seven Native nations.

MASHANTUCKET
Mashantucket Pequot Museum and Research Center

The Mashantucket Pequot Museum and Research Center, founded in 1998, is owned and operated by the Mashantucket Pequot Tribal Nation. It has a permanent collection that includes artifacts of Native American peoples of eastern North America from the sixteenth to the twentieth centuries as well as commissioned artworks and traditional crafts by modern Native Americans. A series of interactive exhibits and life-size, three-dimensional dioramas depicts the lifeways and history of the Mashantucket Pequot and their ancestors from the last glacial period through modern times. One highlight is a twenty-two-thousand-square-foot walk-through re-creation of a coastal Pequot village around the year 1550, shortly before the first contact with Europeans. The village is populated by fifty-one life-size figures of Indians engaged in activities such as building wigwams, sharpening arrows, and weaving mats. A six-hundred-foot photomural of an oak-hickory forest surrounds the village. The Trading Post Gift Shop has a large selection of jewelry, art, books, CDs and videos, clothing, postcards, and greeting cards.

In 2012, a reviewer for *Connecticut Magazine* described the museum as "rival[ing] anything in the nation" and commented that the Pequot village reconstruction and other dioramas "almost put EPCOT to shame."

Info: 110 Pequot Trail, P.O. Box 3180, Mashantucket, CT 06338 • 800.411.9671 • http://www.pequotmuseum.org

UNCASVILLE
Shantok Village of Uncas

Fort Shantok was the principal Mohegan settlement between 1636 to 1682 and the sacred ground of Uncas, one of the most prominent and influential Mohegan leaders

A life-size diorama at the Mashantucket Pequot Museum. Contemporary Pequot citizens served as models for the artists.

and statesmen of his era. Originally part of Mohegan reservation lands, the property was taken by the State of Connecticut in the twentieth century and converted Shantok into a state park in 1926. In 1995, following legal action by the tribe to recover its lands, the state returned the park to Mohegan control. The tribe now operates the area, part of its reservation, as a local park. The grounds were declared a National Historic Landmark in 1993.

The Mohegans remained on the English side through King Philip's War in the 1670s, but with all other Indian threats removed from the area, the Mohegans were of no further use as allies and by the eighteenth century had lost their ancestral lands. Most eventually moved to New York into Oneida country. It was here that young James Fenimore Cooper grew up and heard bits and pieces of the story of the Mohegans and Uncas's alliance with England. In later life, he moved the event about one hundred years ahead in time and in *The Last of the Mohicans* portrayed Uncas as fighting with the Redcoats in the French and Indian War. Because of the popularity of Cooper's novel in America and Europe, Uncas, a Pequot dissident, achieved an influence that lasted far beyond his own life. His policies could not save his own people, but they made him immortal.

Info: 200 Fort Shantok Rd., Uncasville, CT 06382 • 860.862.6100 •
https://mohegan.nsn.us/explore/heritage/our-history/sachem-uncas

Tantaquidgeon Indian Museum

At the height of the Great Depression, a Mohegan named John Tantaquidgeon decided to build a dream. Although blind in one eye and on crutches, he and his children, Gladys and Harold, founded Tantaquidgeon Indian Museum on September 29, 1931. Featuring Mohegan and other New England Indian objects, the museum's mission is to showcase objects from a Native American perspective. The museum is the oldest Indian-owned-and-operated museum in the United States.

Also born near Uncasville was Samson Occum, the first ordained minister from the Mohegan tribe. His preaching caused such a sensation in England that money was raised to found the first school of higher education for Indian youths in America, an institution that developed into Dartmouth College.

Info: 1819 Norwich-New London Turnpike (Route 32), Uncasville, CT 06382 • 860.848.0594 • https://mohegan.nsn.us/

Wigwam Festival

This annual festival and powwow is hosted by the Mohegan Tribe during the third weekend in August as a corn harvest celebration. Traditional dancing, storytelling, exhibits, and handmade Indian arts are part of this joyous gathering.

Info: Fort Shantok Rd., Uncasville, CT 06382 • 860.862.6100 • https://www.mohegan.nsn.us/explore/heritage/wigwam-festival

WASHINGTON
Institute for American Indian Studies Museum and Research Center

Located in Washington, Connecticut, the Institute for American Indian Studies (IAIS)—formerly the American Indian Archaeological Institute (AIAI)—was incor-

A replica of traditional Mohegan buildings at the Tantaquidgeon Indian Museum.

porated in 1975 as an outgrowth of local efforts to recover New England's then-largely unknown Indigenous history. Since then, IAIS has surveyed or excavated over five hundred sites, including the remarkable discovery of a ten-thousand-year-old site—the earliest known archaeological site in Connecticut.

Respect for the earth and all living things central to Native American lifeways is reflected throughout the museum, which is nestled in fifteen acres of woodlands and trails. The Three Sisters and Healing Plants Gardens is outdoors as well as a replicated, sixteenth-century Algonkian Village. The appearance and construction of the village is based upon traditional knowledge and archaeological research and is built from local, natural resources. The Four Directions Gift Shop carries hand-crafted jewelry, books, pottery, prints, dolls, and many other items. A variety of events and workshops are offered.

Info: 38 Curtis Rd., P.O. Box 1260, Washington, CT 06793 • 860.868.0518 • http://iaismuseum.org

DELAWARE

Around 11,800 Native citizens and one association are in Delaware.

MILLSBORO

Nanticoke Indian Association's Annual Powwow

For over forty years, the Nanticokes have been holding a powwow every September.

Info: 27073 John J. Williams Hwy., Millsboro, DE 1966 • 302.945.3400 • http://nanticokeindians.org/

Nanticoke Indian Museum

The survival of the Nanticokes is a tribute to the perseverance of a small group of individuals who, over the generations, refused to surrender their tribal identity. The Nanticokes once occupied the middle section of the Delmarva Peninsula, building their villages on the rivers that ran inland from Delaware and Chesapeake bays. John Smith visited them from Jamestown in 1608 and noted their industrious habits.

However, with the settlement of the Maryland colony, successive encroachments were made on their lands. Reservations were set aside, redrawn, and shrunk. Finally, in 1742, the Nanticokes were accused of taking part in a rebellion plot and forced to relinquish the right to choose a chief, or emperor. Finding it impossible to conduct tribal affairs under those conditions, they requested permission from the Iroquois to move into their lands on the Susquehanna River in southern New York. Eventually, they joined them in exile to Canada after the Revolutionary War.

One tiny remnant of people chose to stay in southern Delaware to cling to their identity as Nanticoke. They formed a tightly knit community in the area known as Angola Neck, ridiculed by both their white and black neighbors for what was regarded as a spurious claim to Indian ancestry. During the days of segregation, the state set up four separate school systems in the area: white, black, "Moor" (a group who considered themselves an Indian-Negro mixture), and Nanticoke. The community of Harmon School, midway between Millsboro and Angola, preserves the name of the "Moor" school. Nonetheless, the Nanticokes tried to keep alive certain rituals they had come to associate with their Indian identity. Finally, in 1922, with the help of testimony from University of Pennsylvania anthropologists, they were given the legal right to incorporate as a tribe. They now operate this small museum and hold an annual gathering.

Housed in what was once a community schoolhouse, the museum displays many artifacts, implements, and traditional clothing that have been passed down from our elders, who have since perished, as well as donations that have been made over the years. The public is invited to the annual Native American Heritage Day held in May at the museum. Admission is free, and guests are treated to performances, speakers, traditional food, and games.

Info: 27073 John J. Williams Hwy., Millsboro, DE 19966 • 302.945.7022 • http://www.nanticokeindians.org/page/museum

MAINE

A bout 18,700 Native citizens and four Native governments are in Maine.

BAR HARBOR
Abbe Museum

The Abbe Museum first opened to the public in 1928. The museum is named for its founder, Dr. Robert Abbe (1851–1928), an eminent New York physician known for his pioneering use of radiation therapy. The Abbe has since grown from a small trailside museum, privately operated within Acadia National Park, to a contemporary museum in the heart of downtown Bar Harbor and in Acadia National Park. In 2013, the museum became the first and only Smithsonian affiliate in the State of Maine.

At the Abbe's downtown museum, exhibitions and activities deal with the history and cultures of Maine's Native people, the Wabanaki. Also, special events, teacher workshops, archaeology field schools, and craft workshops are available for children and adults. From spring through fall, the Abbe's historic trailside museum at Sieur de Monts Spring offers visitors a step back in time to early twentieth-century presentations of Native American archaeology in Maine.

"People of the First Light," the Abbe Museum's core multimedia exhibit, introduces visitors to twelve thousand years of history, conflict, adaptation, and survival in the Wabanaki homeland through oral traditions, personal stories, cultural knowledge, language, historical accounts, photographs, objects, and interactive digital displays. The gift shop has a selection of exquisite baskets and other Native American-made crafts as well as books.

Info: Downtown Bar Harbor: 26 Mt. Desert St., Bar Harbor, ME 04609 •
207.288.3519 • Acadia National Park: 49 Sweetwater Cir., Bar Harbor, ME 04609 •
https://www.abbemuseum.org

DAMARISCOTTA
Whaleback Shell Midden State Historic Site

The upper Damariscotta River is famous for its enormous oyster shell heaps, also
called middens. For centuries and well into the twentieth century, Abnaki peoples
gathered near the river's mouth to harvest foods from the sea. They and other more
ancient peoples created the middens between 2,200 and 1,000 years ago. Middens
are rubbish dumps of soil and discarded shells along with related cultural materials,
such as bones, ceramic pots, and stone tools, and are about six feet deep. Middens
can range in size from thin scatterings of shells along the shore to deep, layered ac-
cumulations, which have built up over many, many years, and the unearthed middens
give an astonishing picture of the work of perhaps one thousand summers by the
Abnaki on the Maine coast.

Info: Opposite 559 Main St., Damariscotta, ME 04543 • 207.287.3200 •
http://www.damariscottariver.org/trail/whaleback-shell-midden-state-historic-site/

INDIAN ISLAND
Penobscot Nation Museum

The Penobscot Nation Museum is housed in the old Indian Agent's Office on Indian
Island, part of the Penobscot Reservation. When the Maine Indian Claims Settlement
Act was passed in 1980, the Penobscots received justice and restitution for the loss

The entrance to Whaleback Shell Midden State Historic Site.

Penobscot Nation Museum.

of millions of acres of land. The passage of the act affirmed the Penobscots' inherent right to govern their own affairs.

The Penobscot Nation Museum is dedicated to preserving and sharing the rich cultural heritage of the Penobscot and Wabanaki people. The museum houses collections that span thousands of years of history. Birch bark canoes, walking sticks, root clubs, numerous historical photos, traditional garments and ceremonial wear, basketry materials, and tools as well as contemporary art chronicle Penobscot history and current events.

Those with a taste for sports history will want to know that Louis Sockalexis was born on the Penobscot Reservation. An outstanding athlete at Holy Cross University, he was regarded as the finest Native American baseball player of his era. When he joined the Cleveland Spiders in 1897, he was met with horrendous displays of racism every time he entered the field. Sockalexis just wanted to play ball and was devastated by the hatred hurled at him during games. He finally gave up and went home. Ironically, the Spiders changed their name to the Indians in his honor. However, today's Native leaders feel the name and the logo is an insult and trivializes Native cultures. Sockalexis died on the reservation in 1913. His hometown honored his legacy by constructing the twenty-five-hundred-seat Sockalexis Ice Arena, where Indian Island youth can carry on his love of sports and thrill of challenge.

Info: 12 Down St., Indian Island, ME 04468 • 207.827.4153 • http://www.penobscotnation.org/penobscot-nation-museum

PERRY
Passamaquoddy Reservation

The Passamaquoddy are the easternmost tribe of the Abnaki, and they still retain that distinction within the United States. The Point Pleasant Reservation, just southeast of Perry, is the administrative center for all of Maine's coastal Native lands. Shops here feature intricately handwoven baskets. In the cemetery, the Daughters of the American Revolution have erected a monument in memory of the Passamaquoddy who fought with the colonials during the War for Independence.

A Waponahki Museum and Resource Center preserves Passamaquoddy culture and traditions for future generations.

Info: 59 Passamaquoddy Rd., Perry, ME 04667 • 207.853.2600, Ext. 227 • http://wabanaki.com/wabanaki_new/museum.html

MARYLAND

Around 18,500 Native citizens and three Native entities are in Maryland.

BALTIMORE
Baltimore American Indian Center

The Baltimore American Indian Center (BAIC) has been serving Native Americans in the Baltimore metropolitan area and surrounding areas since 1968. It was established to serve as a social and cultural "home base" for American Indians in the region. It assists and supports American Indian and Alaska Native families moving into an urban environment and adjusting to the culture change they will experience. The BAIC also educates non-Native people about the cultures of the North American Indian and Alaska Native communities. Plans for a museum are underway.

The Baltimore American Indian Center Museum will introduce the stories of the experiences, cultures, and histories of the original inhabitants of Maryland and the Mid-Atlantic region as well as other tribal communities that have, over several centuries, made Baltimore and Maryland their home. The story of the North Carolina Lumbees, who created the Indian center and are the largest Native American community in Maryland, will be one of the museum's most important themes.

Through exhibitions, programming, events, and the sale of culturally appropriate merchandise in the gift shop, the BAIC Museum will expand the knowledge of both

Lumbee artist Dean Tonto Cox Sr. painted the mural on the side of the Baltimore American Indian Center.

Native and non-Native people about the richness of these living cultures and the tenacious efforts to maintain those cultures. BAIC hosts an annual powwow in November, Native American Heritage Month, at Towson University.

Info: 113 S. Broadway, Baltimore, MD 21231 • 410.675.3535 • http://www.baic.org/home/4582130324 and http://www.baicmuseum.org/aboutus.htm

MASSACHUSETTS

A round 62,800 Native citizens, two Native governments, and seven Native entities are in Massachusetts.

Massachusetts Native American Trail Project

The Massachusetts Office of Travel and Tourism (MOTT), the Massachusetts Commission on Indian Affairs, the University of Massachusetts/Amherst, and the North American Indian Center of Boston collaborated on designing the Massachusetts Native American Trail Project. The aim is to promote, educate, and bring awareness about the Massachusetts Native American Indians, from a cultural tourism point of view, to the Massachusetts visitors. The Native American Trail provides travelers with important Native American events (historic and contemporary) and site markers that exist across the state.

Info: https://www.massvacation.com/blog/2015/11/massachusetts-native-american-trail/

Approximately 100 million years old, Aquinnah's clay cliffs are among the most sacred places on Earth to the Wampanoag people.

AQUINNAH
Aquinnah Cultural Center

The mission of the Aquinnah Cultural Center, Inc. (ACC) is to preserve, interpret, and document the Aquinnah Wampanoag self-defined history, culture, and contributions past, present, and future. A nonprofit organization, the ACC is a special place that expresses Wampanoag beliefs and lifeways as well as provides a place where visitors can learn about the tribe's cultural heritage, including their glorious pottery made from Aquinnah's famous multicolored clay cliffs. Public events include exhibits that highlight four hundred years of Wampanoag history, guest speakers, and art demonstrations.

Info: 35 Aquinnah Cir., Aquinnah, MA 02535 • 508.645.7900 • http://mvol.com/listings/aquinnah-cultural-center/

BOSTON
Boston Children's Museum

One of the few children's museums to maintain a collection, the Boston Children's Museum has Passamaquoddy artifacts as well as clothing and objects of many North American First Peoples. Special events are offered.

Info: 308 Congress St. (Perkins St., off Centre, behind Whole Foods in Hyde Square), Boston, MA 02210 • 617.426.6500 • http://www.bostonchildrensmuseum.org/

BOURNE
Aptuxcet Trading Post

Seven years after landing at Plymouth, the basics of survival secured, the Pilgrims were ready to get down to business. Their contacts with the Native Americans to

The Aptuxcet Trading Post has been replicated for visitors to enjoy and appreciate.

the south, between Buzzards Bay and Narragansett Bay, had been sociable thanks to the personal relationship between the leaders of the Plymouth Colony and the Wampanoag chief, Massasoit. In 1627, the colonists opened the Aptuxcet Trading Post at the shoulder of Cape Cod. The Dutch, who had set up a colony at Manhattan Island the previous year, also came to Aptuxcet.

While the post survived just a few years, it was the prototype of the sort of business that would precede European expansion across the continent. The trading posts introduced the concept of goods that were valued not because they served any basic necessity but because they were scarce. That undercut the Native way of life, which was based on need and availability. It drew them into the rivalries and trade wars between the colonial powers, but they also acquired weapons and tools that altered their worldview. Although Aptuxcet is an early trading post, it is probably not the first. Evidence exists that the Dutch had set up a similar operation before actually establishing their colony of New Amsterdam, but Aptuxcet is the oldest to have been restored, and it gives an indication of what one such business looked like in the 1620s at the dawn of Indian–European trade.

Info: 24 Aptuxcet Rd., Bourne, MA 02532 • 508.759.8167 • http://www.bourne-historicalsociety.org/aptucxet-museum/

CAMBRIDGE
Peabody Museum of Archaeology and Ethnology

From towering Native American totem poles and Maya sculptures to finely woven textiles and everyday utensils, the Peabody Museum is among the oldest archaeological and ethnographic museums in the world with one of the finest collections of human cultural history found anywhere. The Peabody is strongest in the cultures of North, Central, and South America and the Pacific Islands.

Info: 11 Divinity Ave., Cambridge, MA 02138 • 617.496.1027 • https://www.peabody.harvard.edu/

A Mi'kmaw birchbark box on display at the Peabody Museum of Archaeology and Ethnology.

GRAFTON
Hassanamisco Indian Museum

As the principal repository of Nipmuc history and culture, the museum represents a rare and valuable cultural resource. Its artifacts, documents, and research library communicates the culture of the Eastern Woodland Indian and the interactions between the Nipmucs and the dominant culture of central Massachusetts. The museum opened its doors in 1962, nicknaming itself the "Memorial to the Eastern American Indian." It consisted of two buildings on the Hassanamisco Reservation, the original nineteenth-century Homestead and a new longhouse built specifically for the museum's exhibits.

The rate of deterioration of the Homestead has increased due to lack of knowledge in preservation techniques on the part of the tribe and limited funds. The artifacts have suffered as well and are presently at risk. Severe damage to the Homestead last year forced the removal of all items from the structure. These items are now in a climate-controlled storage unit or are being exhibited in other venues. Museum programs are held in rented space at the Nipmuc Nation tribal office.

Info: 80 Brigham Hill Rd., Grafton, MA 01519 • 774.317.9138 • http://www.nipmucmuseum.org/

MASHPEE
Old Indian Meeting House

In 1684, the Old Indian Meeting House was founded by Shearjashub Bourne as part of English efforts to Christianize the Wampanoag. In 1741, it was moved to its present location and expanded. In the past three centuries, the Old Indian Meeting House has been a gathering place, a church, a spiritual stronghold for the Mashpee Wampanoag Tribe, a tool for Christianizing Wampanoags, and a source of great controversy past and present, but in December 2009, it was a cause for celebration for a broad cross-section of Mashpee. The little white meeting house, considered one of the most significant historic buildings on Cape Cod, was reopened after being closed for six years.

Old Indian Meeting House, Mashpee.

This New England church, with its box pews and organ gallery, is among the oldest surviving Indian houses of worship in the country. The burial grounds hold the remains of many early members of the congregation.

Info: 410 Meetinghouse Rd., Mashpee, MA 02649 • 508.477.0208 • http://www.mashpeewampanoagtribe-nsn.gov/meetinghouse

PLYMOUTH
Massasoit Memorial

About three months after the landing of the Pilgrims in Plymouth, Massasoit, the chief of the Wampanoag, received word of their arrival at his home, atop Mount Hope, near what is now Bristol, Rhode Island. Drawn by curiosity about these newcomers, he and several Wampanoag representatives walked the 60 miles (97 kilometers) to their encampment in March 1621. The party included Squanto, who had been kidnapped by a party of English slavers years before and managed to escape, after picking up the rudiments of the language, so in this first meeting of Indians and Europeans in Massachusetts, the Englishmen were astonished to be addressed in their own tongue.

A statue of Sachem of the Wampanoag tribe in Plymouth.

Before returning home, Massasoit signed a treaty of alliance with King James I. He really had no choice: it was not a good time for his people. A mysterious illness, now believed to have been jaundice, had swept over the community and reduced their fighting capacity to about sixty men. Massasoit badly needed allies to help his people fend off any possible assaults from their neighbors. The English with their guns and armor seemed perfectly suited for this task. For his part, Massasoit had no idea how desperate the colonists were. They had lost more than half the 102 original members of the settlement during the first winter and buried them secretly in Cole's Hill, so it was two emaciated groups of human beings who met here and decided to help each other.

The story about Squanto teaching the English how to plant corn is probably untrue, although he may have shown them the technique of using dead fish as fertilizer. A series of visits between the two groups ensued, culminating in the mythic Thanksgiving feast, probably held in December 1621, to which Massasoit contributed several deer.

Massasoit permitted the English to send missionaries among his people, although he himself held on to traditional beliefs. He also agreed to land purchases, which weakened the Wampanoag hold on the best hunting and fishing grounds. The relationship deteriorated and could not survive his death in 1661. The terrible King Philip's War, which almost eradicated the Indian presence in southern New England, followed (see entry on "King Philip's War," Bristol, Rhode Island).

Nevertheless, the memory of Massasoit's friendship and how it enabled the colony to take root is part of American legend. His statue, sculpted by Cyrus Dallin, was placed, fittingly enough, at the crest of Cole's Hill, where the victims of the first Pilgrim winter, 1620–1621, in America are interred in a sarcophagus. Cole's Hill was declared a National Historic Landmark in 1960.

Info: Carver St., Plymouth, MA 02360 • 508.746.1620 • http://www.legendsof america.com/ma-plymouthrock.html

Plimoth Plantation

Telling the iconic story of Plymouth Colony fulfilled a young archaeologist's boyhood dream. With help and support from friends, family, and business associates, Henry Hornblower II started the museum in 1947 as two English cottages and a fort on Plymouth's historic waterfront. Since then, the museum has grown to include *Mayflower II* (1957), the English Village (1959), the Wampanoag Homesite (1973), the Hornblower Visitor Center (1987), the Craft Center (1992), the Maxwell and Nye Barns (1994), and the Plimoth Grist Mill (2013).

Plimoth Plantation offers powerful, personal encounters with history built on thorough research about the Wampanoag people and the colonial English community in the 1600s. Today, it provides an experiential outdoor and indoor learning envi-

The Plimoth Plantation Living Museum.

ronment on its main campus at the State Pier on Plymouth's waterfront and at the Plimoth Grist Mill on Town Brook. Permanent exhibits tell the complex and interwoven stories of two distinct cultures: English and Wampanoag. The main exhibits are enhanced with special events, public programs, and workshops that offer a diverse exploration of the seventeenth century.

Info: 137 Warren Ave., Plymouth, MA 02360 • 508.746.1622 • http://www.plimoth.org

SALEM
Peabody Essex Museum

Originally called the East India Marine Society, the Peabody Essex Museum was founded in 1799 by "collecting" sea captains who returned with a wealth of Native art. Salem also became the headquarters of the American Board of Commissioners for Foreign Missions, whose missionaries also collected Native art, which became part of the Peabody's collection. The Peabody has one of the country's oldest collections, with pieces dating from the seventeenth through the twentieth centuries.

Info: 161 Essex St., Salem, MA 01970 • 866.745.1876 • http://www.pem.org

Pioneer Village

Dubbed the country's "first living history museum," the three-acre village features various examples of colonial architecture: dugouts, wigwams, thatched-roof cottages, and the Governor's Faire House. Culinary and medicinal gardens and a blacksmith shop further illustrate early seventeenth-century colonial life. The museum offers a variety of activities.

Info: 98 West Ave., Salem, MA 01970 • 978.744.8815 • http://www.pioneervillagesalem.com/

WEST TISBURY
Mayhew Chapel

After the disastrous King Philip's War, the remnant of the Wampanoag people survived on the island of Martha's Vineyard. The rest were either dead, sold into slavery, or absorbed by the Saconnet tribe; the island branch of the Wampanoag had refused to join the war.

Set on less than one acre, the grounds are all that remain of the "one mile square given by Sachem Josias for a praying town for Indian converts to Christianity." The chapel, which dates to 1680, is named for Thomas Mayhew, Jr., the first minister to Christianize any of the Indigenous peoples of New England, beginning in 1643.

Most were converted to Christianity by the Reverend Thomas Mayhew and were referred to as "praying Indians." That designation had not been enough to save most mainland converts. The colonists were zealous to destroy any Indians they could reach, whether allied with Philip or not, but the praying village established by Mayhew on the Vineyard in 1659 escaped the worst of the bloodshed.

Many Vineyard Natives are of Wampanoag ancestry, and they maintain a tribal council in Aquinnah, formerly called Gay Head. The little chapel in West Tisbury is a memorial to the praying Indians who kept the Nation's identity alive on the island.

Info: Christianown Rd., West Tisbury, MA 02575

NEW HAMPSHIRE

New Hampshire is home to thirteen hundred Native citizens and three Native nations.

HANOVER
Dartmouth Powwow

Dartmouth College's Native American Program has been sponsoring a powwow for almost fifty years. The May event celebrates the history of Native presence at the school. Over one thousand Native Americans from more than two hundred different nations have attended Dartmouth.

Info: The Green, 1 E. Wheelock St., Hanover, NH 03755 • 603.646.2110 • http://www.dartmouth.edu/~nap/powwow/

Hood Museum of Art, Dartmouth College

Representing the cultural complexity, artistic diversity, and historic and contemporary cultural expressions of the Indigenous peoples across the United States, Canada, and Greenland, a collection of four thousand works is an integral part of Dartmouth's Native American Studies curriculum and also reflects the college's commitment to the education of Native Americans since 1970.

Grand Entry at Dartmouth Annual Powwow.

Info: 6 E. Wheelock St., Hanover, NH 03755 • 603.646.2808 • http://www.hood museum.dartmouth.edu

WARNER
Mt. Kearsage Indian Museum

The museum has several themed rooms depicting Native American life in different sections of North America. It contains artifacts, clothing, tools, canoes, and other implements of everyday life as well as a self-guided tour and an introductory eight-minute video. Many works of art by locals are displayed. Educational walking trails surround the ten acres of museum property.

Info: 18 Highlawn Rd., Warner, NH 03278 • 603.456.2600 • https://www.indian museum.org

NEW JERSEY

A bout 92,650 Native citizens and five tribal governments are in New Jersey.

MONTCLAIR
Montclair Art Museum

Built in 1914, the Montclair Museum is home to a collection of American and American Indian art spanning the past three centuries. The Native art is drawn from seven major regions: the Woodlands, Southeast, Plains, Southwest, Northwest Coast, California, and Arctic. Exhibitions, which include contemporary works, support the idea that Indian art is fine art rather than ethnographic objects.

Info: 3 Mountain Ave., Montclair, NJ 07042 • 973.746.5555 • http://www.mont clairartmuseum.org

PATERSON
Native American Indian Heritage Festival

The Sand Hill Band of the Lenape and Cherokee Indians, the Paterson Museum, and the National Park Service cohost this annual event, which celebrates the culture of the Indigenous community of Paterson: the Lenape Indians. Dance, storytelling, exhibits, and traditional food as well as tours of the Paterson Museum and the Great Falls make this annual event a special day.

Info: 72 McBride Ave., Paterson, NJ 07501 • 973.523.0370 • https://www.nps.gov/pagr/index.htm

Paterson Museum

The museum's Native American exhibit covers New Jersey, New York, and Connecticut. Exhibits include maps, murals, arrowheads, traditional housing, canoes, and tools. It also includes a display of contemporary Native residents of Paterson.

Info: 2 Market St., Paterson, NJ 07505 • 973.321.1260 • http://www.thepaterson museum.com/

A diorama of a Lenape family on display at the Paterson Museum.

RINGWOOD
Ramapough Lenape Nation Powwow

For more than three hundred years, members of the Ramapough Lenape have been separated from the other Lenape, who were pushed out of the area. Their mountain home, shared by two states, gave them refuge and helped them maintain strong family ties. For the past several years, they have been enjoying a resurgence of their traditional culture and reconnecting to other Lenape in the Diaspora. The Ramapough hold an annual powwow.

Info: Sally's Field, Ringwood State Park, 1304 Sloatsburg Rd., Ringwood, NJ 07456 • 973.981.1954 • http://www.ramapoughlenapenation.org/

NEW YORK

New York State has around 304,000 Native citizens and thirteen Native nations.

COOPERSTOWN
The Fenimore Art Museum

The Fenimore Art Museum is home to a major collection of American Indian art: the Eugene and Clare Thaw Collection that spans twenty centuries of North American artistic expression. The Thaws focused on collecting objects as works of art, not as cultural, ethnographic, craft, or decorative objects. Examples include baskets from

The Fenimore Art Museum in Cooperstown, New York.

California, masks from the Arctic, pottery from the Southwest, and beadwork from the Plains and Great Lakes regions.

Info: 5798 State Highway 80, Cooperstown, NY 13326 • 607.547.1400 • http://www.fenimoreart.org

FONDA
The National Shrine of Kateri Tekawitha

Kateri's father was Mohawk, her mother a Christian of Algonquian descent. When a smallpox epidemic swept their village in 1660, both of Kateri's parents were killed and she was left facially scarred for life. Taken to live with an uncle at the nearby village of Caughnawaga, she came under the influence of Christian teaching. She was baptized, took vows of virginity, and set about to live a life of dedicated piety. Forced by her relatives to wed, she fled to a Christian Mohawk settlement near Montréal. Her religious ardor continued until her death at age twenty-four in 1680.

For centuries, the location of the village in which St. Kateri grew up and was baptized was lost, but in 1950, archaeologists working in cooperation with the Albany Archdiocese determined that it had been located just west of Fonda, on the north bank of the Mohawk River, a few miles upstream from Ossernenon. A barn on the property was converted into a shrine and a small museum, in which the story of Kateri is related. It is a place of pilgrimage for Catholic Native Americans from around the Americas.

Also called the Lily of the Mohawks, Kateri is the Mohawk form of Catherine, which she took from St. Catherine of Siena St. Kateri Tekakwitha was canonized by Pope Benedict XVI on October 21, 2012, as the patroness of ecology and the environment, people in exile, and Native Americans. She became the first Native American to become a saint.

Info: 3628 State Highway 5, Fonda, NY 12068 • 518.853.3646 • http://www.kateri shrine.com/kateri.html

GREENFIELD CENTER
Ndakinna Education Center

The center's programs teach how to integrate Native values and lifeways into one's daily life to improve conflict resolution, team building, and character. Visitors can explore the many educational exhibits of Native tools, baskets, rattles, drums, shelters, and clothing as well as full-scale birch bark canoes and bark longhouses. Ndakinna also offers bird and tree walks at the adjacent 80-acre (32-hectares) Marion F. Bowman Bruchac Memorial Nature Preserve.

Info: 23 Middle Grove Rd., Greenfield Center, NY 12833 • 518.583.9958 • http://www.ndakinnacenter.org/

HOGANSBURG
Akwesasne Cultural Center

The collection of the Akwesasne Museum includes over two thousand photographic objects and over seven hundred ethnographic objects of various kinds related to the Mohawk community of Akwesasne. One of the priorities of the museum continues to be the traditional arts program. Classes for the Akwesasne Mohawk community help to keep traditional arts skills alive and well. Their top ten priorities are: work baskets, fancy baskets, cornhusk dolls, feather fans, raised beadwork techniques, moccasins, beaded crowns, beaded yokes, beaded skirts, and cradleboards.

Info: 321 State Route 37, Hogansburg, NY 13655 • 518.358.2240 • http://akwes asneculturalcenter.org/

HOWES CAVE
Iroquois Indian Museum

The stunning Iroquois Indian Museum, which opened in 1992, is built in the shape of an Iroquois longhouse. Through artifacts, artwork, crafts, and ceremonies, it tells the story of the Iroquois from the founding of the confederacy to contemporary time. A hands-on section has been set up to make the exhibits more meaningful for children. The exhibits show what everyday life was like in the traditional villages and the role each tribal member played in the group. Special displays explore the role of women, who determined clan affiliation and were also given a voice in political affairs. All members of the confederacy are represented in the museum, although the displays are particularly strong in Mohawk items, since the museum is located in "the Eastern Door," which was once their stronghold. The museum shop has hand-made Iroquois objects, children's items, jewelry, and more.

Info: 324 Caverns Rd., Howes Cave, NY 12092 • 518.296.8949 • http://www.iroquoismuseum.org

ITHACA
Public Art

Ithaca, a small city on Cayuga Finger Lake in upstate New York, is dedicated to in-clusivity as evidenced by its public-funded murals and monuments. Onondaga artist Brandon Lazore's murals grace two significant walls in the city. One mural pictures the Two Row Wampum Treaty, an agreement of peace between the Haudenosaunee and Dutch in 1613. The painting signifies both contemporary and historic Iroquois culture. Another one of Lazore's murals is on the Green Street Parking Garage. Ithaca is also located on the homelands of the Cayuga, the only federally recognized Nation that does not have any land in the United States and struggles to regain territory.

Info: Seneca at Aurora St., Ithaca, NY • http://www.cityofithaca.org/353/public-art-commission

NEDROW
Tsha' Hoñ'noñyeñ'dakhwa' (Where They Played Games) Onondaga Nation Arena

The two-thousand-seat Lacrosse Arena is located on Onondaga Territory and home to the Onondaga Nation's lacrosse team and the Onondaga Athletic Club (OAC) RedHawks. It is the site of many tournaments. Tsha' Hoñ'noñyeñ'dakhwa' also serves as an ice arena from September through March, where local high schools and colleges as well as youth hockey (Valley Youth Hockey Association) consider Tsha' Hoñ'noñyeñ'dakwha' their home ice.

The colors of the arena are purple and white, the colors used in the Hau-denosaunee wampum belts, which are replicated on the facade. One shows the union of five nations (the Haudenosaunee): the Seneca, Cayuga, Onondaga, Oneida, and Mohawk. Another depicts the two-row wampum belt, which represents two people: the Haudenosaunee and "their new white brothers living together in peace, separate, and equal."

Info: 4000 State Route 11, Onondaga Nation via Nedrow, NY 13120 • 315.498.6813 • http://onondagaarena.com/

NEW YORK CITY
American Museum of Natural History

One of the largest museums in the world, the museum opened the Hall of Northwest Coast Indians in 1900 under the name "Jesup North Pacific Hall." It is currently the oldest exhibition hall in the museum, though it has undergone many renovations in its history. The hall contains artifacts and exhibits of the tribes of the North Pacific Coast cultural region (southern Alaska, northern Washington, and a portion of British

Northwest Canoe Figurehead at the American Museum of Natural History.

Columbia). Featured prominently in the hall are four "House Posts" from the Kwak<u>wa</u>ka'wakw Nation and murals by William S. Taylor depicting Native life.

The Hall of Plains Indians focuses on tribes as they were in the mid-nineteenth century. The Hall of Eastern Woodlands people details the lives and technology of traditional Native American peoples in the woodland environments of eastern North America. Particular cultures exhibited include Cree, Mohegan, Ojibwe, and Iroquois.

Info: Central Park West and 79th St., New York, NY 10024 • 212.769.5100 • https://www.amnh.org/

Children's Cultural Center of Native America (CCCONA)

CCCONA offers an exciting, interactive program for schoolchildren that augments curricula about Indigenous peoples of the Americas, with a focus on New York State Indian nations. Two-hour presentations include a puppet show, a Lenape language lesson, and an exploration of the past, present, and future of Native peoples of the Americas. The cultural interpreters are Indigenous artists from different regions of the Americas; programs are by reservation only. CCCONA seeks to counter negative stereotypes and racism about Native peoples in school-age children.

Info: 550 W. 155th St., New York, NY 10032 • 646.330.2125 • http://www.cccona.nyc/

Drums Along the Hudson Festival

The Drums Along the Hudson Festival continues a centuries-old tradition of being a key gathering place for Native peoples and their guests in Inwood Park, Upper Manhattan. Called Shorakapok (edge of the river) in Lenape, Inwood was the site of the first oyster bar in the country, and the Lenape served up the tasty mollusks to customers of all backgrounds. The oysters themselves were the foundation of a valuable

A woman dressed for the Drums Along the Hudson Festival.

ecosystem that cleaned the waters and provided habitats for other marine creatures; they are almost extinct, but environmental activists struggle to bring them back.

Jumping ahead a few centuries, Shorakapok was the spot where the first American Indian Day was observed. Arapahoe activist Reverend Sherman Coolidge (1862–1932) led the push for a pan-Indian organization to both represent and celebrate Native peoples. He founded the Society of American Indians (1911–1923), forerunner of the National Congress of American Indians, and on September 28, 1915, he issued a proclamation designating the second Saturday of each May as American Indian Day (AID) and urged Indians to observe it as a memorial to their "race." The first celebration took place in Inwood Park under the great tulip tree, which became iconic of Indian New York. Over the decades, Native New Yorkers turned the annual serious event into a festive occasion, which for the past several years has been sponsored by Lotus Music and Dance. Indigenous dance troupes from around the world entertain guests on the main stage; the powwow arena gives tribute to a dizzying display of fancy footwork by Native dancers, and the park is packed with Native vendors, demonstrations, and camaraderie.

Info: 218th St. and Indian Rd., Inwood Park section of Upper Manhattan, New York, NY • 212.627.1076 • http://www.drumsalongthehudson.org/

George Gustav Heye Center, National Museum of the American Indian

The George Gustav Heye Center opened in 1994 at the Alexander Hamilton U.S. Custom House, a Beaux Arts–style building designated a National Historic Landmark and a New York City landmark. The center serves as an exhibition and education facility of the National Museum of the American Indian in Washington, D.C. The museum's over one million artifacts were originally housed in the Museum of the American Indian on Broadway at 155th St. (in the Audubon building) and in the museum's research annex in the Bronx. The collection was assembled over a fifty-four-year period, beginning in 1903, by George Gustav Heye (1874–1957), a New York banker who traveled throughout North and South America accumulating the collection.

In May 1989, the Heye Foundation and the Smithsonian Institution signed an agreement to transfer the collections of the Museum of the American Indian to the Smithsonian. Later that year, an act of Congress established the National Museum of the American Indian as part of the Smithsonian, making it the first national museum dedicated to the Native peoples of this hemisphere. The National Museum of the American Indian opened in Washington, D.C., on September 21, 2004. (See entry on "National Museum of the American Indian [NMAI]," Washington, D.C.)

The Heye Center's permanent and temporary exhibitions—as well as a range of public programs, including music and dance performances, films, and symposia—explore the diversity of the Native people of the Americas. The museum shop carries exquisite, handmade ceramics, jewelry, books, CDs, postcards, and other objects.

Info: One Bowling Green, New York, NY 10004 • 212.514.3700 • http://www.nmai.si.edu/visit/newyork

Thunderbird Powwow

New York City's oldest and largest powwow brings out thousands of visitors a day and has almost two hundred dancers from every corner of the Americas. During the dances, a narrator explains what they represent and where they are from along with the meaning of the dancers' outfits. A couples' group dance and a Thunderbird hoop dance have been featured at the powwow before, as have caribou, grass, and shawl dances. The powwow includes tables of Native American crafts, food, and other items made by artists from throughout the Americas.

Info: 73-50 Little Neck Pkwy., Floral Park, Queens, New York • 718.347.3276 • http://www.queensfarm.org

ONCHIOTA
Six Nations Indian Museum

The Six Nations Indian Museum provides for the viewing of three-thousand-plus artifacts, with an emphasis on the culture of the Six Nations of the Iroquois Confederacy (Haudenosaunee). Ray, Christine, and John Fadden opened the museum for its first season during the summer of 1954. The wood that went into the lumber of the initial structure was milled at a local sawmill from trees felled by Ray Fadden.

The museum, originally two rooms large, expanded to four rooms, producing a building approximately 80 by 20 feet (24 by 6 meters). The museum's design reflects the architecture of a traditional Haudenosaunee (Six Iroquois Nations Confederacy) bark house. The long bark house is a metaphor for the Six Nations Confederacy, symbolically stretching from east to west across ancestral territory. The Six Nations are: Mohawk, Oneida, Onondaga, Cayuga, Seneca, and Tuscarora.

The museum houses a myriad of precontact and postcontact artifacts, contemporary arts and crafts, diagrammatic charts, posters, and other items of Haudenosaunee culture. The objects within the museum are primarily representative of the Haudenosaunee, but other Native American cultures are represented as well.

Many objects are within the museum. The floors are decorated with Haudenosaunee symbols and motif, and within the rooms are cases exhibiting artifacts. The walls are laden with informative charts, beaded belts, paintings, and other Indigenous items of interest.

The museum features a gift shop with books, southwest jewelry, and other crafts. Some of the items are local, such as beadwork, Mohawk baskets, and painted rocks. T-shirts are available, along with baseball caps with Native images and greeting cards.

Info: 1466 County Route 60, Onchiota, NY 12989 • 518.891.2299 • http://www.sixnationsindianmuseum.com

ONEIDA
Shako:wi Cultural Center

Constructed in 1993, the Shako:wi Cultural Center is a hand-crafted, white, pine log building on Oneida homelands. Guests can experience thousands of years of Oneida history, from the key role they played as allies of General George Washington during the Revolutionary War to the current day, as the Oneida people have worked to revitalize their community and regain control of more than thirteen thousand acres (53 square kilometers) of ancestral Oneida homelands—more than they have had since 1824. Exhibits focus on lacrosse, basketry, and wampum. Panoramic displays created by renowned anthropologist Arthur Parker depict Haudenosaunee life in central New York. One display was devoted to each of the Six Nations in the Haudenosaunee Confederacy. The cultural center has a spectacular, all-Iroquois gift shop.

Info: 5 Territory Rd., Oneida, NY 13421 • 315.829.8801 • http://www.oneidaindiannation.com/shakowiculturalcenter/

SALAMANCA
Seneca-Iroquois National Museum

The Seneca-Iroquois National Museum, located on the Alleghany Reservation, showcases both permanent and temporary exhibits that introduce visitors to the culture and history of the Onöndowa'ga:' and Hodinöhsö:ni'. Exhibits give visitors a glimpse of this rich tribal history from ancient to contemporary times, with examples of wampum belts and various clan animals and a sampling of both traditional and contemporary crafts. The museum shop carries 100 percent Seneca-made items, including cornhusk dolls, beadwork, carvings, sculptures, regalia, books, CDs, DVDs, and more.

Info: 814 Broad St., Salamanca, NY 14779 • 716.945.1760 • http://www.seneca museum.org

SANBORN
The Native American Museum of Art

The Native American Museum of Art (NAMA), located on the Tuscarora Indian Reservation, offers innovative and creative Native art exhibits and collections. It features the works of Joseph Jacobs (Cayuga) and his Narratives in Stone, including soapstone, alabaster, limestone, and clay sculptures as well as bronze castings.

Info: 2293 Saunders Settlement Rd., Sanborn, NY 14132 • 716.261.9241 • http://www.nativeamericanmuseummart.com

SOUTHAMPTON
Shinnecock Nation Cultural Center and Museum

The Shinnecock Nation Cultural Center and Museum, established in 2001, is the only Native American-owned-and-operated not-for-profit organization on Long Island dedicated to honoring both Native ancestors and today's Algonquian descendants. When the ground was broken for the museum in 1998, Elizabeth Haile Thunder Bird noted: "Everyone has been telling our story but us."

The museum chronicles the ten-thousand-year Shinnecock history of the area now called Long Island. Built from Adirondack white pine with a magnificent, carved door, the five-thousand-square-foot facility features a permanent exhibition, located in the east and west wings of the longhouse, numerous artifacts and objects including implements from the Shinnecock whaling history, woven Native baskets, a wickiup, and an Indigenous animal display. The curved stairwell of halved pine logs descends to a gallery lined with portraits of Shinnecock people.

In 2011, the museum added some cultural material items to the permanent display "A Walk with the People." These items help illustrate the different time periods of Shinnecock history. In 2013, "The Wikun Village" had its grand opening, which is an interactive Eastern Woodland homesite that represents Shinnecock culture from the years 1640–1750.

In 2010, the Shinnecocks became federally recognized. Their eight-hundred-acre reservation occupies a peninsula jutting into Shinnecock Bay. The tribe hosts an annual powwow on Labor Day weekend with traditional dances and crafts. A museum shop offers handmade items and books.

Grounds surrounding the Shinnecock Nation Cultural Center and Museum.

Info: 100 Montauk Hwy., Southampton, NY 11968 • 631.287.4923 •
https://www.facebook.com/shinnecockmuseum/

VICTOR
Native American Winter Arts Weekend

The center hosts an annual Native American Arts Weekend with traditional story-tellers, talented Native American artists, and fun children's activities.

Info: 7000 County Road 41 (Boughton Hill Rd.), Victor, NY 14564 • 585.924.5848 •
http://www.ganondagan.org/winterartsfestival

The Seneca Art and Culture Center at Ganondagan

The Seneca Art and Culture Center is a permanent, year-round interpretive facility at Ganondagan that tells the story of the Seneca and Haudenosaunee (Iroquois) contributions to art, culture, and society from more than two thousand years to the present day. The center, which includes a reproduction of the Seneca Bark Longhouse, sits on a historic site located on the land of the Seneca Nation. The dedication of the longhouse at the Ganondagan State Historic Site took place on July 25, 1998. The Seneca Bark Longhouse represents the return of a traditional Seneca dwelling to a site razed in 1687 by the French Marquis de Denonville. The longhouse is furnished as closely as possible to an original 1670 longhouse, complete with replicas of European and colonial trade goods and items created and crafted by the Seneca. Also in the longhouse are crops, herbs, and medicines grown, harvested, and preserved by the Seneca who lived atop the hill at Ganondagan. The center fulfills a vision of Peter Jemison (Seneca), who wants visitors to know, "We are still here. We're not dead and gone. We know what our ancestors ate. We know how they lived."

The gift shop offers Haudenosaunee one-of-a-kind, artisan arts, crafts, and jewelry. It also offers an important selection of informative and engaging books, CDs, and DVDs.

Info: 7000 County Road 41 (Boughton Hill Rd.), Victor, NY 14564 • 585.924.5848 •
http://www.ganondagan.org/sacc

PENNSYLVANIA

Around 96,600 Native citizens and four Native entities are in Pennsylvania. The state does not recognize Native Americans, which makes it difficult for the original people who still live there.

AIRVILLE
Indian Steps Museum

The Indian Steps Museum is a one-of-a-kind destination set along the Susquehanna River. Originally an arts-and-crafts-style cabin, it was built in 1912 by an eccentric York, Pennsylvania, lawyer, John Vandersloot. He was enamored with Native American artifacts, history, and culture and built the cabin as a testament to the long history of American Indians.

An annual festival takes place in September that celebrates the arts, culture, history, and heritage of the First Nations.

Info: 205 Indian Steps Rd., Airville, PA 17302 • 717.862.3948 • http://www.indiansteps.org/

ALLENTOWN
Museum of Indian Culture

The Museum of Indian Culture was inaugurated in 1980 and is housed in a 1750 farmhouse. The building consists of a German stonehouse and a springhouse, which is two-storied. The museum aims at portraying the history of the Lenape and other Native Indian American tribes. It has on display various collectibles, pottery, costumes, etc., which denote the rich Indian culture in the area. It also offers various educational programs.

Info: 2825 Fish Hatchery Rd., Allentown, PA 18103 • 610.797.2121 • http://www.museumofindianculture.org/

BUSHKILL
Pocono Indian Museum

The British called them the Delaware, after the name they had given to the great river on which most of the tribe's villages were found. They called themselves Lenni Lenape, which roughly translates to "real men." The other Algonquian tribes referred to them as "grandfather" in recognition of their ancient origins and position of pre-eminence in the area between the Delaware and Hudson rivers.

They first came into contact with Europeans in 1609, when they encountered Henry Hudson on his first voyage up the river that bears his name. The competition for manufactured goods that Hudson set in motion involved the area tribes in the fur trade and in the colonial ambitions of the European powers. This was ruinous to the Delaware: by the late seventeenth century, they had become dominated by the more powerful Iroquois, and their lands had been reduced to eastern Pennsylvania.

Their chief village, Shackamaxon, was located within what is now Philadelphia. It was there that they signed a treaty with William Penn in 1686. Penn was a decent man who respected Indian claims, but his successors were more devious. One provision of the treaty was the Walking Purchase, which permitted white land claims over a territory that could be covered in a walk of a day and a half. Penn observed the spirit of the agreement, and his walk was done in a leisurely fashion.

In 1737, the governor asked for the clause to be reopened, and the Delaware obliged. This time, the governor hired trained walkers, provided with packhorses, who covered more than 60 miles (97 kilometers) in the stipulated time. One of the walkers, Edward Marshall, made his own claim in the area; a town a few miles south, Marshalls Creek, is named for him.

The Delaware were defrauded of their homeland and in a few more years were totally displaced by the Iroquois in negotiations with whites. The Walking Purchase began the slow western migration of the Delaware, with tragic interludes in Ohio (see entries in Gnadenhutten and New Philadelphia, Ohio) and Kansas. Today, tribal members are scattered across portions of New Jersey, Pennsylvania, Oklahoma, Wisconsin, and Ontario, while many more have been absorbed by the Cherokee.

The Pocono Indian Museum, near the Delaware Water Gap, lies amid the lands taken from the tribe in the notorious purchase. The museum contains displays of Delaware housing and tools, most of which were uncovered in nearby excavations. The museum shop offers handmade objects and books.

Info: 7005 Milford Rd., Bushkill, PA 18302 • 570.588.9338 • http://www.poconoindianmuseumonline.com

CARLISLE
Indian Industrial School

On October 6, 1879, in the rolling hills of central Pennsylvania, the people of Carlisle turned out to watch the most extraordinary parade in anyone's memory. A group of eighty-four children from the Sioux tribe, from the faraway Dakota Territory, marched from the railroad depot to the old army barracks. Most were still dressed in blankets and leggings, just as they had been when taken from their families on the Rosebud and Pine Ridge agencies. Most of the children had no idea why they were there. Many of them had been virtually kidnapped when Indian agents "volunteered" them for the school.

This first all-Indian school of higher education was the dream of Lieutenant Richard H. Pratt, a Civil War veteran who had been dispatched to Oklahoma for frontier duty. Pratt was convinced that training Native children to accept the white world's cultural values would be more efficient than fighting them in deadly battles. Historian Oliver LaFarge wrote: "The idea was to break (the children) down completely away from their families and their tribes, forbid any speaking of their native language or any manifestation of their Native culture, and put them through a course of sprouts that would make them over into white men." All items of Native dress were discarded, students were given English names, and, since Pratt believed in discipline, they were put through military drills.

Pratt first sent the Indians in his program to Hampton Institute, a Virginia college for black students founded right after the Civil War. Having decided that the ethnic gap was too great and that the Indians needed a school of their own, he petitioned the government and soon won permission to adapt the Carlisle barracks for his school.

In its thirty-nine-year existence, more than 10,500 children from almost every Native nation were taken from their homes and transported to Carlisle. Only one in seven actually received a degree. While it identified itself as a college, the courses were more of a vocational nature on the level of a high school. Some students managed to adjust to the white world, but many others returned to their reservations and found themselves alienated from both the Indian and white cultures. Countless died and were buried in unmarked graves.

Ironically, Carlisle's greatest fame came during its last years, when Jim Thorpe (see entry on "Jim Thorpe," Jim Thorpe, Pennsylvania) helped to turn its teams into leaders in college football and track. Pratt, who was gone by then, had hired Glenn "Pop" Warner as coach in his determination to have the school compete at the highest level of athletics.

In 1918, with reservation schools being established across the country, the Carlisle barracks were returned to military use to serve the effort for World War I. It now houses the Army War College, and markers on the premises explain the role the barracks played in Native American history. The grounds also has a small cemetery. In it rests those children who succumbed sooner to disease than to the white man's culture.

Info: P.O. Box 1773, Carlisle, PA 17013 • 717.245.1399 • http://www.carlisleindian.dickinson.edu/

EASTON
Lenape Cultural Center

The Lenape Cultural Center represents the Lenape Nation of Pennsylvania, descendants of the original people of the area. Most Lenape people were forced off their ancestral homelands through the Walking Purchase Treaty of 1737, but small pockets of communities and families remained, managing to survive. The center is an educational, cultural, and historical outreach promoting Lenape history.

Info: 169 Northampton St., Easton, PA 18042 • 610.253.1222 • https://www.facebook.com/lenapeculturalcenter/

JIM THORPE

Jim Thorpe was voted the best American athlete of the first half of the twentieth century in a 1950 Associated Press poll. Not much has changed since then to alter the standings. He won both the pentathlon and decathlon at the 1912 Olympics, led the Carlisle Indian School to victories over the greatest powers in college football, played in a World Series for the New York Giants, and helped to establish and then starred in the organization that grew into the National Football League. Jim Thorpe remains the stuff of legend.

Thorpe was born in Oklahoma, a member of the Sauk and Fox Tribe. Orphaned at an early age, he became a federal ward and was sent to the Haskell Indian Institute in Kansas to learn a trade. While he was there, his athletic skills attracted the attention of school officials, who notified Glenn "Pop" Warner, coach of the Carlisle Indian Industrial School (see entry on "Indian Industrial School," Carlisle, Pennsylvania). Warner persuaded the nineteen-year-old to enroll at Carlisle in 1907. Thorpe kicked three field goals to beat Penn State, and his sixty-yard run tied a heavily fa-

The Jim Thorpe Memorial.

vored Pennsylvania team. He did not care for the rigors of academia and dropped out of school for three years, but Warner persuaded him to return in 1911.

He was named to the All-American football teams in 1911 and 1912, beating Harvard with a forty-eight-yard drop kick field goal with his injured leg encased in bandages and beating Army on a one-hundred-yard kickoff return right after a ninety-five-yard return was nullified by a penalty. When the Carlisle track team showed up for a meet with Lafayette, only Thorpe and four other men got off the train: Thorpe alone took five first-place finishes and one second-place finish. At the Olympics in Stockholm, his unprecedented sweep of the grueling fifteen events in the decathlon and pentathlon still stands as a mark of strength and endurance. Many shared the sentiment of King Gustav V, who had said to the Olympian, "Sir, you are the greatest athlete in the world." Thorpe's reply was, "Thanks, King."

Within a few months, however, Thorpe was forced to return his medals. Officials had learned that for a few months in 1909, after he had dropped out of Carlisle, Thorpe had played semiprofessional baseball. This nullified his amateur status. Although it was fairly common in those days for college athletes to pick up some extra money by playing professionally under an assumed, different name, the International Olympics Committee returned replicas of Thorpe's old medals to the Thorpe family. They are displayed under a portrait of Thorpe that hangs in the rotunda of Oklahoma's State Capitol in Oklahoma City.

Giants manager John McGraw, always looking for a gate attraction, signed Thorpe to play big-league baseball, but this was not his best game: his inability to hit the curveball kept him from stardom, although he did hit over .300 in his final season with the Boston Braves.

While still playing for the Giants, Thorpe went to Canton, Ohio, and organized a team of professional football players. The Bulldogs are now recognized as the first pro team in history, which is why Canton was chosen as the site for the Professional Football Hall of Fame. Other teams soon joined them, and Thorpe was named president of the new league, the predecessor of the NFL. He went on to star with the football Giants in New York, and along with Red Grange, he became the premier gate attraction of the new sport. Those who saw him play say that he had no equal in that era in combining speed, power, and an instinctive ability to find the hole; it was impossible for a single tackler to bring him down. In 2000, a majority of respondents to an ABC *World of Sports* Internet poll voted for Thorpe as the twentieth century's greatest athlete.

After retiring from sports, however, Thorpe drifted from job to job. When he was admitted to a hospital in 1952 for surgery, his wife stated that he was destitute. He died a few months later of a heart attack.

Originally, Thorpe was to be buried in Oklahoma near his birthplace. A campaign to erect a memorial there failed to raise the necessary funds, and his wife had his body exhumed and reburied at the site of the current memorial in an emotional ceremony in 1954. The town's name, Mauck Chunk, was changed a few months later to Jim Thorpe.

Info: Route 903, Jim Thorpe, PA 18229 • https://www.jimthorpe.org/

PHILADELPHIA
University of Pennsylvania Museum of Archaeology and Anthropology

In "Native American Voices: The People—Here and Now," a long-term exhibition at the Penn Museum, visitors can see over two hundred objects from its expansive North American collections. The exhibition challenges common Native American stereotypes and explores the many ways in which today's Native leaders are creating and maintaining religious, political, linguistic, and artistic independence. The two-thousand-square-foot exhibition tells important stories of Native American successes in achieving independence as sovereign (self-governing) Nations. Through old and new objects, video and audio recordings, and digital, interactive opportunities, this exhibition allows visitors to develop a new understanding of the original inhabitants of this land as told through Native American voices. Four main themes are presented in the exhibition: Local Nations, Sacred Places, Continuing Celebrations, and New Initiatives. These themes are presented through the lens of several overarching topics, including language loss and revitalization, identity, representation, and ongoing political activism in support of sovereignty and self-determination.

Info: 3260 South St., Philadelphia, PA 19104 • 215.898.4000 • http://www.penn.museum/sites/nativeamericanvoices

PITTSBURGH
Alcoa Foundation Hall of American Indians, Carnegie Museum of Natural History

The Alcoa Hall of the American Indians celebrates Native cultures from four geographical areas of the country and their relationship with the natural world: the Tlingit of the Northwest Coast, Hopi of the Southwest, Lakota of the Plains, and Iroquois of the Northeast. Concentrating on the nineteenth and twentieth centuries, the Alcoa Hall exhibits American Indian cultures of the recent past and the present. Nearly one thousand historical and contemporary artifacts are displayed, most of which have never been seen by the public. About fifty Native people partnered with Carnegie Museum of Natural History to develop the exhibit and interactive displays.

Their historical and cultural knowledge, personal experiences and belongings, talents, artwork, guidance, and time shaped the messages and impact of the hall. An important topic included in the Alcoa Hall is Native experiences in urban areas, such as the steelwalkers in Pittsburgh.

Info: 4400 Forbes Ave., Pittsburgh, PA 15213 • 412.622.3131 • http://www.carnegiemnh.org/exhibitions/permanent/alcoa-foundation

RHODE ISLAND

Rhode Island has around 17,500 Native citizens and two Native nations.

EXETER
The Tomaquag Indian Memorial Museum

One of the oldest tribal museums in the country, the Tomaquag Indian Memorial Museum was established in the 1950s by anthropologist Eva Butler and Narragansett/Pokanoket Wampanoag historian and educator Mary E. Glasko, also known as Princess Red Wing. The museum opened in its present Exeter site in 1969. Today, the Colonial-style home includes over ten exhibits focused on the Indigenous peoples of America, many focusing on the Narragansett and other southern New England tribes. An archive of documents contains information about events impacting the Narragansett community since the 1880s.

In 2016, Tomaquag was awarded the National Medal for Museum and Library Service, the nation's highest honor given to museums and libraries to service in the community. The award celebrates institutions that respond to societal needs in innovative ways, making a difference for individuals, families, and their communities.

Info: 390 A Summit Rd., Exeter, RI 02822 • 401.491.9063 • http://www.tomaquagmuseum.org

PROVIDENCE
Haffenreffer Museum of Anthropology, Brown University

The Haffenreffer Museum has its origins in the early twentieth century with the Native American collections of Rudolf F. Haffenreffer Jr., an entrepreneur and philanthropist who lived in Fall River, Massachusetts. In 1903, he purchased the King Philip amusement park and summer resort in Bristol, Rhode Island, for use as a summer home. The property is important historically due to its associations with King Philip (Metacom), the famous Wampanoag (Pokanoket) leader.

Haffenreffer became deeply interested in Native American archaeology and history. He purchased local collections of Indian artifacts and made collecting trips to the Southwest. In order to house his growing collection, he built a museum, which he named the "King Philip Museum." Haffenreffer interacted with the local Native American tribes and sponsored meetings of the Algonquin Indian Council of New England. He was also active in the museum community and served for twenty-two

The Haffenreffer Museum of Anthropology.

years on the board of George Gustav Heye's Museum of the American Indian in New York City (now the National Museum of the American Indian). After Haffenreffer's death in 1955, his wife and children donated the collections to Brown University. Brown, in turn, used them as the basis for the museum and introducing anthropology as an academic discipline.

The Haffenreffer Museum also has a Collection Research Center, located in Bristol, which is strong in Native North American ethnographic objects and New England archaeological material. Under Brown's stewardship, the original Haffenreffer collections have grown enormously in breadth and depth.

Info: P.O. Box 1965, Providence, RI 02912 • 401.863.5700 • https://www.brown.edu/research/facilities/haffenreffer-museum

VERMONT

Vermont has around sixty-four hundred Native citizens and three Native governments.

ADDISON
Chimney Point State Historic Park

Chimney Point on Lake Champlain is one of the earliest and most strategic sites in the Champlain Valley, with human habitation dating back as far as nine thousand years ago.

The site explores the history of the area's three earliest cultures: the Native Americans, French Colonial, and early American history. In the "People of the Dawn, People of New France" permanent exhibit, the Abenaki and French history are revealed through items from ancient stone tools to other cultural objects and short films. The "Light of Dawn" rotating exhibit showcases contemporary Abenaki arts and crafts, including masks and other art pieces by Gerald Rancourt Tsonakwa, basketry, jewelry, rattles, drums, and more.

Info: 8149 VT Route 17W, Addison, VT 05491 • 802.759.2412 • http://historicsites.vermont.gov/directory/chimney_point

Chimney Point porch with panoramic views of Lake Champlain.

BENNINGTON
The Bennington Center for the Arts

The collection of Native American and Southwestern artwork is the product of over three decades of serious collecting on the curators' part and includes more than three hundred paintings, fifty bronzes, fifty Hopi Kachinas, eighty-five hand-woven Navajo rugs, and numerous pieces of Native American pottery, jewelry, and baskets. The collection was put together to show the old along with the new.

Info: 44 Gypsy Ln., Bennington, VT 05201 • 802.442.7158 • http://www.thebennington.org/native-american-arts/

VERGENNES
Abenaki Heritage Celebration

The annual weekend organized by the Vermont Abenaki Artists Association and presented at the Lake Champlain Maritime Museum gives visitors an Abenaki perspective on life in the Champlain Valley. Dancing, drumming, storytelling, crafts, and cooking demonstrations are presented by members of Vermont's Abenaki Tribes.

Info: 4472 Basin Harbor Rd., Vergennes, VT 05491 • 802.475.2022 • http://www.abenakiart.org/events

Lake Champlain Maritime Museum

The "Contact of Cultures" exhibit reflects the maritime skills and traditions of Lake Champlain's first navigators. It contains a dugout canoe, full-sized and miniature birch bark canoes, some of the tools used to make them, and an array of canoe paddles as well as traditional fishing nets, hooks, and sinkers. The relationship between Samuel de Champlain and the First Nations is explored and how his personal diplomacy helped shape the world of today.

Info: 4472 Basin Harbor Rd., Vergennes, VT 05491 • 802.475.2022 • http://www.lcmm.org

WASHINGTON, D.C.

A round five thousand Native citizens live in Washington, D.C. Many are descendants of the area's First Nations; others are government employees from across the country.

The Interior Museum

The Interior Museum houses photographs and historic and contemporary artifacts that tell the story of the department's nine bureaus, including the Bureau of Indian Affairs. Holdings include two thousand American Indian artifacts, although only a small portion of those are currently on display in a small gallery. The building also contains New Deal murals. The Indian Craft Shop on the premises sells handmade treasures by emerging and established Native artists and has been around since 1938.

Info: 1849 C St. NW, Washington, DC 20240 • 202.208.3100 • http://www.doi.gov/interiormuseum/

National Museum of the American Indian (NMAI)

In May 1989, the Heye Foundation and the Smithsonian Institution signed an agreement to transfer the collections of the Museum of the American Indian to the Smithsonian. Later that year, an act of Congress established the National Museum of the American Indian (NMAI) as part of the Smithsonian. The National Museum of the American Indian opened on September 21, 2004, built on the last available space on the National Mall in Washington, D.C., across the street from the National Air and Space Museum.

The National Museum of the American Indian houses one of the world's largest and most diverse collections of its kind, spanning more than ten thousand years. It contains objects from the entire Western Hemisphere, from the Arctic to Tierra del

National Museum of the American Indian.

Fuego. The museum's sweeping, curvilinear architecture, its Indigenous landscaping, and its exhibitions, all designed in collaboration with tribes and communities from across the hemisphere, combine to give visitors the sense and spirit of Native America. The collections also include film and audiovisual works, paper archives, and photographs both historic and contemporary.

The museum's Mitsitam Native Foods Cafe provides visitors the opportunity to enjoy the Indigenous cuisines of the Americas and to explore the history of Native foods. The cafe features Native foods found throughout the Western Hemisphere. *Mitsitam* means "Let's eat!" in the Native language of the Delaware and Piscataway peoples.

In accord with the museum's mission, NMAI recognizes the historical and contemporary cultures and cultural achievements of the Natives of the Western Hemisphere by consulting, collaborating, and cooperating with Natives and by recognizing the museum's special responsibility through innovative public programming, research, and collections to protect, support, and enhance the development, maintenance, and perpetuation of Native cultures and communities.

The museum's collection policy takes great care to respect the cultural and spiritual values of the Native peoples. The collection includes materials of not only cultural, historic, aesthetic, and scientific significance but also of profound spiritual and religious significance. For this reason, public access may be restricted if such access offends the religious or cultural practices of a tribal or cultural group. Religious and ceremonial objects are exhibited only after consultation with the appropriate culturally affiliated group, and the planning of an exhibition's format is done in consultation with representatives of the tribe and/or culture involved to assure historical and cultural accuracy and to avoid desecration, insensitive treatment, and inappropriate interpretation of religious or ceremonial materials. The Roanoke Museum Store presents Native American items from the past and present, illustrating how different artists interpret cultural traditions and art forms. On the museum's second level, the store features jewelry, textiles, and other works by Native artisans; souvenirs; and children's books and toys.

In addition to the Washington, D.C., site, the museum operates a significant exhibition and education facility in lower Manhattan in the Alexander Hamilton U.S. Custom House, known as the George Gustav Heye Center of the National Museum of the American Indian. (See entry on "George Gustav Heye Center," Manhattan, New York.) A collections research center for the museum is located at the Smithsonian's Museum Support Center in Suitland, Maryland. It accommodates activities such as research, collections conservation, exhibition support functions, and community services.

Info: Fourth St. and Independence Ave. SW, Washington, DC 20560 • 202.633.1000 • http://www.nmai.si.edu

Po'pay Statue, National Statuary Hall, U.S. Capitol

In 2005, the statue of a Puebloan leader who led an insurrection against Spanish conquerors in 1680 became the one hundredth and final work added to the U.S. Capitol National Statuary Hall.

An 1864 law authorized the U.S. president to invite each state to furnish two statues, in marble or bronze, of deceased persons who were "illustrious for their historic renown or for distinguished civic or military services." Seven sculptural figures, located throughout the U.S. Capitol building and House of Representatives, honor two Native women (Nevada's Sarah Winnemucca and North Dakota's Sakakawea) and five Native men (Hawaii's King Kamehameha; New Mexico's Po'pay; Oklahoma's Will Penn Adair Rogers and Sequoyah; and Wyoming's Chief Washkie).

This photo of the unveiling of the Po'pay statue pictures the sculptor, Cliff Fragua, at right.

The statue by Jemez Pueblo sculptor Cliff Fragua, located in the Capitol Rotunda, is the only sculpture created by a Native artist. The 7-foot (2-meter)-tall statue of Po'pay (Tewa for "Ripe Pumpkin") is fashioned from Tennessee marble. Fragua said about his rendition of Po'pay: "There is no record of what he looked like. No drawings. I'm just capturing his image as the stone speaks to me."

Info: E. Capitol St. NE and First St. SE, Washington, DC 20004 • 202.226.8000 • https://www.visitthecapitol.gov/

SOUTHEAST

As a Native American, I am proud to share my heritage and the culture of the Muscogee Creek with our community ... a road to remembering the past and celebrating the future.

—Lower Muscogee Creek Elder Debbie Bush

Southeast

The great Southeastern region of the United States is peppered with ancient mounds, the engineering feats of long-ago peoples through different historical stages. Beaches, mountains, and rivers surround lands where early agronomists invented and raised a variety of crops. Ruins of not-so-ancient towns mourn the loss of its citizens, entire nations that were ripped from Southern homelands and forced westward less than two hundred years ago. From Virginia to Florida, evidence of great civilizations remain, and many are tourist stops. However, the entire region is dynamic, rich with contemporary landmarks, festivals, and events that illustrate the moxie, valor, and courage of First Peoples.

Much of the Southeast region was devastated by land-hungry Europeans, and later Americans, who wanted to possess Indian landholdings, centuries-old villages, and thriving farms. Despite thousands and thousands of First Peoples being forced west, a stronghold of Indian culture remains in America's southern states. Many descendants of people who managed to escape forced eviction have reorganized into thriving communities with impressive governments. Others continue the struggle to have land and rights repatriated, but all have a deep and ancestral connection to the area.

Along with museums chock full of archaeological treasures, visitors can enjoy a variety of dance and theater performances, workshops, modern architecture, protected flora and fauna, water activities, interpretative trails, art exhibits, and festivals, and most are hosted by today's Native Americans, who represent a wide array

Jenna Billie (Hollywood, FL), Mensa member (top 2 percent of the most intellectually gifted in the world), is shown here with her parents and wearing a Seminole design crosspatch skirt.

of abilities and interests from alligator wrestling to clogging to conserving wildlife to archiving to being Mensa members!

Trail of Tears National Historic Trail

The Trail of Tears National Historic Trail winds through nine U.S. states (Tennessee, North Carolina, Georgia, Alabama, Kentucky, Illinois, Arkansas, Missouri, and Oklahoma), over mountains, and across rivers and other difficult terrain. It was the route by which the Andrew Jackson administration forcefully exiled one hundred thousand Native American people from their territories east of the Mississippi, beginning in 1831 and lasting a decade. By exiling most members of the five southeastern nations (Cherokee, Choctaw, Seminole, Chickasaw, and Creek) to Indian Territory, their 25 million acres (10.1 million square kilometers) of land with farms, buildings, and businesses were opened to white settlement and to slavery.

Trail of Tears National Historic Trail sign, Hwy 71, Fayetteville, Arkansas.

The impact to the five nations was disastrous, eventually made even worse by Indian Territory being made into the State of Oklahoma, once more disrupting and displacing people. Hundreds perished during removal; thousands more died of its consequences. In 1987, Congress created the Trail of Tears National Historic Trail (TOTNHT): "a trail consisting of water and overland routes traveled by the Cherokee Nation during its removal from ancestral lands in the East to Oklahoma during 1838 and 1839." TOTNHT is managed by the National Park Service and includes many sites. One can map out a route with the interactive map. Sometimes, places on the trail offer activities and events.

Info: https://www.nationalparks.org/explore-parks/trail-tears-national-historic-trail

ALABAMA

The Poarch Band of Creek Indians is the only federally recognized tribe in Alabama. An estimated 33,980 Native residents are in the state.

ATMORE
Poarch Band of Creek Indians

The Poarch Creek Indians are descendants of a division of the original Creek Nation, whose homelands spanned most of the state and parts of Georgia. They escaped removal to the West, and with great difficulty, they were able to maintain their community on what is known today as the Poarch Creek Indian Reservation. For almost half a century, the Poarch Band of Creek Indians have been hosting a powwow on Thanksgiving Day. In addition, they welcome people to their Magnolia Branch Wildlife Reserve for camping, fishing, ziplining, canoeing, horseback riding, water blobbing, birding, and enjoying six hundred acres of protected timberland; the reserve is recognized by *National Geographic* as a geotourism site.

Info: 5811 Jack Springs Rd., Atmore, AL 36502 • 251.368.9136 • http://pci-nsn.gov/westminster/index.html

DANVILLE
Oakville Indian Mounds Education Center

The center is composed of part of the Black Warriors' Path (a major trading route), the largest Woodland ceremonial Indian mound in Alabama (site of a historic cultural center) and the Cherokee Council House Museum (with over ten thousand artifacts), built in the same design as a traditional, seven-sided Cherokee council house. Spanning a timeline of human history of over fourteen thousand years and a diversity of cultures, the park preserves, protects, and presents artifacts dating as far back as 10,000 B.C.E. as well as ancient geological evidence of the people of this region of present-day Alabama. Creek, Yuchi, Shawnee, Chickasaw, and Cherokee were the five historic nations to live in the Oakville area.

Contemporary Native culture is presented at the center also, and every spring, the Lawrence County Native American Student Club collaborates with the park to host the Lawrence County Multicultural Indian Event. People can extend their landmark visitation at the William B. Bankhead National Forest, the western boundary of the Appalachian Mountains and premier site of wildlife, waterfalls, deep gorges, caves, petroglyphs, historic drawings, and rock carvings.

Info: 1219 County Road 187, Danville, AL 35619 • 256.905.2494 • http://oakvilleindianmounds.com/home.html

DECATUR
Point Mallard Park:
Native American Indian Interpretative Walking Trails

Located in this river city's public park are 5 miles (8 kilometers) of pathways named after Cherokee, Chickasaw, and Creek chiefs that educate walkers about First Peoples of the Tennessee Valley. At one time, Point Mallard was the site of a Creek community, and nearby Rhodes Ferry Park is where twenty-three hundred Cherokee landed after being forced off their homelands and marched west on what is called the Trail of Tears.

Info: 2901 Point Mallard Dr., Decatur, AL 35602 • 256.341.4900 • http://www.decaturparks.com/tyfoon/site/accounts/A/2/7/A/7/D/6/1/E/B/file/Pt_Mal_Walk_Trail1d1_1.pdf

MOUNDVILLE
Moundville Archaeological Park

The grouping of mounds at Mound State Monument, on a bluff above the Black Warrior River, so dominates the landscape that it was unquestionable what to name the town built adjacent to it.

This was a metropolis by twelfth-century standards, built by an accomplished agrarian people. They left behind a vast array of beautiful pottery, tools, and ornaments, artfully displayed in the museum on-site. Anthropologists say that this copper and stone craftsmanship skill level is unmatched at any historic site north of Mexico. The twenty mounds here were the cultural and religious center for a large group of surrounding villages, much as a core city is surrounded by its suburbs today. The mounds range from 3 to 58 feet (.9 to 18 meters) in height and once were crowned by temples and homes of religious leaders. One of the temples, Wallsboro, has been reconstructed elsewhere, figures have been placed depicting inhabitants engaging in daily activities.

A carved crested wood duck diorite rock bowl on display at Moundville Archaeological Park.

For thirty years, the Moundville Native American Festival has brought back Native celebrations to the mounds in October. Cherokee, Creek, Choctaw, Chickasaw, and Seminole performing artists, craftspeople, and musicians entertain and educate visitors in this four-day homecoming in what was once America's largest city north of Mexico.

Info: 634 Mound State Pkwy., Moundville, AL 35474 • 205.371.2234 • http://moundville.ua.edu/

TUSCALOOSA
Alabama Museum of Natural History

The museum holds over one million artifacts, associated documents, and photographic images documenting human history in the southeastern United States and beyond.

Info: 427 6th Ave., Tuscaloosa, AL 35487 • 205.348.7550 • https://almnh.ua.edu/

ARKANSAS

No federally recognized Native nations are in Arkansas; 29,268 residents identify as Native American.

BENTONVILLE
Museum of Native American History

Exhibits are divided into five different time periods from fourteen thousand years ago to more recent times. The museum houses a large collection of artifacts from across the Americas and hosts various events like the Native American Cultural Symposium, featuring Native musicians, speakers, and writers.

Info: 202 SW 'O' St., Bentonville, AR 72712 • 479.273.2456 • http://www.monah.us/index.html

LITTLE ROCK
The Sequoyah National Research Center

The Sequoyah National Research Center (SNRC) houses a remarkable repository of unique resources by and about Indigenous peoples where researchers can study in a creative and supportive environment. SNRC is part of the Collections and Archives Division at the University of Arkansas at Little Rock. Collections and Archives supports the academic success of the university community by taking part in research and dialogue through three organizations: The Center for Arkansas History and Culture, Ottenheimer Library, and the Sequoyah National Research Center.

Info: 500 University Plaza, University of Arkansas at Little Rock, 5820 Asher Ave., Little Rock, AR 72204-1099 • 501.569.8336 • http://ualr.edu/sequoyah/

SCOTT
Toltec Mounds State Park

While many Native American remains throughout the West were linked with the Aztec people by white settlers with vivid imaginations (see entries on "Montezuma Castle National Monument," Camp Verde, Arizona, and "Aztec Ruins National Monument,"

The Museum of Native American History in Bentonville, Arkansas.

The Toltec Mounds.

Aztec, New Mexico), the non-Native people of Arkansas were more subtle. When they found these mounds, they named them for the Toltec, a Mexican people who preceded the Aztec. The Toltec actually were prolific mound builders, and many of their monuments may be found around Mexico City.

John Baldwin, a nineteenth-century historian who wrote extensively on the origins of mounds in the United States, was convinced that the Toltec had migrated north, taking their mound culture with them. Although many anthropologists now believe that some Mississippi Valley groups were influenced by trade contact with the Toltec, no evidence links them to Arkansas. The religious and governmental complex at Toltec Mounds State Park was probably associated with the temple mound culture, which flourished in many areas of the American South. This community peaked between 700 and 950 C.E. The site has guided tours, a small museum, and gives visitors the chance to watch archaeologists at work.

Info: 490 Toltec Mounds Rd., Scott, AR 72142 • 501.961.9442 • https://www.arkansasstateparks.com/toltecmounds/

WILSON
Hampson State Museum

Amid the cotton fields of the delta, the remains of a temple mound people were found along the Mississippi River. Researchers uncovered Nodena, a 15-acre (60,703-square meter) palisaded farming village, which was occupied from about 1350 to 1700 C.E. by ancestors of the Chickasaw. In the 1930s and 1940s, Dr. James K. Hampson headed the excavations, and after his death, the archaeological materials were donated to the State of Arkansas.

The museum houses an impressive selection of artifacts from a number of different culture periods. Collections include rare head pots, which have a unique design and specialized technology and are believed to have been made only during the Mississippi time period; the function of these pots is still a mystery to anthropologists.

Examples of pottery found on site near the Hampson State Museum.

The many items of personal adornment—such as imported shell, copper, animal claws, teeth, and bones, fashioned into beads, pendants, and ear spools—were, according to the evidence, worn in great quantities by the Nodena people. Exhibits aim to place objects within their cultural context: the pottery exhibit, which includes the distinctive Nodena red-and-white pottery, describes the process of creating a pottery vessel, and the tool exhibit illustrates the function of the implements, comparing them to their modern counterparts.

Info: 10 Lake Dr., Wilson, AR 72395 • 501.655.8622 • https://www.arkansasstateparks.com/hampsonmuseum/

FLORIDA

The Seminole are the largest group of Native peoples in the state, and 101,060 Natives live in Florida.

BUSHNELL
Dade Battlefield State Historic Site

The Seminole of Florida are actually made up of many groups, exiles from their own lands in American-appropriated territory to the north. Oconee Indians were known to be living in the area early in the eighteenth century, and within a few years, they were joined by Yamasee from South Carolina. Finally, the Creek arrived after their disastrous defeat in 1813, swelling the number of those identified as Seminole to about five thousand.

Andrew Jackson invaded the area in 1818 on the pretext of recovering escaped, enslaved Africans and subduing the refugee Creek. This First Seminole War was actually a pretext to grab Florida for the United States. The States gained Florida, and the Seminole were pushed further south. In the next generation, the influx of white settlers brought the groups into conflict again. American policy toward the Indians in other parts of the South was expulsion to the West, and the same course was pursued in Florida. In 1832, the Seminole signed a treaty by which the tribe agreed to removal. However, in 1835, several younger leaders denounced the treaty, and the Second Seminole War began.

Although Osceola (see entry on "Osceola Historic Site," St. Augustine, Florida) was the most celebrated of the Seminole leaders, a brilliant piece of generalship came three days after Christmas in 1835 when the forces of Micanope and Jumper encountered a detachment of 108 American soldiers under Major Francis Dade. Caught near here in an open pine barren, only one of Dade's men survived. Oddly enough, the Seminole resistance and the ability of their leaders fueled the imagination of the American press. For the first time, public sympathy swung to the side of the Indians in their fight for independence, and Americans avidly followed the seven-year war. While some observers genuinely sympathized with the Seminole, most others saw it as a way for Northern opinion leaders to embarrass the South at a time of growing sectional tension. The remarkable feature of this park is that the natural flora and fauna that existed during these wars is protected today.

Info: 7200 CR 603, Bushnell, FL 33513 • 352.793.4781 • https://www.floridastate parks.org/park/dade-battlefield

CLEWISTON
Ah-Tah-Thi-Ki Museum

Located on the Big Cypress Seminole Indian Reservation in the Everglades, the museum houses almost two hundred thousand artifacts and archives that detail the history and contemporary culture of the Seminole. Ah-Tah-Thi-Ki is Seminole for "a place to learn, a place to remember." Besides the amazing displays, visitors are

Ah-Tah-Thi-Ki Museum (photo courtesy of the Ah-Tah-Thi-Ki Museum).

treated to a variety of events from the annual American Indian Arts Celebration to workshops by Native artists to a mile-long trek on a raised boardwalk through a beautiful, sixty-acre cypress dome in the incredible Everglades.

Info: Big Cypress Seminole Indian Reservation, 34725 W. Boundary Rd., Clewiston, FL 33440 • 877.902.1113 • http://www.ahtahthiki.com/

CRYSTAL RIVER
Crystal River Archaeological State Park

The Crystal River Mounds complex, composed of six burial and temple mounds, is considered to be one of the longest continually occupied sites in Florida. According to some Native traditionalists, the area was the "Club Med" of ceremonial sites and visited by many people over the centuries. The most impressive of the structures are two great platform mounds that were built at different stages but seem to be part of an alignment that incorporates the other mounds into an immense astronomical observatory that was used to keep track of the seasons, sun, and stars throughout the year.

Temple Mound at Crystal River Arch Park.

The structures, called midden mounds, were elaborately constructed of sand mixed with shell and organic debris. At its heyday, the largest would have been 210 feet (64 meter) wide at the base with sharply tapered edges, 40 feet (12 meters) high with a brightly colored building on the top. Among the artifacts discovered on the site are two types of upright limestone slabs (stele) that remain a mystery. They align with the mounds, and one has a faded carving of a human face.

It is estimated that the area was used until about 1400 c.e. and was probably built around 250 b.c.e. Excavations in the early twentieth century confirm that extended trade occurred from Ohio to Mexico that included present-day Florida, even including items as far away as the Rocky Mountains.

Info: 3400 N. Museum Point, Crystal River, FL 34428 • 352.795.3817 • https://www.floridastateparks.org/park/crystal-river-archaeological

DADE CITY
Silverhawk Flute Gathering

This annual, two-day festival is centered around the tradition of Native flute music and the flutes themselves. This family-friendly event, featuring Native food, workshops on flute construction, performances, and Native vendors, promises something for everyone.

Info: Withlacoochee River Park, 12449 Withlacoochee Blvd., Dade City, FL 33525 • 813.763.2118 • http://www.silverhawkflutegathering.com/

MELBOURNE
Native Rhythms Festival

An annual, two-day event, headline performers feature GRAMMY, NAMMY (Native American Music Award), and ISMA (Indian Summer Music Award) winners and nominees. Legendary musicians Robert Mirabel, Ed WindDancer, and Arvel Bird have been center stage at past festivals.

Info: Wickham Park, 2500 Parkway Dr., Melbourne, FL 32935 • 321.452.1671 • http://nativerhythmsfestival.com/

MIAMI
Miccosukee Indian Village

The Miccosukee began moving into central Florida even before the migrations of the 1700s. By the turn of the eighteenth century, they had begun to push further and further south into Florida, partly as a response to the establishment of Spanish missions and forts across northern Florida during the seventeenth century. Within Tamiami Station, in less than a hundred years, the Timucua and Apalachee Indians living in the Spanish mission settlements were wiped out, largely by sickness.

Diorama of Famous Alligator Wrestling, Miccosukee Indian Village.

Sometime between 1715 and 1730, the main ancestors of the Miccosukee were back in the area of the Florida Panhandle, some of whom settled in the Apalachee Bay region, others along the Chattahoochee and Apalachicola rivers.

In 1821, Spain sold Florida to the United States. The Americans, who recognized the rights of the Indians over much of the peninsula at that time, negotiated for land in the Treaty of Moultrie Creek in 1823. Tantamount to a land grab, the treaty forced the Miccosukee to pull back to a reservation in central Florida, where they were allowed to live in peace for twenty years.

In 1829–1830, agitation by new Anglo-American settlers led the government to dictate that all the Indians in the Southeast had to move west. The Second Seminole War, which lasted from 1835 to 1842, left many of the Miccosukee dead or deported, and the Third Seminole War, which lasted from 1855 to 1858, further decimated the tribe. After the wars, about three hundred Seminole went off the grid by relocating deep into the Everglades, and the federal government abandoned hope of ever finding them. Since the war had already cost more than one thousand soldiers and millions of dollars, the government left the remaining Seminole alone and eventually established these reservations. The remainder of the Miccosukee who escaped removal to Oklahoma reside on four Seminole reservations. By 1860, only about 150 to two hundred Mikasuki speakers were still living in Florida; sixty years earlier, more than six thousand Indians had been in the area.

Although Miccosukee is the smallest reservation—a strip of 333 acres (1.3 square kilometers) along the Tamiami Trail—most public activities are held here, including the annual Green Corn Ceremonial. (Call in advance for dates.) A museum displays the traditional chickees, open-sided cypress houses built on stilts and thatched with palmetto fronds. Traditional craft shops showcase unique Seminole clothing, and a restaurant serves traditional Native American dishes. The adjacent Everglades National Park offers airboat rides. Also, one can visit the casino and resort.

Info: Mile Marker 35, U.S. Hwy. 41, Tamiami Trail, Miami, FL 33194 • 305.223.8380 • Casino: 500 SW 177th Ave., Miami, FL 33194 • 305.222.4600 • http://www.miccosukee.com/indian-village/

TALLAHASSEE
Mission San Luis

When the first Spanish explorers made their way across the Florida panhandle, they described the fields of the Apalachee, which spanned for acres and acres between prosperous villages. At the time, the Apalachee numbered more than six thousand and were acknowledged to be the wealthiest group in what is now Florida. They were part of the extensive trade network that stretched thousands of miles to parts of Mexico and the Midwest. The De Soto expedition arrived in 1539 looking for plunder after having been told by other Indigenous peoples that the Apalachee owned great stores of gold. "Pass through, robbers and traitors," they were told; the conquistador dared not challenge the Apalachee show of strength.

However, a century later, the Apalachee were Christianized when a series of missions were established in their homeland. The capital of the Apalachee missions, San Luis de Talimali, built in 1656, was located in present-day Tallahassee. In 1703–1704, an alliance of South Carolina militia and southern Creek invaded Apalachee country and shattered them, destroying half of their communities and enslaving hundreds. The rest escaped west, eventually settling in Louisiana, where the French welcomed their agrarian expertise. Descendants of these survivors are represented by the Talimali Band of Apalachee.

Archaeologists have uncovered evidence of a seventeenth-century, Catholic mission and its associated village, San Luis Mission, where work is still in progress. It is one of the eight major Apalachee towns and situated just outside what is now the state capital. Today, the National Historic Landmark site is a living history museum with reconstructed colonial buildings and interpretive guides in period outfits. The impressive, thatched Apalachee Council House is 125 feet (38 meters) in diameter and five stories tall and is the center of many activities at San Luis, including solstice celebrations, archery demonstrations, and multicultural events. A small exhibit gallery displays artifacts from the site.

Info: 2100 W. Tennessee St., Tallahassee, FL 32304 • 850.245.6406 • https://www.missionsanluis.org/visitorinfo/index.cfm

GEORGIA

No federally recognized tribes are in the state. Georgia's Indian population is 51,405.

ATLANTA
Michael C. Carlos Museum—Emory University

The Carlos Museum is one of the Southeast's premier ancient art museums with a major collection of art objects from the ancient Americas. On display are changing exhibits like "Threads of Time: Tradition and Change in Indigenous American Textiles" and "Coiling Culture: Basketry Art of Native North America."

Info: 571 S. Kilgo St., Atlanta, GA 30322 • 404.727.4282 • http://carlos.emory.edu/

AUGUSTA
Augusta Museum of History

One exhibit hall is dedicated to the First Peoples of Augusta, mainly the Yamasee.

Info: 560 Reynolds St., Augusta, GA 30901 • 706.722.8454 • http://www.augustamuseum.org/augustasstory

BLAKELY
Kolomoki Mounds State Park

Kolomoki is the most southern of the state's significant mound groupings and features the oldest and largest Woodland Indian site in the southeastern United States.

Plaque and lookout of Kolomoki mounds.

The oldest great temple mound is 57 feet (17 meters) high, towering over two smaller burial mounds and several ceremonial mounds. The museum is built around an excavated mound; you can see how the archaeologists made their cuts when most of the work was done in the 1930s and 1940s. Numerous artifacts and films detail the historic period during which the mounds were built, which lasted from 5000 B.C.E. into the thirteenth century.

Info: Kolomoki Mounds State Park, 205 Indian Mounds Rd., Blakely, GA 39823-4460 • 912.723.5296 • http://www.gastateparks.org/kolomokimounds

CALHOUN
New Echota State Historic Site

This Southeast site illustrates the tragedy and victimization of the Cherokee Nation. The reconstructed village of New Echota is just a few miles from the busiest interstate highway in Georgia and follows the same route that once ran north through the Cherokee heartland from the Standing Peachtree, in what is now Atlanta, a landmark that once marked the separation between the territories of the Creek and the Cherokee. According to historic accounts, the Cherokee lost the lands to the South in a series of ball games.

New Echota was the capital of the Cherokee from 1825 to 1838, the seat of a nation within a nation. Its legislature resided here, making laws and electing leaders in a form of government modeled after that of the United States. The nation had been promised by the Americans that if they modeled their government on the federal system, the two groups could live together in amity. Strange, as the U.S. government itself was based on the traditional Haudensaunee (Iroquois) government.

The Cherokee emphatically stuck to their word, expecting the white government to do the same. During this era, they hung on to a much-reduced territory that extended across the north Georgia highlands and into adjacent areas of Tennessee, North Carolina, and Alabama. In traditional times, they controlled a vast region, including what is now parts of the Virginias, Kentucky, the Carolinas, Tennessee, Alabama, and Georgia. Many of the Cherokee had fought with white settlers against the Creek during the War of 1812. Because of that alliance against their Creek brothers, Cherokee leaders felt safe from expulsion even as the Creek were being pushed out of Georgia in the 1820s. President John Quincy Adams supported them, despite Georgia's governor's insistence that the federal government adhere to an 1802 agreement that called for the removal of all Indians from the state. Washington recognized the Cherokee as a self-governing nation. At New Echota, the Cherokee shaped a democratic republic, with a bicameral legislature and a principal chief elected by the upper house.

It was apparent by 1828, however, that Andrew Jackson would be elected president in that year's election. The Georgia legislature passed a law extending its jurisdiction over the Cherokee lands and revoking the Indian government. When Jackson took over, he immediately turned on his former comrades-in-arms and embraced the Georgia law.

Even worse for the Cherokee, gold was discovered on their lands almost simultaneously with Jackson's election. No diplomatic niceties would stop the prospectors who poured into the Cherokee Nation and often settled land claims by murdering the Indian occupants. Any hope for Cherokee resistance ended in 1832. The state simply subdivided and sold their lands out from under them, passing a law forbidding them to hold public assemblies. The prospect of Indians living under their own self-governance, publishing a newspaper in their own language, seemed to enflame white suspicion and hatred: the more the Cherokee tried to cooperate with their white neighbors, the more they were feared as an impediment to unrestricted white settlement.

Recognizing the futility of further resistance, some tribal leaders accepted an offer of five million dollars and new lands in the West in 1835. These treaty signers were a minority, but when the federal government approved the treaty, the entire

Inside the Council House, New Echota.

Indian population was given two years to leave the state. Jackson ignored a U.S. Supreme Court decision that favored the Cherokee and ordered the expulsion to proceed. By 1838, New Echota had been exiled, forced westward along the Trail of Tears. The buildings were torn down and the land plowed for crops. Only a home built by the Reverend Samuel A. Worcester, a missionary from Boston who had come to New Echota in 1827 and followed the Cherokee west on their exile, remained standing to mark the site.

About 120 years later, some residents of Calhoun, the town that had grown up nearby, purchased 200 acres (809,371 square meters) on what was determined to have been the site of New Echota. In 1955, a tavern once owned by Cherokee leader James Vann was moved there to save it from destruction by a man-made lake. The Worcester House was restored in 1959, and offices of the Cherokee national newspaper, *The Phoenix*, were rebuilt. New Echota was made a state historic site in 1962, and the Cherokee Nation Supreme Court Building and a typical home site in the village were reconstructed. That same year, the Georgia legislature also repealed the laws that had taken these lands away from their rightful occupants.

Twelve original and reconstructed buildings, including the Council House, Court House, Print Shop, Missionary Samuel Worcester's home, and an 1805 store as well as smokehouses, corn cribs, and barns, mark the grounds on the original capital. The site has nature trails, a gift shop, and interpretative exhibits. A monument to the Trail of Tears was erected on its sesquicentennial in 1988.

Info: 1211 Chatsworth Hwy. NE, Calhoun, GA 30701 • 706.624.1321 • http://www.gastateparks.org/newechota

CARTERSVILLE
Etowah Mounds State Historic Site

In 1871, the Etowah Mounds began to be systematically excavated. Archaeologists determined that the mounds dated from about 1000 to 1500 c.e. and had been used as temples, burial places, and residences for the priest-chiefs. Several smaller mounds were rich in artifacts, including stone effigies of human beings lavish with ornamentation. Trade items from Michigan's Upper Peninsula and Mexico were also found on this site. The whole complex, surrounded by a moat, could be fortified.

Info: 813 Indian Mounds Rd. SW, Cartersville, GA 30120 • 770.387.3747 • http://www.gastateparks.org/etowahmounds

CHATSWORTH
Chief Vann House Historic Site

James Vann is one of those shadowy figures who turns up repeatedly on the southern frontier in the late eighteenth century. Although Georgia was one of the original thirteen states, its northern area, the Cherokee lands, was still free from colonial rule. Frequently, men on the run from the seaboard cities or the neighboring Carolinas would seek refuge in the area and begin new lives. Vann was one such man. He turned up in the Cherokee lands in the years after the revolution and married an Indigenous woman. He made a fortune as a trader and eventually became a chief. Something was dangerous in his makeup, contemporaries observed, that inspired respect but not love.

Chief Vann's House.

Almost as if in penance for the actions of his past, Vann dedicated himself to converting the Cherokee to Christianity. He imported Moravian missionaries from North Carolina in 1802 and sent his own children to their school. Two years later, he built this home across the road from the mission. The two-story, red, brick mansion stands on a slight elevation and was obviously built to inspire awe and a sense of stability. A hanging staircase and Native carvings are its finest interior features.

Although Vann urged his tribe to take up Christianity, he was a polygamist with three wives, and in 1809, he was killed in retaliation for having shot one of his brothers-in-law in a duel. His son, Joseph, inherited the house and the family fortune. Soon, however, having violated a newly passed state law when he hired a white man to work for him, Vann's property was seized, and he was sent west with his expelled people.

While on a visit to this house in 1835, John Howard Payne, the author of "Home Sweet Home," was arrested by Georgia guardsmen and charged with sedition. Payne insisted that he was simply writing a history of the Cherokee and was released after twelve days.

Info: 82 Highway 225 N., Chatsworth, GA 30705 • 706.695.2598 • http://gastateparks.org/chiefvannhouse

EATONTON
Rock Eagle Mound

Rock Eagle is the best-preserved animal sculpture mound in the state, measuring 120 feet (37 meters) across its outspread wings. Built of quartz stones, the bird is painstakingly proportioned, right up to the relative size of the feathers in its wings. The shape becomes apparent only when viewed from above; visitors may gain that perspective from an adjacent tower.

An aerial view of Rock Eagle Mound.

Info: 350 Rock Eagle Rd., Eatonton, GA 31024 • 706.484.2862 • http://caes2.caes.uga.edu/georgia4h/rockeagle/about.html

FLOVILLA
Indian Springs State Park

For centuries, the Creek used the spring water here for healing, as it had restorative powers. It later became associated with their final disaster. Following the British withdrawal from the region after the War of 1812, the Creek were subjected to the fury of the U.S. government. Many of the southern Creek had allied themselves with England, and Georgia demanded that they be expelled from the state under the terms of an 1802 agreement with the federal government. Early in 1821, in a treaty signed at this spring, the Creek ceded most of their lands under extreme pressure. They retained only a few tracts, including one surrounding the spring.

That was not enough for Georgia's governor, George Troup. Demanding the total expulsion of all Indians from the state, he bullied the government into obtaining the rest of the land. Creek leader William McIntosh, who had fought with the Americans in the war and was Troup's cousin, complied. In a second treaty signed in 1825 at Indian Springs, he agreed to the cession of the remaining Creek lands and expulsion to the west. The tribal leaders were outraged and ordered McIntosh executed a few months later. Nevertheless, the agreement was upheld by the U.S. government, and the Creek were displaced across the Mississippi. The spring was turned into a state park immediately after the signing of the second treaty and has remained one ever since.

Info: 678 Lake Clark Rd., Flovilla, GA 30216 • 770.504.2277 • http://www.gastate parks.org/indiansprings

LAGRANGE
Lamar Dodd Art Center

The center is known for the Josephine Altman Case Collection of Plains and Southwest American Indian Art.

Info: 601 Broad St., LaGrange, GA 30240 • 706.880.8000 •
http://www.lagrange.edu/academics/art/lamar-dodd.html

MACON
Ocmulgee National Monument

Higher and more numerous mound groupings exist in the Southeast, but none contain such a clear record of continuous habitation, or are so impressively situated, as those at Ocmulgee. Located on the Macon Plateau just to the east of the central Georgia city of Macon, the view over modern Macon from the ancient mounds adds to their sense of majesty.

Evidence of human occupancy, like spear points of ancient hunters, dates back to at least 9000 B.C.E. The fertile bottomlands, rich game, and elevated location attracted one group after another to the place for ten millennia, but the residents who left the most lasting impression were the early Mississippians, who lived there for just two hundred years. Given their name because the culture arose in the Mississippi River Valley, they arrived here around 900 C.E. and were brilliant agronomists, had an extremely complex religious life, and built towns for one thousand people or more. It is believed through both tribal histories and archaeological finds that many different nations are descended from this amazing culture: Alabama, Apalachee, Caddo, Chickasaw, Cherokee, Choctaw, Muscogee Creek, Guale, Hitchiti, Houma, Kansa, Missouria, Mobilian, Natchez, Osage, Quapaw, Seminole, Tunica-Biloxi, Yamasee, and Yuchi. Around 1100 C.E., the community was abandoned for no clear reason, and a

Ceremonial Mound at Ocmulgee.

new settlement was built nearby by a people who adapted many elements of the Mississippian culture. Finally, a Creek village was established in the late seventeenth century and a British trading post operated here until 1715.

The visitor center at the park entrance contains a historic overview of the site, including displays of the local artifacts. A reconstruction of an original ceremonial building features a thousand-year-old clay floor that could hold large meetings. Nearby is the Cornfield Mound and the clear evidence of an ancient field, one of the oldest examples of cultivation in the Southeast. The Great Temple Mound, which rises 45 feet (14 meters) has a staircase to its summit; in ancient times, a rectangular, wooden structure stood at its top. A Funeral Mound was built up over seven successive stages; more than half the mound was destroyed when a railroad cut through the area in the 1870s, more than half a century before the first archaeological examination of the site began.

Visitors can attend the annual fall Ocmulgee Indian Celebration, learn to construct ancient Mississippian pottery, or grab a lantern and stroll along the luminary-lined path from the Visitor Center to the Great Temple Mound during the annual spring Lantern Light Tour.

Info: 1207 Emery Hwy., Macon, GA 31217 • 478.752.8257 • https://www.nps.gov/ocmu/index.htm

ROME
Chieftains Museum

Major Ridge, a leading tribal statesman, was a controversial figure in the final years before the Cherokee expulsion to the West. He built this log cabin in 1794; it now lies at the core of the mansion that grew up around it in what was the village of Chiaha, one of the most populous Cherokee settlements in northern Georgia. Operating a ferry service in the late nineteenth century, Ridge turned his riverside home into a gathering place.

Ridge allied himself with the American forces in the war against the Creek, and his name probably reflects the rank he held in that conflict. As pressure grew for a state takeover of Indian lands, he joined John Ross, the leading advocate of resistance to the white incursion. Late in 1835, however, Ridge reversed his position and signed the treaty of New Echota, relinquishing all Cherokee land claims east of the Mississippi, thinking, perhaps, that his people would be spared. He accompanied his people on the Trail of Tears but was executed in 1839 in accordance with a tribal mandate that sentenced to death all who had signed the treaty. His descendants feel that he was misjudged by his people and was a scapegoat for the removal. Ridge's home is now a museum of the area's Indian heritage.

Info: 501 Riverside Pkwy., Rome, GA 30161 • 706.291.9494 • https://chieftainsmuseum.org/

SANDERVILLE
Washington County Historical Society

On permanent loan from Muscogee elder Debbie Bush, the museum has an extensive Muscogee Creek Indian display of several artifacts: pottery, baskets, trade items, fur skins, traditional clothing, ceremonial items, weapons, and art. The collection is currently housed in the Train Museum Building adjacent to the main museum.

Info: 268 N. Harris St., Sandersville, GA 31082 • 478.552.1965 • http://wacohistorical.org/

WALESKA
Funk Heritage Center at Reinhardt University

The center offers several exhibits on Southeast Indigenous peoples, particularly the Cherokee, including "Life along the Etowah" and "History Beneath Our Feet," with dioramas depicting different historical eras and an account of the Trail of Tears. Also, the Rogers Contemporary Native American Art Gallery is an extensive collection of remarkable works by today's Native artists.

Info: 7300 Reinhardt Cir., Waleska, GA 30183-2981 • 770.720.5970 • https://www.reinhardt.edu/funkheritage/index.php

WHIGHAM
Tama Intertribal Powwow

Although some of the Lower Muskogee Creek were given back some of their own land for their services to the U.S. government in the War of 1812, they were adversely affected by the laws that followed the Indian Removal Act of 1826. Muskogee people were not allowed to be hired by a white man; their hunting and fishing rights were

Funk Heritage Center.

denied; their identity was changed from Muskogee to "persons of color"; and they were banned from practicing their religion. The South Swamps of Attapulgus became a haven for the Creek who had migrated from central Georgia, Alabama, and north Florida. Often called border trotters, they traveled from Florida to Georgia to Alabama to flee persecution of state laws. In spite of white hostility, the Creek helped their white neighbors during the War of 1836 by taking care of their livestock while the whites themselves went into Fort Bainbridge. William Williams, a Muskogee, was trained in an Indian boarding school and used his knowledge of written English to help his people get the right to work as sharecroppers on his property. Another tribal leader, William Brown, spent his life persuading Congress to return Muskogee land. That never happened. However, the Muskogee served in every war, including the current conflicts in the Middle East. Today, the Lower Muskogee Creek Tribe has been recognized as a legal entity within the State of Georgia and is a state-recognized tribe by the Georgia General Assembly. They are headquartered in their traditional town of Tama. Every fall, they hold an intertribal powwow.

Info: 106 Tall Pine Dr., Whigham, GA 39897 • 229.762.3165 • http://lowermuskogeetribe.com/home.html

KEnTUCKY

Native people number 13,012 in Kentucky; tribes are state recognized.

CORBIN
Kentucky Native American Heritage Museum

The museum began as a mobile outreach to schools, libraries, museums, festivals, and powwows and promotes understanding of Indigenous peoples' lifeways from both historic and contemporary perspectives. Focusing on Eastern Woodlands culture, particularly Appalachian heritage, the museum holds community events like powwows and classes.

Info: 4116 Cumberland Falls Hwy., Corbin, KY 40701 • 606.526.5635 • http://www.knahm.org/support.html

FRANKFORT
Kentucky Native American Heritage Commission

November is Native American Heritage Month, and the commission offers different events each year. For a listing, visit its website.

Info: 505.564.7005, Ext. 120 • http://heritage.ky.gov/knahc/

HOPKINSVILLE
Trail of Tears Commemorative Park

This park is located on one of the few documented sites (1838–1839) of the actual trail and campsites used during the forced removal of the Cherokee people to "Indian Territory." Two Cherokee chiefs, Fly Smith and Whitepath, who died during the removal, are buried here. Memorial statues to the fallen leaders were created by local artist Steve Shields and unveiled by delegations from the Eastern Band of Cherokee and local Cherokee. The park was created by a 1987 bill by President Ronald Reagan creating the Trail of Tears as a National Historical Trail. Hopkinsville, Kentucky, was the first nonfederal property to receive such designation (1996), and Kentucky was once part of Cherokee lands. The Heritage Center dates back to the time of removal and is filled with the history, maps, and relocation accounts of "The Trail Where They Cried." Seven red Cherokee chief dogwoods were planted in honor of each clan; each is marked by a carved, redwood sign. For over thirty years, the Trail of Tears Powwow has been held in the park on the weekend after Labor Day.

Info: 1730 E. 9th St., Hopkinsville, KY 42240 • 270.885.9096 • http://trailoftears.org/index.php/home

LOUISVILLE
Speed Art Museum

The museum's collection of Native American art is often part of changing exhibits.

Info: 2035 S. Third St., Louisville, KY 40208 • 502.634.2700 • http://www.speedmuseum.org/

RICHMOND
Richmond Powwow Association

This organization holds an annual powwow every spring. The site may change, but it is currently held at Battlefield Park.

Info: 859.623.6076 • http://www.richmondpowwow.org/

WICKLIFFE
Wickliffe Mounds State Park

These mounds are the site of a Mississippian community that existed from 1110 to 1350 C.E. Homes surrounded a central plaza overlooking the Mississippi River. Today, this area is on the National Register of Historic Places and is a designated Kentucky Archaeological Landmark. Along with a museum that exhibits items excavated on the site, the area features mounds surrounded by abundant wildlife, a walking trail, and a spectacular view of the bluff area on top of the Ceremonial Mound, the largest mound on the site. Special exhibits, hands-on displays, events, demonstrations, and educational programs occur at various times throughout the year. For example, one fun, popular summer event is an archaeology day camp for kids.

Info: 94 Green St., Wickliffe, KY 42087 • 270.335.3681 • http://parks.ky.gov/parks/historicsites/wickliffe-mounds/

LOUISIANA

Over 35,648 Natives call Louisiana home; four federally recognized tribes are in the state.

CHARENTON
Chitimacha Museum and Cultural Center

Displays at the Chitimacha Tribal Museum and Cultural Center include traditional arts, history, education, and government. Historical artifacts exhibited include clothing, blowguns, a detailed house diorama, pottery, arrowheads, and the famous Chitimacha baskets. The baskets were extremely valuable, even as early as the seventeenth century, and are still prized by collectors. The Chitimacha are known as the best basket makers in all of the Gulf, and visitors are sometimes treated to a basket-weaving demonstration. Artifacts and videos present a view of historical and contemporary Chitimacha culture.

A double basket on display at the Chitimacha Museum and Cultural Center.

Info: 3289 Chitimacha Trail, Charenton, LA 70523 • 337.923.4830 • http://www.chitimacha.gov/

GONZALES
Louisiana Indian Heritage Association Powwow

For over fifty years, this large powwow has been a celebration of Native cultures in the southeast part of the state. The Louisiana Indian Heritage Association, a statewide, nonprofit organization founded in 1967, has helped revive traditions among Louisiana First Peoples.

Info: Lamar-Dixon Expo Center, 9039 S. St. Landry Ave., Gonzales, LA 70737 • 225.621.1700 • http://liha.webs.com/

GRAY
United Houma Nation Cultural Center

Ground has been broken for the new multimillion-dollar culture center, which will display the history and culture of the United Houma Nation. Check the website for progress of the facility.

Info: 4425 Park Ave., Gray, LA 70359 • 985.275.0820 • http://www.unitedhoumanation.org/

KINDER
Coushatta Powwow

One of the country's biggest Native gatherings, the annual powwow is held every June. The Coushatta are a testimony to survival under the worst conditions of oppression and colonialism. However, they remain on their homelands and, in spite of great odds, still speak their language in its purest form. They also operate a casino, where guests can learn more about their history and heritage as well as do activities for the entire family.

Info: 777 Coushatta Dr., Kinder, LA 70648 • 800.584.7263 • http://www.coushattapowwow.com/

MARKSVILLE
Marksville State Historic Site

This is one of the oldest mound sites in the mid-South, dating from about 100 to 400 C.E. Of greater importance is the clear evidence found here of extensive contact with the Hopewell culture (see entry on "Mound City National Monument," Chillicothe, Ohio) far to the north. The practice of building enclosures for mounds and creating a central plaza are definitely Hopewell attributes, and Marksville is the earliest-known site at which it was copied in the South. The mounds here were built in a conical shape, rather than the flat-topped variety favored by the temple mound people who later came to dominate this part of the country. An on-site museum features the history of the area.

Info: 837 Martin Luther King Dr., Marksville, LA 71351 • 225.342.8111 • http://www.crt.state.la.us/louisiana-state-parks/historic-sites/marksville-state-historic-site/

Tunica-Biloxi Cultural and Educational Resources Center

The center's museum is home to the "Tunica Treasure," a vast collection of Native American European trade items and other artifacts buried in over a hundred graves

Tunica-Biloxi Cultural and Educational Resources Center.

by the Tunica from 1731 to 1764 near present-day Angola Prison. It is also the birth-place of the repatriation movement and the subsequent passing of the Native American Graves Protection and Repatriation Act of 1990 (NAGPRA). Before NAGPRA, Native people had little power to defend their sacred and material objects; grave looters and artifact hunters were profiting from Indian cultural items, robbing First Nations of their histories. The Tunica initiated a long and arduous legal battle to regain and conserve their historic items. They also trained several tribal members to be conservators for the collection. Not only have Tunica conservators honed the patience and skill to painstakingly restore these ancient items that were in deplorable condition, but they have also saved the tribe thousands of dollars in restoration fees.

The museum is located in the Tunica-Biloxi Cultural and Educational Resources Center (CERC), a 40,000-square-foot (3,716-square-meter) building that also includes a conservation and restoration laboratory, gift shop, library, auditorium, classrooms, distance learning center, meeting rooms, and tribal government offices. Every spring, the Tunica-Biloxi host a powwow at the Earl J. Barbry Sr. Convention Center at Paragon Casino Resort, a tribal entity.

Info: 151 Melancon Rd., Marksville, LA 71351 • 318.240.6400 • http://www.tunicabiloxi.org

PIONEER
Poverty Point National Monument

Poverty Point (1650–1100 B.C.E.) was the center of a vast trading and industry network that extended hundreds of miles across the present-day states of Louisiana, Mississippi, Arkansas, and parts of Tennessee and eastward to Florida's Gulf Coast, but its importance was not understood until the 1950s, when aerial photos were taken in by the U.S. Army Corps of Engineers and analyzed the American Museum of Natural History. Museum staff discovered that when viewed from the air, the group of mounds

Aerial view of Poverty Point (photo by Susan Guice).

along the bayous of northeastern Louisiana resolved itself into a shape that could not be grasped from the ground. From the air, one can appreciate the engineered, gigantic earthworks consisting of five mounds and six rows of semicircular, concentric ridges. Moreover, from the outlines visible in the pictures, the researchers estimated that the original structure may have been 11 miles (1.6 kilometers) long, 6 feet (1.8 meters) high, and 80 feet (24 meters) thick. The largest of the mounds is bird-shaped and rises to a height of 70 feet (21 meters). To move the amount of earth required to build all this would have taken twenty million basketloads of soil, each weighing 50 pounds (23 kilograms), and at least five million hours of labor to build. Perhaps the ridges provided housing for those coming to trade. The middle area is perfectly flat, made so by an incredible engineering feat. Possibly, it was a giant amphitheater with raised stages. Surrounding mounds overlook the Mississippi flood plain.

As the area is studied, even more proof has been found that it was a huge market and gathering place for a far-reaching economic system. A wide variety of objects have been unearthed. Some of the projectile points and tools, ground stone plummets, fired clay figurines and vessels, gorgets, and shell and stone beads are made from materials found nearby, but other objects were constructed from imported soapstone, hematite, magnetite, slate, galena, copper, and other materials from far away. This thriving culture, ancestors of modern-day Southeasterners, was a hub of ancient peoples—the mall or farmers market of its time. No one knows why Poverty Point was abandoned—natural disasters or a change in trends, maybe, but by the time the Europeans arrived, it was already a historical site. Poverty Point was the name of the cotton plantation located on the grounds and has nothing to do with the ancient community. In 1962, Poverty Point Park in Louisiana was designated a National Historic Landmark by the U.S. Department of the Interior. In 2014, it became the 1,001st property on the World Heritage List (UNESCO), giving it equal status with other ancient treasures like the Pyramids of Giza and the Great Wall of China.

An on-site museum has artifact displays, and visitors may climb an observation tower to get some idea of what it looks like from the air. Various activities like flint knapping and ranger-guided hikes are offered. Archaeologists also work here during the summer months.

Info: 6859 LA-577, Pioneer, LA 71266 • 318.926.5492 • https://www.nps.gov/popo/index.htm

ROBELINE
Adai Caddo Cultural Center

The center chronicles the historical and contemporary lives of the Adai Caddo Indian people, who live in both Louisiana and Texas.

Info: 4460 Hwy. 485, Robeline, LA 71469 • 318.472.1007 • http://adaicaddoindiannation.com/adai-caddo-cultural-center/

SHREVEPORT
Louisiana State Exhibit Museum

The Caddo have been continuously documented in the area along the Red River from 900–1050 C.E. to the present day. The Caddo people built mounds along the river to cover sacred sites and burial areas and as platforms for buildings or special events; the biggest are located in Gahagan and Mounds Plantation in Caddo Parish and Crenshaw Mound, in Miller County, Arkansas. Haley and Belcher, along with similar other smaller mounds, have been found between Crenshaw and Mounds plantations. Each site is about equidistant from the others, with 75 miles (121 kilometers) between each along the river. Most were excavated by a team led by Dr. Clarence H. Webb.

Ceremonial pottery, shell beads, pipes, copper ornaments, and stone tools unearthed at these sites are all on display in the museum's Webb Native American Gallery. One of the most spectacular artifacts is a cypress canoe from around 1005 C.E., which shows the great artistry of the Caddo ancestors and their far-reaching travel for trade, hunting, leisure, and lifeways.

Info: 3015 Greenwood Rd., Shreveport, LA 71109 • 318.632.2020 • http://www.laexhibitmuseum.org/

MISSISSIPPI

A population of 17,810 Native people is in Mississippi.

CHOCTAW
Mississippi Band of Choctaw Indians

Thirty-five thousand acres (142 square kilometers) of trust land spread over ten counties in east-central Mississippi comprise the Choctaw Indian Reservation, home to around ten thousand members who live in one of eight reservation communities. When Europeans began invading the area in the sixteenth century, the Choctaw had agricultural villages spread throughout central Mississippi; government was handled on the local level. The people prospered, growing enough food to export staples to their neighbors and developing a reputation for their business acumen. Known as a formidable power, their towns were fortified, but they preferred settling conflicts through stickball games and diplomacy.

The nation allied with the French during the eighteenth-century conflicts between the French and the British colonial powers. Following the defeat of the French in the French and Indian War (1754–1763), the British took some Choctaw land, forcing many westward in search of new territory.

The Mississippi Choctaw have always maintained a strong business tradition, and as early as 1700, they had a thriving economy based on selling livestock, goods, and agricultural products to Europeans as well as their custom of trade with other Native peoples. They continued to prosper throughout the eighteenth century and had large

The Mississippi Band of Choctaw Indians World Series of Stickball champs (2013).

land holdings. However, the formation of the United States of America created more and more pressures for the Choctaw as the new nation began to expand onto Choctaw land. Mississippi became a territory in 1798; two years later, Thomas Jefferson was elected president and set his sights on acquiring all lands bordering the eastern Mississippi River as a defense against France, Spain, and England. In 1801, the Treaty of Fort Adams was signed, forcing the Choctaw to cede 2,641,920 acres (10,691 square kilometers) of land from the Yazoo River to the thirty-first parallel to the United States. It was just the first of a series of treaties between 1801 and 1830; eventually, more than 23 million acres (93,078 square kilometers) were ceded to the United States. The Treaty of Dancing Rabbit Creek in 1830 marked the final secession of lands and outlined the terms of Choctaw removal to the West. Indeed, the Choctaw Nation was the first American Indian tribe to be removed by the federal government from its ancestral home to land set aside for them in what is now Oklahoma. The Choctaw was the first of the "Five Civilized Tribes" to be removed from the southeastern United States. In 1830, the Treaty of Dancing Rabbit Creek, signed by a small minority of the Choctaw when most leaders walked out of the negotiations in disgust, committed the Choctaw to give up their lands and be removed to the West. The phrase "Trail of Tears" originated from a description of the removal of the Choctaw Nation in 1831, although the term is also used in reference to the Cherokee removal in 1838–1839. However, Indigenous people called it "The Trail Where They Cried."

Unlike neighboring states, however, Mississippi did not require all Indians to leave. A small number remained on their homelands while thirteen thousand were forced out of their territory (1831–1833), and more followed in later years. The title to their property was seized; their government was disbanded by the United States. The result was economically ruinous. Promises of aid for land acquisition were not kept, and the Choctaw were reduced to sharecropping or squatting on their original lands. They also were victimized by Mississippi's rigorous Jim Crow laws. Members of the Mississippi Band of Choctaw Indians are descendants of those who refused to be removed to present-day Oklahoma. The nation has self-governed since 1945.

The Mississippi Band of Choctaw Indians (MBCI) owns and operates diverse enterprises. In 1949, they hosted the first Choctaw Fair, now a major Indian event in the South and held each July. Historical and cultural displays, social dancing, traditional arts, World Series of Stickball, Choctaw traditional food, and the Choctaw Indian Princess Pageant entertain visitors. The Choctaw Museum showcases the nation's culture, history, government, and traditional art forms, along with events like demonstrations by Choctaw artisans and craftsmen. In addition to the museum, the Chahta Immi Cultural Center provides cultural education, an archives collection, and displays of a variety of Choctaw art as well as classes and events. MBCI owns the Pearl River Resort with three spectacular casinos, two award-winning golf courses, a water theme park, a relaxing spa, and gourmet restaurants.

The Choctaw Nation is a major employer in Neshoba County, operating several manufacturing enterprises. Visitors are both educated and entertained, as they have lots to do within the Choctaw Nation boundaries.

Info: 101 Industrial Rd., Choctaw, MS 39350 • 601.656.5251 • http://www.choctaw.org/tourism/index.html

GREENVILLE
Winterville Mounds State Park

The Mississippi delta is among the flattest places in America, and the view from the top of the central mound seems almost alpine amid the surrounding flatness. The mounds are worth a visit if for no other reason than to see the dramatic appearance they make in the otherwise level landscape.

Winterville represents a major community of the temple mound people, a religious center that flourished around 1000 C.E. Fifteen mounds are in the group, the highest being 55 feet (17 meters) tall. The mounds were built by women carrying basketloads of dirt, and individual loads are visible within the mounds. When the mounds were completed, a temple or a chief's house was constructed on top of it. Eventually, these buildings were ceremonially destroyed by fire, covered over with more earth, and another building was erected on top of the mound. In this way, the mounds grew in successive layers over as many as eight hundred years. A museum displays articles recovered from the area, in addition to some donated by private collectors. Artifacts include rare pipes, weapons, beads, and tiny effigy owl and game stones.

Info: 2415 MS-1, Greenville, MS 38701 • 662.334.4684 • https://www.nps.gov/nr/travel/mounds/win.htm

NATCHEZ
Emerald Mound

The Natchez Trace was one of the most important roads in pre-European contact culture, running 444 miles (715 kilometers) northeast from Natchez through the lands of the Chickasaw and Choctaw all the way to present-day Nashville, Tennessee. Used for generations as a trade route between tribes of the Mississippi and Tennessee valleys in 1801, Native peoples gave the U.S. government the rights to run a wagon road through their lands along the old trail. It became a crucial link between the lower Mississippi and the rest of the country. Flatboat crews would transport goods down the big river but could not return by water because the bulky crafts were useless against the strong current, so they went back overland along the trace, and it became a legendary trail (see entry on "Chickasaw Indian Village," Tupelo, Mississippi). Today, almost every major road in the United States was first mapped out by Native peoples.

Just a few miles from the start of the trace was the Emerald Mound, the great ceremonial center of the Natchez tribe. This 35-foot- (11-meter-) high mound covers 8 acres (32,375 square meters) and is the second largest in area in the country. It was built around 1300 c.e.

Info: 10 miles northeast of Natchez, MS (milepost 10.3) on Natchez Trace Pkwy., Route 553 intersection; follow signs to mound • 800.305.7417 • https://www.nps.gov/nr/travel/mounds/eme.htm

Grand Village of the Natchez

The Natchez were the last of the Mound Builders to survive until the coming of the Europeans, an arrival that proved devastating to them. In the late seventeenth century, when the French reached their home in the lower Mississippi Valley, the Natchez

An artist's rendition of what Emerald Mound may have looked like in its heyday.

were still practicing a religion built around the construction of temple mounds. Each Natchez village had a temple mound and a residential mound for its leader. What was unique about the Natchez, setting it apart from all other known absolutist societies, was that members of the nobility were required to marry commoners. Every member of the community had both a noble and commoner background, which seemed to make for a stable society.

By this time, most of the tribes who inhabited former Mound Builder land had forgotten the origin of these earth hillocks, but around 1700, French missionaries started living among the Natchez and left detailed accounts of the Mound Builder culture. (Curiously enough, the writings, which explained the significance of the mounds, were themselves forgotten in the next century. Many Anglo scientists who later studied the mounds refused to believe that Indians were capable of building them.)

The impact with France was fatal to the Natchez. Within six years, almost one-third of the tribe had fallen victim to smallpox or measles. One French observer professed to see a design in this. "So true is it," he wrote, "that it seems God wishes to make them give place to others." To speed the process, France established Fort Rosalie in the area of the great Natchez village in 1716 and began the systematic exploitation of Native citizens. Finally, in 1729, the Natchez rebelled, took the garrison, and wiped it out. The French response was quick and ruthless. A military expedition was sent into the Natchez country the following year on a campaign of extermination and enslavement. Only a few families escaped death or transport to the Caribbean as slaves; they joined the Chickasaw and Creek and, apparently, were welcomed into those nations as possessors of special knowledge. The Natchez influence among the Chickasaw was especially strong. It was one reason for that nation's ongoing hostility toward France, blocking the way to the French dream of unifying their colonies in the southern and Midwestern portions of the Mississippi. Between 1682 and 1729, the Grand Village of the Natchez was the center of activities for the Natchez people, who based their calendar on the sustaining elements of their culture.

Although the Grand Village was eradicated during the 1730 French campaign of genocide, the reconstructed town is on the same site. Mounds have been renovated and many of the buildings erected according to the descriptions left by European observers. A museum tells the story of the Natchez and displays items recovered in digs on the site.

Info: 400 Jeff Davis Blvd., Natchez, MS 39120 • 601.446.6502 • https://www.nps.gov/nr/travel/mounds/gra.htm

TUPELO
Chickasaw Indian Village

The Natchez Trace Parkway, designated one of America's National Scenic Byways by the Federal Highway Administration, winds its way through Alabama, Mississippi, and Tennessee along an American Indian historic travel corridor. One stop on the parkway is the Chickasaw Village site. The Chickasaw had one of the strongest militaries in the country before Europeans arrived on the continent. Although they were much smaller in population than their neighbors, their stellar military skills secured their hunting rights throughout Kentucky and Tennessee. After the European arrival, they were pulled into the competing colonial ambitions of England and France, often warring against their Native allies.

Chickasaw Statue outside Chickasaw Village (photo by Catherine Wright and A Wandering Wombat [2015]).

The Choctaw were allies of the French, but the Chickasaw saw that their interests lay in keeping the French out of the Mississippi Valley, so they cast their lot with Britain. It was France's peculiar misfortune in both the northeastern and southwestern corners of its colonial empire to arouse the enmity of some of the most effective fighters among Native Americans—the Haudenosaunee and the Chickasaw, the only Indigenous nations that the French could never befriend or conquer.

When the United States overtook the land, past alliances made no difference. The Chickasaw were also forced to relinquish their vast holdings through a series of treaties, between 1801 and 1832, and then expelled to the West along the Trail of Tears.

The northern portion of the Natchez Trace ran through Chickasaw heartland; this fortified village outside of Tupelo is a memorial. Interpretive displays explain how the village was designed, and audio stations relate Chickasaw history. A nature walk identifies plants the Chickasaw used for food and medicine.

Info: 2680 Natchez Trace Pkwy., Tupelo, MS 38804 • 800.305.7417 • https://www.nps.gov/natr/index.htm

NORTH CAROLINA

North Carolina's Native population of 156,173 is the largest one east of the Mississippi River. The Eastern Band of Cherokee Indians is federally recognized; the others are state recognized.

CHEROKEE
Museum of the Cherokee Indian

In place of the living history concept, the museum (a nonprofit corporation owned by the Eastern Band of the Cherokee Indians) takes a decidedly modern approach. Extensive collections of tribal artifacts, clothing, and crafts are presented within the framework of their historical and cultural contexts, supplemented by an impressive range of audio- and videotapes. Six minitheaters offer presentations about historic through modern times. "Hearphones" allow visitors to listen to ancient accounts in the Cherokee language; a display illuminates each written character of the syllabary (Cherokee alphabet) as it is pronounced so that visitors may learn about the language while hearing it being spoken. A presentation in the museum's auditorium provides an inside glimpse into the present-day Cherokee community.

Info: 589 Tsali Blvd., Cherokee, NC 28719 • 828.497.3481 •
http://www.cherokeemuseum.org

Oconaluftee Indian Village

A recreated Cherokee village of the eighteenth century, Oconaluftee is one of the best living history museums on Native Americans. Authentically costumed members of the tribe demonstrate traditional crafts in a setting that is meant to reflect an actual Indian community. The eastern Cherokee are noted for their skills in basketry, and examples of this art are given frequently each day. Also, a reconstructed, seven-

A diorama of Cherokees visiting London at the Museum of the Cherokee Indian.

sided council chamber and several typical dwellings are filled with items that would have been used during the daily work routine. An authentic herb garden also is on the site.

Info: 218 Drama Rd., Cherokee, NC 28719 • 866.554.4557 • http://www.cherokeehistorical.org/oconaluftee-indian-village/

Qualla Arts and Crafts Mutual

Located on Qualla and across from the Cherokee Museum, Qualla Arts and Crafts is the oldest Native American cooperative. Founded in 1946, it showcases the artwork of over 250 tribal members and offers exhibits that give the tradition, history, and materials used for each medium, including baskets, wood and stone carvings, bead-work, and more. A vast array of art from jewelry to utensils to baskets and much more are featured and for sale.

Baskets on display at the Qualla Arts and Crafts Mutual.

Info: 645 Tsali Blvd., Cherokee, NC 28719 • 828.497.3103 • http://www.quallaartsandcrafts.com/

Qualla Reservation

Cherokee is the administrative center of the Qualla Reservation, home of the Eastern Band of Cherokee. Since it adjoins the most popular facility in the National Park system, the Great Smoky Mountains, the reservation also has become one of the top Indian attractions in the country.

It exists, primarily, by accident. In the 1830s, the land of the Cherokee spread across four states—Alabama, Georgia, Tennessee, and North Carolina. At the inception of the Trail of Tears, the forced expulsion of the Cherokee to Oklahoma, it was a fairly easy matter for federal troops to round up the Cherokee from their farms and businesses, but as word began trickling back about the cruelty and deprivation that awaited them on the forced march, groups of Indians began to elude the Army and make their way into the mountains. By 1838, as the last of the Cherokee left their homeland, about fourteen hundred members of the tribe remained hidden in these ancestral hills.

General Winfield Scott, who was charged with completing the expulsion, knew it was hopeless to try to find them, so he struck a deal with Yonaguska, the chief of this remnant, through his agent, Colonel William Thomas, a white man who was sympathetic to their situation. A man named Tsali and some of his relatives had been charged with murder for killing a soldier during their escape. Tsali testified that the soldier had prodded his wife with a bayonet, and he had acted to protect her. Nonetheless, in the best interests of the tribe, he agreed to surrender himself to Scott if the other fugitives could remain unmolested. Through this heroic act, the Cherokee remained here and eventually purchased the reservation lands through a congressional grant.

The nation has several entertaining and educational venues, including a museum, arts and crafts collective, theater, casino, restaurants, and shops.

Info: Cherokee Welcome Center • 498 Tsali Blvd, Cherokee, NC 28719 • 800. 438.1601 • http://visitcherokeenc.com/#home

Unto These Hills

This annual summer pageant recreates the history of the Cherokee, with special emphasis on the story of the group that broke away from the Trail of Tears to make their home here. The outdoor drama has been presented each year since 1950 from a script written by Kermit Hunter.

The focus of the drama is the story of Tsali, who surrendered himself to an uncertain white justice so that his tribe could live in peace in their new home. The actors are residents of the Cherokee reservation, many of them direct descendants of the characters being portrayed.

Info: The pageant takes place in the Mountainside Theater, adjacent to Oconaluftee Village. • http://www.cherokeehistorical.org/theatre.html

CULLOWHEE
Mountain Heritage Center

The center presents Mountain Heritage Day on the last Saturday in September. It is a celebration of southern Appalachian music, arts, dance, and culture with demonstrations of traditional mountain crafts and skills, Cherokee stickball games, over one hundred arts and crafts vendors, and numerous children's activities along with nonstop music and dance performances. In addition, temporary exhibits are displayed on a variety of themes, including Cherokee culture and history.

Info: 176 Central Dr., Western Carolina University, Cullowhee, NC 28723 • 828.227.7129 • https://www.wcu.edu/engage/mountain-heritage-center/index.aspx

FRISCO
Native American Museum and Natural History Center

This quirky museum located on a North Carolina outer bank island has many surprises. It has the most comprehensive collection of photographs on Geronimo's people, the

Chiricahua Apache, along with exhibits on the Croatians, the original Indigenous folks of the area. In addition, the museum has many events.

Info: 53536 NC-12, Frisco, NC 27936 • 252.995.4440 • http://nativeamericanmuseum.org/

LAURINBURG
Indian Museum of the Carolinas

The Indian Museum of the Carolinas highlights Carolina Indian life featuring many different groups, including the Lumbee, Cheraw, Cherokee, Tuscarora, Waccamaw, and Catawba. Forty exhibits provide insight into historical Native American culture through contemporary times. Items from Carolina bays, Indian mounds, and fishing villages are featured.

Info: 13043 X-Way Rd., Laurinburg, NC 28352 • 910.277.2456 • http://nc-rural-heritage.com/indian_museum_of_the_carolinas/

MOUNT GILEAD
Town Creek Indian Mound State Historic Site

Town Creek is the only significant mound grouping in the state and is thought to be the work of a tribe related to the Creek. During the fifteenth century, it was a cere-monial center for surrounding agricultural villages. Many Native towns that fringed the site have been located by archaeologists, and much of the area at Town Creek has been excavated, including the mound itself, which has been rebuilt. The major temple on top of the mound, and the minor temple, or priest's dwelling, have also been reconstructed.

The exhibit area has special displays that interpret the way of life of the In-dians of Town Creek with audiovisual shows that complement the artifacts. Exam-

Town Creek Mound.

ples of pottery made by Pee Dee women with the coil method are displayed, which makes the clay bowls look as though they're made of wood. The archaeological section gives an idea of the work that has been done at the site since it was first excavated in the 1930s and includes photographs of early excavations and explanations of techniques, such as dating artifacts. A five-panel depiction of life during the Town Creek period—illustrating the crops they grew, the games they played, and other aspects of their daily life—places artifacts within their social and cultural context.

Info: 509 Town Creek Mound Rd., Mt. Gilead, NC 27306 • 910.439.6802 • http://www.nchistoricsites.org/town/town.htm

PEMBROKE
Lumbee Homecoming

For a half a century, the Lumbee have hosted Lumbee Homecoming for a week every summer. Activities include a powwow, a Miss Lumbee Pageant, a market featuring Lumbee food and art, a gospel sing, bike rides, games, a golf tournament, and a parade.

Miss Lumbee at Lumbee Homecoming, 2018.

Info: 636 Prospect Rd., Pembroke, NC 28372 • 910.521.8602 • http://lumbeehomecoming.com/

Museum of the Southeast American Indian

The museum is located on the University of North Carolina Pembroke campus and is a scholarly research and community resource. Exhibits contain Indigenous artifacts, arts, and crafts from Indian communities all over the Americas, especially from the American Southeast. Many items come from North Carolina Native communities, with special emphasis on Robeson County Indian people.

Info: 1 University Dr., Pembroke, NC 28372-1510 • 910.521.6000 • http://www.uncp.edu/about-uncp

University of North Carolina Pembroke

The Lumbee were treated as a separate entity and classified as "free persons of color" during the era of slavery but were made to use segregated facilities, separate from both white and black, in the Jim Crow days. During the Jim Crow era, the Lumbee had their own school system, centered around the Lumbee Normal School, which grew into what is today the University of North Carolina Pembroke (UNCP). The university houses a repository of tribal history called the Lumbee Collection.

UNCP also hosts an annual play portraying the story of Lumbee hero Henry Berry Lowry (1845–c. 1872). During the early years of Reconstruction, predecessors of the Klan murdered his unarmed father. Henry went underground for the next ten years and with a band of raiders struck back at the whites he thought were responsible for his father's death. He was considered the Lumbee Robin Hood, as his band helped the area's poor black, white, and Indian people. Lowry's story, first dramatized in 1922, is an annual outdoor pageant called Strike at the Wind.

The Lumbee continued the intrepidness of Lowry. For almost a century after the Civil War, this Native community fought for some sort of legal recognition. Finally, in 1953, they were recognized as the "Lumbee Indians of Robeson County" by an act of the North Carolina legislature. The name stems from the river that runs through the county. Early in 1958, the Lumbee Indians suddenly burst from generations of obscurity into the headlines of the nation's newspapers. On the evening of January 13, the Ku Klux Klan decided to burn a cross in the nearby town of Maxton. The era of civil rights demonstrations had begun throughout the South. While African Americans were the targets of most of their racial intimidation and violence, the local Klan decided to send a message to the large Indian population of Robeson County to frighten them from possibly becoming involved with the Civil Rights movement, but the Klan got a big surprise. As it prepared its white-sheeted parade, they were suddenly attacked by a shouting, rifle-brandishing crowd of Lumbee Indians. The Klansmen bolted and ran, and newspapers across the country happily ran front-page pictures of their flight. It was the first time the Lumbee, descendants of the Cheraw, had attracted much attention beyond North Carolina, although they had formed a major presence in this southeastern county for centuries, but it was not the first time they protected their homelands against white supremacists.

The fifty-five-thousand members of the Lumbee Tribe of North Carolina reside primarily in Robeson, Hoke, Cumberland, and Scotland counties, and it is not only the largest tribe in North Carolina but the largest east of the Mississippi and the ninth largest in the country. Pembroke, North Carolina, is the economic, cultural, and political center of the tribe.

Info: 1 University Drive, Pembroke, NC 28372-1510 • 910.521.6000 • https://www.uncp.edu/

WINSTON-SALEM
Wake Forest University Museum of Anthropology

The museum's permanent collection of nearly thirty thousand includes archaeological and ethnographic artifacts from the Americas. Workshops and special events are offered as well.

Info: 1834 Wake Forest Rd., Winston-Salem, NC 27109 • 336.758.5000 • http://moa.wfu.edu/

SOUTH CAROLINA

A mong the sixteen separate tribal entities in South Carolina, the Catawba are federally recognized, and the state contains over twenty-six thousand Native citizens.

CHARLESTON
Charleston Museum

The Lowcountry Gallery features artifacts and displays related to the Yamasee and other Native peoples living in the low country of South Carolina. In addition, various activities have been offered, like the Native American Jewelry Workshop with artist Susan Hayes-Hatcher, Waccamaw.

Info: 360 Meeting St., Charleston, SC 29403 • 843.722.2996 • http://www.charlestonmuseum.org/

LANCASTER
Native American Studies Center

The center exhibits feature a collection of over thirteen hundred pieces of pottery, archaeological artifacts, and other Native American art. The center also sponsors various events.

Info: 476 Hubbard Dr., Lancaster, SC 29720 • 803.777.0169 • https://www.sc.edu/about/system_and_campuses/lancaster/study/student_opportunities/native_american_studies_center/

RIDGEVILLE
Edisto Natchez-Kusso Powwow

For almost fifty years, the Edisto Natchez-Kusso have been hosting a powwow on their tribal lands. State recognized, they have endured centuries of misunderstanding and struggles to maintain their tribal unity. Today, the annual festival helps raise money to support their health clinic and other tribal programs.

Info: 1125 Ridge Rd., Ridgeville, SC 29472 • 843.871.2126 • https://www.facebook.com/natchezkussotribe/

ROCK HILL
Catawba Cultural Center

The center is the hub of the Catawba reservation and features an exhibit of the nation's history, culture, and current information. The glorious Catawba pottery, a six-thousand-year-old craft, is a special treat; displays highlighting the process offer visitors an understanding of this unique art form. Catawba children take classes in pottery making so the art can be preserved. The pots were so popular with the early white settlers that many refused to prepare food in any other vessels. Today, about fifty artists sell their prized creations at the center's gift shop and through other venues.

Info: 1536 Tom Steven Rd., Rock Hill, SC 29730 • 803.328.2427 • http://catawbaindian.net/about-us/our-culture/catawba-cultural-center/

TENNESSEE

Eight tribal groups and almost thirty thousand Native people are in Tennessee.

CLEVELAND
Red Clay State Historical Area

In the fall of 1838, the Cherokee tribal council assembled at Red Clay. Georgia had outlawed any public gathering by Native peoples three years earlier. Leaders were forced to abandon the capital at New Echota to continue the fight against expulsion. A three-year delaying action was led from Red Clay by Chief John Ross, but time had run out on the Cherokee Nation. Mass removals to the West began that summer. The hardships in the heat were so great that federal authorities decided to wait until October before exiling most of the nation. Still, one in four would die on the forced march.

Gathering in despair, representatives of the dissolved nation met to resolve last matters in their ancestral land. Then they were divided into thirteen groups and herded away on the Trail of Tears. The site has been designated a State Historical Area, with a museum and interpretive center and a reconstruction of the last council house.

Info: 1140 Red Clay Park, Cleveland, TN 37311 • 423.478.0339 • http://tnstateparks.com/parks/about/red-clay

MANCHESTER
Old Stone Fort State Park

Old Stone Fort, measuring more than a mile around on the bluffs above the Duck River, illustrates the incredulity with which white settlers viewed ancient remains. The work on these earth walls is so skillful and intricate that the pioneer mentality could not grasp that Indians were capable of such an achievement. Instead, they attributed the fort to the expedition of Hernando De Soto in 1541, which is unlikely. When the technique of tree-ring dating became known centuries later, a local historian determined that the trees growing on the ruins of the fortification would have been almost one hundred years old when De Soto landed. The story typifies the condescending attitude of most European settlers. Well into the twentieth century, they attributed such ancient monuments to some "vanished race," rather than the First Peoples (see entry on "Seip

Mound State Memorial," Bainbridge, Ohio). The walls, which enclosed a religious center, are thought to have been built between 100 and 300 C.E.

Info: 732 Stone Fort Dr., Manchester, TN 37355 • 931.723.5073 • http://tnstateparks.com/parks/about/old-stone-fort

MEMPHIS
Chucalissa Indian Museum

When Hernando De Soto became the first European in recorded history to view the Mississippi River, he saw it from bluffs occupied by Chickasaw villages. The site would become Tennessee's largest city. A veteran looter in Peru and Mexico, De Soto passed on to Arkansas in search of gold, leaving the Spanish flag behind as a claim to the land. The Chickasaw ignored it until they were disturbed by the next European incursion more than a century later.

When De Soto arrived, the Chickasaw were the dominant people of the Mississippi Valley. Their extensive hunting rights, which extended across most of western Tennessee and Kentucky, had been won through their skill as military strategists.

Even before the Chickasaw reached the Mississippi bluffs, however, the site of Memphis had been occupied by an older people. Chucalissa Village had been inhabited for half a millennium before De Soto's appearance, and only in the early years of the sixteenth century were its residents displaced by the Chickasaw. Chucalissa, an archaeological site of Memphis State University, has several reconstructed dwellings, including a chief's home. Native American history and culture workshops plus festivals are offered at the interpretive center, which explains the town's historic significance.

Info: 1987 Indian Village Dr., Memphis, TN 38109 • 901.785.3160 • http://www.memphis.edu/chucalissa/

A reconstruction of a Chicasaw village at Chucalissa Indian Museum.

NASHVILLE
Native American Indian Association of Tennessee

The Indian Education Powwow and Fall Festival's three-day educational event celebrates the cultures of the twenty thousand Indians who live in Tennessee and attracts thousands of visitors. The association has a capital funds campaign to construct a cultural center "Circle of Life" building at 1466 Bell Rd., Antioch, Tennessee.

Info: 230 Spence Ln., Nashville, TN 37210-3623 • 615.232.9179 • http://www.naiatn.org/

Native History Association

The association chronicles Native history and areas in Tennessee. It provides tours and advocates for the preservation of historic sites like the foundation of the first bridge in Nashville, which was also the first bridge over the Cumberland River, built in 1823. By the late 1830s, thousands of Cherokee crossed this bridge on the Trail of Tears.

Info: 512 Stevenson St., Nashville, TN 37209-1835 • 423.892.1499 • http://www.nativehistoryassociation.org/

PINSON
Pinson Mounds State Archaeological Park

This cluster of twelve mounds, the highest being 73 feet (22 meters), along the Forked Deer River is the most significant mound grouping in Tennessee. Like many other southern mounds, they served primarily as a ceremonial center for surrounding agricultural villages. A number of cremation and activity areas have been found nearby, and mound sites contain related earthworks.

A Tennessee state park, Pinson Mounds is listed on the National Register of Historic Places and is protected by the Tennessee State Antiquities Act. It consists of

Saul's Mound at at Pinson Mounds State Archaeological Park.

1,162 acres (4.7 square kilometers) of field and forest, wild flowers, creeks, and a nursery of the Division of Forestry. Hiking trails run through the area.

The museum is designed to replicate an Indian mound; it houses the park offices, an archaeological library, a theater, 4,500 square feet (418 square meters) of exhibit areas, and the West Tennessee Regional Archaeology Office.

Info: 460 Ozier Rd., Pinson, TN 38366 • 731.988.5614 • http://tnstateparks.com/parks/about/pinson-mounds

TOWNSEND
Great Smoky Mountains Heritage Center

The 1966 National Historic Preservation Act ensures that archaeological evacuations must be done on road improvement projects. A road-widening project on Highway 321 through Tuckaleechie Cove unearthed tens of thousands of artifacts belonging to First Peoples in eastern Tennessee. The collection eventually became the Great Smoky Mountains Heritage Center. Many of the treasures were everyday items used by the Cherokee and are on display in the center's main building. Tuckaleechee Cove can be traced back five thousand years through the tools, ceremonial masks, housing, cooking utensils, plants, furniture, medicine, and more housed in the center.

Info: 123 Cromwell Dr., Townsend, TN 37882 • 865.448.0044 • http://www.gsmheritagecenter.org/

VONORE
Sequoyah Birthplace Museum

Undoubtedly, Sequoyah is recognized as a cultural icon—he is one of the few Native people who appears in American schoolbooks, being credited with inventing a Cherokee written language, but differing accounts exist of this brilliant man's life. Some of Sequoyah's descendants maintain that the Cherokee already had a written language, but he improved it and made it accessible to every person in-

Great Smokey Mountains Heritage Center.

stead of just to the traditional scribes. Indeed, he trained several teachers, and in a short time, the Cherokee Nation was literate in their own language, producing newspapers, books, and a constitution written in the eighty-five- to eighty-six-character syllabary. Some say Sequoyah was a revolutionary, finding a way to out-smart the encroaching Americans by leaving messages of resistance that they could not decipher. Some say he was hunted by the Americans and even tortured, but he prevailed, and because the Americans couldn't sully his image, the whites Angli-cized him, making him an acceptable hero to whites in order to downplay the symbol of Cherokee nationalism Sequoyah represented. Ironically, the literacy of the Cherokee only made them seem more threatening to the white settlers who were hungry for Native territory.

Sign at Sequoyah Birthplace Museum.

Whatever the true Sequoyah story is, a visit to this Eastern Cherokee-owned museum is worth the trip. Visitors learn about the national newspaper, the *Cherokee Phoenix*, which was born in New Echota. An annual Cherokee Fall Festival takes place as well as workshops in Cherokee arts and language.

Info: 576 TN-360, Vonore, TN 37885 • 423.884.6246 • http://www.sequoyahmuseum.org/

VIRGINIA

There are twelve tribal entities in Virginia; seven are federally recognized, but only the Pamunkey and Mattaponi have reservations. Over forty-five thousand Virginians are Native.

AMHERST
Monacan Ancestral Museum

Open by appointment only, this small museum keeps the history of the Monacan alive, one of the few Southeastern American Indian nations that still remains in its ancestral homelands.

Info: 2009 Kenmore Rd., Amherst, VA 24521 • 434.946.0389 • https://www.monacannation.com/ancestral-museum.html

CAPRON
Nottoway Indian Tribe of Virginia's
Community House and Interpretive Center

This center/museum tells the story of the Nottoway Indians through artifacts, lectures, storytellers, artisans, and performances. The Nottoway also host an Indian Corn Harvest Powwow in November.

Info: 23186 Main St., Capron, VA 23829 • 757.653.7932 •
http://www.nottowayindians.org/interpretivecenter.html

HAMPTON
Hampton University Museum

In 1991, Hampton unveiled its astounding Native American exhibit, curated by Dr. Paulette Molin (Minnesota Chippewa). At one time, Hampton University had a campus for Native students from across the country, who left behind a treasure trove chronicling their history at the historically African American college. Adding to the memorabilia, Native nations and individuals gifted many remarkable items to this beautiful and informative exhibit.

Info: 14 Frissell Ave., Hampton, VA 23669 • 757.727.5000 •
http://museum.hamptonu.edu/

JAMESTOWN
Powhatan Indian Village

This reconstructed village is part of Jamestown Settlement, a museum complex adjoining Jamestown that was established during the colony's 350th anniversary in 1957. Based on a living history style, it chronicles the daily life of both First Peoples and Europeans during the time of the first English colony.

A historical interpreter fletching a hand-made arrow at Jamestown Settlement Powhatan Indian Village.

At one time, the Powhatan were a confederacy of about thirty nations stretching along the eastern shore of Chesapeake Bay and the great tidal rivers of Virginia. They numbered over twenty thousand in two hundred separate villages in 1607, but within a century, the towns had been reduced to a dozen. Disease and war created by Europeans devastated the population; Virginia's 1924 Racial Integrity Act victimized the Powhatan even more. Pushed forward by eugenicist and Virginia Bureau of Vital Statistics director Walter Plecker, the act not only upheld a colonial law forbidding marriage between whites and others, but it virtually changed the "race" of the state's Native population to "colored" and "Negro" overnight. Virginia's Indigenous peoples have been recovering from this "paper genocide" for almost a century. Today, around seven thousand people are enrolled Powhatan members, representing just eleven of the original thirty nations of the great Confederacy: Mattaponi; Pamunkey; Chickahominy; Eastern Chickahominy; Rappahannock; Upper Mattaponi; Nansemond; Monacan; Cheroenhaka; Nottoway; and Patawomeck.

In historic times, the Powhatan built long log houses behind palisades as tall as 12 feet (30.5 centimeters). They were skilled agronomists, and their pottery and basketry styles are still popular today. Englishman John Rolfe admired and wanted their proficiency in tobacco cultivation and processing. However, since tobacco use and its making was a sacred and spiritual art, the Powhatan would not allow it—that is, until after his marriage to the paramount Chief Wahunsonacock's daughter, Pocahontas. Their marriage was not the Disney love story or the legend often told to children. It has been determined that Pocahontas was a captive and violated by the British, a crime not tolerated by the Powhatan. She did marry John Rolfe, and some feel that the marriage brought a decade of peace to her people, a brief respite from the invasive and out-of-control English, but she died in England in 1617, and her father, Wahunsonacock, passed away the following year. His brother, Opechancanough, fearing the growing strength of the colony, tried to drive the Europeans off with a surprise assault in 1622. He came very close to succeeding, but Jamestown, the largest settlement, received advance warning and survived. The resulting counterattack was so severe that most of the Powhatan were driven back to the falls of the James. Twenty-two years later, Opechancanough tried again, but this time, the cause was hopeless, and while the Powhatan managed to inflict some damage on the most far-flung European settlements, they were easily defeated. Opechancanough was brought back to Jamestown for trial but was murdered by a colonist before it began. The tragic event ended armed conflict between the two groups.

Ten thousand years of artifacts are on display at Powhatan Village. There are also changing and temporary exhibits like "Werowocomoco," the original capital city of the Powhatan Confederacy as well as the primary residence of its paramount chief.

Info: 2110 Jamestown Rd., Route 31 S., Williamsburg, VA 23185 • 888.593.4682 • http://www.historyisfun.org/jamestown-settlement/powhatan-village/

KING WILLIAM
Pamunkey Indian Museum and Cultural Center

The museum focuses on the Pamunkey way of life from the Ice Age to the present. Tools and artifacts are displayed, with information on how they were made and used. Pamunkey women demonstrate pottery making, which is still crafted in the same way since ancient times from the digging of clay in the Pamunkey River to traditional coil construction to ancient embellishments. The beautiful ceramics are sold in the museum gift shop.

Former Pamunkey chief Kevin Brown at Pamunkey Museum.

Info: 175 Lay Landing Rd., Pamunkey Indian Reservation, King William, VA 23086 • 804.843.4792 • http://www.pamunkey.net/museum.html

NORFOLK
Norfolk Botanical Garden

In 1938, the Norfolk Botanical Garden was created by African American workers as part of the Works Progress Administration. The 155-acre (627,263 square meters) garden has received national recognition and is the site of many Native events throughout the year, held at the Eagle Tribute Plaza. In addition, walking tours center on the eagles.

Info: 6700 Azalea Garden Rd., Norfolk, VA 23518 • 757.441.5830
• http://norfolkbotanicalgarden.org/

RICHMOND
Virginia Museum of Fine Art

Temporary exhibits like "Hear My Voice: Native American Art of the Past and Present" feature the work of contemporary Native artists like Kay WalkingStick (Cherokee). On display are many items from the museum's permanent Native American collection of ceramics, baskets, and rugs from the Pacific northwest coast, Southwest United States, and Plains cultures. In addition, it includes an impressive collection of Indigenous art from South and Meso America.

Info: 200 N. Blvd., Richmond, VA 23220 • 804.340.1400 •
https://vmfa.museum/collections/ancient-american-art/

WEST VIRGINIA

The state has 4,459 Native citizens and one tribal organization. Many Native people have tribal membership in other states—the majority are Shawnee and Cherokee descendants.

CORE
Mountain Spirit Powwow

Held every summer in Mason-Dixon Historical Park, this event showcases the Appalachian Native peoples in West Virginia.

Info: 79 Buckeye Rd., Core, WV 26541 • 304.662.6496 •
https://www.facebook.com/pg/Native-American-Community-Center-Inc-1454772
78855253/about/

MOUNDSVILLE
Grave Creek Mound

In the mid-nineteenth century, Grave Creek Mound became the most controversial
mound in America as scientists, both authentic and spurious, waged a furious debate
over what was found here. The 79-foot (24 meter)-high mound, with a circumference
at the base of more than 300 yards (274 meters), is one of the largest in North
America. For generations, it was a familiar landmark to Native peoples of the Ohio
Valley and westward-moving Anglo settlers.

In 1838, to resolve the mystery, the owner of the land sponsored an excavation,
the first systemic examination of a mound. A shaft was sunk from its summit, and as
the investigation went deeper, a variety of objects and remains were found, including
a richly ornamented skeleton, log-walled chambers, and horizontal shafts that turned
up several more chambers, with dozens of human remains. The biggest surprise for
the investigators was a sandstone tablet written in an unknown alphabet.

It was at about this time that Joseph Smith was spreading the teachings of the
Book of Mormon, which held that the Indians were descended from the Ten Lost
Tribes of Israel. The Grave Creek tablet caused a sensation, and investigators rushed
to take a crack at translating it. One professed that it was Sumerian characters, another said that it was definitely Phoenician, and yet another declared that it was
unquestionably Canaanite.

Of all the experts, only Henry Schoolcraft discerned that both the mound and
the tablet were of Native origin. He was ignored, as Native intelligence, cultures,
and inventions have always been trivialized. The Grave Creek mound, however, was
an important milestone in the effort to sort out the history of First Nations. Scholars agreed that it belonged to the late Adena culture, centered in mid-Ohio, and

Grave Creek Mound.

that this was one of its easternmost outposts. The burials and artifacts have been dated at about the fifth and sixth centuries C.E. The mound has been protected by the state since 1907, and an on-site museum exhibits artifacts found in the mound. Although these excavations are done in the spirit of "discovery and science," many Indigenous people take offense at having their ancestors' resting places disturbed.

Info: 801 Jefferson Ave., Moundsville, WV 26041 • 304.843.4128 • http://www.wvculture.org/museum/gravecreekmod.html

MIDWEST

On my reservation, we had one of the most abundant fisheries in the world and hundreds of thousands of acres of wild rice beds. We've lost a lot of it, but there's still natural wealth that could support our communities.

—Winona LaDuke

The celebrated Mississippi River, one of the world's largest, twists south from northern Minnesota as it cuts through the United States separating east and west. On the north, the iconic Great Lakes push into Canada, dividing the two biggest countries on the North American continent. These waterways, along with other major rivers, such as the Missouri and the Ohio, have been trade routes that sustained and connected First Peoples since the end of the Ice Age. Midwestern woodlands boast sugar maple, nut trees, and berry bushes, while lakes show off many species of fish, water birds, and Mahnomen (wild rice), harvested and stewarded in the same thoughtful way by the Ojibwe and Menominee as it has been for centuries.

Farms, farms, and more farms decorate the pastoral countryside today, but many groups were farmers long before Europeans arrived; the land is accustomed to agriculture. The esteemed Winona LaDuke (Ojibwe) lives and works on Minnesota's White Earth Reservation, where she helped start Native Harvest, which revives and protects Native seeds, heritage crops, naturally grown fruits, animals, wild plants, traditions, and knowledge of Indigenous land-based communities. Through Native Harvest, White Earth Nation community members harvest and sell foods free from genetic engineering, providing a healthy alternative to the Midwest's scores of agribusinesses.

A few big cities pop up from the miles of soybeans and corn throughout the Midwest, and Native people are not new to cities. In historic times, Cahokia, located just a few hours south of Chicago, was one of the largest cities in the world in 1250 C.E.! The center of trade and commerce for early people, its structures are preserved wonders and well worth a visit. Jumping into this century, plenty of contemporary Native arts, festivals, and events are scattered throughout the region, many in cities. Minneapolis is the site of the "American Indian Corridor," both a place and a dream in progress to create Indigenous tourism as a viable economic endeavor for the city's Native residents. At the center is Franklin Avenue, the most densely populated urban Native neighborhood. Designs on sidewalks, churches, offices, and even electric boxes broadcast that indeed this is Indian Country. Acclaimed Ojibwe author Louise Erdrich owns Birch Bark Books, an incredible shop offering Native books a few blocks from the famed Franklin Avenue. From Kansas City, Missouri's Harvest Moon Festival of today to the plethora of mounds in Ohio built long ago, the Midwest is a travel treasure trove.

ILLINOIS

About thirty-five thousand Native citizens live in Illinois.

CHICAGO
American Indian Center Powwow

The American Indian Center (AIC) in Chicago is the venue of the annual AIC Powwow, held on the third Saturday of September. The powwow features traditional artisans, dance, music, and food. The dancers, drummers, singers, and craft vendors represent more than 175 tribes from across the United States and Canada.

Info: 3401 W. Ainslie St., Chicago, IL 60625 • 800.870.3666 • https://www.aicchicago.org/

Field Museum

Since its founding, the Field Museum has devoted considerable attention to the Native peoples of North America. The result is a series of collections, strong in history and contemporary culture. The staff collaborates with Native American groups, who come to visit and study the collections of their nations.

The museum holds a large collection of material from the Hopewell culture of Ohio, dating back more than two thousand years. "Ancient America" is a permanent exhibit of the innovations that enabled small hunter-gatherer groups to diversify and populate the Western Hemisphere from the Arctic to the tip of South America. More than twenty-two hundred artifacts representing twenty distinct cultural groups illustrate the narrative.

The Hall of Native North Americans includes hundreds of artifacts that demonstrate the diverse lifestyles of Indigenous Americans. Every aspect of life is covered from food storage and clothing to war and spirituality. The Northwest Coast section showcases the artistic talents of Native people in Oregon, Washington, and British Columbia. The Arctic exhibit focuses on how Inuit people survive the harsh cold of the far north. Videos follow an Inuit tribe as people live, hunt, and eat throughout the year.

Info: 1400 S. Lake Shore Dr., Chicago, IL 60605 • 312.922.9410 • https://www.fieldmuseum.org/

First Nations Film and Video Festival

The First Nations Film and Video Festival advocates for and celebrates the works of Native American filmmakers and new works and films that break racial stereotypes and promote awareness of Native American issues. All films are written and/or produced and directed by Native American artists from all of the Americas. Check the website for venue addresses; films are shown in various cities and states, including Chicago and the University of Missouri in Columbia.

Info: 773.262.5503 • http://fnfvf.org/blog/

COLLINSVILLE
Cahokia Mounds State Historic Site

The remains of the ancient Native civilization north of Mexico are preserved at Cahokia Mounds State Historic Site. Within the twenty-two-hundred-acre tract lie the archaeological remnants of the central section of the ancient settlement that is today known as Cahokia. Named for the Cahokia, a subtribe of the Illiniwek, who lived in the area when the French arrived in the 1600s, the Cahokia Mounds are both a UNESCO World Heritage Site and a U.S. National Historic Landmark.

The First Terrace—Monk's Mound, Cahokia Mounds State Historic Site.

One of the greatest cities of the world, Cahokia was larger than London was in 1250 C.E. The Mississippians (800–1550 C.E.) who lived here were accomplished builders, who erected a wide variety of structures from practical homes for everyday living to monumental public works that have maintained their grandeur for centuries. At one time, more than 120 mounds were at Cahokia, but today, only eighty remain. Of these, sixty-eight lie within the Cahokia Mounds site. They are either flat-topped, conical, or linear ridge-topped in shape.

The site was already completely abandoned by the time the first Europeans arrived. In the early nineteenth century, Trappist monks attempted to establish a community at the base of the largest mound but gave up and returned to France in 1813. The mounds were not systematically excavated until 1922.

The museum gift shop carries an assortment of Cahokia Mounds souvenirs and handcrafted Native American-made items.

Info: 30 Ramey St., Collinsville, IL 62234 • 618.346.5160 • https://cahokiamounds.org

EVANSTON
The Mitchell Museum of the American Indian

The Mitchell Museum of the American Indian, founded in 1977, is one of the few museums across the country that focuses exclusively on the art, history, and culture of First Nation peoples from throughout the United States and Canada. It promotes public understanding of cultural diversity through first-voice perspectives.

The museum's collection includes archaeological, ethnographic, and art objects of American Indian and Inuit people from the Paleo-Indian time period through the present day. The museum serves as a resource for the Evanston community, for the greater Chicago area and its schools, for Native peoples, and for researchers from other educational and cultural institutions. The museum shop features Native American arts and crafts items, books, music, and videos; many are for children.

Info: 3001 Central St., Evanston, IL 60201 • 847.475.1030 • http://www.mitchellmuseum.org/

LEWISTOWN
Dickson Mounds Museum

The Dickson Mounds Museum, a branch of the Illinois State Museum and a National Register Historic Site, is one of the major on-site archaeological museums in the United States. It provides a journey through twelve thousand years of American Indian history in the Illinois River Valley through archaeological records. Displays focus on the daily life of the Mississippian culture (800–1550 c.e.), illustrating the ways in which people used their environment to obtain food, clothing, and shelter and how they organized their communities, created their buildings, and conducted their ceremonies.

Dickson Mounds was built to display what chiropractor Don Dickson unearthed on his farm southeast of Lewistown. Leaving the eight-hundred-year-old remains right where he uncovered them, Dickson turned the site, which contained some 234 open graves, into a popular, private museum. Indians protested at the site for years and appealed to state officials to close the display, calling it sacrilegious, racist, and demeaning. Supporters called it a respectful display of history and a tourist draw. In 1989, a World Archaeological Congress meeting held in South Dakota declared the exhibit unacceptable. A movement away from open burials had already prompted the closing of similar exhibits in response to Native American pressure to repatriate Native burial sites. In April of 1992, the state closed the display. Balancing the concerns of activists who wanted the skeletons reburied and local residents who worried that the museum would disappear without them, the State of Illinois gave the museum $4 million to reinvent itself.

Info: 10956 N. Dickson Mounds Rd., Lewistown, IL • 309.547.3721 • http://www.illinoisstatemuseum.org/content/welcome-dickson-mounds

NAPERVILLE
Annual Harvest Powwow

The Midwest Soarring Foundation has sponsored many local powwows in northern Illinois. The largest of these is the Annual Harvest Powwow, held in September at the Naperville Settlement. In addition to dancing, drumming, and storytelling, vendors display and sell Native arts and crafts and Native foods.

Info: 523 S. Webster St., Naperville, IL 60540 • 708.257.4300 • http://www.midwestsoarring.org/

ROCK ISLAND
Hauberg Museum and the Black Hawk Historic Site

The collection of Dr. John Hauberg, a Rock Island philanthropist, forms the basis of the museum's collection, which features full-size replicas of Sauk winter and summer houses. Dioramas with life-size figures depict activities of the Sauk and Meskwaki (Fox) people typical of the period 1750 to 1830. Many artifacts, including authentic trade goods, jewelry, and domestic items, are displayed. The Black Hawk State Historic Site is located at the Sauk village that was the chief's home. The museum contains historical displays on the Black Hawk War, briefly described below.

In 1804, five Sauk and Fox chiefs traveled to St. Louis to meet with federal officials in an effort to win the release of a young Indian charged with murder. During these discussions, the chiefs signed an agreement ceding rights to their lands in Illinois for an annual payment. They retained hunting and residential privileges as long as the federal government controlled the land.

Statue of Black Hawk at the Hauberg Indian Museum.

When the treaty was renewed in 1816, Black Hawk was horrified to learn what his predecessors had signed. Black Hawk saw the influx of miners pouring into the northern part of the tribal lands when lead deposits were opened for private development.

Leaders of the Sauk and Fox had debated what to do. Keokuk counseled peace. Black Hawk, however, decided that immediate confrontation would secure Indian rights to the land. In 1831, he challenged white farmers, whom he accused of digging up Indian burial grounds to plant their corn. The farmers appealed to the governor, who declared that Illinois was "in a state of actual invasion." A volunteer army attacked the Indian village in Rock Island, but Black Hawk had already moved his followers to safety. The following spring, Black Hawk crossed back into Illinois with the intent to plant crops. Their movements led to conflict with state soldiers. Both sides attacked, and the white troops were routed at the Battle of Stillman's Run. When federal troops were sent into the campaign, Black Hawk tried to retreat to the Mississippi. The troops ignored his appeals for a truce, and he was forced into a guerrilla action. As he reached the river, however, near the present-day city of La Crosse, Wisconsin, Black Hawk was attacked in force, and the Indians were overrun. A federal gunboat fired on those who tried to cross the river. A few reached the opposite shore.

As a result of the war, all Indians were expelled from Illinois; it was only a matter of time before the onrush of white intruders forced the Indians off the land. Black Hawk was captured and taken on a tour of the East. For the first time, he realized the numbers that opposed him. He dictated an autobiography and dedicated it to the general who had defeated him: "That you may never experience the humility that the power of the American government has reduced me to, is the wish of him, who in his native forests was once as proud and bold as yourself."

Info: 1510 46th Ave., Rock Island, IL 61201 • 309.788.0177 • http://www.blackhawkpark.org/museum

SPRINGFIELD
Illinois State Museum

The Anthropology/Archaeology Collections of the museum consist of more than eight million archaeological specimens and ethnographic objects. The collections are housed in Springfield and the Dickson Mounds Museum (Lewistown). Ancient Native artifacts range in age from three hundred to about twelve thousand years ago.

Info: 1011 E. Ash St., Springfield, IL 62703 • 217.785.0037 • http://www.illinoisstatemuseum.org/

INDIANA

A round fifty-seven thousand Indian citizens and nine tribal councils are in Indiana.

BATTLE GROUND
Tippecanoe Battlefield and Museum

This National Historic Landmark is located in a 96-acre (0.4 square kilometers) park setting in Battle Ground, complete with picnic areas, a nature center, and historic and scenic hiking trails. The 85-foot (0.3 square kilometers) marble obelisk monument was erected in 1908 and marks the site of the November 7, 1811, Battle of

Tippecanoe between the United States's forces, led by William Henry Harrison, and representatives of Tecumseh's Native American confederation of Shawnee, Delaware, Miami, Potawatomi, and Wyandot tribes.

The museum tells the story of the battle with exhibits, a fiber-optic map of the action, and information about the dynamic leaders: Tecumseh; his brother, Tenskwatawa, known as the Prophet; and Harrison.

Tippecanoe Battlefield Monument.

Tecumseh urged other leaders to halt land cessions. In defiance, older leaders of other tribes signed the Fort Wayne Treaty in 1809, giving up more land rights in Indiana. They ridiculed Tecumseh and the Shawnee as interlopers who had no right to tell them what to do with their lands. The Wyandot and Potawatomi, together with young men who had left the Miami and Delaware tribes, flocked to Prophet's Town to join Tecumseh.

In 1810, the governor of Indiana Territory, William Henry Harrison, requested a parley with Tecumseh. Neither could agree on a formula for peace. In the following year, the governor received orders from President James Madison, under pressure from alarmed westerners, to strike at Prophet's Town.

Harrison set out from the territorial capital of Vincennes early in the fall of 1811 with a force of about one thousand men. He arrived at the Tippecanoe River on November 6. Tecumseh was absent, having left to visit the Creek, and no effective war leader replaced him at home. The Indian alliance retreated, and although Harrison took heavy losses, he had managed to destroy Prophet's Town.

The Battle of Tippecanoe undermined the prestige Tecumseh had garnered. Although Tecumseh became an effective British ally in the War of 1812, the tribal unity he had stitched together unraveled at Tippecanoe. Tecumseh was killed in the war. In its aftermath, the white flood gathered momentum, and the Shawnee were forced into Kansas. Harrison rode his victory to the White House in the election of 1840 in a campaign that featured the slogan "Tippecanoe and Tyler, too."

Info: 200 Battle Ground Ave., Battle Ground, IN 47920 • 765.567.2147 •
http://www.tippecanoehistory.org/our-sites/tippecanoe-battlefield-museum/

EVANSVILLE
Angel Mounds State Memorial

The Angel Mounds community, located on the banks of the Ohio River, was settled by Mississippian people known as the Mound Builders. Raised between 1200 and 1400 c.e., the site is the largest grouping of mounds in the state. Excavation, which did not begin until 1939, revealed that the area was a substantial farming community with a few thousand inhabitants and was occupied for nearly 250 years. The Mississippians probably chose this site because of the nearby river, the abundant food supply, and the great number of plants and animals available to them.

The town originally covered 103 acres and served as an important religious, political, and trade center for people living within a 50-mile (81 square kilometers) radius. This society built eleven earthen mounds for elevated buildings; no burial mounds are present. The community was abandoned over a period of years before white explorers came to America; archaeologists can offer no explanation for the community's abandonment, since no evidence exists of warfare or disease. Some family accounts say that people decided as a group to walk away from these cities for various reasons: overcrowding, pollution, change in values, etc. Several typical buildings from this settlement have been reconstructed from archaeological evidence, including winter houses, a round house, summer houses, and a temple as well as a portion of a stockade wall similar to the one that surrounded the village. The interpretive center exhibits artifacts recovered from the mounds, and a nature walk traverses the 103-acre (0.4 square kilometer) site.

Info: 8215 Pollack Ave., Evansville, IN 47715 • 812.853.3956 •
https://www.indianamuseum.org/angel-mounds-state-historic-site

INDIANAPOLIS
The Eiteljorg Museum of American Indians and Western Art

The Eiteljorg Museum of American Indians and Western Art was founded by Indianapolis businessman and philanthropist Harrison Eiteljorg. Its mission has been to inspire an appreciation and understanding of the art, history, and cultures of the American West and the Indigenous peoples of North America.

The Eiteljorg collects and preserves high-quality Western art and Native American art and cultural objects. Its collection includes Native artists such as T. C. Cannon, Allan Houser, and Kay WalkingStick. The institution's contemporary Native art collection has been ranked among the world's best.

Every other year since 1997, the Eiteljorg Contemporary Art Fellowship has selected five Native contemporary artists and provided them grant support so they can continue to pursue their art professionally and receive greater exposure. The museum has purchased approximately four hundred works of contemporary art since 1999 to add to its permanent collections. These works challenge conventional notions that Native American art is limited to particular styles or materials or focused on particular eras. Instead, they reveal how thought-provoking contemporary art can be and how relevant it is to issues of today. The Katrina Basile Museum Store carries a vast array of unique products, many produced by Native American artists and companies. The store features one-of-a-kind turquoise, silver, and precious stone jewelry as well as pottery, sculpture, paintings, beaded items, and posters by award-winning artists. Books detail Native American artistry from weaving to pottery to jewelry. Each year in June, the Eiteljorg Museum Indian Market and Festival takes place on the weekend after Father's Day. Composed of two full days of cultural activities, the market focuses on a juried presentation of art for sale.

Info: 500 W. Washington St., Indianapolis, IN 46204 • 317.636.9378 • https://www.eiteljorg.org/

PENDLETON
Falls Park Memorial

Early in 1824, a small group of witnesses gathered quietly at dawn to watch an execution. Three white men, found guilty of murdering a party of nine Indians the previous year, had been sentenced to hang. Among the observers were several Miami tribesmen from the surrounding area.

Indiana had been a state for just eight years, and its central portion, the New Purchase territory, had only been open to Anglo settlement since 1820. Most white and Indian residents remembered the bitter warfare that had swept across this frontier during the previous decade.

The execution settled nothing. Agitation for removal of remaining Indians continued, and by 1838, most Miami and Potawatomi had been expelled from Indiana to the west. Nonetheless, in the first such decision in American jurisprudence, white men had been sentenced to death for a capital crime against Indians. Indiana-born novelist Jessamyn West dramatized the incident in her book *Massacre at Falls Creek*.

Info: 460 Falls Park Dr., P.O. Box 221, Pendleton, IN 46064 • 765.778.2222 • https://www.fallspark.org/

TERRE HAUTE
Native American Museum

The Native American Museum is located in Dobbs Memorial Park. It is the only museum of its kind to be operated by a city parks department in the Midwest. One permanent display features the lifeways of Northeast Woodlands Native peoples; numerous temporary exhibits are also on display.

Info: 5170 E. Poplar Drive–Dobbs Park, Terre Haute, IN 47805 • 812.877.6007 • http://www.terrehaute.in.gov/departments/parks/city-parks/dobbs/nam

Steve Witt Memorial Annual Gathering of the People Powwow

An annual two-day powwow consists of intertribal dancing, storytelling, drumming, flint knapping, and other activities.

Info: Vigo County Conservation Club, 10382 Grotto Rd., Terre Haute, IN 47805 • 812.236.1692 • https://www.crazycrow.com/site/event/steve-witt-memorial-gathering-of-the-people-powwow/

IOWA

Iowa's Native citizens number around 27,450, and one Native nation is headquartered in the state.

IOWA CITY
University of Iowa Powwow

The University of Iowa Powwow was founded in 1990 by a Native American student association. Held every spring, the powwow has grown from a one-day event to a three-day event with a wide range of dance categories, drummers, and arts and crafts vendors.

Info: University Field House, 225 S. Grand Ave., Iowa City, IA 52242 • http://powwow.uiowa.edu

MARQUETTE
Effigy Mounds National Monument

On a bluff above the Mississippi River, in the hilliest part of Iowa, a long-departed people shaped the earth into animal forms. Over two hundred mounds are in this 2,500-acre (10-square-kilometer) monument, the most extensive such grouping in the Midwest. Running almost 6 miles (9.6 kilometers) along the bluffs, it is divided into two separate sections by the Yellow River.

America the Beautiful 2017 dollar coin depicting Effigy Mounds National Monument.

One of the largest bear effigies ever found is here, measuring 70 feet (21 meters) across at the shoulders and 137 feet (42 meters) long. It is part of the Fire Point Mound group. Other effigies are in the shapes of wolves, serpents, and birds. The structures range from five hundred to more than two thousand years in age. Footpaths lead from the visitor center to the effigy groups and to scenic overlooks atop the bluffs into neighboring Wisconsin.

President Harry Truman designated the area a monument in 1949. Research has revealed evidence that the mound-building cultures existed here for at least eighteen hundred years. The mound-building cultures of the upper Midwest built their mounds sometime between 800 B.C.E. and 1200 C.E. The effigy mounds were built in the latter half of that time period.

Info: 151 Hwy. 76, Harpers Ferry, IA 52146 • 563.873.3491, x.123 • https://www.nps.gov/efmo/index.htm

TAMA
Meskwaki Cultural Center and Museum

The Meskwaki Cultural Center and Museum opened in 2010 (in part) as part of the Iowa Great Places designation received by Tama County. The museum gives visitors a glimpse into the Meskwaki (also spelled Mesquakie and translated to "red earth people") Nation's rich cultural legacy. The nation is also referred to as the Sac and Fox Tribe of the Mississippi in Iowa.

Artifacts that have been passed down, as well as other reacquired and repatriated items, are arranged in appealing displays. Exhibits include arrowheads, bowls, spoons, other pottery, tools, clothing, jewelry, photographs, and other objects.

Info: 303 Meskwaki Rd., Tama, IA 52339 • 641.484.3185 • https://www.meskwaki.org/about-us/museum/

Mesquakie Powwow

For over one hundred years, the Mesquakie have held a four-day powwow every August, which originated with their harvest ceremonial, the Green Corn Dance. Although it is not a religious gathering anymore, it is a time of reaffirmation and hope, of worship and kinship, and, above all, a time of friendship. Visitors can purchase floral-design beadwork, for which the tribe is noted. This celebration of Native culture is the only one of its kind in Iowa.

Info: Battleground Rd., Tama, IA 52339 • 641.484.4678 • http://meskwakipowwow.com

MICHIGAN

Around 147,000 Native citizens and fourteen Native councils are in Michigan.

ANN ARBOR
University of Michigan Museum of Anthropological Archaeology

The museum's collections of more than ten thousand ethnographic objects include artifacts and artworks collected over the last 150 years from diverse cultures and regions. Strengths include collections of birch bark, wooden baskets, and basswood, cattail, and sedge mats from the Great Lakes and a collection of micaceous pottery from Puebloan, Apache, and Hispano villages in the American Southwest.

Info: 1109 Geddes Ave., Ann Arbor, MI 48109-1079 • 734.764.0485 • http://outreach.umich.edu/programs/museum-of-anthropology-umma

CASS CITY
Sanilac Petroglyphs Historic State Park

Within the 240-acre parcel historic site are the Sanilac Petroglyphs, Michigan's only known ancient rock carvings attributed to Native American workmanship in the Lower Peninsula of Michigan.

Info: 8251 Germania Rd., Cass City, MI 48726 • 989.856.4411 • http://www.michigandnr.com/parksandtrails/details.aspx?id=490&type=SPRK

DETROIT
Detroit Institute of Arts

Covering nearly three thousand years of history, the Detroit Institute of Arts' Native American collection includes pieces from North, Central, and South America. The collection comprises early religious artifacts, ceremonial attire, and domestic objects from the nineteenth and twentieth centuries.

Info: 5200 Woodward Ave., Detroit, MI 48202 • 313.833.7900 • https://www.dia.org/

The Native Hands Gallery

The North American Indian Association (NAIA) serves the Native community of Metro Detroit. The gallery showcases local artisans and displays their beadwork, basketry, ribbon work, regalia, and many other items. Most are also for sale. In addition, the NAIA hosts many events and activities.

Info: 22720 Plymouth Rd., Redford Charter Twp., MI 48239 • 313.535.2966 • http://naiadetroit.org/

Penobscot Building

The building is named for the Penobscot, a Native American tribe from Maine, far away from this area. Native American motifs in art deco-style ornamentation are

The Penobscot Building in downtown Detroit.

used on the exterior and the interiors. The Penobscot Building became a potent symbol of Detroit's industrial might. It is certainly a magnificent piece of architecture, but it is also a glaring example of the appropriation of Native cultures and design elements from the Plains Indian style headdresses to Southwest Indian geometric patterns to the use of animal motifs featuring foxes, turtles, and eagles. These bits and pieces of pop culture sprinkled throughout the country affirm the fascination America has with First Peoples as well as the perpetuation of the stereotype that Indians are relics of the past.

Info: 645 Griswold St., Detroit, MI 48226 • https://www.penobscotbuilding.com/

GRAND RAPIDS
Grand Rapids Public Museum

On permanent display is the "Anishinabek" (the people), chronicling the story of West Michigan's original Ottawa, Potawatomi, and Chippewa peoples. The multimedia exhibit celebrates their voices from their ancestors to present-day residents of the area through memorabilia, documents, and a vast array of objects handed down through their families.

Info: 272 Pearl St. NW, Grand Rapids, MI 49504 • 616.929.1700 • http://www.grpm.org/

HARBOR SPRINGS
Andrew J. Blackbird Museum

Andrew J. Blackbird was born in what is now Harbor Springs around 1815; he was the son of the Ottawa chief Mack-e-te-be-nessy (Makade-binesi, "black hawk"). The name was mistranslated as "Blackbird," which became the family's English name.

Chief Andrew J. Blackbird Museum.

Mack-e-te-be-nessy was chief of the Arbor Croche, or Middle Village, band of the Ottawas. Andrew was trained as a blacksmith but enjoyed formal education and attended Twinsburg Institute in Ohio and Michigan State Normal School, now Eastern Michigan University.

During the 1850s, Blackbird was a counselor for both the United States and Ottawa and Ojibwa peoples and worked to help Native American veterans receive pensions. He helped settle land claims and worked to achieve citizenship for Native Americans. He married, bought a house in Harbor Springs, and became the town's second postmaster in 1858.

Today, Blackbird's mark on Harbor Springs as well as the Native American influence on northern Michigan is preserved at the Andrew J. Blackbird Museum, listed on the National Register of Historic Places. Native American artifacts fill the museum space.

Info: 368 E. Main St., Harbor Springs, MI 49740 • 232.526.0612 • http://www.visitharborspringsmichigan.com/stories/andrew_j_blackbird_museum_harbor_sprin

MACKINAC ISLAND
Indian Dormitory

Built in 1838 on Mackinac Island, the Indian Dormitory provided Native Americans a place to stay when arriving on the island to receive payment and supplies as part of the 1836 Treaty of Washington. The Mackinac Island United States Indian Agency called for improvements due to a treaty in which Indian nations of the Great Lakes deeded significant portions of Michigan's upper and lower peninsulas to the United States.

Around 1844, it was converted into the Mackinac Island schoolhouse and served as the Mackinac Island Public School for nearly one hundred years. In 1964, the Mackinac State Historic Parks purchased the Indian Dormitory from the Mackinac Island Board of Education. Exhibits about Native American crafts and historic maps were installed, and it was opened to the public from 1966 to 2002. It was closed in 2003.

Henry Schoolcraft, a young Detroiter, worked here as an Indian agent. After several years at Mackinac, he published *History and Statistical Information of the Indian Tribes of the United States*. The first book to attempt a systematic study of Native Americans, it became a best-seller.

The book also excited the imagination of Henry Wadsworth Longfellow, who took many of the Chippewa legends recorded by Schoolcraft and composed his epic poem, "Hiawatha," around them. While the poem has little to do with the historic Hiawatha, a Mohawk from New York, the lines "by the shores of Gitche-Gumee, by the shining Big-Sea-Water" are familiar to generations of Americans. One room of the Indian Dormitory is decorated with depictions of scenes from Longfellow's poem.

Info: Huron St., Mackinac Island, MI 49757 • 906.847.3328 • http://www.mackinacparks.com/attractions/historic-indian-dormitory/

MOUNT PLEASANT
Ziibiwing Center of Anishinabe Culture and Lifeways

The Saginaw Chippewa Indian Tribe (composed of three bands of Ojibwe: Saginaw, Black River, and Swan Creek) operates this 34,000-foot (10-kilometer) center designed in the traditional Woodland-style dwellings of the Anishinabe people. The center's signature exhibit, "Diba Jimooyung: Telling Our Story," interprets past, present, and future of the Saginaw Chippewa and other Great Lakes Anishinabe through artifacts, computer technology, hands-on opportunities, and language learning. A photographic retrospective exhibit of the Saginaw Chippewa is also displayed in the center.

Bbaamoseg Gitiganing (All Will Walk about the Plants That Grow) Plant Walk is available from June to September. Visitors explore the Ziibiwing Center grounds to observe many of the plants that have been traditionally used by Anishinabe people and are still used today. This outdoor exhibit includes plants used for many different purposes, including medicines, foods, and dyes, many native to Michigan and the surrounding region.

Info: 6650 E. Broadway Rd., Mt. Pleasant, MI 48858 • 989.775.4750 • http://www.sagchip.org/ziibiwing/

NILES
Fort St. Joseph Museum

Sitting Bull returned from his Canadian exile in 1881, five years after he led the Indian alliance that had annihilated General George Custer's forces at the Little Big Horn (see entry on "Little Big Horn Battlefield National Monument," Crow Agency, Montana). Although he had heard that a pardon would be forthcoming after he surrendered to U.S. troops, he was imprisoned for two years at Fort Randall, South Dakota. To get through the long months of confinement, Sitting Bull began to paint. A German newspaper illustrator, Rudolph Cronau, gave him drawing lessons.

Sitting Bull set out to illustrate the story of his life in a series of vividly colored and energetic pictographs. The drawings primarily depicted the achievements of Sitting Bull and his tribe at war as they defeated both their traditional Indian enemies and cavalry officers. Alice Quimby, the daughter of the fort commandant, befriended Sitting Bull, and when he was released from confinement, he gave her the pictures as a gift. She kept them for the rest of her life and left them to the Fort St. Joseph Museum in her hometown when she died in 1947. Sitting Bull's saddle and gun were also part of her bequest, and they now form a remarkable exhibit in this small museum dedicated mainly to local history.

Info: 508 E. Main St., Niles, MI 49120 • 269.683.4702 • http://www.nileshistorycenter.org

OKEMOS
The Nokomis Learning Center

The Nokomis Learning Center is a nonprofit Native American cultural learning center located near Lansing dedicated to the preservation and presentation of Anishinabe culture. For nearly two decades, the center has been educating Michigan residents about Anishinabe (Ojibwa, Odawa, and Potawatomi) arts, culture, and history.

Info: 5153 Marsh Rd., Okemos, MI 48864-1198 • 517.349.5777 • http://nokomis.org/

PESHAWBESTOWN
Eyaawing Museum and Cultural Center

The Eyaawing Museum and Cultural Center was created by the Grand Traverse Band of Ottawa and Chippewa Indians to establish, gather, interpret, and maintain a record of the Grand Traverse Anishinabe history. The museum Odaawa Gamik (gift shop) features the work of local and tribal artists.

Info: 2605 N. West Bay Shore Dr., Peshawbestown, MI 49682 • 231.534.7768 • http://www.gtbindians.org/eyaawing.asp

ST. IGNACE
Museum of Ojibwa Culture

The Ojibwa are now the most heavily represented group in part of the Upper Peninsula. A former church next to Marquette Park has been turned into the Museum of the Ojibwa Culture. Exhibits illustrate the history of the people, the structure of their families, and their relationship to their natural surroundings. Of special note is the new Anishinabe Sculpture Park with its glorious, contemporary statues created by Jennifer DeVos. Her "Clan System" sculptures placed Third Best in the World in the International Mural/Exhibits Contest juried by *Signs of the Times* magazine. The gift shop represents over one hundred Native American and Native Canadian artists. The museum hosts a Native American Festival brimming with activities, demonstrations, and music to share Ojibwa culture.

A sculpture at the Museum of Ojibwa Culture.

Info: 500 N. State St., St. Ignace, MI 49781 • 906.643.6076 • http://museumofojibwaculture.net/index.html

TRAVERSE CITY
The Dennos Museum Center

The Dennos Museum Center houses a collection of more than two thousand works of art, with over half composed of Inuit prints and sculptures. Significant holdings also include twentieth-century Great Lakes Indian and Canadian Indian art. The art collections are shown on a rotating basis as part of the museum's changing exhibitions.

Info: 1701 E. Front St., Traverse City, MI 49686 • 231.995.1055 • http://www.dennosmuseum.org/

MINNESOTA

M innesota's Native citizens number around 108,800, and thirteen Native governments are in Minnesota.

COMFREY
Jeffers Petroglyphs

The Jeffers site lies at the top of Red Rock Ridge, a rock formation extending from south-central Minnesota to southeastern South Dakota. The red quartzite rocks situated along the Little Cottonwood River are covered with about two thousand pictorial carvings that chronicle the history of this area's ancient people. The carvings form one of the largest groups of petroglyphs found in the Midwest. The word "petroglyph" comes from the Greek words *petros* (rock) and *glyphe* (carving).

Historians estimate that these petroglyphs were carved during the Late Archaic–Early Woodland (3000 B.C.E. to 500 C.E.) and the Late Woodland (900 to 1750 C.E.) periods. They recorded important events, pastimes, and sacred ceremonies.

The visitor center offers a video presentation and exhibits about American Indian culture and prairie ecology. The "Packing a Travois" display gives guests a chance to interact with American Indian tools, clothing, and games. The gift shop includes American Indian gifts.

Info: 27160 County Road 2, Comfrey, MN 56019 • 507.628.5591 • http://sites.mnhs.org/historic-sites/jeffers-petroglyphs

An arrow is one of many pictures to be found among the Jeffers Petroglyphs.

DULUTH
Tweed Museum of Art, University of Minnesota Duluth Campus

The museum exhibits pieces from the Richard E. and Dorothy Rawlings Nelson Collection of American Indian Art that includes baskets, birch bark, beadwork, quillwork, tourist art, and treaty portraits, primarily by the Great Lakes Ojibwe and Eastern Woodlands people from 1850–1950. These objects reflect the visual culture of this region's Anishinabe people. They also provide historical context for the museum's expanding collection of contemporary works by Native American artists.

Info: 1201 Ordean Ct., Duluth, MN 55812-2496 • 218.726.8222 • http://www.d.umn.edu/tma/

FARIBAULT
Sioux Window in Cathedral of Our Merciful Saviour

Episcopal bishop Henry Whipple, who had established a school and mission at Faribault, had become sympathetic to the dilemma of the Sioux located in the southwestern part of the state. When clauses that had been attached to treaties were suddenly enforced, the Sioux were made to give up half their reservation lands. Crop failures occurred. While the government debated on whether to pay treaty annuities in gold or paper money, the agent refused to give out food until money arrived. Chief Little Crow was told that his people "would eat grass or their own dung."

In August, four young men of the tribe suddenly fired into a party of whites, killing five. Authorities demanded that the tribe surrender the men for justice. The Sioux refused and, under the leadership of Little Crow, raided settlements of the Minnesota River Valley. Finally, the state organized a fourteen-hundred-man force and defeated Little Crow at the Battle of Wood Lake.

The government rounded up all Native men suspected of participating in the campaign, even those who were neutral. In courts, 303 of the men were sentenced to death. Bishop Whipple interceded on behalf of the Sioux, making a personal plea to President Lincoln. As a result, 265 of these men had their sentences reduced to prison terms, but the remaining thirty-eight, erroneously accused of either murder or rape, were hung at a public ceremony on December 26, 1862. The reservation lands then were broken up and the remaining Sioux dispersed. This was the largest government lynching in history.

Construction on Whipple's cathedral included a stained-glass window showing a ceremonial pipe and a broken war club, a token of gratitude from the Sioux for Whipple's efforts on their behalf.

Info: 515 2nd Ave. NW, Faribault, MN 55021 • 507.334.7732 • http://www.inhonorofthepeople.org/cathedral-our-merciful-saviour

GRAND PORTAGE
Grand Portage National Monument

During the great era of the fur trade, the area around the present-day Grand Portage National Monument site was one of the most important places on the Great Lakes.

Grand Portage National Monument.

At Grand Portage ("great carrying place"), voyagers from French Canada made their way to the bountiful trapping country to the northwest. The area was known to European explorers by 1722.

Every spring, French trappers and their Native American guides and companions would come to Grand Portage with the year's supply of pelts for Rendezvous. They met with company representatives from Montréal. Deals were struck, trade goods from the East purchased, and celebrations held. For the Ojibwa who lived in the area, Rendezvous was a time to stock up on the manufactured goods that were playing an increasingly important part in their lives.

The Grand Portage Rendezvous was held for nineteen years, from 1784 to 1803, until the company opened a new base at Fort William, across the Canadian border. Within a few years, the buildings had crumbled into disuse, and in time, the very site was almost forgotten, but in 1958, the Ojibwa, who had been given the surrounding lands as a reservation, donated the Grand Portage location to the federal government for use as a historic park. The major buildings were reconstructed according to the records of archaeologists and historians who went over old journals. Now this first permanent settlement in Minnesota stands again, with exhibits that pay particular attention to the roles of Native Americans in the fur-trading era. Examples of their beadwork and other crafts are sold at gift shops within the national monument.

Info: P.O. Box 426, Grand Portage, MN 55605 • 218.475.0123 • https://www.nps.gov/grpo/index.htm

HUTCHINSON
Little Crow Memorial

Little Crow was among the Santee bands that could not bear to stay away from their ancestral homes after the Sioux War. During the resistance, he had reluctantly led the Indian forces. He seemed to recognize that the resistance was futile, but his stature among the Santee was such that he could not refuse the demands of leadership placed upon him. It is unclear whether it was his plan to attack the isolated farms along the Minnesota River in an attempt to drive white farmers out.

The attacks stirred up outrage in St. Paul, as well as throughout the East, where lurid newspaper stories on the Sioux resistance caused enormous excitement. When the state managed to assemble an army against Little Crow, his demand for amnesty was refused. The public thirst for revenge was too great to allow it.

After his defeat at Wood Lake, Little Crow escaped to the Dakota Territory, but the following year, he returned to his homeland. Hutchinson was not the safest place to be because it was in this vicinity that the first shots of the war had been fired. A farmer, learning that Little Crow was in the area, ambushed him while he was picking berries with his son. Little Crow died on July 3, 1863.

In 1937, when firsthand memories had faded and new perspectives were gained on the grievances of the Sioux, the town erected a monument to the Native leader who was gunned down here. It was created by Hutchinson sculptor Les C. Kouba. In 1982, Kouba accepted a commission to create an updated Chief Little Crow statue. The original statue can be found at the McLeod County Historical Museum in Hutchinson.

Info: County Road 18, Hutchinson, MN 55250

MINNEAPOLIS
All My Relations Gallery

The All My Relations Gallery features Native contemporary art as well as workshops. Founded by Shirlee Stone as Mitakuye Oyasin (Dakota phrase for All My Relations) in 1999, the gallery has more than a decade-long history of producing quality contemporary American Indian fine arts exhibits. It is located on Franklin Avenue in the center of the American Indian Cultural Corridor. Since its founding, All My Relations Arts has created more than twenty-five exhibits.

Info: 1414 E. Franklin Ave., Minneapolis, MN 55404 • 612.235.4970 • http://www.allmyrelationsarts.com

American Indian Cultural Corridor

The American Indian Cultural Corridor, an endeavor of the Native American Community Development Institute, was inaugurated on April 30, 2010, with a ribbon cutting and community walk, but the idea of creating an American Indian district on Franklin Avenue has been around for many years. Franklin Avenue has been a commercial corridor in the city of Minneapolis for over a century. Through the federal relocation period of the 1950s and 1960s, during which time the federal government encouraged thousands of American Indian people to leave their reservations and move to cities, Franklin Avenue became an important gathering place for Indian people. Franklin Avenue developed a national reputation as the heart of Minneapolis's urban

Mural in the American Indian Corridor.

American Indian community. To this day, the area surrounding the cultural corridor is the densest concentration of urban American Indian people in the country. This important history has led to many "firsts" occurring around Franklin Avenue, including the development of the first urban American Indian health clinic, the first American Indian preference housing project, and the location of one of the oldest American Indian centers in the country. In addition, Franklin Avenue is the birthplace of the American Indian Movement, a national protest movement founded in the 1970s for American Indian civil rights.

Info: 1414 E. Franklin Ave., Minneapolis, MN 55404 • 612.235.4976 • http://aiccorridor.com/

Augsburg Native American Film Series

The Augsburg Native American Film Series (ANAFS) grew out of a love for film and a desire to increase the number of venues for Native American filmmakers in Minneapolis. The energy that drives the ANAFS is based on a commitment to affecting the world through artistic collaboration and a belief in the power of film to inform, affect, and stimulate vastly different groups of people.

Info: Augsburg College, CB 115, 2011 Riverside Ave., Minneapolis, MN 55454 • 612.330.1523 • http://www.augsburg.edu/filmseries/

Two Rivers Gallery

Two Rivers Gallery is located at the Minneapolis American Indian Center along the American Indian Cultural Corridor. Its mission is to expose local emerging Native artists by providing a space to exhibit work, nurture creativity, and provide professional development.

Info: 1530 E. Franklin Ave., Minneapolis, MN 55404 • 612.879.1780 • http://tworiversarts.com/

ONAMIA
Mille Lacs Indian Museum and Trading Post

The Mille Lacs Indian Museum and Trading Post, which opened in 1965, is dedicated to telling the story of the Mille Lacs Band of Ojibwe. Adjacent to the museum is a restored 1930s trading post where visitors can buy art created by Mille Lacs artisans.

In 1996, a new facility was constructed, built in cedar with an exterior highlighted by a copper dome and tile installation designed by Mille Lacs artist Batiste Sam. Exhibits use multimedia interactive displays and artifacts to present tribal history as well as contemporary issues such as sovereignty, treaty rights, veterans, casino operations, and maintaining cultural practices facing seven Ojibwe communities located throughout the state. A Four Seasons Room depicts the traditional seasons of the Ojibwe people.

The core of the Ojibwe cultural materials are items from the collection of Henry and Jane Ayers, who operated a local trading post in the early 1900s where they bought and traded items from the local community. The collection is best known for exceptional examples of birch bark items, bandolier bags, deer-hide garments, and beaded and quilled personal objects.

Info: 43411 Oodena Dr., Onamia, MN 56359 • 320.532.632 • http://sites.mnhs.org/historic-sites/mille-lacs-indian-museum

PIPESTONE
Pipestone National Monument

Among every group of Native Americans in the Northern Plains, the red, stone pipe became a sacred item. Certain pipes carried religious significance, were stored in special animal skin bundles, and were associated with ancient stories that sought to explain the origin of the tribes. Many pipes were buried with their owners. Pipe smoking

Mille Lacs Indian Museum.

Pipe quarry at Pipestone National Monument.

was a ritual that accompanied almost every important event, from going to war to making peace, from trading goods to making medicine. The T-shaped pipe, known as the calumet, was smoked at ceremonial events, such as the signing of treaties, and became known to white settlers as "the peace pipe." The tradition continues.

The most highly prized source for these pipes was a soft-red-stone quarry in southwestern Minnesota. Evidence exists that digging here began in the seventeenth century. The territory was always controlled by some division of the Sioux. While the Sioux managed the distribution of the pipestone, the land around the quarry was regarded as a stewardship, held for the use of all tribes.

As white settlers moved onto the land, they encroached on the stone. Many public buildings in the nearby town of Pipestone were built with stone quarried from Indian lands. In 1928, the Yankton ceded their unrestricted access to the quarry to the federal government. In 1937, the Pipestone National Monument was formed, and only people of Native ancestry are permitted to quarry the pipestone at the monument.

In the visitor center, Native Americans give demonstrations of the traditional art of pipe making, which has changed little since Western artist George Catlin first described the process in the 1840s. The Upper Midwest Indian Cultural Center operates craft displays here. The gift shop sells a wide variety of objects.

Info: 36 Reservation Rd., Pipestone, MN 56164 • 507.825.5464 • https://www.nps.gov/pipe/index.htm

TOWER
Bois Forte Heritage Center and Cultural Museum

The Bois Forte Ojibwe people have preserved their heritage and culture in a museum that opened in 2002. The entry displays a Carl Gawboy mural, which depicts the migration of the Ojibwe with their travel route shown in a red pictograph overlay. Exhibits include their art and beadwork, dress, and their association with the white settlement throughout the eras of fur trade, mining, and timbering to the present day. Videos are also available for viewing. The museum's outdoor exhibits include a birch bark dwelling and tipi.

Info: 1500 Bois Forte Rd., Tower, MN 55790 • 218.753.6017 • https://ironrange.org/attractions/bois-forte-heritage-museum-and-gift-shop/

MISSOURI

About 76,700 Native citizens live in Missouri, and it contains eight Native entities.

JACKSON
Missouri's American Indian Cultural Center in Van Meter State Park

Visitors can view both permanent and temporary displays that interpret the cultural history of the nine tribes that called Missouri home in the early nineteenth century. These tribes include the Otoe-Missouria, Osage, Delaware, Ioway, Illini-Peoria, Kanza, Kickapoo, Sac and Fox, and Shawnee. Today, those tribes have been relocated to reservations in Kansas and Oklahoma. In addition, information is displayed about William Clark, superintendent of Indian affairs in 1813. A large display of early maps of North America depict early European exploration and contact with American Indian tribes.

Info: 429 Moccasin Springs, Jackson, MO 63755 • 573.290.5268 • https://mostateparks.com/location/55530/missouris-american-indian-cultural-center

Trail of Tears State Park

The tragic history that gives Trail of Tears State Park its name provides a sharp contrast to the peaceful, serene setting enjoyed by visitors today. The 3,415-acre (14-square-kilometer) park is a memorial to the Cherokee Indians who lost their lives in a forced relocation. The park is located on the site where nine of the thirteen groups of Cherokee Indians crossed the Mississippi River in harsh winter conditions in 1838–1839. Thousands lost their lives on the trail, including dozens on or near the park grounds. Legend says that Nancy Bushyhead Hildebrand died and was buried within the park boundaries. The Bushyhead Memorial is a tribute to all the Cherokee who died on the trail. The park's visitor center features exhibits that interpret the forced relocation.

Info: 429 Moccasin Springs, Jackson, MO 63755 • 573.290.5268 • http://www.visitcape.com/discover/trail-of-tears-state-park/

KANSAS CITY
Harvest Moon American Indian Festival

The annual Harvest Moon Indian Festival celebrates culture, arts, and tradition in Kansas City; it showcases Native performers, dancers, artists, and artisans. The festival aims to break stereotypes and introduce visitors to an urban Indian community.

Info: 31st and Troost Aves., Kansas City, MO 64109 • 816.216.1181 • http://harvestmoonfestivalkc.com/

Nelson-Atkins Museum of Art

The American Indian collection of the Nelson-Atkins Museum of Art features more than two hundred objects, including pottery, basketry, quill- and beadwork, textiles, painting, and sculpture. The holdings are distinguished by numbers of recognized masterworks. Beyond individual pieces, strengths lie in historical works from the Pacific Northwest Coast, Plains, and Southeastern Woodlands and in both historical and contemporary works from the Southwest. In 2001, a gift of 170 objects, a private collection of Pacific Northwest Coast art, other gifts, and a fund for acquisitions, added to the growing collection. In 2009, a suite of three galleries dedicated to the art of Native peoples opened at the museum. The collection continues to expand.

Info: 4525 Oak St., Kansas City, MO 64111 • 816.751.1278 • https://nelson-atkins.org/collection/american-indian

MIAMI
Missouria Indian Village in Van Meter State Park

Van Meter State Park features remnants of the Missouria Indian village that sat at the Great Bend of the Missouri River, marked on a map by Jacques Marquette and Louis Jolliet in 1673. A hand-dug earthwork—Old Fort—and several burial mounds lie within the park's boundaries. The village has been excavated by teams from the University of Missouri. The village is estimated to date back as far as 10,000 B.C.E.

Info: 32146 N. Hwy. 122, Miami, MO 65344-9613 • 660.886.7537 • https://mostateparks.com/park/van-meter-state-park

ST. LOUIS
St. Louis Art Museum

The St. Louis Art Museum has collected Native North American art since the first decades of the twentieth century. Over the next several decades, the collection built

The Nelson-Atkins Museum of Art.

strengths in Native arts from the Northwest Coast, Arctic, Plains, and Southwest. The Native American art collection now encompasses almost seven hundred objects that span ancient and historic periods. The museum has also collected prints, photographs, and other works by contemporary Native artists since the 1970s. In addition, the museum collaborates with contemporary Native artists to present the collection in relation to Indigenous ways of seeing. Painter Dyani White Hawk visited the museum and then traveled to the Rosebud and Pine Ridge reservations in South Dakota to interview cultural specialists and tribal elders. Dyani White Hawk curated an installation of Lakota art inspired by these experiences. These works were installed in July 2017 and will be on view for two years.

Info: 1 Fine Arts Dr., St. Louis, MO 63110 • 314.721.0072 • http://www.slam.org/collections/nativeamerican.php

WALKER
Osage Village Historic Site

The site was the location of a large, Osage Indian village between 1700 and 1775, when the Osage were first encountered by Europeans. The village was home to two to three thousand people. The site features a self-guided interpretive trail with exhibits and information about Osage Indians.

Info: Route C, Walker, MO 64790 • 417.751.3266 • https://mostateparks.com/park/osage-village-state-historic-site

OHIO

About 95,800 Native residents and eight Native nations are in Ohio.

BAINBRIDGE
Seip Mound State Memorial

At one time, archaeologists wrote about an Adena culture and a Hopewell culture and concluded that they were early and late aspects of one culture, not two distinct cul-

Seip Mound.

tures. "Adena" became associated with the culture because of a mound excavated on a 2,000-acre (8-square-kilometer) estate, Adena, owned by Thomas Worthington, an early governor of Ohio. "Hopewell" refers to the farmlands of Mordecai Hopewell. Adena/Hopewell people are noted for building large burial mounds.

The people of the Hopewell culture began moving into Ohio from the Northeast in about 400 B.C.E. and reached their peak of influence about one thousand years later. Seip Mound, named for the brothers on whose farm it was discovered, is one of the largest of the Hopewell mounds, measuring 30 feet (9 meters) high and 240 by 130 feet (73 by 40 meters) wide. The findings of the mound—thousands of river pearls, along with a 28-pound (13-kilogram) ceremonial ax, richly ornamented breastplates, and items made of silver, copper, and mica—created a sensation, prompting the press to name the mound "the great pearl burial."

Info: Bainbridge, OH 45612 • http://www.stateparks.com/seip_mound.html

CHILLICOTHE
Hopewell Culture National Historic Park (Mound City)

So little appreciated were these mounds along the Scioto River that during World War I, they were almost obliterated to create an army training base. Many of them were leveled to make room for Camp Sherman. Only after the war did systematic excavation begin, and the site was not protected as a national treasure until 1923.

The present Hopewell Culture National Historical Park evolved in part from the former Mound City Group National Monument. The national monument was established by a proclamation signed by President Warren G. Harding in 1923 to preserve prehistoric mounds of "great historic and scientific interest." The National Park Service recommended expanding the boundaries of the monument by adding four additional sites. Hopewell Culture National Historical Park was thus established in 1992 by a law that renamed it.

The monument was assembled by the Hopewell culture between 200 B.C.E. and 500 C.E. During that period, the inhabitants erected twenty-three burial mounds within a 13-acre (52,609-square-meter) enclosure. Although the site was examined—and raided for artifacts—as early as 1846, another seventy-five years passed before serious study began. Among the findings were a mound with a mica-covered grave, another that contained more than two hundred effigy pipes, and yet another containing copper figurines and a death mask.

The National Park Service's visitor center has excellent displays with walking paths, trailside exhibits, and an observation deck overlooking the area.

Info: 16062 State Route 104, Chillicothe, OH 45601 • 740.774.1126 • https://www.nps.gov/hocu/index.htm

Tecumseh Outdoor Drama

The life of Tecumseh, the extraordinary Shawnee leader, is also a part of Indiana history (see entry on "Tippecanoe Battlefield and Museum," Lafayette, Indiana).

Nonetheless, during the years of the white settlement of Ohio, Shawnee leaders led the fight against European expansion. Their capital, Chillicothe, was occupied until 1795, and it is likely that Tecumseh was born there. The contemporary city of Chillicothe—in Greene County, several miles to the southeast of the original city—stages an annual outdoor pageant that dramatizes Tecumseh's leadership and the Shawnee struggle to retain their lands.

Info: 5968 Marietta Rd., Chillicothe, OH 45601 • 740.775.0700 • http://www.tecumsehdrama.com

COLUMBUS
Ohio Historical Center

Many of the art objects recovered from Ohio mounds were scattered among various museums over the years. Some of them even wound up in the British Museum. One of the best collections, however, is in Columbus, in Ohio's state museum. While its exhibits are not strictly limited to Native American culture, the museum offers an outstanding glimpse into the wealth and skills of these ancient cultures.

Info: 800 E. 17th Ave., Columbus, OH 43211 • 614.297.2300 • https://www.ohiohistory.org

DAYTON
Sun Watch Indian Village/Archaeological Park

Sun Watch Indian Village/Archaeological Park is a partially reconstructed Fort Ancient period American Indian village along the Great Miami River in Dayton, Ohio. The Fort Ancient culture as defined by archaeologists occupied the Middle Ohio River Valley between about 1000 and 1650 C.E. from what is now southeastern Indiana east to modern-day West Virginia.

These people have been named the Fort Ancient culture because many of their villages were clustered around the earthworks of that name (see entry on "Fort Ancient State Memorial," Lebanon, Ohio). However, the earthworks were in fact built by the Hopewell people, and the "Fort Ancient" farmers occupied the land much later.

In the 1960s, two amateur archaeologists learned that the site was scheduled to be turned into a sewage treatment plant. The Dayton Museum of Natural History conducted emergency excavations, and by 1971, the site was considered to be so significant that the sewage plans were revised. Sun Watch became a National Historic Landmark in 1990.

The interpretive center exhibits many artifacts that have been recovered from the site. Continuing analysis is being done of the artifacts (pottery, stone tools, bone tools, textile fragments, and others) as well as the locations of houses, trash pits, and other features at the site.

Info: 2301 W. River Rd., Dayton, OH 45417 • 937.268.8199 • http://www.sunwatch.org/about-us

GLENFORD
Flint Ridge Ancient Quarries and
State Memorial and Museum

Flint Ridge is a nearly 8-mile (13-kilometer)-long vein of high-quality flint located in Licking and Muskingum counties of eastern Ohio. Hundreds of quarry pits and workshop sites are scattered across more than 2,000 acres (8 square kilometers) of ridgetop in these Appalachian foothills. It has been called the "Great Indian Quarry of Ohio."

Flint Ridge seems to have been well known in the ancient world, as small amounts of it have been found at American Indian sites across the present-day eastern United States. Because of this flint's great beauty, it has been respected throughout the ages in the tools, weapons, and ceremonial objects of Native cultures and in modern times in the production of jewelry.

Within the museum is information about the importance of flint in ancient Indian cultures. Also, visitors learn about Ohio's official gemstone and the shaping of flint into tools, known as knapping.

Info: 15300 Flint Ridge Rd., Glenford, OH 43739 • 740.787.2476 • http://www.flintridgeohio.org

GNADENHUTTEN
Gnadenhutten Historical Park

Gnadenhutten was founded by a Moravian missionary, David Zeisberger, in 1772. His goal was to convert Lenape Indians to Christianity. He succeeded in converting around four hundred people.

On March 8 and 9, 1782, a group of Pennsylvania militiamen under the command of Captain David Williamson attacked the Moravian Church mission. The militia assaulted the Christian Delaware in retaliation for the deaths and kidnappings of several white Pennsylvanians, although this particular group was not responsible for the attack.

On March 8, the militia placed men and women in separate buildings and voted to execute their captives the following morning. Informed of their impending deaths, the Christian Delawares spent the night praying and singing hymns. The next morning, Williamson's soldiers murdered twenty-eight men, twenty-nine women, and thirty-nine children. Only two people survived, who informed the Moravian missionaries and other Christian American Indians as to what had occurred.

Today, the park includes a large obelisk that stands in memory of the massacred Indians. It includes a museum with many local artifacts, and a mission house and copper shop have been constructed on the site of the original cabins that served as the execution locations.

Info: 352 S. Cherry St., Gnadenhutten, OH 44629 • 740.254.4143 • http://traveltusc.com/directory/listing/gnadenhutten-museum-historical-park

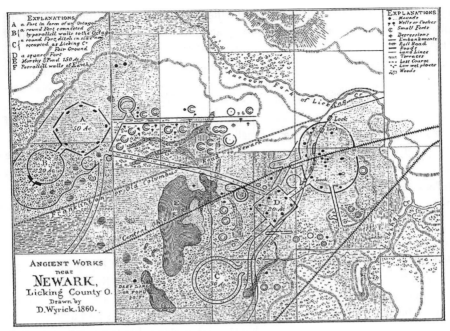

An 1860 illustration of the Newark Earthworks.

HEATH
Newark Earthworks (Moundbuilders State Memorial)

Built by people of the ancient Hopewell culture between 100 B.C.E. and 500 C.E., this architectural wonder of ancient America was part cathedral, part cemetery, and part astronomical observatory. The entire Newark Earthworks originally encompassed more than 4 square miles (6.4 square kilometers). Over the years, the growth of the city of Newark destroyed many of the Newark Earthworks, but three major segments survived because of the efforts of interested local citizens:

- Great Circle Earthworks—Formerly known as Moundbuilders State Memorial, it is nearly 1,200 feet (366 meters) in diameter.

- Octagon Earthworks—Enclosing 50 acres (0.2 square kilometers), it has eight walls, each measuring about 550 feet (168 meters) long and from 5 to 6 feet (1.5 to 2 meters) in height.

- Wright Earthworks—It consists of a fragment of a geometrically near-perfect square enclosure and part of one wall which led from the square to a large, oval enclosure. Originally, the sides of the Newark square ranged from about 940 to 950 feet (287 to 290 meters) in length.

In 1982, professors Ray Hively and Robert Horn of Earlham College in Indiana discovered that the Hopewell builders aligned these earthworks to the complicated cycle of risings and settings of the moon. They recovered a remarkable wealth of Indigenous knowledge relating to geometry and astronomy encoded in the design of these earthworks.

The Newark Earthworks are the largest set of geometric earthen enclosures in the world. Designated a National Historic Landmark, in 2006, the State of Ohio also designated the Newark Earthworks as "the official prehistoric monument of the state." The Great Circle Museum includes an interactive video explaining the significance of the site, an exhibit that includes a timeline of Ohio's ancient cultures, and an explanation of why American Indians regard the Newark Earthworks as a sacred site. The exhibit also details how the earthworks align with the rising and setting of the moon.

Info: 455 Hebron Rd., Heath, OH 43056 • 740.344.0498 • https://www.ohio history.org/visit/museum-and-site-locator/newark-earthworks

HILLSBORO
Fort Hill State Memorial

Fort Hill is one of the best-preserved examples of an ancient hilltop enclosure. Fort Hill was built by American Indians of the Hopewell culture, who lived in Ohio about two thousand years ago. Despite the name, Fort Hill was not an actual fort used for warfare but more likely a ceremonial gathering place. Fort Hill is also a nature preserve, and the 1,300 acres (5 square kilometers) are home to one of southern Ohio's largest mature forests, with many towering, old trees.

Fort Hill State Museum.

People of the ancient Hopewell culture (100 B.C.E.–500 C.E.) built the 1.5-mile- (2.4-kilometer-) long earthwork, which was as much as 20 feet (6 meters) high, as well as at least two ceremonial buildings and probably a village in the Brush Creek Valley. Lying at the western edge of the Allegheny Plateau, immediately south of the glacial boundary, this hilly area contains an impressive diversity of bedrock, soils, flora, and fauna. 11 miles (18 kilometers) of hiking trails are at the preserve. A museum houses exhibits on the geology and archaeology of the area.

Info: 13614 Fort Hill Rd., Hillsboro, OH 45133 • 800.283.8905 • https://www.ohiohistory.org/visit/museum-and-site-locator/fort-hill-earthworks

KELLEYS ISLAND
Inscription Rock Petroglyphs

Now a resort getaway in Lake Erie, this island was once inhabited by the people for whom the lake is named. Having been wiped out in wars with the Iroquois in the middle of the seventeenth century, the Erie left little but that name behind. At one time, however, the Erie inhabited the entire sweep of the lake's southern shore, from the present-day New York border to what is now Toledo.

Rediscovered partly buried in the shoreline in 1833, the rock is now entirely exposed and protected by a roof and viewing platform. Inscription Rock Petroglyphs is accessible daily in season, weather permitting, via the Kelleys Island Ferry. The petroglyphs on Inscription Rock are attributed to the Erie and are believed to depict the history of these people. Rising 11 feet (3.4 meters) above the water and measuring 32 by 20 feet (10 by 6 meters), the rock drawings are among the finest of their kind in the East. Listed on the National Register of Historic Places, Inscription Rock Petroglyphs is believed to have been created sometime between 1200 and 1600 C.E.

Info: Kelleys Island, Port Clinton, OH 43452 • 866.921.5710 • https://www.ohio history.org/visit/museum-and-site-locator/inscription-rock-petroglyphs

MARIETTA
Mound Cemetery

With the end of the American Revolution, the great land hunger of the seaboard colonies could be sated. Prior to that time, British law had prohibited settlement west of Pittsburgh in territory reserved for First Peoples. The new government, however, was eager to promote western expansion. The Shawnee, who had backed Britain in the war, could no longer retain their lands in southeastern Ohio. The Ohio Company was one of the first organized groups to take advantage of the "new" lands. In the spring of 1788, General Rufus Putnam, a trained surveyor and member of George Washington's military staff, and others arrived and established Marietta. They named the city in honor of Queen Marie Antoinette, which became the capital of the newly organized Northwest Territory.

Putnam had no idea who built the mounds or what they represented, but he suspected that they were associated with burials. Many of the mounds occupied a central position on the land where the newcomers intended to build their town; Putnam took the novel approach of incorporating the mounds in his town plan, whereas many early Ohio cities leveled the mounds they encountered. Marietta's founders preserved the Great Mound, the largest of the mounds, from destruction by surrounding it with a burial ground for citizens of the town. The cemetery is believed to have the highest number of burials of American Revolutionary War officers in the country.

Info: 5th St. and Scammel St., Marietta, OH 45750 • 800.288.2577 • https://en.wikipedia.org/wiki/Mound_Cemetery_(Marietta,_Ohio)

MIAMISBURG
Mound State Memorial

This is the largest conical mound in Ohio, and it baffled the early mound-builder theorists. Because most other mounds in the area are rounded or flat-topped, many nineteenth-century pseudohistorians were convinced that these 68-foot (21 meter)-high mounds were linked to an ancient race originating in Egypt or Meso America. Later investigation established, however, that these mounds—related to the Grave Creek Mound in Moundsville, West Virginia—were the work of the Adena culture. Archaeological investigations of the surrounding area suggest that the mound was constructed between 800 B.C.E. and 100 C.E. Monuments like Miamisburg Mound served as cemeteries for several generations of ancient Ohioans.

Miamisburg Mound.

The Miamisburg Mound is one of the two largest conical mounds in eastern North America. Listed on the National Register of Historic Places, the mound is 65 feet (20 meters) tall and eight hundred feet in circumference and contains 54,000 cubic yards (49,378-cubic-meters) of earth. The mound is visible from several miles away because it stands atop a 100-foot (20 meter)-high ridge above the Great Miami River. Steps have been built to the top observation platform, where one can enjoy a wonderful view of the area.

Info: 900 Mound Ave., Miamisburg, OH 45342 • 937.866.4532 • https://www.ohiohistory.org/visit/museum-and-site-locator/miamisburg-mound

NEW PHILADELPHIA
Schoenbrunn and "Trumpet in the Land" (Outdoor Pageant)

"Trumpet in the Land," written by Pulitzer Prize-winning playwright Paul Green, has been Ohio's longest-running outdoor theater production. The outdoor pageant brings to life the inspiring story of David Zeisberger and his Christian Indian followers as they struggled to preserve their peaceful settlement despite the growing violence of the Revolutionary War.

In 1772, Zeisberger, a Moravian minister from Pennsylvania, arrived in the Ohio Valley with dreams of building the first European settlement Schoenbrunn ("beautiful fountain" in German). When the Revolutionary War broke out, Zeisberger and his followers found themselves caught between the British at Fort Detroit and the Americans at Fort

Pitt. By refusing to take sides in the struggle, Zeisberger and his people incurred the wrath of both parties, eventually leading to the brutal massacre of ninety-six Christian Indians at Gnadenhutten in 1782 by a band of colonial militiamen (see entry on "Gnadenhutten Historical Park," Gnadenhutten, Ohio). President Teddy Roosevelt, a noted historian, called the event "a stain on the frontier character that time cannot wash away."

In 1923, archaeologists discovered the outline of Zeisberger's house, around which the state reconstructed much of the Moravian–Native American village. The church and schoolhouse, the first such structures west of Pittsburgh, have been rebuilt, as have many of the residential log cabins.

Info: Schoenbrunn Amphitheatre, P.O. Box 450, New Philadelphia, OH 44663 • 330.339.1132 • http://www.trumpetintheland.com

OREGONIA
Fort Ancient State Memorial

In Warren County, Ohio, an isolated peninsula rises about 260 feet (293 meters) above the muddy banks of the Little Miami River. This is an immense monument to the dedication and technological savvy of the original inhabitants of ancient North America. Fort Ancient features 18,000 feet (5,486 meters) of earthen walls built two thousand years ago by American Indians, who used tools made of shoulder blades of deer, split elk, and antler and clam shells to dig earth. They then transported loads of 40 pounds (18 kilograms) in baskets. Portions of these walls were used in conjunction with the sun and moon to provide a calendar system for these peoples. The Hopewell, known for their engineering expertise, built these walls and many other features both within the enclosure and on the steep valleys that surround the site: conical and crescent-shaped mounds, limestone pavements and circles, and many subsurface elements that are currently coming to light. The earthworks at Fort Ancient are among the most impressive military works of ancient North America. Today, the Fort Ancient State Memorial is listed on the National Register of Historic Places.

The Museum at Fort Ancient contains 9,000 square feet (2,743 meters) of exhibits, many interactive, that focus on fifteen thousand years of American Indian history in the Ohio Valley. The museum also contains a classroom, a research area, and a sales shop with many fine American Indian items.

Info: 6123 State Route 350, Oregonia, OH 45054 • 513.932.4421 • http://fortancient.org/archaeology

PEEBLES
Serpent Mound State Memorial

Serpent Mound is an internationally known National Historic Landmark built by the ancient American Indian cultures of Ohio. It is an effigy mound (a mound in the shape of an animal) representing a snake with a curled tail. Nearby are three burial mounds—two created by the Adena culture (800 B.C.E.–100 C.E.) and one by the Fort Ancient culture (1000–1650 C.E.).

Archaeologists are still puzzled by when and why the Serpent Mound was built. Most effigy mounds were more recently constructed and were concentrated far to the north, in the upper Mississippi Valley (see entries on "Effigy Mounds National Monument," Marquette, Iowa, and "Panther Intaglio Mound," Fort Atkinson, Wisconsin).

About 20 feet (6 meters) wide at the base, the mound stands 5 feet (1.5 meters) high in some places. The figure writhes seven times in gigantic loops and ends with an open mouth, about to swallow a smaller, oval mound. Some interpret this smaller mound as an egg, others as a frog. The undulating body, measuring 1,348 feet (411 meter) long, cannot be fully appreciated from the ground. To see the entire serpent and grasp its size, it is necessary to climb a 25-foot (7.6-meter) observation tower. A museum is located in the 61-acre (0.25-square-kilometer) park that surrounds the mound.

Info: 3850 State Route 73, Peebles, OH 45660 • 800.752.2757 • https://www.ohiohistory.org/visit/museum-and-site-locator/serpent-mound

PIQUA
Historic Indian Museum

This fertile, well-watered area was the homeland of several Native communities in the eighteenth century. The Miami moved in from the north early in the century and established their main community, Pickawillany, which became a crossroads for several neighboring tribes to trade. A historic recreation of the trading post at Pickawillany—which gave its name, in shortened form, to the present-day town of Piqua—now stands near the site of the former Miami and Shawnee villages.

Among the restorations is the Historic Indian Museum, which gives a historic overview of the Native people who occupied this land at the time of European settlement. It exhibits artifacts and graphics related to American Indians, with emphasis on the tribes associated with the Ohio country from the seventeenth to the nineteenth centuries. Displays show how the introduction of European culture led to the exchange and substitution of tools, weapons, and other objects between Indians and white settlers.

Info: 9845 N. Hardin Rd., Piqua, OH 45356 • 937.773.2522 • http://www.johns tonfarmohio.com/the_museum_-_native_american_frontier_and_canal_history

Wyandotte Mission

In 1816, John Stewart, a recovered alcoholic who found solace in the Methodist church, arrived at the main settlement of Wyandotte Indians at present-day Upper Sandusky. A man of mixed race, he was living in Marietta when he fell seriously ill in 1814. He vowed that if he recovered, he would dedicate his life to church service, and later, while walking in the fields outside town, he heard a voice that told him, "You must declare my counsel faithfully." The voice seemed to come from the northwest, and Stewart, taking this as a sign, headed in that direction to carry the word to the First Peoples. He first came to Delaware lands, who were already Christianized.

They told him of the Wyandotte, an unconverted tribe who lived further on, and Stewart concluded that this was where he was meant to go.

In 1824, the year after Stewart's death, a stone chapel was built here where the Wyandotte worshipped. When the Wyandotte were finally forced to relinquish their lands in 1843, part of the treaty stipulated that the chapel remain under the auspices of the Methodist church. The chapel that stands today was built in 1889 from the stones of the original mission, and the Methodists now recognize it as a shrine. Surrounding the chapel is a Wyandotte graveyard, where tombstones of Stewart and nine Delaware are located, members who stayed while their kinsmen were removed to the west.

Info: 200 Church St., Upper Sandusky, OH 43351 • 419.294.4841 • http://uppersanduskyoh.com/history.php

WISCONSIN

About ninety-three thousand Native citizens and ten tribal governments are in Wisconsin.

BLACK RIVER FALLS
Ho-Chunk Powwows

Ho-Chunk powwows are the oldest powwows in the Midwest and among the oldest in the nation, beginning in 1902 outside Black River Falls. Now the Ho-Chunk Nation holds several events throughout the year, none more promoted than the gatherings held at the Andrew Blackhawk Memorial Powwow Grounds on Memorial and Labor Day weekends. The powwows held during these celebrations feature respected warriors from all nationalities, raising over one hundred flags in honor of the veterans who've proudly served.

The Ho-Chunk welcome all visitors to attend their powwow, held as a celebration of thanks. It provides a time to gather and enjoy drums, dancing, and a wide variety of crafts available from vendors across the country.

The Ho-Chunk casino in Wisconsin Dells is adorned with design elements of Ho-Chunk culture (http://www.ho-chunkgaming.com/wisconsindells/).

Info: State Hwy. 54 E., Black River Falls, WI 54615 • 715.284.9343 • https://www.travelwisconsin.com/events/native-culture/ho-chunk-pow-wow-39030

BOWLER
Mohican Veterans Annual Powwow

The Stockbridge-Munsee Community Band of Mohican Indians hosts a three-day Veterans Annual Powwow that honors all veterans.

The Stockbridge-Munsee Tribe also hosts an annual Mohican Nation Traditional Powwow in August.

The powwow celebrates the Mohican Nation's heritage and culture through dancing, singing, prayer, crafts, and other activities.

Info: Many Trails Park on MohHeConNuck Rd., Bowler, WI 54416 • 715.524.2139 • http://www.mohican-nsn.gov/

Stockbridge-Munsee Historical Library/Museum

The Stockbridge-Munsee Community Band of Mohican Indians has a historical library/museum that is the official depository for the public records of the Mohican Nation, the Stockbridge-Munsee Band. The primary goal is to preserve the history and culture for tribal members and the general public. A research library consists of written materials, such as books, manuscripts, correspondence, handwritten letters, notes, maps, microfilm, microfiche, scrapbooks, photographs, videotapes, language tapes, and much more!

The museum part has a collection of cultural and historical artifacts from pre-contact to the mission school eras. The tribe's bible is on display. The library and museum have a gift shop located in the museum.

The Stockbridge-Munsee Band of Mohican Indians were pushed from the eastern seaboard across half a continent, forced to uproot and move many times to their present land in Wisconsin.

Info: N8476 MoHeConNuck Rd., Bowler, WI 54416 • 715.793.4834 • http://www.mohican.com/librarymuseum/

CRANDON
Forest County Potawatomi Cultural Center, Library, and Museum

The Forest County Potawatomi Cultural Center, Library, and Museum was primarily created to educate the public with a permanent exhibit outlining significant historical events and to pass the culture and traditions of the Potawatomi to the next generations.

The core of the museum is the collection of historical and contemporary photographs, audio/video, books, treaties, manuscripts, language material, and other memorabilia.

Info: 5460 Everybody's Road/P.O. Box 340, Crandon, WI 54520 • 715.478.4841 • https://www.fcpotawatomi.com/culture-and-history/

DE PERE
Oneida Nation Museum

The Oneida Nation Museum opened in 1979 with a small collection obtained from community members. In 1994–1995, the museum purchased a large portion of the closed Turtle Museum Collection in Niagara Falls, New York, and doubled its collection. Traditional Oneida homelands are in upstate New York; they are part of the Haudenosaunee (Iroquois).

The Oneida Nation Museum provides accurate information about the Oneida and Iroquois cultures, histories, and nationhoods. This is accomplished by developing, preserving, and expanding resources and collections and by providing exhibits, especially tribal history, and other educational programming. The museum also displays and promotes Iroquois artwork.

Besides experiencing original Iroquois artwork, visitors can see nature trails and the Three Sisters Garden. The museum gift shop offers contemporary Oneida and Iroquois arts and crafts, corn husk dolls, music, books and DVDs, beadwork, jewelry, clothing, art cards, and more.

The Oneida have become very active in the Green Bay area and own several tribal enterprises, including a casino.

Info: W. 892 Cty. Hwy. EE, De Pere, WI 54115 • 920.869.2768 • https://oneida-nsn.gov/our-ways/museum

FORT ATKINSON
Panther Intaglio Mound

In 1850, when Increase Lapham published his *Antiquities of Wisconsin,* he documented a remarkable series of Indian mounds that ran along Riverside Drive in Fort Atkinson. At the end of the group was the most interesting one of all: an effigy mound in reverse, or cut into the ground. This intaglio—as it's called—in the shape of a panther is now marked by a state historic marker in the 1200 block of Riverside Drive.

Back in 1850, when Lapham did his survey, a total of eleven of these intaglios existed in Wisconsin, but now, thanks to thoughtful city officials back in the early 1900s, the City of Fort Atkinson can boast that it has the only intaglio left in the entire United States. It was added to the National Register of Historic Places in 1970.

A historical marker reads: "Discovered in 1850 by Increase A. Lapham, this is the only known intaglio effigy mound in the world. It was excavated for ceremonial purposes by American Indians of the Effigy Mound culture in about 1000 C.E. A part of the tail has been covered. Of ten other recorded intaglios, all now destroyed, eight were similar in representing the panther and two represented bears."

Info: 1236 Riverside Dr., Fort Atkinson, WI 53538 • 920.563.7769

GREEN BAY
Oneida Powwow

An annual powwow, Native American dancers from around the country meet over the weekend to compete for prize money at the Oneida Powwow. This event not only has Native American dancers and singers but also offers Native American foods, crafts, and lacrosse exhibitions.

Info: N7210 Seminary Rd., Oneida, WI 54155 • 920.713.0608 • https://www.travelwisconsin.com/events/native-culture/oneida-pow-wow-41286

Walk of Legends

The Walk of Legends, sponsored by the Oneida Nation, is one of the most popular attractions in the Greater Green Bay area. In addition to cataloguing the history of the Green Bay Packers football team, the statues on the Walk of Legends educate viewers on the history of its sponsor, the Oneida Nation of Wisconsin (whose members were some of the first marquee players in Green Bay football history). You'll be able to read vignettes outlining tribal history, practices, and customs on each statue.

Info: Block east of Lambeau Field, Green Bay, WI 54304 • 920.497.5944 • https://www.greenbay.com/directory/oneida-nation-walk-of-legends/

HAYWARD
Honor the Earth Homecoming Celebration and Powwow

The Lac Courte Oreilles host the Honor the Earth Homecoming Celebration and Powwow. Ojibwe tradition and celebration are the centerpieces of the homecoming. Music, dancing, crafts, and food create an authentic tribal experience.

Info: 8575 N. Round Lake School Rd., Hayward, WI • 715.634.8934 • https://www.travelwisconsin.com/events/native-culture/lco-honor-the-earth-pow-wow-38913

KESHENA
Menominee Cultural Museum

Completed in the spring of 2010, this new, state-of-the-art, environmentally controlled facility is the focal point of Menominee culture, history, and language. The 6,000-square-foot (1,829-meter) facility is home to Menominee artifacts the tribe has repatriated from museums through the Native American Graves Protection and Repatriation Act. The gift shop is filled with Native American–made items.

Info: W3426 Cty. Hwy., West Keshena, WI 54135 • 715.799.5258 • http://www.menominee-nsn.gov/culturepages/culturalmuseum.aspx

Menominee Nation Powwows

The Menominee Nation hosts an Annual Nation Contest Powwow and Annual Veterans of Menominee Nation Powwow "Gatherings of Warriors." Contestants and spectators from across the nation and Canada gather to enjoy the finest in dance competition and in live singing and drumming. Each vendor offers a diverse array of merchandise inspired by Native American artwork, beadwork, and apparel as well as a variety of traditional Native American and contemporary cuisine.

Info: Woodland Bowl, Fairgrounds Rd., Keshena, WI 54135 • 715.799.5114, x.1267 • https://www.travelwisconsin.com/events/native-culture/menominee-nation-contest-pow-wow-39804

LAC DU FLAMBEAU
George W. Brown Ojibwe Museum and Cultural Center

The George W. Brown Ojibwe Museum and Cultural Center is owned and operated by the Lac du Flambeau Band of the Lake Superior Chippewa. In 1995, the band chose to distinguish an elder who has been a lifelong proponent of cultural preservation by naming the center in his honor. The center preserves and promotes local history and culture through the collection of data and artifacts and through the development of exhibits and educational programs. Exhibits are structured around two general themes: 1) Ojibwe history and culture and 2) the fur trade period and the Ojibwe.

The museum and cultural center was opened in June of 1989. Since then, more than two hundred thousand visitors have come to participate in cultural programming and research the collections and archives. Lac du Flambeau is one of three Ojibwe (or Chippewa) Wisconsin bands of the tribe and located in the inland lake country. The name itself derives from a Chippewa practice, observed by French explorers, of fishing at night with the aid of birch torches meant to attract fish.

Info: 603 Peace Pipe Rd., Lac du Flambeau, WI 54538 • 715.588.3333 • http://ldfmuseum.com/

MADISON
On Wisconsin Annual Spring Powwow

The UW-Madison's American Indian student organization, Wunk Sheek, hosts the On Wisconsin Annual Spring Powwow. It is cosponsored by multiple departments, units, and programs and the Native American student groups at UW-Madison.

Info: 215 N. Brooks St., Madison, WI 53706 • 414.229.5880 • https://amindian.wisc.edu/aiscc/

MILWAUKEE
Hunting Moon Powwow

The Hunting Moon Powwow, hosted by the Forest County Potawatomi Community, is held every October. The powwow lasts three days, bringing together dancers, drummers, and singers from many Native American cultures for a celebration in the heart of downtown Milwaukee.

The Indian Summer Festival in Milwaukee, Wisconsin, is a traditional, two-day Native American powwow that celebrates Native heritage. The event features traditional dancing, musical performances, bow and arrow demos, boxing exhibitions, authentic Native cuisine, lacrosse, cultural instruction workshops, and a fireworks display.

Info: 400 W. Wisconsin Ave., Milwaukee, WI 53203 • 414.229.5880 • http://www.huntingmoonpowwow.com

Milwaukee Public Museum

Both archaeology and ethnology materials are strongly represented in the Milwaukee Public Museum (MPM) collections. The museum's archaeology collections are heavily weighted toward North America (82 percent of archaeology holdings), with smaller but important collections from Meso and South America (14 percent of archaeology holdings).

Within North America, major strengths are in the archaeology of Wisconsin (77 percent of MPM North American archaeology holdings), Illinois, and the American Southwest. Material from over thirty major Wisconsin excavations is represented, showing major periods of the state's ancient history.

Milwaukee Public Museum.

Non-Wisconsin North American archaeological collections include significant collections of Mandan village material, Middle Woodland Hopewellian material from both Illinois and Ohio, a valuable collection of material from Spiro Mound in Oklahoma, and sizeable collections of ceramics from both Mississippian period sites in the American midcontinent and Ancestral Puebloan sites in the American Southwest. Particularly strong collections represent Great Lakes tribes, groups from the American Southwest, Plains, Northwest Coast, and West Coast and a variety of Iroquoian, Subarctic, and Arctic groups.

Info: 800 W. Wells St., Milwaukee, WI 53233-1478 • 414.278.2728 • https://www.mpm.edu/

ODANAH
Bad River Manomin Celebration and Traditional Powwow

Since 1980, the Bad River Manomin Celebration and Traditional Powwow has been a public event for the entire family. Enjoy Native American food, dancing, and singing throughout the weekend. Manomin, or wild rice, is an integral part of Ojibwe history, and the Bad River Tribe celebrates the growth and harvest of this natural staple with traditional dancing, singing, canoe races, marathons, and plenty of food.

Info: Historic Old Odanah Powwow Gounds, Odanah, WI 54861 • 715.682.7111 • http://www.badriver-nsn.gov/

ONEIDA
Buffalo Overlook

The Oneida Nation's Buffalo overlook offers an eye-catching view of the buffalo herd from a covered observation deck equipped with picnic tables and informative signage about the buffalo. Take a picture with the 6-foot (1.8-meter)-tall bronze buffalo!

Info: N7633 Cooper Rd., Oneida, WI 54155 • 920.833.7952 •
http://www.exploreoneida.com/?s=buffalo

RED CLIFF
Red Cliff Powwows

The Red Cliff Band of Lake Superior Chippewa host the annual Red Cliff Traditional
Powwow (July) and the Red Cliff Days Powwow (Labor Day). The public is invited to
enjoy dancers in colorful regalia, singers, drums and drumming, artists, and vendors.

Info: Red Cliff Powwow Grounds, Hwy. 13, Red Cliff, WI 54814 • 715.779.3700 •
https://www.crazycrow.com/site/event/annual-red-cliff-traditional-pow-wow/

SPOONER
Wisconsin Canoe Heritage Museum

The Wisconsin Canoe Heritage Museum features canoes and canoe-related ephemera.
This eclectic assemblage of boats is exciting in its diversity and includes significant
crafts from the golden age of North American canoeing as well as work by important
contemporary builders. The building traditions of the eastern seaboard, the Midwest,
and Canada are all represented, providing the museum visitor a fascinating opportunity to experience the evolution of canoe design and manufacture in proper historical context.

Info: P.O. Box 365, Spooner, WI 54801 • 715.635.2479 •
http://www.wisconsincanoeheritagemuseum.org/

WEST BEND
Lizard Mound State Park

This Washington County park features twenty-eight effigy mounds—out of an original sixty—and takes its name from the most outstanding mound: a lizard mound

A canoe display at the Wisconsin Canoe Heritage Museum.

that's hundreds of feet long. This park has one of the largest, most diverse groups of effigy mounds, some in the shape of animals and geometric patterns, open to the public in Wisconsin. Visitors can take a self-guided, mile-long tour of twenty-six mounds, which are well preserved and clearly marked with information.

The mounds at Lizard Mound are remnants of an ancient culture unique to Wisconsin. In 2011, Washington County constructed an interpretive center with signage and audio exhibited to tell the story of the site.

Info: 2121 County Highway A, West Bend, WI 53090 • 262.335.4445 • https://www.travelwisconsin.com/county-parks/lizard-mound-county-park-195047

PLAINS

As Indigenous people we have "Traditional Ecologic Knowledge," but here is the secret: "common sense." Whatever happens to one person happens to all of us.

—Kandi Mossett, Mandan, Hidatsa, Arikara activist

One can see from one end of the horizon to the other on the Great Plains—the immense sky makes humans feel small. Winters court frigid blizzards while summers sing of intense, almost unbearable, heat. This legendary landscape teeming with prairies, steppes, grasslands, and wetlands stretches from the Missouri River to the Rocky Mountains.

The Plains has different types of cultures, but most people only know about those nations that were buffalo hunters. For this well-known culture, the Plains was an efficiently tuned ecosystem in the same way that a great symphonic orchestra produces musical masterpieces. The environment, including First Peoples, was based on a cycle. As the great bison herds migrated, they fertilized the land, which supported plants that sustained them and other species. The people followed, relying on the great beasts and using every single part of the animals for food, clothing, tools, homes, and household items—multiuse conservation. These people—Lakota, Santee, Comanche, Pawnee, and others—have become legendary in anglicized, romantic notions of what Indians are. All other Natives are compared to them—their homes, their horsemanship, their ceremonies, and accounts of their military prowess. Of course, it is not by their design but contrived by Hollywood machinations and the film industry's perpetuation of stereotypes, relegating Indians to the past, and, of course, the Great Plains always reflected the diversity of the many different groups; some, like the Missouri, were farmers living in geothermal earth lodges, for instance. The Plains was and is an enormous place.

The Plains became a land of forced exodus for many eastern tribes as they were wrenched from their territories by land-hungry Anglos. They were moved to the Southern Plains to what was designated Indian Territory (present-day Kansas/Oklahoma) as per the Indian Removal Act of 1830. It was a culture shock for the new-comers as well as those whose lands were being appropriated to make room for them. Others, like the Ojibwe and the Potawatomi, whose traditional lands were farther northeast, ended up farther north in this region as well. Many came earlier than the times of forced removal in 1830s and 1840s.

The bison herds have been regaining their numbers as different tribes act as stewards to restore the environment. Some statistics suggest that more Indians and buffalo are around now than have been there since 1870, when white adventurers slaughtered the animals by the thousands, robbing many Plains people of their main food source. The buffalo are getting healthier, but the Plains peoples have been meeting a new challenge as they try to keep the oil companies from polluting their rivers and drinking water. In 2016, thousands of Native people and their supporters blocked pipeline construction on the Missouri River near the Standing Rock Reservation. The struggle continues.

Travelers in the Plains today have a variety of sights and activities to experience. Rapid City, South Dakota, is the site of the Lakota Nation Invitational, which draws Native teams from around the country to compete in basketball, traditional games, and even a poetry slam. Across town, the Journey Museum is a hubbub of contemporary Indian art and events. Oklahoma is a place where one can celebrate Southeastern culture at the Cherokee National Holiday in Tahlequah or honor the "Lords of the Plains" at the Comanche National Museum and Cultural Center in Lawton. Wherever one travels in the Plains, the horizon is never far away.

KANSAS

Almost thirty-five thousand Native people live in Kansas today, with four tribal organizations.

COUNCIL GROVE
Council Oak

In March 1825, the Congress of the United States of America passed an act to authorize President John Quincy Adams to appoint three commissioners to carry out the process of marking a road to Santa Fe and secure a treaty with the Indians. The three commissioners met with chiefs of the Great and Little Osage nations at Council Grove on August 10, 1825. Gathered in the shade of what came to be known as the Council Oak on a hot August day, agents of the Osage Tribe and the U.S. government signed a treaty giving Americans and Mexicans safe passage along the Santa Fe Trail through Osage Territory in return for $800. Before the Council Oak blew down in a windstorm in 1958, the tree stood 70 feet (21 meters) tall and measured 16 feet (5 meters) around. A shelter east of the Neosho River Bridge in Council Grove, Kansas, protects the stump of the Council Oak.

Info: Main St., City Park, Council Grove, KS 66846 •
http://www.santafetrailresearch.com/trail-photo-01/council-oak.html

FAIRWAY
Shawnee Mission

As the federal government became committed to a policy of transporting Native people from the East to the unsettled lands west of Missouri, the question became where to put them. The answer, eventually, was Oklahoma, which was known for many years as Indian Territory, but for seventeen years, from 1825 to 1842, the Kansas Territory was the preferred resettlement site, and twenty-eight tribes signed treaties that granted them new lands there. Kansas, however, became a political prize in the sectional differences that led to the Civil War. As both pro- and antislavery forces vied for political control of the territory, white settlers on both sides of the issue were encouraged to move there and establish a presence for their faction. In 1854, the entire territory was opened to white settlement, and the Native American position became impossible. Another removal resulted, this time to the final destination of Oklahoma.

In the early years of Kansas history, the Indian settlements and the missions sent out to educate and convert their inhabitants became the focus of growth. Shawnee Mission was the first and the most important. In 1838, the Missouri Conference of the Methodist Episcopal Church sent out Rev. Thomas Johnson to minister to the Shawnee, the first of the eastern tribes to settle in Kansas. This was the tribe that had fought expansion of the white frontier for a century throughout Ohio and Indiana.

The mission thrived for a time, actually enlarged with new dormitories in 1845, but as the slavery question started to override all other considerations, Shawnee Mission was swept up in it. The school was closed, and the government took over the grounds. While meeting at Shawnee Mission, the legislature passed the laws that legalized slavery in Kansas, touching off a round of violence that swept the state and was a bitter prelude to the Civil War. By the time the capital left Shawnee Mission for good, so had the Shawnee as well as most of the other tribes. Disturbed by the growing circle of violence in a quarrel that did not involve them, many individuals sold their lands here and moved to Oklahoma of their own volition. Johnson, however, remained and, although a slaveholder, he pledged his loyalty to the Union. He was gunned down by Confederate raiders in 1865 and is buried nearby in the Shawnee Cemetery.

One of the remaining mission buildings tells the story of the emigrant Indians in Kansas, such as the Iowa, Kickapoo, Potawatomi, and Sac and Fox. Exhibits include woven baskets, beadwork, drums, and other art forms made from techniques passed down through generations of Kansans with American Indian ancestry. Many historical items relate to both the Native people who attended classes at the mission and the political strife that shut the mission down.

Info: 3403 W. 53rd St., Fairway, KS 66205-2654 • 913.262.0867 • https://www.kshs.org/shawnee_indian

KANSAS CITY
Huron Indian Cemetery

For a short time, no more controversial piece of urban real estate existed in the country than this cemetery plot in downtown Kansas City. This is the area to which the Huron, also known as the Wyandots, finally came in 1842, almost two hundred years after they had been driven from their traditional homeland on Canada's Georgian Bay by the Iroquois. They had traveled all around the Great Lakes, settled for a time in northern Ohio, and finally ceded those lands to come to Kansas, but little more than a decade later, as settlers poured into Kansas, they were forced to move again to Indian lands in Oklahoma. In the treaty that extinguished their claims in the Kansas City area, it was stipulated that their burial ground here would be preserved.

In 1906, when business was booming in Kansas City, a group of urban developers pushed a bill through Congress that permitted the site to be sold. The approximately four hundred bodies buried there were to be moved to a new cemetery. The case reached the U.S. Supreme Court four years later and the court upheld the bill, but the public outcry against it was so great that Congress repealed the bill in 1913 and created a city park around the burial ground instead. The cemetery today is in the heart of the business district, part of a central downtown plaza.

Info: 7th St. and Ann St., Kansas City, KS 66101 • 913.721.1078 • http://www.kansastravel.org/kansascitykansas/huronindiancemetery.htm

LAWRENCE
Haskell Indian Nations University Cultural Center and Museum

In 1884, the doors to Haskell officially opened under the name of the United States Indian Industrial Training School. The educational program focused on agriculture and education in grades one through five. Enrollment quickly increased from its original twenty-two to over four hundred students within one semester's time. The early trades for boys included tailoring, wagon making, blacksmithing, harness making, painting, shoe making, and farming. Girls studied cooking, sewing, and homemaking. Most of the students' food was produced on the Haskell farm, and students were expected to participate in various industrial duties.

Ten years passed before the school expanded its academic training beyond the elementary grades. By 1927, high school classes were accredited by the State of Kansas, and Haskell began offering post-high school courses in a variety of areas. Part of Haskell's attraction was not only its post-high school curriculum but also its success in athletics. Haskell football teams in the early 1900s to the 1930s are legendary, and even after the 1930s, when the emphasis on football began to decrease, athletics remained a high priority to Haskell students and alumni. Today, Haskell continues to pay tribute to great athletes by serving as the home of the American Indian Athletic Hall of Fame.

By 1935, Haskell began to evolve into a post-high school, vocational-technical institution. Gradually, the secondary program was phased out, and the last high school class graduated in 1965. In 1970, Haskell began offering a junior college curriculum and became Haskell Indian Junior College.

In 1992, after a period of planning for the twenty-first century, the National Haskell Board of Regents recommended a new name to reflect its vision for Haskell as a national center for Indian education, research, and cultural preservation. In 1993, the assistant secretary for Indian affairs (U.S. Department of the Interior) approved the change, and Haskell became "Haskell Indian Nations University (HINU)."

Haskell's 6,000-square-foot (557-square-meter) Cultural Center and Museum is dedicated to the memory of the first students who attended Haskell. The center's permanent exhibit, "Honoring Our Children Through Seasons of Sacrifice, Survival, Change, and Celebration," recounts the many evolutions of HINU from a vocational-technical school to a junior college and finally a four-year university.

The museum's archives and collections hold more than one million documents and photographs and more than two thousand works of art created by Native artists.

HINU is the only U.S. government boarding school to become a four-year university. Today, it has an average enrollment of over one thousand students each semester. Students represent federally recognized tribes from across the United States. The entire campus is a National Historic Landmark, with several buildings dating from the nineteenth century. In addition, it hosts events like the annual Haskell Indian Art Market held during the second weekend in September, which provides an economic opportunity for Native artists and a forum for intercultural exchange.

Info: 155 Indian Ave., P.O. Box #5013, Lawrence, KS 66046-4800 • 785.832.6686 • http://www.haskell.edu/cultural-center/

MEDICINE LODGE
Peace Treaty Park

Peace Treaty Park commemorates one of the largest gatherings in the history of the relations between Native and white people. In the fall of 1867, war on the western Plains had been going on for three years. The government wanted to secure a right of way for railroads, and the tribes could not carry on the fight through another winter. This place in southern Kansas was chosen as a conference site. Well within Indian lands, the area had been recognized as neutral ground among the Plains tribes for generations. The river waters were believed to have curative powers, and many nations came here for healing. The Arapaho, Cheyenne, Comanche, Kiowa, and Kiowa-Apache sent delegations to the conference. About fifteen thousand Native people showed up to meet with six hundred representatives from Washington.

A full list of Indian grievances was discussed with Little Raven, an Arapaho, making an address so moving that almost half a century later, white participants in the conference could quote from it. After two weeks of negotiations, the southern

Medicine Lodge Peace Treaty Amphitheater.

border of Kansas was fixed and the lands to the south given to Native peoples as their territory "for all time." The agreement, signed in 1867, opened western Kansas to settlement. Congress refused to ratify several parts of the treaty, and within a year, warfare had broken out again, but the gathering still went down as the largest of its kind in American history.

A citizens' committee decided to commemorate the event with a historical pageant. The celebration that was first presented in 1927 was usually held every three years and, since 2006, every five years. The twenty-fifth presentation of the Medicine Lodge Peace Treaty reenactment took place in 2015.

Info: Medicine Lodge Indian Peace Treaty Association, 103 E. Washington Ave., Medicine Lodge, KS 67104 • 620.886.9815 • http://www.peacetreaty.org

REPUBLIC
Pawnee Indian Museum State Historic Site

The Pawnee Indian Museum State Historic Site is an archaeological site and museum. At the site are the remains of a village once occupied by the Kitkehahki, or Republican, Band of the Pawnee Tribe. It is one of four known Kitkehahki sites in the Republican River Valley. The dates of occupation of this particular village are not known; the Kitkehahki intermittently occupied the Republican Valley from the 1770s to the 1820s.

The site includes a small museum store with Plains Indian-related items.

Info: 480 Pawnee Trail, Republic, KS 66964 • 785.361.225 • http://www.kansastravel.org/pawneeindianmuseum.htm

ST. MARYS
Potawatomi Pay Station Museum Marker

An Indian Agency for the Potawatomi was established at St. Marys Mission in 1857. In accordance with the terms of the Treaty of 1861, the payment to the Potawatomi was made here on October 29, 1870.

Through the cooperation of the City of St. Marys and the St. Marys Historical Society, this unique and historical site was designated in 1969 as the Potawatomi Pay Station Museum. It is listed on the National Register of Historic Sites.

Info: 102 E. Mission St., St. Marys, KS 66536

WICHITA
Mid-America All-Indian Center and Museum

The Mid-America All-Indian Center, established in 1969, is the only facility of its kind in Kansas that is solely dedicated to preserving and promoting the rich cultural history of American Indians in North America. The centerpiece of the Indian Center is the museum that houses work from American Indian artists from around the country. From the more than three-thousand-piece collection, multiple exhibits are on display inside the museum. The Indian Center is home to the largest public collection of work by artist Blackbear Bosin. Exhibits are changed quarterly and yearly, which promote the exploration of many areas of American Indian life.

Outdoor exhibits, which include a full-size tipi and grass houses, illustrate how Plains Indian families lived in the 1850s. Events are held regularly at the Indian Center, including powwows that attract American Indian dancers from across the United States.

A gift shop features American Indian-made items.

Info: 650 N. Seneca St., Wichita, KS 67203 • 316.350.3340 • http://www.theindiancenter.org/pages/default.aspx

Wichita Kansas Intertribal Warrior Society Veterans Powwow

The Wichita Kansas Intertribal Warrior Society Veterans Powwow takes place at the Mid-America All-Indian Center in Wichita. The powwow is an annual event that features plenty of gourd dancing and intertribal powwow dancing during the two-day event. The powwow features Native American vendors on the site.

Info: 650 N. Seneca St., Wichita, KS 67203 • 316.350.3340 • http://www.theindiancenter.org

NEBRASKA

N ebraska is home to 26,492 Native people and four tribal councils.

BANCROFT
John G. Neihardt Center State Historic Site

The John G. Neihardt Center seeks to educate the public using the literary and thematic legacy of John G. Neihardt and to preserve the heritage of the Great Plains and the voices of Native Americans and pioneers, both past and present. The Neihardt State Historic Site is also for the study and preservation of the works of John G. Neihardt and the history and cultures of the Great Plains.

John G. Neihardt Center and surrounding garden.

John Neihardt's series of epic poems about Nebraska, many of them incorporating stories he had gathered on the Omaha and nearby Sioux reservations, earned him the title of poet laureate. His home in Bancroft was made into a museum after his death in 1973. It contains many items of Native origin and a Sioux prayer garden.

Info: 306 W. Elm St., Bancroft, NE 68004 • 888.777.4026 • http://www.neihardtcenter.org

MACY
Umonhon Hedewachi or Harvest Celebration

The Omaha Tribe of Nebraska has hosted its Umonhon Hedewachi, or Harvest Celebration, for over two hundred years. It originated this form of the powwow, known as the Hethuska in the Omaha language.

The four-day Macy event features a variety of Native American performers singing and dancing, including tail dances and gourd dances. The event is open to the public and presents an opportunity to appreciate the Omaha Tribe's heritage, culture, regalia, and people.

When Lewis and Clark passed the Omaha villages on their voyage up the Missouri River in 1803, they witnessed the tribe's ceremony. It has been held ever since and is regarded as the oldest such Native American observance in the country.

Info: Omaha Nation, Macy, NE 68039 • 402.837.5728

NORTH DAKOTA

Four tribal entities and over forty-one thousand Native people are located in North Dakota.

BISMARCK
United Tribes International Powwow

The United Tribes International Powwow is one of the biggest gatherings in the north-central states. The four-day September powwow draws more than fifteen hundred dancers and representatives from seventy tribes. In addition to dance contests, the powwow includes sporting tournaments, arts and crafts, and food vendors.

Info: 3315 University Dr., Bismarck, ND 58504 • 701.255.3285 • http://unitedtribespowwow.com/

FORT TOTTEN
Fort Totten State Historic Site

Located on the southeastern edge of the town of Fort Totten, this site preserves a military post built in 1867 and was used continuously as a military reservation until 1890, when it became a boarding school for Indian children. The brick buildings, which replaced an earlier log fort, appear much as they did when built of locally made brick in 1868. Original buildings now house museum exhibits.

Constructed as a military post, Fort Totten became an Indian boarding school, Indian health care facility, and a reservation school. Initially, the fort policed the surrounding reservation. The soldiers enforced the peace, guarded overland transportation routes, and aided Dakota (Sioux) who lived near Devils Lake after 1867. Fort Totten was decommissioned in 1890.

On January 5, 1891, the former post became the property of the Bureau of Indian Affairs. The post served as an Indian boarding school until 1935. For four years (1935–1939), the site was used as the Tuberculosis Preventorium, run by the federal government. This successful program was aimed at small groups of Dakota children who had or were susceptible to tuberculosis. They were taught basic studies as well as being treated for tuberculosis. When this program was shut down, the site returned to being a community and day school for the reservation with gradually more input and control being given to the tribal leaders of the reservation.

Fort Totten became a North Dakota State Historic Site in 1960 and was listed on the National Register of Historic Places in 1971. It is located on the Spirit Lake Reservation (formerly Devils Lake) land.

Traditional tribal dances are held at Fort Totten/Spirit Lake in July during the Fort Totten Day Powwow observance.

Info: P.O. Box 359, Fort Totten, ND 58335 • 702.766.4221 • http://www.spiritlakenation.com

MANDAN
Slant Village at Fort Abraham Lincoln State Park

On-A-Slant Indian Village includes reconstructed earth lodges that depict the lifestyle of the Mandan, who occupied this site from about 1575 to 1781. The Mandan village that preceded Fort Abraham Lincoln on this site has been preserved just inside the state park entrance. It is built on a narrow point of land above the river, with bluffs guarding the water approach and moats protecting the other sides. A museum interprets the history of the fort and the Mandans.

Partially reconstructed Mandan On-A-Slant Village at Fort Abraham Lincoln State Park.

Info: 4480 Ft. Lincoln Rd., Mandan, ND 58554 • 701.667.6340 • http://www.parkrec.nd.gov/parks/falsp/falsp.html

NEW TOWN
Three Affiliated Tribes Museum

The Three Affiliated Tribes Museum displays and preserves the history and culture of the Mandan, Hidatsa, and Arikara people. This educational facility explains the origins and relationships of the three groups who live at Fort Berthold.

Upheaval is nothing new to these nations. The Mandan and Hidatsa, both long-time inhabitants of North Dakota, unified in 1845 after smallpox and war had nearly wiped them out. They were joined by the Arikara in 1862. This tribe was most closely related to the Pawnee, while the other two belonged to the Siouan family. They were all predominantly agricultural people and lived in earth lodge villages. The three separate groups established a community on a bend of the Missouri, called Fishhook. Then, in 1870, they moved onto the Fort Berthold lands, which were diminished over the decades by congressional acts, executive orders, and, finally, flooding by the opening of the Garrison Dam on the Missouri River.

Four Bears Bridge is the main connecting link within the reservation. The bridge, named for a Mandan chief, honors all three affiliated tribes. Plaques pay tribute to eighteen other chiefs affixed to the bridge. Four Bears Memorial Park is on the western side of the bridge, and within it is the museum.

Info: 404 Frontage Rd., New Town, ND 58763 • 701.627.4781 • http://www.ndtourism.com/new-town/attractions/three-affiliated-tribes-museum

STANTON
Knife River Villages National Historic Site

The Knife River Indian Villages National Historic Site, which was established in 1974, preserves the historic and archaeological remnants of the Northern Plains Indians.

This area was a major trading and agricultural area and location of three Hidatsa villages.

During the first winter of Lewis and Clark's voyage up the Missouri, they stopped for the season near a group of Hidatsa villages at the mouth of the Knife River. These villages already had been occupied for hundreds of years by the Hidatsa, who were talented farmers and traders. Long before the arrival of white trade goods, a network of Indian trade arrangements carried implements from this area all through the continent. Seashell ornaments have been found here, while flint goods made at Knife River have been uncovered as far away as Georgia.

The Hidatsa villages were the major population centers in North Dakota, but by 1804, the Hidatsa had been severely reduced by smallpox epidemics introduced by non-Indians. It was at the Knife River that the explorers met Sakakawea, the Shoshone woman who would guide them into the homeland of her people far to the west. A discrepancy exists regarding the spelling of her name. In North Dakota, it is Sakakawea, according to state researchers, because that is the Hidatsa rendering. In their language, it means "bird woman." In Shoshone, it usually is spelled Sacajawea, meaning "boat launcher."

The National Park Service has expanded this site. In 1992, a new Native American interpretive center opened. Imaginative displays recreate what daily life was like in Hidatsa villages and the impact that the Lewis and Clark Expedition had on the tribes of the region. Walking tours are laid out around the three villages located here. Markers clearly indicate the sites of homes, cache pits, and fortification ditches, some of which may be thirty-five hundred years old. In the summer months, several events are connected with the fur trade, Indian life, and the Lewis and Clark visit. The visitor center sells locally made Indian art.

Info: P.O. Box 9, Stanton, ND 58571 • 701.745.3300 • https://www.nps.gov/knri/index.htm

OKLAHOMA

The Oklahoma Native population is over 355,000. Not surprisingly, thirty-eight nations are headquarted in Oklahoma, but most were not historically located in the state, which was once called Indian Territory.

ANADARKO
American Indian Exposition

Every August, hundreds of Native American people from all over come to Anadarko, the home of the American Indian Exposition, one of the largest gatherings of Plains Indians in Oklahoma.

The exposition shows off Native American arts and crafts and helps preserve their cultural heritage. Visitors sometimes camp out in traditional tipis and wear historic clothing.

Attendees experience Native contest dancing, a carnival, parades, dance contests, pageants, a fry bread contest, talent presentations, crafts, concessions, and immersion in the history and ways of the present-day heritage of fourteen Plains nations.

Info: 453 Post Office Rd., Anadarko, OK 73005 • 580.678.1282 • http://www.americaslibrary.gov/es/ok/es_ok_parade_1.html

Delaware Tribal Museum

Until 1960, the Delaware—who by now had changed their name from the Absentee Delaware to the Delaware Tribe of Western Oklahoma—had no territory, even though they once controlled much of the land in the eastern United States. The Delaware now have a headquarters situated on land that they own jointly with the Wichita and Caddo. The facility includes a small museum, archive, and a library, with photographs of scouts, leaders, chiefs, and their descendants as well as maps and charts explaining the history of the Lenni-Lenape people. It was the Delaware who signed the famous treaty with William Penn, and it was they who signed the first Indian treaty with the United States in 1778.

Info: 31064 U.S. Hwy. 281, Building 100, Anadarko, OK 73005 • 405.247.2448 • http://delawarenation.com/cultural-preservation/

Kiowa Murals

The historic Anadarko post office building houses a massive mural depicting the ceremonial and social life of the Plains peoples. The work consists of sixteen variously sized panels of tempera-on-canvas designed by Stephen Mopope, one of the original Kiowa Five artists. Commissioned by the U.S. Treasury Department in June 1936, this was the largest mural commission ever awarded to a Southern Plains Indian artist. Oscar Jacobson, who was in charge of WPA projects for Oklahoma, commissioned Mopope and "Kiowa Five" associates James Auchiah and Spencer Asah to paint the murals in the newly constructed post office in Anardako, previously the site of the Kiowa Indian Agency of the Bureau of Indian Affairs that is listed on the National Historic Register. (See entry on "Carnegie, Kiowa Tribal Museum.")

Info: 120 S. First St., Anadarko, OK 73005 • https://livingnewdeal.org/projects/post-office-mural-anadarko-ok/

National Hall of Fame for Famous American Indians

The National Hall of Fame for Famous American Indians (also known as the American Indian Hall of Fame) was established in 1952 in Anadarko, Oklahoma. The National Hall of Fame has bronze busts mounted outdoors. Forty-one Native Americans from various tribes are honored for their contributions and places in American history.

Info: 851 E. Central Blvd., Anadarko, OK 73005 • 405.247.5555 • https://www.yelp.com/biz/national-hall-of-fame-for-famous-american-indians-anadarko

The Southern Plains Indian Museum.

Southern Plains Indian Museum

The Southern Plains Indian Museum displays richly varied arts of western Oklahoma Native peoples, including the Kiowa, Comanche, Kiowa-Apache, Southern Cheyenne, Southern Arapaho, Wichita, Caddo, Delaware, and Ft. Sill Apache. Their historic clothing, shields, weapons, baby carriers, and toys highlight the exhibits. They also include displays of the traditional fashions of Southern Plains men, women, and children as well as art forms related to both everyday and ceremonial life. Events include exhibits and talks by contemporary artists representing the area.

The museum was founded in 1947–1948 through federal and Oklahoma State governments' cooperative efforts and is operated by the Indian Arts and Crafts Board of the U.S. Department of the Interior.

Info: 715 E. Central Blvd., Anadarko, OK 73005-4437 • 405.247.6221 • https://www.doi.gov/iacb/southern-plains-indian-museum

Wichita Annual Tribal Dance

A Wichita Tribe tradition since 1974, this annual event showcases a series of traditional dance competitions as well as food and vendor booths.

Info: Wichita Tribal Park Highway 281, Anadarko, OK 73005 • 405.247.2425 • http://www.wichitatribe.com/culture/annual-dance-committee.aspx

CACHE
Quanah Parker Star House

The Quanah Parker Star House was the residence of the last chief of the nonreservation Comanche, and his story may strike a familiar chord with fans of John Ford movies. Ford adapted elements of the story in his classic film *The Searchers*.

Built around 1890 for the renowned Comanche warrior, leader, and statesman, the house is a testament to the respect Quanah commanded. He skillfully balanced his roles as a leader within the Comanche Nation and as an emissary to white culture while maintaining his own beliefs. The Star House is an excellent example of this balance, displaying Quanah's success and wealth while also allowing him to continue practices such as sleeping outside on a second-story wraparound porch. The large stars on the roof give the house another special twist.

While other members of the Comanche agreed to resettlement in Oklahoma, Parker fought on against buffalo hunters and federal troops. Finally, seeing that further battle was hopeless, he accepted resettlement in 1875. He built this home fifteen years later and spent the rest of his life there. In his later years, he became something of a national celebrity and even developed a friendship with Theodore Roosevelt. He died at the house in 1911, which contains mementos of his life and of that era in Oklahoma history. The Star House is listed on the National Register of Historic Places and is also on Oklahoma's list of Most Endangered Historic Places. Currently, the Comanche Nation is attempting to preserve Star House; it is owned privately, and the owners are not able to pay for repairs.

Info: N. 8th St., Cache, OK 73527 • http://comanchenation.com/

CARNEGIE
Kiowa Tribal Museum

The Kiowa Museum seeks to "protect, preserve, and perpetuate the Kiowa way." Programs are focused on preserving Kiowa language, art, song, history, and traditions.

The Kiowa have a long, artistic tradition, including talented muralists (see entry on "Kiowa Murals," Anadarko, Oklahoma). In the 1980s, the Kiowa Business Committee hired three Kiowa artists (Parker Boyiddle, Mirac Creepingbear, and Sherman Chaddlesone) to paint ten murals for the museum that would show Kiowa history.

The Tribal Museum displays many of the works of six Kiowa internationally known artists, previously known as the Kiowa Five: Spencer Asah, James Auchiah, Jack Hokeah, Stephen Mopope, Lois Smoky, and Monroe Tsatoke. Other exhibits show and explain Kiowa cultural items.

Info: Highway 9 W., Carnegie, OK 73015 • 580.654.2300 • https://www.kiowatribe.org/kiowa-museum.html

CHEYENNE
Washita Battlefield National Historic Site Visitors Center

The Washita site protects and interprets the setting along the Washita River where Lt. Col. George A. Custer led the 7th U.S. Cavalry on a surprise dawn attack against the Southern Cheyenne village of Peace Chief Black Kettle on November 27, 1868. It was an important event in the tragic clash of cultures of the Indian Wars era. (The Black Kettle Museum moved to the Washita Battlefield National Historic Site Visitors Center.)

The museum includes Cheyenne history, Oklahoma history, art and artifacts, and area information, with a gift shop featuring books, children's books, dolls, and Native American art.

Info: 18555 Hwy. 47A, Cheyenne, OK 73628 • 580.497.2742 • https://www.nps.gov/waba/index.htm

ELGIN
Fort Sill Cemetery

Fort Sill includes various cemeteries with their own histories and significance. The most famous is the Post Cemetery at the intersection of Macomb and Geronimo roads. Many Indian chiefs who signed the Medicine Lodge treaty came to rest at Fort Sill Post Cemetery. Unlike most cemeteries of its day, it was never segregated. Troopers of the 10th Cavalry Regiment, known as the "Buffalo Soldiers" who died at Fort Sill, lie next to these chiefs. Officers, soldiers, spouses, and children lie side-by-side, regardless of their race or social status.

The most famous person buried at Fort Sill is the Apache warrior Geronimo, interred in the Apache Cemetery on East Range. Because his grave is off the beaten path, the route is marked with signs. Others buried at Fort Sill include Kiowa Chief Satanta and Comanche Chief Quanah Parker.

Geronimo came to Fort Sill in 1894 after eight years of imprisonment in Florida and Alabama. He had surrendered in Arizona in 1886, probably the most famous Native American in the country at the time. His five-year campaign against the military in southeastern Arizona was trumpeted by the eastern press as the "last Indian war," and its lurid coverage turned the Chiricahua leader into a national figure. The number of combatants involved was actually quite small, and too large of a white presence was already in Arizona for Geronimo to have had any chance of success. For the last years of his life, he toured the country as a celebrity guest at countless Wild West shows, while curious crowds shuddered. Geronimo lived out his years in what amounted to house arrest at Fort Sill. He was not confined and was free to roam the military base, but he could not leave the post unless under special guard. He died here in 1909 and is buried in the Apache Cemetery in the Old Post section of the base. His few remaining followers were then returned home to reservations in Arizona. Other Native people who died in captivity are buried on Chiefs Knoll in the Old Post Cemetery.

Info: 2648 NE Jake Dunn Rd., Elgin, OK 73538 • 580.492.3200 • https://www.cem.va.gov/cems/nchp/ftsill.asp

GORE
Tahlonteeskee (Cherokee Courthouse)

The site was named for Chief Tahlonteeskee, who presided over the Cherokee Nation from 1809 to 1818. He was part of the Old Settler band of Cherokee who were removed from ancestral lands in the southeast United States. Tahlonteeskee became the Old Settler capital of the Cherokee Territory from 1828 to 1839 and is considered the oldest governmental capital in Oklahoma. The restored courthouse became the nation's administrative center until 1843, when the capital was moved to Tahlequah (see entry on "Cherokee National Capitol," Tahlequah, Oklahoma).

Info: Highway 64, Gore, OK 74435 • 918.489.5663, 877.779.6977 • http://www.cherokeetourismok.com/attractions/pages/tahlonteeskee.aspx

LAWTON
Comanche National Museum and Cultural Center

The Comanche National Museum and Cultural Center (CNMCC), which opened in 2007, seeks to provide communities with programs and exhibits that deepen the understanding and appreciation of the Great Comanche history, culture, and fine art. Through collections, preservation, and education, the museum is a recognized resource for information about the Nʉmʉnʉʉ (Comanche people).

Exhibits focus on the resiliency of the Comanche people from their early lives as "Lords of the Plains" to the transition period of the Reservation Era in the late 1800s. Visitors are treated to heroic accounts of twentieth-century warriors, including the seventeen Comanche men who served as "Code Talkers" during World War II, and get to hear firsthand how the Nʉmʉnʉʉ language helped defeat Hitler's army on D-Day. One exhibit explores the role the Native American Church plays in Comanche culture.

Info: 701 NW Ferris Ave., Lawton, OK 73507 • 580.353.0404 • http://comanchemuseum.com/visit

MUSKOGEE
Ataloa Lodge

Ataloa Lodge Museum features one of the largest privately owned collections of Native American history and culture in the United States. The Ataloa Lodge Museum, built in 1932 on the campus of historic Bacone College, is Native American-operated and houses more than twenty thousand pieces of traditional and contemporary Native American art, including a large Kachina doll collection, a large collection of Maria Martinez's San Ildefonso pottery, Native baskets from all parts of the North American continent, and items of daily and ceremonial use as well as Civil War memorabilia. A gift shop offers Native-made art, clothing, and accessories. The museum is also a cultural and Native American genealogical resource for local schools and surrounding communities.

Info: 2299 Old Bacone Rd., Muskogee, OK 74403 • 918.781.7283 • https://roadtrippers.com/us/muskogee-ok/attractions/ataloa-lodge-museum

Five Civilized Tribes Museum

The purpose of the Five Civilized Tribes Museum is to preserve the history, culture, and traditions of the five tribes—Cherokee, Chickasaw, Choctaw, Creek, and Seminole—through the acquisition of art, artifacts, documents, books, correspondence, and other materials. The museum promotes interest, knowledge, and appreciation of tribal heritage through exhibits, tours, programs, writings, and other media and is housed in the historic Union Indian Agency building built in 1875.

Info: 1101 Honor Heights Dr., Muskogee, OK 74401 • 918.683.1701 • http://www.fivetribes.org/5contactus.html

NORMAN
Jacobson House Native American Center

Oscar B. Jacobson's name is synonymous with early twentieth-century art in Oklahoma. Educated in Europe and America, he tirelessly promoted all arts to the young state. One genre, traditional Plains Indian art, is now inexorably bound to him and to the University of Oklahoma. Because Jacobson held Indian people in good regard and treated them with respect, he became their champion and mentor. In the late 1920s, he and Professor Edith Mahier, also of the OU art school, worked with a small group of five Kiowa men and briefly with one Kiowa woman. These artists and their style became world famous and have always been associated with Jacobson.

The Native American artists—James Auchiah (1906–1974), Spencer Asah (1905/1910–1954), Jack Hokeah (1902–1969), Stephen Mopope (1898–1974), Monroe Tsatoke (1904–1937), and Lois (Bougetah) Smoky (1907–1981)—were Kiowa tribal members from the Anadarko area of Oklahoma. Because of their talent and the opportunities afforded them at the University of Oklahoma, they became international celebrities. It is well remembered that these young artists were occasionally homesick for their Kiowa cultural heritage and that during those times, they would gather at the Jacobson House to sing, dance, and share cultural stories.

Info: 609 Chautauqua Ave., Norman, OK 73069 • 405.366.1667 • https://jacobsonhouse.org

Native Crossroads Film Festival and Symposium

This two-day themed festival features the best new Indigenous cinema from around the world. The event evokes discussions among academics, media creators, and community and tribal organization representatives. The annual festival is usually in April and held in different locations in Norman.

Info: 640 Parrington Oval #302, Norman, OK 73019 • 405.325.302 • http://www.nativecrossroads.org/

OKLAHOMA CITY
Red Earth Festival

A popular annual event in Oklahoma City for thirty years, the Red Earth Festival is held in June. The award-winning festival features hundreds of American Indian artists and dancers from throughout North America who celebrate the richness and diversity of their heritage with the world. Thousands of visitors watch one of the country's most unique grand parades, led by Native representations in regalia, through downtown Oklahoma City. The dance competition at Red Earth is one of the rare occasions when dancers from America's northern and southern tribes can be seen together in one venue.

Info: Cox Convention Center, One Myriad Gardens, Oklahoma City, OK 73102 • 405.602.8500 • https://www.travelok.com/listings/view.profile/id.18211/type.event

Red Earth, Inc.

Red Earth, Inc., began in 1978 with the establishment of the Center of the American Indian, a museum dedicated to showcasing Native American arts. In 1987, a group of influential community and tribal leaders founded the Red Earth Festival to showcase Native dance and art. The two groups merged in 1992 to create Red Earth, Inc., which is now one of the most respected organizations of its type in the United States.

Red Earth is home to an esteemed, permanent collection of more than one thousand items of traditional and contemporary fine art, pottery, basketry, textiles, and beadwork. Collection pieces are rotated for viewing throughout the year.

A major component of this attraction is a sales gallery featuring original, handmade artwork. Visitors can sample the work of some of the nation's most celebrated artists with opportunities to purchase contemporary and traditional examples of beadwork, basketry, jewelry, pottery, sculpture, paintings, graphics, and cultural attire during the juried art show and market.

Info: 6 Santa Fe Plaza, Oklahoma City, OK 73102 • 405.427.5228 • https://www.redearth.org/contact/

OKMULGEE
Creek Council House Museum

The Council House that stands today was built in 1878 and served as the Creek capitol for the last twenty-eight years of nationhood. It was here that the final issues of self-rule versus land concessions to the federal government were debated, often painfully, as the realization dawned that Washington was going to get what it wanted anyhow. After statehood, the building served as a courthouse until 1916. It is now a museum of the Creek Nation, containing priceless early documents of the tribe as well as other cultural and historical items and displays relating to the events that occurred in this building.

The Creek Council House received designation as a National Historic Landmark in 1961 and was listed in the National Register of Historic Places in 1966.

Info: 112 W. 6th St., Okmulgee, OK 74447 • 918.756.2324 • http://creekculturalcenter.com/2014/05/muscogee-creek-nation-council-house/

PARK HILL
Cherokee Heritage Center

The Cherokee Heritage Center is the premier cultural center for Cherokee tribal history, culture, and the arts, located in the heart of the Cherokee Nation in Tahlequah, Oklahoma. It was established in 1963 by the Board of Trustees of the Cherokee National

Historical Society to preserve and promote the Cherokee culture while sponsoring dynamic educational programs, reconstructed historic villages, engaging exhibits, and scholarly research stimulating interest in the enduring legacy of the Cherokee people.

The center is the repository for the Cherokee National Archives, the nation's foremost collection of historic, tribal-related documents and artifacts cataloging the rich history of the Cherokee people from the 1700s through the present day. The center is also home to the Cherokee Family Research Center, assisting Oklahoma Cherokee descendants to reconnect with their lineage.

Cherokee Heritage Center.

The Cherokee Heritage Center is on the National Register of Historic Places, as it is located on the grounds of the Cherokee Female Seminary, c. 1851, one of the first institutions of higher learning for women west of the Mississippi. The center is designated by the National Park Service as the interpretive site for the western terminus of the Trail of Tears for the Cherokee and other nations forcibly removed to Oklahoma during the 1800s. Apart from the Trail of Tears permanent exhibit, a fine offering of other educational exhibits is included as well as nationally recognized art shows.

Visitors can time-travel to Diligwa, a 1710 Cherokee village that opened on June 3, 2013, on the grounds of the center. The outdoor-living exhibit provides guests with an enhanced experience of authentic 1700s Cherokee life and history. The Adams Corner Rural Village recreates an 1890s setting to illustrate Cherokee society in Indian Territory.

Info: 21192 S. Keeler Dr., Park Hill, OK 74464 • 918.456.6007 • http://www.cherokeeheritage.org/

John Ross Museum

The John Ross Museum is devoted to the story of John Ross, principal chief of the Cherokee Nation for more than thirty-eight years, and houses exhibits and interactive displays on the Trail of Tears, Civil War, Cherokee Golden Age, and the Cherokee Nation's passion for the education of its people. The museum also has a gift shop and research area.

The museum was originally built in 1913 to operate as a rural school in Cherokee County just after Oklahoma statehood. The school served Cherokee and non-Cherokee students, and the facility remained open through the 1950s.

Info: 22366 S. 530 Rd., Park Hill, OK 74451 • 918.431.0757 •
http://visitcherokeenation.com/ATTRACTIONS/Pages/john-ross-museum.aspx

PAWHUSKA
Osage Tribal Museum

Dedicated on May 2, 1938, the Osage Tribal Museum is the oldest tribally owned museum in the United States and was one of the first projects of the Osage Tribal Council. Intended to preserve the language and traditions of the people, it was the first museum of its kind in the country. Its current home exhibits a fine collection of documents, artifacts, and exhibits on the history of the tribe, which figured prominently in American history.

Info: 819 Grandview Ave., Pawhuska, OK 74056 • 918.287.2495 •
https://www.osagenation-nsn.gov/museum

PONCA CITY
Standing Bear Museum and Education Center

The Standing Bear Museum and Education Center, which opened in 2007, promotes intercultural understanding. The facility has permanent and revolving art displays created by Native artists. A gift shop sells books, crafts, and a variety of Native artwork.

The center includes a large, permanent structure for the annual Standing Bear Powwow held on the last Friday and Saturday of September. Eight plaques are inlaid surrounding the dance area containing photos and text explaining the styles of dance most commonly seen in the region.

Info: 601 Standing Bear Pky., Ponca City, OK 74601 • 580.762.1514 •
https://www.facebook.com/Standing-Bear-Museum-Education-Center-89306514861/

Osage Tribal Museum.

Standing Bear Park

In 1996, Ponca City unveiled a 22-foot (6.8 meter) bronze statue of Ponca Chief Standing Bear. A tribute to all Native Americans, it was created by Oreland C. Joe Sr. A colorful, 60-foot (18.3 meter) diameter, circular viewing court is located at the feet of Standing Bear and contains large, sandstone boulders around its perimeter affixed with the official brass seals of the six area tribes: Osage, Pawnee, Otoe-Missouria, Kaw, Tonkawa, and Ponca. The names of eight clans of the Ponca Tribe are inlaid in the floor of the plaza.

Info: Standing Bear Park, Ponca City, OK 74056 • 580.762.1514 • http://standingbearpark.com/

Standing Bear Sculpture

To commemorate his life and landmark civil rights courtroom victory, a 10-foot (3-meter), bronze sculpture of Standing Bear, created by sculptor Benjamin Victor, was unveiled on October 15, 2017, in a ceremony at Centennial Mall. The sculpture captures the powerful image of Standing Bear in 1879 as he stood in the courtroom with his right hand outstretched, fighting for the freedom to return to his homeland to bury his son. Standing Bear convinced a federal judge to allow him to leave Indian Territory (Oklahoma) and return to his homelands in northeast Nebraska, a decision that is today considered an important civil rights victory for Native Americans.

Info: Centennial Mall, Ponca City, OK 74601

SALLISAW
Sequoyah's Cabin Museum

Sequoyah built a one-room, log cabin in 1829, shortly after moving to Oklahoma. The actual cabin is located inside a stone memorial building built by the Works Progress Administration in 1936 and is surrounded by a 10-acre (40,469-square-meter) park. The cabin is furnished to appear as it might have when Sequoyah lived there. Personal artifacts and documents associated with his life are on display.

Sequoyah, also known as George Guess or George Gist, was born in Tennessee around 1778. He was among the "Old Settlers" of the Cherokee Nation who migrated to present-day Oklahoma in approximately 1818. (See entries in Sequoyah, Tennessee.) He is usually credited with bringing literacy to the Cherokee, although other accounts say that the Cherokee always had a written language; Sequoyah just simplified it. The Cherokee had become the first fully literate Native American people with their own newspaper and a means of communication between the eastern and western branches of the tribe. That was a critical factor in easing the reunification process when the eastern remnant was forced onto the Trail of Tears in 1838. By that time, the Cherokee were already operating the first schools in Oklahoma, and shortly thereafter, in 1843, a newspaper was reestablished there as well.

Info: 470288 Highway 101, Sallisaw, OK 74955 • 877.779.6977 • http://visitcherokeenation.com/ATTRACTIONS/Pages/sequoyahs-cabin.aspx

SPIRO
Spiro Mounds Archaeological Center

The mounds site opened to the public in 1978 and is located outside of Spiro, Oklahoma. It is the only ancient American Indian archaeological site in Oklahoma. The mounds are one of the most important American Indian sites in the nation. The ancient Spiro people created a very complex society that influenced the entire Southeast. Artifacts indicate an extensive trade network, an intricate religious center, and a political system that controlled the entire region. Located on a bend of the Arkansas River, the site was a natural gateway from which the Spiro people exerted their influence.

From 900 to 1300 c.e., the leaders at Spiro Mounds thrived. The mound center declined and was eventually abandoned by 1450 c.e., although the city continued to be occupied for another 150 years. The people of the Spiro Mounds are believed to have been Caddoan speakers, like the modern Wichita, Kichai, Caddo, Pawnee, and Arikara. The site remained unoccupied from 1600 c.e. until 1832.

During the 1930s, commercial, and later academic, excavations revealed one of the greatest collections of artistic and utilitarian ancient American Indian artifacts in the United States. Early looting of the site led to laws making Oklahoma one the first states in the United States to preserve and scientifically research archaeological sites.

Info: 18154 First St., Spiro, OK 74959 • 918.962.2062 • http://www.okhistory.org/sites/spiromounds.php

SULPHUR
Chickasaw Cultural Center

The Chickasaw Cultural Center serves as a cultural home of the Chickasaw people's legacy. This world-class destination is dedicated to helping people of all ages and

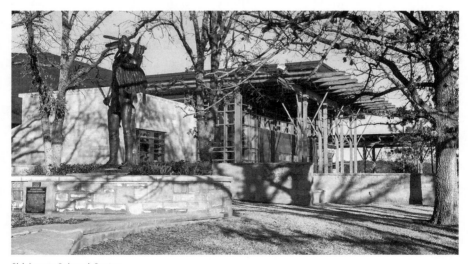

Chickasaw Cultural Center.

backgrounds share in and celebrate Chickasaw history and culture through natural architecture and interactive exhibits.

In historic Chickasaw towns, the Council House was the hub of the community. In addition to showcasing an authentic piece of Chickasaw culture, the center's Council House hosts showings of *Chickasaw Renaissance*, a short film designed to welcome guests to the Chickasaw Cultural Center. The "Itti' Anonka' Nannakat Oktani" ("Spirit Forest") exhibit re-creates the treasured bond with the natural world. The Exhibit Gallery takes one on an adventure through Chickasaw history with Native American interactive stations, reproductions, and graphic and text displays. The Removal Hallway and the Stomp Dance areas tell the story of the Chickasaw people's ability to express emotion through dance and song. Artwork, sounds, and accounts guide visitors along the difficult route thousands of Native Americans took after President Andrew Jackson passed the Indian Removal Act of 1830. The center also includes daily live stomp dance demonstrations by Chickasaw cultural interpreters.

Info: 867 Cooper Memorial Dr., Sulphur, OK 73806-8697 • 580.622.7130 • http://chickasawculturalcenter.com/

TAHLEQUAH
Cherokee National Capitol

The Cherokee National Capitol currently houses the judicial branch of the Cherokee Nation. After the Civil War, the tribal council provided for a new building to commemorate the achievement of the Cherokee in overcoming the hardships of removal and merging their tribal legislative offices until 1906, when the Five Civilized Tribes began abolishing their tribal governments in accordance with the Curtis Act of 1898.

Info: 101 S. Muskogee Ave., Tahlequah, OK 74464 • 877.779.6977 • http://visitcherokeenation.com/ATTRACTIONS/Pages/cherokee-national-capitol.aspx

Cherokee National Holiday Powwow

The multiday Cherokee National Holiday Powwow celebrates Cherokee heritage, cultural awareness, and reuniting families. Thousands of Cherokee and visitors from across the United States and beyond travel to the historic Cherokee Nation capital in Tahlequah. The holiday has been observed in early September since 1953, commemorating the signing of the 1839 Cherokee Constitution and the Act of Union reuniting Cherokee both east and west after the Trail of Tears. With an array of entertainment and cultural and athletic events, the Cherokee National Holiday has grown into one of the largest festivals in Oklahoma, attracting more than one hundred thousand visitors.

The powwow is packed with sports activities for all ages, from traditional games such as Cherokee marbles, the cornstalk shoot, and the blowgun competition to the more familiar golf and softball tournaments. Hundreds of vendors and craftspeople set up booths where visitors may view and purchase authentic Native American-made products and foods.

The nation's holiday also coincides with the annual State of the Nation address from the Cherokee principal chief.

Info: West 810 Rd., Tahlequah, OK 74464 • 918.207.4991 • https://www.crazycrow.com/site/event/cherokee-national-holiday-powwow/

Cherokee National Supreme Court Museum

The Cherokee National Supreme Court Museum features three historic areas, including the Cherokee judicial system, the *Cherokee Advocate* and *Cherokee Phoenix* newspapers, and the Cherokee language with a variety of historical items including photos, stories, objects, and furniture.

The building housed the printing press of the *Cherokee Advocate*, the official publication of the Cherokee Nation and the first newspaper in Oklahoma. It is the oldest government building in the State of Oklahoma.

Info: 122 Ketoowah St., Tahlequah, OK 74464 • 918.207.3508 • http://visitcherokeenation.com/ATTRACTIONS/Pages/cherokee-national-supreme-court-museum.aspx

John Hair Museum and Cultural Center

The Keetoowah Cherokee Tribe opened the John Hair Museum and Cultural Center, named after the former United Keetowah Band chief, in 2011. The museum is named for John Hair, who devoted most of his life to the Gaduwa Cherokee cause and unselfishly worked without pay to help continue the Keetoowah Cherokee traditions and preserve and document its history. Keetowah records, papers, ephemera, photos, publications, and other items are part of the center's collections.

Info: 18627 W. Ketoowah Cir., Tahlequah, OK 74464 • 918.772.4389 • http://www.keetoowahcherokeemuseum.org/museum-history.html

TISHOMINGO
Chickasaw Council House Museum

Located on the Capitol Square, the Chickasaw Council House Museum holds one of the largest collections of Chickasaw art, historic items, and archive materials. Visitors experience the first Chickasaw Council House built in Indian Territory, artifacts tracing the history and culture of the Chickasaw people, and contemporary Chickasaw artwork.

Tishomingo was the capital of the Chickasaw Nation through its entire Oklahoma existence (see entry on "Chicasaw Cultural Center," Sulphur, Oklahoma).

Info: 209 N. Fisher Ave., Tishomingo, OK 73460 • 580.371.3351 • https://www.chickasaw.net/Services/Chickasaw-Council-House-Museum.aspx

Chickasaw National Capitol

The Chickasaw National Capitol Building in Tishomingo, built in 1898 out of red granite from the Pennington Creek quarry of Governor R. M. Harris, served as the

Chickasaw Nation's Capitol until Oklahoma statehood in 1907. The Victorian, gothic-style building was later sold to Johnston County in 1910 and was used as the Johnston County Courthouse. In 1992, the museum was reclaimed by the Chickasaw Nation. The building's historic significance and unique architecture led to its addition in the National Registry of Historic Buildings in 1971.

Today, this 8,000-square-foot (743-square-meter), historical building is a testament to Chickasaw identity and the struggle for independence. The largest exhibit focuses on Chickasaw government history from 1856 to 1907 with accurate replicas of Chickasaw Governor Douglas Johnston's office. Other exhibits include the Chickasaw Governor's Portrait Exhibit on the first floor, the rotating photography exhibit on the second floor, and the Chickasaw National Well Exhibit outside of the Capitol.

Info: 411 W. 9th St., Tishomingo, OK 73460 • 580.371.9835 • https://www.chickasaw.net/Services/Chickasaw-National-Capitol.aspx

TONKAWA
Tonkawa Tribal Museum

The Tonkawa Tribal Museum is a tribute to a small nation that seemed on the verge of extermination several times in their history. They moved often in historic times, spoke a language related to no others, and were called by a name that means "they all stay together." They were driven from their Texas homes when the state voted to expel all Native people, and they traveled throughout the Indian Territory with no fixed place of residence.

Finally, tiny slivers were carved from the westernmost Cherokee lands after the Civil War and allotted to several small groups, among them the Tonkawa. In the early 1940s, the tribal census listed only eighteen persons surviving, but since then, the Tonkawa have tried to reaffirm an identity. Among the measures taken to accomplish that was this museum, which shows off Tonkawa artifacts and photographs. It is also the place where Chief Joseph and several of his Nez Perce followers were imprisoned following their surrender in 1879.

Info: 1 Rush Buffalo Rd., Tonkawa, OK 74653 • 580.628.5301 • http://www.tonkawatribe.com/museum.html

TULSA
Gilcrease Museum

The Gilcrease Museum houses one of the world's most extensive and renowned collections of Native American and western art and artifacts. Museum founder Thomas Gilcrease (Creek) believed that the story of the American West could be told through art and that the history of the Native Americans and his own American Indian heritage could be preserved through painting, sculpture, and other forms of art. He purchased over five hundred paintings by twentieth-century Native American artists alone.

Gilcrease Museum has a long-term Native American exhibition, "Enduring Spirit: Native American Artistic Traditions," in which the museum showcases some of the

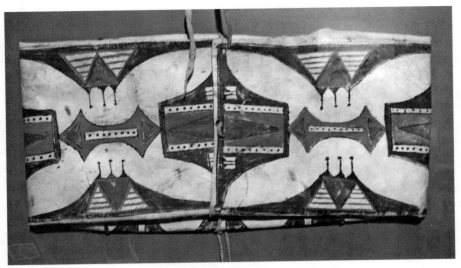

A Sioux parflesche (1900) on display at the Gilcrease Museum.

major strengths of the permanent collection, including objects thousands of years old as well as modern paintings and sculptures. One-third of the exhibit covers contemporary Native painting and sculpture.

Also noteworthy are the museum's archaeological collections from the Mississippi Valley region (present-day Illinois and Arkansas), the southwestern United States (Colorado, New Mexico, and Arizona), and ancient Mexico. Gilcrease Museum has one of the most important collections of ancient projectile points (arrow- and spearheads) in North America.

Info: 1400 N. Gilcrease Museum Rd., Tulsa, OK 74127 • 918.596.2700 • https://gilcrease.org/

Philbrook Museum of Art

Philbrook's collection of Native American art has always been a cornerstone of the museum. With the addition of the Eugene B. Adkins Collection, the Philbrook boasts one of the finest surveys of twentieth-century Native art and features iconic pieces by artists from across Indian Country with particular strengths in basketry, pottery, paintings, and jewelry.

The Philbrook Indian Annual, a monthlong exhibition that occurred every year from 1946 to 1979, was recognized as the most prestigious competition of Native paintings for its time, and its impact can still be seen today. Over the years, nearly one thousand artists from two hundred Native American communities entered almost four thousand works of art for judging, exhibition, awards, and sale. The Philbrook Indian Annual played a pivotal role in the definition of twentieth-century Native American fine art. The jurors consisted mostly of Native American artists reviewing the work of their peers, rather than exclusively non-Native art critics evaluating work emerging from Native American communities.

Info: 2727 Rockford Rd., Tulsa, OK 74152 • 918.749.7941 • http://philbrook.org/explore/collections/native-american-art

Red Fork Native American Film Festival and Powwow

This annual spring event held on the campus of Tulsa Community College brings the best of new Native American/First Nations independent films to the public. The celebration culminates in a powwow.

Info: 7505 W. 41st St., South Tulsa, OK 74107-8633 • 918.595.7118 • http://www.tulsacc.edu/about-us/news-and-events/events/2017-red-fork-native-american-film-festival-powwow

TUSKAHOMA
Choctaw Nation Capitol Museum

The Choctaw Nation Capitol Museum is located in the Choctaw Capitol Building on the Tvshka Homma grounds. This impressive red-brick structure was built in 1884 and served as the capitol of the Choctaw Nation until 1907. Today, it is on the National Register of Historic Places. Choctaw Nation Tribal Court is still held here. The museum features displays on Choctaw history before European contact, the Trail of Tears, Choctaw life in Oklahoma, the Lighthorsemen, the Choctaw Code Talkers, Choctaw basketry, a gift shop selling Choctaw-made artwork, and much more.

The physical structure of the council building is impressive and reflects the old Choctaw governmental structure: the large rooms with 18-foot (5.5-meter) ceilings housed the Senate, the House of Representatives, and the Supreme Court. A room above a walk-in vault provided an observation point for armed guards; the attic, which included a cistern, was sometimes used as a jail. The Choctaw Nation Capitol Museum building, also known as the original Council House, is listed on the National Registry of Historic Places.

Info: Council House Rd., Tuskahoma, OK 74574 • 918.569.4465 • ttp://choctawnationculture.com/museum/choctaw-nation-capitol-museum.aspx

Choctaw Nation Tvshka Homma (Labor Day) Festival

The Choctaw Nation Labor Day Festival invites visitors to enjoy tribal heritage activities, an intertribal powwow, Choctaw cultural exhibitions, stickball games, a fine arts show, free concerts, and carnival rides. This annual Tuskahoma event offers activities for all ages, including sports tournaments, quilting demonstrations, live performances, buffalo tours, a princess pageant, and more.

Info: Choctaw Nation Capital Grounds, Tuskahoma, OK 74574 • 580.924.8280 • https://www.travelok.com/listings/view.profile/id.19030

WEWOKA
Seminole Nation Museum

The Seminole Nation Museum, which opened in 1974, documents and interprets the history and culture of the Seminole Nation of Oklahoma and the people and events that make its capital, Wewoka, one of the most historically significant and culturally diverse communities in Oklahoma. Through the use of select artifacts, historic photographs, and interpretive exhibits, the events and stories that shaped the home of the Seminole for more than a century are chronicled in an educational and enlightening experience. The museum also contains exhibits about the oil boom of the 1920s, which turned these lands into some of the richest in Oklahoma.

The Seminole Nation exhibit tells the story of the nation's ancient origins across the Southeast through the development of their cultural identity in the Florida Everglades to their determined search for a new homeland in the Indian Territory (present-day Oklahoma). Other exhibits deal with the history of the Wewoka community and men and women who served in the military.

The annual, award-winning Sorghum Festival every fall is cosponsored by the Seminole Nation Museum and Wewoka. Crowds from around the United States show up to celebrate the age-old art of sorghum making.

Originated by the Wewoka Rotary Club in 1976 to promote the Seminole Nation Museum, the event has grown to become one of Oklahoma's premier attractions. Historic re-enactors, Native American foods, children's crafts, live music, and entertainment, as well as pioneer and Native American living demonstrations, are to be found on the museum grounds.

Info: 524 S. Wewoka Ave., Wewoka, OK 74884 • 405.257.5580 • https://www.seminolenationmuseum.org/

YALE
Jim Thorpe House

The Oklahoma Historical Society and the Jim Thorpe Foundation preserve the former home of the Olympian and celebrated athlete, Jacobus Franciscus "Jim" Thorpe (Sac and Fox [Sauk]).

Thorpe, who was born near Prague on the Sac and Fox Nation in Oklahoma, and his wife, Iva, purchased the house in 1917 and left in 1923. The house has much of the original decor, which serves as backdrop to the iconic athlete's photographs, memorabilia, awards, family items, and a display that illustrates his life story. The home is on the National Registry of Historic Places and attracts visitors from around the world. The Oklahoma Historical Society purchased the Jim Thorpe House in 1968. Thorpe's 1912 Olympic medals are at the Oklahoma History Center.

After his death in 1953, original plans called for a permanent memorial to be erected to him in this area, but when fundraising hit a snag, his widow had the body removed to Pennsylvania after two towns voted to combine and rename the new town in his honor.

Info: 706 E. Boston St., Yale, OK 74085 • 918.387.2406 • http://www.okhistory.org/sites/thorpehome.php

SOUTH DAKOTA

The state is headquarters to nine nations and home to eighty-three thousand Native citizens.

CHAMBERLAIN
Akta Lakota Museum And Cultural Center

In 1992, the Akta Lakota Museum and Cultural Center, an educational outreach located at St. Joseph's Indian School, opened to promote knowledge about the Northern Plains Indian cultures through the preservation of historical artifacts and contemporary works of art. The phrase "Akta Lakota," meaning "to honor the people," was chosen because of the museum's intention to honor and preserve the extraordinary culture of the Lakota people for the students at St. Joseph's Indian School and for the thousands who visit the museum each year.

The center's 14,000 square feet (4,267 square kilometers) of art, artifacts, and educational displays are housed in an octagon-shaped building. Much of the museum's original collection came from gifts given to St. Joseph's by alumni and friends since the school opened in 1927. Since the museum opened, it has acquired many new pieces and continually strives to add relevant pieces to the collection—all strive to honor the dignity and incredible heritage of the Lakota. Contemporary artists are featured as well.

St. Joseph's School, established in Chamberlain, is based on a Catholic education with the elements of Lakota culture. The school's residential living program is for Native American children in grades one through twelve. An annual powwow and extracurricular activities like traditional Lakota hand games are part of the curriculum.

Info: 1301 N. Main St., Chamberlain, SD 57325 • 800.798.3452 • http://aktalakota.stjo.org/site/PageServer?pagename=alm_homepage

CUSTER
Crazy Horse Memorial

Crazy Horse Memorial is located in the heart of the southern Black Hills. Sculptor Korczak Ziolkowski began the world's largest mountain carving in 1948. Henry Standing Bear, a nephew of Crazy Horse, had asked him to create a stone-carved memorial for the deceased Lakota military leader.

Zolkowski died in 1982, leaving his sons to carry on the work. Members of his family and their supporters are continuing his artistic intent to create a massive statue that will be 641 feet (195 meters) long and 563 feet (172 meters) high. Workers completed the carved 87.5-foot (27-meter) -tall Crazy Horse face in 1998.

The Crazy Horse Memorial as of 2017.

When it is completed, the sculpture will depict Crazy Horse, arms extended across the land, sitting astride a war pony. Ziolkowski's inscription for the memorial was "Where My Dead Lie Buried." Visitors can watch work in progress, view plans for its final appearance, and see an exhibit on the history of the memorial and displays of Lakota tribal materials.

The image is not that of Crazy Horse since no images were ever made of him. The statue is meant to represent all American Indians.

Info: 12151 Avenue of the Chiefs, Crazy Horse, SD 57730-8900 • 605.673.4681 • https://crazyhorsememorial.org/

Indian Museum of North America

When Ziolkowski agreed to carve Crazy Horse at the invitation of Henry Standing Bear, a Lakota elder, he wanted an educational institution to sit at the base of the mountain, complete with a center showcasing examples of Native American culture and heritage. The Indian Museum of North America (IMNA) opened in 1973. Although the Plains Indian is the most strongly represented, all regions are represented in the museum. IMNA features drawings, photographs, artifacts, clothing, personal items, and documents from tribes across North America.

Info: 12151 Avenue of the Chiefs, Crazy Horse, SD 57730 • 605.673.4681 • http://www.crazyhorse.org

Native American Educational and Cultural Center® at Crazy Horse Memorial

The Native American Educational and Cultural Center® provides a number of unique educational opportunities geared to enhance the visitors' experience at Crazy Horse. One-of-a-kind exhibits are displayed, Native American artisans are showcased, and special activities and games are featured. The distinctive stone building was completed in 1996 from rock blasted from the Crazy Horse mountain carving.

The center hosts and encourages many hands-on activities with staff and vendors providing instruction in American Indian history and culture through storytelling, flute playing, song, and dance. Native American artists throughout North America spend much of the summer in residence at Crazy Horse to create, share, and sell their work while interacting with visitors, which provides a valuable cultural exchange.

The lower level houses a display of a large collection of Edward S. Curtis photographs of Native Americans, taken around the end of the nineteenth century. As part of the Indian Museum of North America, the cultural center building is also the home of many museum exhibits.

One wall of the lower level of the cultural center houses an exhibit of the American bison. The story begins with the history of the bison in North America from its ancient beginnings to its near-extinction, the exploits of western figures who helped save the remaining bison at the end of the 1800s, to the cultural significance of the buffalo to tribes across the country.

Info: 12151 Avenue of the Chiefs, Crazy Horse, SD 57730 • 605.673.4681 • https://crazyhorsememorial.org/native-american-educational-cultural-center.html

MITCHELL
Mitchell Prehistoric Indian Village

Designated a National Historic Landmark, the Mitchell Village is the only archaeological site in South Dakota that is open to the public. It was discovered in 1910 by a student from Dakota Wesleyan University. The Mitchell Prehistoric Indian Village Preservation Society was formed in 1975 to preserve the site. It promotes an understanding of the first people to inhabit this region by developing, preserving, and exhibiting a significant collection and archaeological site; by taking a leadership role in research and scholarship; by engaging and providing access for audiences from all nations; and by delivering innovative programs of benefit to the general public and community.

The Boehnen Memorial Museum houses a full-sized reproduction of an earthen lodge, exhibits, a bison skeleton, the Betty Buche Boehnen Roby Audio Visual Technology Center, a student library, staff offices, and the Shoppe Antiquary.

Info: 3200 Indian Village Rd., Mitchell, SD 57301 • 605.996.5473 • http://mitchellindianvillage.org/

Oscar Howe Art Center

Once Mitchell's Carnegie Library, the Oscar Howe Art Center now displays the work of the Sioux artist who worked here and taught at Dakota Wesleyan University. A Yanktonai Sioux, Oscar Howe studied at the Studio of the Santa Fe Indian School in the 1930s. He began to develop a highly personalized style that blended traditional representational art with elements of cubism. His handling of Native symbolism in a contemporary vernacular has become a signature of his work in many public buildings in South Dakota. Howe was hired in 1940 to decorate the dome of this building with Sioux imagery. The entire library now is turned over to displays of his paintings and those of other contemporary Native American artists.

Info: 119 W. 3rd St., Mitchell, SD 57301 • 605.966.4111 • http://www.ohwy.com/sd/h/howemus.htm

MOBRIDGE
Scherr-Howe Arena Murals

The Mobridge Auditorium, completed in 1936, is an impressive example of the Works Progress Administration's (WPA) Art Deco architecture, but of great interest are ten murals mounted inside the auditorium's arena. These works by acclaimed Sioux Indian artist Oscar Howe dramatically recreate the history and culture of the Sioux. Begun in 1941, the five murals mounted on the south wall of the arena depict "Ceremonies of the Sioux" while the five on the north wall portray "History along the Missouri River." Many such "worker-realism" murals were funded by the WPA and mounted in public buildings all across America in the 1930s and 1940s. A Save America's Treasures grant will help preserve the Howe murals by improving the environmental conditions under which they are displayed.

Info: 212 N. Main St., Mobridge, SD 57601 • 605.845.3700 • https://oscarhowetour.wordpress.com/

Sitting Bull Memorial

As the Hunkpapa Lakota chief and leader of the Native alliance that destroyed George Custer's command, Sitting Bull (Tatanka Iyotake) found himself a fugitive in Canada

Sitting Bull Monument.

six months after the Little Big Horn. Pursued relentlessly by federal forces, he had crossed the international border with the remnants of his band in December 1876, but he could not hold the group together. Game was scarce, and many discontented young men returned to the United States. In 1881, upon hearing that a pardon would be forthcoming, Sitting Bull turned himself in at Fort Buford, North Dakota. Instead of being pardoned, he was imprisoned for two years while the rest of his band was settled on the Standing Rock Reservation, a tract along the Missouri River and extending across both Dakotas.

On December 15, 1890, nine years after surrendering to the U.S. government, he was shot to death by Indian police who had been executing an arrest warrant in order to prevent Sitting Bull from attending a Ghost Dance ceremony. Sitting Bull was buried about 500 yards (457 meters) south of the agency cemetery in present-day Fort Yates, North Dakota.

In 1953, one of Sitting Bull's descendants by marriage and a group of business-men from Mobridge obtained an opinion from the Bureau of Indian Affairs (BIA) that the descendants of Sitting Bull should determine his final burial site. On April 8 of that year, the group used the BIA letter as justification for the clandestine re-location of the great chief's remains to a site in the southern portion of the Standing Rock Reservation that overlooks the Missouri River near Mobridge.

Less than five months later, South Dakota dedicated a memorial to Sitting Bull on the site of the relocated remains. A bust created by sculptor Korczak Ziolkowski (sculptor of the Crazy Horse monument in the Black Hills) was erected to commem-orate the gravesite.

Both the original gravesite in Fort Yates and the current site have tremendous significance today. Sensitive to the exploitation of Native Americans and the suspect way Sitting Bull's remains were handled in the past, a commitment has been made not to exploit or commercialize the Sitting Bull monument for financial gain. The statue is in an isolated park that remains serene and free to visitors.

Info: Hwy. 1806, Mobridge, SD 57601 •
https://www.mobridge.org/mobridge.php?subid=8

PINE RIDGE
Red Cloud Heritage Center

One of the earliest cultural centers and museums located on a U.S. Indian reserva-tion, the Red Cloud Heritage Center represents the complex and storied heritage of North America's Native community and the skill and creativity that are still mainstays of the local Lakota and other Native American cultures. The center, named for Oglala Lakota Chief Red Cloud, works to strengthen cultural pride and celebrate, as well as preserve, the local Lakota culture and artistic tradition. A permanent art collection is displayed along with the school's splendid Star Quilts. The Oglala Nation Wacipi Rodeo Fair, held here on the first weekend of each August, is famous for its tradi-tional dancing and drumming.

Through the center's renowned gift shop and online store, local artists are em-powered to increase their own economic self-sufficiency by making their work available to a wider community and, in doing so, preserve their work and extend appreciation for their artistry to all corners of the globe.

Info: 100 Mission Dr., Pine Ridge Reservation, SD 57770 • 605.867.1105 • https://www.redcloudschool.org/museum

RAPID CITY
Journey Museum and Learning Center

The Native American art exhibits in the Journey Museum and Learning Center that opened in May 1997 introduce the public to Native American culture and artistry, both traditional and contemporary. The collection is composed of materials of high aesthetic quality and includes numerous items of rare historic value acquired from notable Sioux individuals, artists, and artisans. Today's Sioux artwork incorporates a diversity of Native and trade materials, including glass beadwork, porcupine quillwork, hide painting, featherworking, wood and pipestone carving, and metalworking. These mediums, as well as some of the traditional forms—decorated garments, ceremonial regalia, personal adornments, and containers such as bags and parfleches—were all developed by the Sioux during their hunting days of the early 1800s.

Many of the distinctive tribal styles and lavish surface embellishments in beadwork and quillwork were developed during the early reservation days of the late nineteenth century and the first decades of the twentieth century. Included in the collection of contemporary Native American arts and crafts is work by the late Oscar Howe, Herman Red Elk, Robert Penn, Sophie New Holy, Emil and Alice (New Holy) Blue Legs, Nellie Menard, Dwayne Wilcox, and many more. In addition to the permanent exhibits, the museum features a series of rotating promotional exhibits featuring contemporary American Indian artists.

In 2016, The Great Race installation featured thirty-two contemporary Lakota artists of different mediums—painters, poets, musicians, and sculptors, who illustrated the epic story of the race between the four-leggeds and the two-leggeds to determine which group would have precedence over the other as recounted by James LaPointe (Oglala Lakota) in his 1976 book, *Legends of the Lakota*.

Info: 222 New York St., Rapid City, SD 57701 • 605.394.6923 • http://www.journeymuseum.org/about-us

Lakota Nation Invitational

From a small start in 1976–1978, the Lakota Nation Invitational (LNI) has taken place for decades at the Rushmore Plaza Civic Center. It has drawn numerous teams from across the nation, who gather to compete in basketball, volleyball, golf, cross-country, archery, traditional hand games, cheerleading, chess, business plans, wrestling, a powwow, a Lakota language bowl, an art show, a knowledge bowl, and a poetry slam, to name a few. Other events at LNI include multiple workshops.

LNI was founded by Bryan Brewer and the LNI board, who organized an annual event that brings together many Native Americans and non-Natives alike in peaceful, wonderful ways.

Info: 444 N. Mount Rushmore Rd., Rapid City, SD 57701 • 605.867.5174 • https://www.lakotanationinvitational.com/

Prairie Edge Trading Company and Gallery

This incredible store is part gallery, part museum, part lounge, part library, part music shop, part clothing boutique, part jewelry bazaar, and part artist's supply store, beautifully decorated and appointed with all things Native. From fine paintings to beaded jewelry repair, something can be found for everyone at this trading post in the heart of downtown Rapid City.

Info: 606 Main St., Rapid City, SD 57701 • 800.541.2388 • https://prairieedge.com/

Sioux Indian Museum

The Sioux Indian Museum, founded in 1939 through the cooperation of the federal and Rapid City governments, houses an extensive collection of historical items and artwork relating to the Sioux Nation. The personal belongings of many of the best-known leaders, religious items that were objects of veneration for centuries, crafts, contemporary paintings—all are presented in this facility, which is administered by the Indian Arts and Crafts Board of the U.S. Department of the Interior. Collections include nineteenth-century medicine bundles and pipe and tobacco pouches as well as items such as a turn-of-the-century vest embroidered with porcupine-quill ap-plique on buckskin, a twentieth-century war bonnet, and the "Big Missouri Winter Count," a pictographic history drawn on an elk hide.

Changing exhibitions feature arts and crafts displays of contemporary Sioux artists and craftspeople. Traditional artistry continues to play an important role in the cultural traditions of the Sioux society, and old skills are applied to the produc-tion of musical instruments, traditional dress, and ceremonial items.

The Sioux are among the few tribes to maintain an unbroken tradition of por-cupine quilling, a craft unique to the North American Indians, and the museum in-cludes both historic and contemporary examples of this art form. Displays of artworks include Native art concepts that have been adapted to a range of non-Native art forms as well as contemporary works that document various aspects of Sioux life. The museum also exhibits works from other tribes.

Info: 222 New York St., Rapid City, SD 57701 • 605.394.2381 • http://www.journeymuseum.org/visit

ST. FRANCIS
Buechel Lakota Memorial Museum and Mission

Named after Father Eugene Buechel, S.J., a missionary, linguist, and ethnologist who came to St. Francis Mission in 1902, the Buechel Lakota Memorial Museum contains unique artifacts, images, and documents. The museum is noted for its exhibits of traditional quillwork. An extensive photographic collection exceeds forty-two thousand items. It is adjacent to the St. Francis Mission, built as a boarding school in 1885 and named in honor of Francis A. Drexel of Philadelphia, a philanthropist who gave widely to minority religious causes. St. Charles Catholic Church, which replaced the original structure in 1920, was built from Native fieldstone by reservation residents. Articles created by local Lakota artists are on sale in the museum gift shop.

Info: 50 S. Oak St., P.O. Box 499, St. Francis, SD 57572 • 605.747.2745 • https://www.sfmission.org/programs/museum/

WALL
Wounded Knee: The Museum

Opened in 2003 by Steve Wyant, the museum cofounder said that he created the museum "to promote tolerance and understanding and share the story of what occurred at the Wounded Knee Massacre." The museum includes a short video to watch about the Massacre at Wounded Knee with summaries of the area, the lead-up to the massacre, the aftermath, and current challenges to Native populations today.

Info: 600 Main St., Wall, SD 57790 • 605.279.2573 • http://www.woundedkneemuseum.org/

WOUNDED KNEE CREEK
Wounded Knee Battlefield (Massacre)

The conflict at Wounded Knee was originally referred to as a battle, but in reality, it was a tragic massacre, not a battle. Inexperienced troops, some members of the Seventh Cavalry who were still out for revenge fourteen years after the Little Big Horn, and the fear of the mysterious passions raised by the Ghost Dance (a religious movement that envisioned Native cultural restoration and disappearance of whites) resulted in the slaughter of more than three hundred Native people. Most were unarmed; many were women and children.

After Sitting Bull's murder on December 15, 1890 (See entry on "Sitting Bull Memorial," Mobridge, South Dakota), his followers joined Big Foot at the Cheyenne River Reservation. Unaware that Big Foot no longer advocated the Ghost Dance, an army detachment captured the combined group as it tried to take refuge on the Pine Ridge Reservation. At Wounded Knee Creek, a scuffle broke out while disarming the Native people, a gun was discharged, and soldiers fired on defenseless Lakotas with Hotchiss guns and rifles. A few survivors managed to escape and recount events. Within two weeks, however, the resistance ended. The final surrender, on January 16, 1891, is the date usually given for the formal end of the wars between Native Americans and federal armed forces in the United States. For this 1890 offensive, the Army awarded twenty medals of honor, its highest commendation.

In 1903, descendants of those who died in the battle erected a monument at the mass grave in which the victims had been buried. The memorial lists many of those who died at Wounded Knee along with an inscription that reads:

Artist Frederic Remington's depiction of the beginning of the Battle of Wounded Knee (1891).

This monument is erected by surviving relatives and other Ogalala and Cheyenne River Sioux Indians in memory of the Chief Big Foot massacre on December 29, 1890. Col. Forsyth is in command of U.S. troops. Big Foot was a great chief of the Sioux Indians. He often said, "I will stand in peace till my last day comes." He did many good and brave deeds for the white man and the red man. Many innocent women and children who knew no wrong died here.

The Wounded Knee Battlefield was declared a U.S. National Historic Landmark in 1965 and was listed on the U.S. National Register of Historic Places in 1966.

Since 1986, Lakota and other Native people have commemorated the tragedy annually by retracing Big Foot's route to Wounded Knee.

Info: Pine Ridge Lakota Reservation, Wounded Knee Creek, SD 57794 • 605.867.5821 • http://oglalalakotanation.info/home.html

MOUNTAINS

We informed the Department of Energy through Tribal Spiritual Leader Corbin Harney that our land and people are being destroyed by the testing of weapons of mass destruction and the development of Yucca Mountain as a high-level nuclear waste repository. Newe Sogobia (Shoshone) cannot endure an increased burden of risk from any source because of our past exposure to fallout from nuclear weapons testing.

—Ian Zabarte (Principal Man for Foreign Affairs
of the government of Newe Sogobia), October 2, 2015

Everything is alive and has a spirit to it. The rocks, the mountains, streams, animals, plants, birds, oceans, and so forth.... We just need to open up the gifts by praying in our own way, singing our own songs and talking to everything out there with love and respect.... This is how everything has been sustained for millions of years. Amazing things will happen if you are patient. This is how we will heal ourselves and our Mother Earth.

—Corbin Harney (1920–2007), Newe Sogobia

Mountain states are not just made of mountains; the region is more diverse than anywhere else in the country. Some of the highest mountain peaks meet up with large, desert lands and rolling plains. The entire area generally features a semi-arid to arid climate, with some alpine climates in the mountains of each state. Some parts of the towering mountains get massive snowfalls and torrential rains while other parts of the area have little rain and often no snow. In this book, only Idaho, Montana, Nevada, and Wyoming are organized into the Mountain Region. As diverse as the landscape is, so is the history and heritage of First Peoples on these lands. Many traditional cultures in these states embraced the lifeways associated with the Great Plains. The economy of some of the other nations in the region were based on fishing. These are the lands through which Meriwether Lewis, William Clark, John Frémont, and Solomon Carvalho navigated their way from one side of the country to the other, with much help from Indigenous peoples.

Traveling in the region, especially visiting tribal museums and events, gives visitors an awe-inspiring glimpse of the varied lifestyles and beliefs. This is cowboy and cowgirl country, and Native people have been cowboying for centuries. Yes, cowboys can also be Indians! The "Olympic" event of Indian rodeoing is the Indian National Finals Rodeo in Nevada, with even a Miss Indian Rodeo event with all the pageantry afforded to mainstream beauty pageants. Both the Cheyenne's Frontier Days and the Crow's Tribe Crow Fair are major destinations to learn about the contemporary presence of Native peoples. The explorative spirit of touring Indian Country should include a concern for the people who live here and on some of the most environmentally fragile lands of the country. For almost a half century, the federal government has been trying to make Nevada's sacred Yucca Mountain a depository for nuclear waste. Yucca Mountain is the Holy Land for the Newe Sogobia (Shoshone) and Paiute, communities already devastated by the testing of weapons of mass destruction and nuclear fallout-related illness. In fact, these Indigenous people are considered to be the "most atom-bombed" nation on earth. Perhaps a visit to "Indian Country" will spark some of the feelings of gratitude for the Earth Mother that many Native people share and INSPIRE commitment from these visitors to help protect the lands, waters, and air and, in the long run, our very species.

IDAHO

Almost thirty thousand Native people live in Idaho, and it contains five tribal councils.

CATALDO
Coeur d'Alene Old Mission State Park

An exhibition called "Sacred Encounters: Father Pierre-Jean De Smet and the Indians of the Rocky Mountain West" at the Coeur d'Alene Mission of the Sacred Heart in Old Mission State Park tells the story of the mission, the tribe, and the missionaries. The Coeur d'Alene Tribe was a major contributor to the exhibit, which is housed in a museum near the mission.

The Mission of the Sacred Heart, the oldest-standing building in Idaho, was built in three years by tribal members between 1850 and 1853. Listed on the National Register of Historic Places, the Sacred Heart Mission and the Coeur d'Alene's Old Mission State Park provide an educational experience giving visitors an opportunity to examine the dynamics and complexities between Native people and Jesuit missionaries. The mission was restored in 1930 and care taken to preserve the elements of Native design. The park features the Sacred Heart Mission Church, a restored parish house, and a historic cemetery. The visitor center includes a gift shop.

Info: 31732 S. Mission Rd., Cataldo, ID 83810 • 208.682.3814 • https://parksandrecreation.idaho.gov/parks/coeur-d-alenes-old-mission

COEUR D'ALENE
Julyamsh Powwow

The annual Coeur d'Alene Julyamsh Powwow, held at the Kootenai County Fairground in Coeur d'Alene, Idaho, is the largest outdoor powwow in the Northwest. Hosted each year by the Coeur d'Alene Tribe and the Coeur d'Alene Casino Resort, the powwow averages about ten thousand people a day, who watch between six hundred and eight hundred dancers. Julyamsh also hosts dozens of drum groups, and visitors can enjoy the spectacle of a horse parade with horses and riders in full regalia.

Info: Kootenai County Fairground, 4056 N. Government Way, Coeur d'Alene, ID 83815 • 800.523.2464 • http://julyamsh.com/

FORT HALL, POCATELLO
Shoshone-Bannock Festival Powwow

Since 1964, the annual Shoshone-Bannock Festival Powwow on the Fort Hall Indian Reservation has been held the second weekend in August. It is a top-rated powwow, complete with traditional Native American dancing, singing, arts and crafts, and traditional food. Thousands of Native Americans from all over North America compete in singing and dance competitions, featuring some of the top dancers and drum groups in North America.

Shoshone-Bannock Festival Powwow activities include: Fort Hall All-Indian Junior/Senior Rodeo, Miss Shoshone-Bannock Contest, All-Indian Festival Parade, Children's Day Powwow, Festival Princess Contest, Traditional Indian Hand Games, Indian Relay Horse Races, Buffalo and Salmon Feast, Indian Art Show, and many others. Elders recount history and culture.

The four-day event is opened with a children's parade that features colorful floats, the Miss Shoshone-Bannock nominees, the Fort Hall travel and safety departments, horse riders, a baby buffalo, children dressed in traditional attire, and everything else that depicts Native American culture at its finest. All events are open to the public.

Info: Fort Hall, Pocatello, ID 83203 • http://shobanfestival.com/

Shoshone-Bannock Tribal Museum

The Shoshone-Bannock Tribal Museum showcases tribal history, old photographs, artifacts from the old Fort Hall, and unique beadwork. Several exhibits feature Chief Pocatello. The museum store offers a variety of Native American books, music, calendars, tribal artwork, and beadwork.

Info: Exit 80, Fort Hall, Pocatello, ID 83203 • 208.237.9791• http://www.sho-ban.com/

LAPWAI
Chief Joseph and Warriors Memorial Powwow

The Nez Perce Tribe hosts the annual Chief Joseph and Warriors Memorial Powwow in June at the Pi-Nee-Waus Community Center. The event brings in a crowd from the area and surrounding states to celebrate and honor those lost in the Nez Perce War of 1877, which was led by Chief Joseph.

Info: Main St. S., Lapwai, ID 83540 • 208.843.7360 • http://powwow-power.com/events/chief-joseph-warriors-memorial-powwow/

MOSCOW
Appaloosa Museum

The Nez Perce are credited with developing this horse breed, famous for its durability and size. It turned the Nez Perce into the Northwest's most accomplished horsemen and made their settlements a special target for raids by their neighbors, who prized the animals. The roan horses marked with spotted rumps have remained very popular over the years, and this museum celebrates the lore that has grown up around them.

Exhibits trace the Appaloosa back to their origin with the Nez Perce. The museum's collections are broken down into materials devoted to Native American horse cultures, the pioneering Northwest, the development of the Appaloosa Horse Club, and contemporary issues of the breed today. The strongest emphasis is placed on how the horse culture was reflected in the Nez Perce way of life through arts, crafts, tools, clothing, and utensils. Among the many fine examples of early Nez Perce horse tack are a woman's saddle dated to 1877, a rare, beaded bridle and apishmore, and several unique horse blankets. A paddock in the back holds a number of Appaloosa horses for visitors to view.

Kathy Whitman-Elk Woman's (Mandan/Hidatsa/Arikara) "Honoring the Warrior Horse" metal sculpture.

Info: 2720 W. Pullman Rd., Moscow, ID 83843 • 208.882.5578 • http://www.appaloosamuseum.com/

Sapaatq'ayn Cinema Native American Film Festival

The Sapaatq'ayn Cinema Native American Film Festival at the University of Idaho has been an annual showcase for Native cinema on the Palouse since 2003. Sapaatq'ayn (suh-pot-kine) is Nimiipuu (Nez Perce) for "to display" or "a motion picture." The festival features new and recently released documentary and feature films made by and about Native peoples and is sponsored by the University of Idaho American Indian Studies Program.

Info: Kenworthy Performing Arts Centre, 508 S. Main St., Moscow, ID 83843 • 208.882.4127 • http://webpages.uidaho.edu/sapaatkayncinema/

SPALDING
Nez Perce National Historical Park, Spalding Visitor Center

Long before the arrival of explorers or missionaries, the Spalding site was home to the Nez Perce (Nimiipuu). Beginning in 1838, Rev. Henry Spalding established his mission there, but this is a short chapter in the story of a site that has seen continuous habitation for generations.

In the nineteenth century, the Spalding site was the center of activities that had a profound effect on the Nez Perce people. The Nez Perce Indian Agency moved to this location in 1861 and remained until 1904. When the agency moved, the town shrank, with its last business closing in 1964. In 1965, Nez Perce National Historical Park was created by an act of Congress and became known as Spalding Park, the headquarters and visitor center for the Nez Perce National Historical Park.

The Nez Perce National Historical Park Visitor Center is located in Spalding. The park consists of thirty-eight sites scattered over four states. Each place illustrates a different aspect of Nez Perce history and culture. Park visits should begin at the

Spalding Visitor Center. A complete list of sites in the park is available there, along with displays on Nez Perce culture.

Info: 39063 U.S. Hwy. 95, Lapwai, ID 83540-9715 • 208.843.7009 • https://www.nps.gov/nepe/learn/historyculture/the-spalding-site.htm

WHITE BIRD
Prairie White Bird Battlefield and Camas Prairie

The opening battle of the Nez Perce War between the Nez Perce Indians and the United States took place on June 17, 1877. The battle was a significant defeat of the U.S. Army. A cavalry detail was sent out from Fort Lapwai to pursue White Bird, the nontreaty leader of the Lamatta Band, when he and his followers refused to move to Lapwai, Idaho, stipulated by the Treaty of 1863. The troopers were routed, with thirty-four killed. The battle was the first indication for the Army that this campaign was going to be long and difficult.

A marker on the road to White Bird Summit explains the role that camas roots played in Nez Perce diet and culture. The blue flowers once grew in profusion in this valley, which is now a major wheat-producing center. The view over this beautiful valley from the 4,245-foot-high summit of White Bird Hill is well worth a stop.

Info: 39063 U.S. Hwy. 95, Lapwai, ID 83540-9715 • 208.843.7009 • https://www.nps.gov/nepe/learn/historyculture/camas-prairie.htm

MONTANA

Montana's Native citizens number around sixty-eight thousand; eight Native nations are headquartered in the state.

ASHLAND
Cheyenne Indian Museum

Located in the historic St. Labre Indian Mission, the museum holds an extensive collection of artifacts and collectibles from the Cheyenne, Crow, and Sioux as well as tribes of the Southwest, Northwest, and Northeast. The museum gift shop offers unique, handmade merchandise created by local Native American artists, including beaded and porcupine quill jewelry.

Info: E. Tongue River Rd., Ashland, MT 59003 • 406.784.4511 • http://www.stlabre.org/about-us/museum/

BILLINGS
Frontier Adventures

Owned and operated by a Crow descendant, Frontier Adventures takes tourists on the same route that William Clark and his men took in 1806. At camps along the Yellowstone River journey, participants learn about Native cultures from Crow ethnobotanists and Cheyenne traditionalists.

Info: Conroy Real Estate, P.O. Box 36, Lincoln, MT 59639 • 406.461.6894 • http://www.exploremontana.com/fa1/

BROWNING
Museum of the Plains Indian

The town of Browning is the administrative headquarters of the Blackfeet Reservation, a reservation in high Plains country. When originally set up in 1855, it stretched from the Continental Divide to the confluence of the Missouri and Yellowstone rivers at the border of the Dakota Territory, but it was sliced up on the east by successive government cessions, and in 1919, the tribe sold the western edge of their lands for $1.5 million to help form Glacier National Park. The thousands of tourists attracted by the park must pass through Browning to reach its eastern gateway and the famous Going-to-the-Sun Highway.

Among the Blackfeet Nation's efforts in the tourist business is the Museum of the Plains Indian founded in 1941. Administered by the Department of the Interior's Indian Arts and Crafts Board, the displays present both traditional and contemporary arts of Northern Plains Indians (Assiniboine, Arapaho, Blackfeet, Chippewa, Cree, Crow, Flathead, Nez Perce, Northern Cheyenne, Shoshone, and Sioux) as well as life-size figures in traditional attire.

The museum series of promotional sales exhibitions introduces contemporary American Indian arts and crafts by emerging artists and craftspeople.

Info: 19 Museum Loop, Browning, MT 59417 • 406.338.2230 • http://www.visitmt.com/listings/general/museum/museum-of-the-plains-indian.html

Museum of the Plains Indian.

North American Indian Days

The annual North American Indian Days observance that takes place each July is one of the largest gatherings of U.S. and Canadian Native nations in the Northwest. Besides traditional dancing, nineteenth-century painted tipis are put up, complete with athletic events, meals, and games.

Info: 1922 1st Ave. N., Browning, MT 59417 • 406.338.7521 • http://www.blackfeetcountry.com/naid.html

CHINOOK
Blaine County Museum

Blaine County Museum is the interim visitor center for the Bear Paw Battlefield, part of the Nez Perce National Park and National Historic Trail, site of the final battle of the four-month Nez Perce War of 1877. Following the breakout of war in Idaho, nearly eight hundred Nez Perce spent a long and arduous summer fleeing U.S. Army troops, first toward Crow allies and then toward refuge in Canada. Forty miles (64 kilometers) short of the Canadian border and following a five-day battle and siege, the Nez Perce ceased fighting at Bear Paw on October 5, 1877, in which Chief Joseph gave his immortal speech: "From where the sun now stands, I will fight no more forever."

The museum houses exhibits of historic artifacts, photographs, and military gear from the late 1800s. A twenty-minute multimedia presentation, "Forty Miles from Freedom," recounts events leading up to the siege of Bear Paw, which ended a remarkable and tragic retreat.

Info: 501 Indiana St., Chinook, MT 59523 • 406.357.2590 • http://www.blainecountymuseum.com/

CROW AGENCY
Crow Fair Celebration Powwow and Rodeo

The annual Crow Fair Celebration Powwow and Rodeo, held at Crow Agency, Montana, by the Apsáalooke people of the Crow Indian Reservation, includes parades, a four-day powwow, a rodeo, and horse races. It is the largest Native American event in Montana and one of the biggest powwows in the country. Also known as the "Tipi Capital of the World" (approximately twelve hundred to fifteen hundred tipis in the encampment during the celebration), the Crow Fair begins on the third Thursday in August and attracts more than fifty thousand spectators and participants from around the world.

The annual Crow Fair Rodeo, sponsored by the Crow Nation, provides a full day's entertainment with youth events, professional Indian cowboys and cowgirls, and horse racing. A parade, which winds its way through the campsites, includes many women on horseback using old-style saddles (many are family heirlooms). Parade participants compete for best traditional dress in more than half a dozen categories.

An overlook of the Little Big Horn Battlefield.

The Crow Fair Powwow emphasizes traditional dance styles. Traditional Crow regalia has changed little since the 1800s.

Info: Crow Agency, MT 59022 • 406.638.3808 • http://www.crow-nsn.gov/

Little Big Horn Battlefield National Monument

This area memorializes one of the last armed resistance efforts of the Northern Plains Indians to being forced onto reservations. They and several thousand Lakota and Cheyenne warriors defeated Lt. Col. George A. Custer and his entire command of the U.S. Army's 7th Cavalry on June 25, 1876.

The park's museum collection includes both cultural and natural history collections. The cavalrymen are buried in the site's national cemetery.

Info: 756 Battlefield Tour Rd., Crow Agency, MT 59022 • 406.638.2621 • https://www.nps.gov/libi/index.htm

LAME DEER
Northern Cheyenne Fourth of July Chiefs Powwow

The Northern Cheyenne Fourth of July Chiefs Powwow is the premier event of the Northern Cheyenne and the largest powwow held on the reservation. In addition to powwow singing and dancing, other activities to observe and participate in include fun runs, hand games, softball and horseshoe tournaments, and health walks. The powwow is held at the Kenneth Beartusk Memorial Powwow Grounds.

Info: Hwy. 212, Lame Deer, MT 54903 • 406.477.4847 • http://www.cheyennenation.com/powwow/powwow.html

MISSOULA
Missoula Art Museum

The museum's Lynda M. Frost Contemporary Art Gallery is dedicated to honoring the creative contributions of American Indians to contemporary art. The American Indian art collection includes works by Jaune Quick-to-See Smith, Corwin Clairmont, Gail Tremblay, George Longfish, Bently Spang, and others.

Info: 335 N. Pattee St., Missoula, MT 59802 • 406.728.0447 • http://www.missoulaartmuseum.org/index.php/

PABLO
The People's Center

The People's Center, sanctioned by traditionalists, is a repository of the histories and cultures of the Salish, Kootenai, and Pend d'Oreille peoples. The museum's largest collection for viewing is entitled "The First Sun the Beginning" and features personal stories as well as artifacts. In August, the center hosts a powwow and artist market.

Info: 56633 Highway 93, Pablo, MT 59855 • 406.675.0160 • http://www.peoplescenter.org/

PRYOR
Chief Plenty Coups State Park and Home

Chief Plenty Coups's (Alek-Chea-Ahoosh) homestead was listed on the U.S. National Register of Historic Places in 1970 and became a National Historic Landmark in 1999. The 195-acre property belonged to Chief Plenty Coups, the last traditional chief of the Apsáalooke (Crow) people. He and his wife, Strikes the Iron, left their home and property to all people in 1928. The only museum of Apsáalooke culture in the United States describes Plenty Coups's long life and achievements. At age seventy-two, Plenty Coups was chosen to represent Native Americans at the dedication of the Tomb of the Unknown Soldier at Arlington Cemetery. He died in 1933.

Info: 1 Edgar Rd., Pryor, MT 59066 • 406.252.1289 • http://stateparks.mt.gov/chief-plenty-coups

THREE FORKS
Madison Buffalo Jump State Monument

The buffalo was always a staple of Plains Indians life, but before Native people acquired the horse, other hunting techniques had to be perfected. One of these involved stampeding herds of the animals over a cliff and then harvesting the carcasses at leisure. One such "buffalo jump" site, a massive, semicircular, limestone cliff situated on the edge of a broad valley carved by the Madison River, was used for two thousand years—ending as recently as two hundred years ago. Every part of the buffalo was used for food, clothing, shelter, and provisions.

Info: 6990 Buffalo Jump Rd., Three Forks, MT 59752 • 406.285.3610 • http://stateparks.mt.gov/madison-buffalo-jump/

Madison Buffalo Jump State Monument.

WISDOM
Big Hole National Battlefield and Visitors Center

Big Hole National Battlefield is a memorial to the people who fought and died there on August 9 and 10, 1877. About 750 nontreaty Nez Perce were fleeing from U.S. Army troops charged with enforcing the U.S. government's demands that all Nez Perce move to a reservation a fraction of the size of their traditional homeland. In doing so, the Army was enforcing a national policy of placing all American Indians on reservations to make way for states. Here, just before daybreak on August 9, 1877, military forces attacked the nontreaty Nez Perce as they rested after six weeks of conflicts and flight from military forces.

The visitor center, which overlooks the battlefield, includes a twenty-six-minute video program and a museum of photographs, quotations, and personal belongings of some of the battle participants and noncombatants. Self-guiding trails wind through the battlefield. Ranger-conducted programs are offered in summer; introductory presentations and exhibits are available year-round.

Info: 16425 Highway 43 W., Wisdom, MT 59761 • 406.689.3155 • https://www.nps.gov/biho/index.htm

NEVADA

Nevada has twenty-eight Native governments and a population of almost forty-eight thousand Indigenous citizens.

BATTLE MOUNTAIN
Hickison Petroglyph Recreation Area

The park features a self-guided trail tour of multiple petroglyph panels, high-desert flora, and views of the Toquima and Toiyabe mountain ranges and the Big Smoky Valley. The ancient art was created by First Peoples who lived near Hickison Summit at the north end of the Toquima Range and the south end of the Simpson Park Mountains.

Info: Battle Mountain District, 50 Bastian Rd., Battle Mountain, NV 89820 • 775.635.4000 • https://aspira.force.com/recreationgov/s/contact-us

CARSON CITY
Nevada State Museum

The museum's center attraction is "Under One Sky," a Native American exhibit from a Native perspective. The story of Nevada's First Peoples is chronicled from the beginning to recent times through Native voice.

Info: 600 N. Carson St., Carson City, NV 89701 • 775.687.4810 • http://nvculture.org/nevadastatemuseumcarsoncity/permanent-exhibits/

Stewart Indian School

The school annually hosts the Stewart Father's Day Powwow in June, which presents traditional competition dancing, arts and crafts, special events, and exhibits. The Washoe Tribe of Nevada Law Enforcement sponsors the powwow.

The Stewart Indian School served as the only off-reservation Indian boarding school in Nevada from 1890 through 1980. In 1985, the school was listed in the National Register of Historic Places as a historic district. The Stewart Indian School Trail is a self-guided walking tour of the campus, with twenty points of interest and audio stories. Using personal cell phones, visitors can access recorded messages from alumni about personal experiences at the school. The goal of the "talking" trail is to preserve the history and memorabilia of the school, which educated youth from more than two hundred nations.

Info: 5500 Snyder Ave., Carson City, NV 89701 • 775.687.8333 • http://stewartindianschool.com/

HENDERSON
Clark County Museum

The museum sits on 30 acres (0.12 square kilometers) of restored, historic buildings depicting life in southern Nevada from precontact times to today. The Anna Robert

Stewart Indian School.

Parks Exhibit Hall boasts a historical journey from the Ice Age to the Age of Entertainment and chronicles the history and culture of the Ancient Puebloan and more recent Paiute people.

Info: 1830 S. Boulder Hwy., Henderson, NV 89002-8502 • 702.455.7955 • http://www.clarkcountynv.gov/parks/pages/clark-county-museum.aspx

HUNGRY VALLEY
Numaga Indian Days Powwow

The annual Numaga Indian Days Powwow, sponsored by the Reno-Sparks Indian Colony, is held over Labor Day weekend. Besides powwow entertainment featuring Native dancers and singers, vendors sell traditional Native foods and handcrafted silverwork, beadwork, baskets, and other American Indian art.

The Numaga Indian Days Powwow is named after Chief Numaga, a Paiute chief known for peace. Numaga tried to preserve the destruction of Paiute aboriginal lands. He called the pine nut groves the Indians' orchards and asked whites to collect fallen timber instead of cutting down healthy trees for firewood. Unfortunately, Numaga's early advocacy for Mother Earth fell on deaf ears. Numaga means "give food."

Info: 9055 Eagle Canyon Dr., Hungry Valley, NV 89441 • http://www.crazycrow.com/site/event/numaga-indian-days-pow-wow/

LAS VEGAS
Indian National Finals Rodeo

Rodeoing is a tough sport, and for almost half a century, rodeo season culminates with a five-day competition of rodeo champions from across Indian Country at the Indian National Finals Rodeo (INFR). Spectators are enthralled with feats in the following categories: Bareback Bronc Riding; Bull Riding; Calf Roping; Cowgirl's Breakaway Roping; Cowgirl's Steer Undecorating; Steer Wrestling; and other dangerous rodeo events. Visitors have lots to see at this annual gathering, including a Miss Indian Rodeo pageant, music/dance performances, and the Indian Cowboy and Cowgirl Art Show. Another treat is the awards ceremony, where champions are inducted into the INFR Hall of Fame.

Info: South Point Equestrian Center, 9777 Las Vegas Blvd., Las Vegas, NV 89183 • 406.338.7684 • http://www.infr.org/

Marjorie Barrick Museum of Art

The museum owns a comprehensive collection of precontact objects, including textiles, jewelry, masks, and baskets from Native peoples of the United States, Mexico, Guatemala, and Bolivia, Changing exhibits present a variety of themes, not just Native.

Info: 4505 S. Maryland Pkwy., Las Vegas, NV 89119 • 702.895.3381 • https://www.unlv.edu/barrickmuseum

NIXON
Pyramid Lake Tribe Museum and Visitor Center

Exhibits at the multipurpose Pyramid Lake Tribe Museum describe the Paiute history and culture and offer insight into the sacredness of the lake and its surrounding landscape to the Paiute people. Other displays focus on Pyramid Lake's natural history and the many creatures that make the lake their home. These include the ancient cui-ui fish and the world-famous Lahontan Cutthroat Trout, which draws anglers the world over.

Info: 709 State St., Nixon, NV 89424 • 775.574.1088 • http://pyramidlake.us/pyramid-lake-visitor-center.html

OVERTON
Lost City Museum

The Lost City Museum, formerly known as the Boulder Dam Park Museum, was built by the Civilian Conservation Corps (CCC) in 1935 and was operated by the National Park Service to exhibit artifacts from the Pueblo Grande de Nevada archaeological sites.

The Lost City Museum shares its location with an ancient site of the Puebloan Indians. In 1981, an extension of the museum was built incorporating some ruins in order to protect them and share them with the public. The museum has displays depicting the excavations of the sites, artifacts unearthed during the project, pictures of the historical excavations, an excavated pithouse, and reconstructions of the Puebloan houses. Pottery, shells, jewelry, and many other examples that showcase the history of the early inhabitants are on display at this museum.

Info: 721 S. Moapa Valley Blvd., Overton, NV 89040 • 702.397.2193 • http://nvculture.org/lostcitymuseum/

Anasazi pueblos at the Lost City Museum.

Valley of Fire State Park

World renowned for its 40,000 acres (162 square kilometers) of bright red, Aztec sandstone outcrops nestled in gray and tan limestone, Valley of Fire State Park contains ancient, petrified trees and petroglyphs dating back more than two thousand years. A visitor center provides exhibits on the geology, ecology, prehistory, and history of the park and nearby region. The park also hosts the annual Atlatl Competition, in which participants test their skills using replicas of ancient spears.

Info: 29450 Valley of Fire Rd., Overton, NV 89040 • 702.397.2088 • http://parks.nv.gov/parks/valley-of-fire

WADSWORTH
Sacred Visions Powwow

The Sacred Visions Powwow is held annually on the Pyramid Lake Paiute Reservation during the second-to-last weekend in July. Founded in 2009, the powwow, which attracts hundreds of dancers and thousands of visitors, helps support the local economies of Pyramid Lake and northern Nevada. It includes food and craft vendors, a parade, hand games, and a junior rodeo.

Info: 50 Big Bend Ranch Rd., Wadsworth, NV 89442 • 775.686.3606 • http://www.sacredvisionspowwow.com

WYOMING

Two tribal councils are located in Wyoming, and almost sixteen thousand Native residents live in the state.

ARAPAHOE
Northern Arapaho Indian Powwow

The town of Arapahoe hosts the Northern Arapaho Indian Powwow, Wyoming's oldest Native American powwow at the Arapahoe Powwow Grounds. Hundreds of dancers compete in full, colorful regalia while dancing to the beats of drum groups.

Info: 15 Great Plains Rd. and 17 Mile Rd., Arapahoe, WY 82510 • 307.840.5805 • https://www.facebook.com/northernarapahopowwow2017/

CHEYENNE
Frontier Days

Every July for over a century, Cheyenne has hosted this eight-day, eye-popping festival that celebrates western life with the world's largest outdoor rodeo, carnival, concerts, midway, grand parade, and an Indian village. Visitors to the village have opportunities to learn about Indigenous cultures, see performances, and participate in a powwow.

Info: 1210 W. 8th Ave., Cheyenne, WY 82001 • 800.227.6336 • http://www.cfdrodeo.com/event/indian-village/

Young girls dance at a Cheyenne Frontier Days celebration.

Wyoming State Museum

"An Unbroken Circle" is the museum's central exhibit that explores the thousands of years of history of Native people in Wyoming. The museum has an extensive collection of Native artifacts; many are on display.

Info: 2301 Central Ave., Cheyenne, WY 82002 • 307.777.7022 • http://wyomuseum.state.wy.us/Index.aspx

CODY

Buffalo Bill Center of the West, Plains Indian Museum

The Plains Indian Museum, one of the five museums in the Buffalo Bill Center of the West, features the stories and objects of Plains Indian people, their cultures, traditions, values, and histories as well as the contexts of their lives today. The majority of the collection is from the early reservation period, ca. 1880–1930. It contains artifacts primarily from Northern Plains tribes, such as the Arapaho, Lakota, Crow, Cheyenne, Blackfeet, and Pawnee. The holdings also include important contemporary objects, ranging from abstract art to star quilts.

In September 2007, the Buffalo Bill Center of the West acquired the Paul Dyck Plains Indian Buffalo Culture Collection, which includes clothing, eagle feather bonnets, bear claw necklaces, buffalo hide tipis, and tipi furnishings, shields, cradles, peace medals, and moccasins. It dates from the late eighteenth century to pre-1890s.

Buffalo Bill Center of the West.

The Plains Indian Museum also sponsors the annual Plains Indian Museum Powwow held each June at the Robbie Powwow Garden at the Center of the West. This event attracts dancers, artisans, and visitors from all over North America.

Info: 720 Sheridan Ave., Cody, WY 82414 • 307.587.4771 • https://centerofthewest.org/explore/plains-indians/

FORT WASHAKIE
Eastern Shoshone Indian Days

Eastern Shoshone Indian Days powwows have been held in late June for over fifty years on the Wind River Reservation. They include dancing and drum competitions, games, a parade, food, and arts and crafts.

The powwow is Wyoming's largest, showcasing more than one thousand dancers and more than thirty drum groups. The event opens with an all-Indian parade. Throughout the weekend, the Coeur d'Alene offers a feast and softball, golf, and basketball tournaments.

Info: Fort Washakie Powwow Arena, Old Wind River Hwy., Fort Washakie, WY 82514 • http://www.pow-wow.org/561/shoshone-indian-days

Shoshone Tribal Cultural Center

The Shoshone Tribal Cultural Center exhibits tribal crafts, art, Shoshone treaty documents, maps, agreements, and other historical artifacts including displays of historical data and photographs. Various events such as walking tours, cultural classes, and workshops are held throughout the year. A gift shop offers Native American handcrafted articles.

Info: 90 Ethete Rd., Fort Washakie, WY 82514 • 307.349.7089 • http://easternshoshonetribe.org

LOVELL
Medicine Wheel/Medicine Mountain
National Historic Landmark

Medicine Wheel is situated atop Medicine Mountain at an elevation of 9,642 feet (2,939 meters) in Wyoming's Bighorn Mountains. The wheel itself measures nearly 80 feet (24 meters) in diameter and consists of twenty-eight alignments of limestone boulders radiating from a central cairn associated with six smaller stone enclosures found around the wheel's perimeter. While the exact purpose of the wheel, its age, and the identity of its makers are unknown, researchers believe that the wheel was constructed over a period of centuries from about five hundred to about fifteen hundred years ago.

The land surrounding the wheel has been used by ancient American Indian groups for at least seven thousand years. In contemporary times, the region's Arapaho, Bannock, Blackfeet, Cheyenne, Crow, Kootenai-Salish, Lakota Sioux, Plains Cree, Shoshone, and other First Peoples hold ceremonies on the site.

Medicine Wheel appears to be part of a much larger network of ancient trails, sites, and important landmarks, encompassing more than 23,000 acres (93 square kilometers). Visitors must hike 1.5 miles (2.4 kilometers) to reach the wheel and, once there, can view the scenic Bighorn Basin and many of the trails and landmarks. Please do not intrude if a ceremony is being observed.

The site, previously known as Bighorn Medicine Wheel, was listed as a National Historic Landmark on August 29, 1970, and was renamed Medicine Wheel/Medicine Mountain National Historic Landmark in 2011.

Info: Hwy. 14A, Lovell, WY 82431 • 307.674.2600 • http://wyoshpo.state.wy.us/NationalRegister/Site.aspx?ID=60

MORAN
Colter Bay Indian Arts Museum

Located in Grand Teton National Park, this little museum houses a small collection of rare Native American artifacts of woven blankets, instruments, beadwork, toys,

Medicine Wheel, a Native American sacred site in Lovell, Wyoming.

moccasins, pouches, sashes, and jewelry. The collection dates from 1875 through the early 1900s and includes pieces from over one hundred nations. Ranger-guided talks are offered twice a day, and once a week, visitors can see the construction of a traditional tipi.

Info: Colter Bay Marina Rd., Moran, WY 83013 • 800.299.0396 • http://www.nationalparkcentralreservations.com/activity/colter-bay-indian-arts-museum

ST. STEPHENS
St. Stephens Church, School, and Museum

St. Stephens Church is a Roman Catholic Church among the Eastern Shoshone and Northern Arapaho on the Wind River Indian Reservation. It features beautiful Native American art and stained-glass windows. The old boys' dormitory and classrooms, rebuilt after a fire in 1928, now serve as a post office, community center, museum, and gift shop.

Info: 33 St. Stephens Rd., St. Stephens, WY 82524 • 307.856.6797 • https://www.yellowstonepark.com/things-to-do/st-stephens-mission

THERMOPOLIS
Gift of the Waters Pageant

The "Gift of the Waters" pageant is a historic Indian pageant held in Thermopolis, Wyoming, on the first weekend in August of every year. Singing, dancing, "The Lord's Prayer" in Native sign language, and a moving scene where an archer sends an arrow into the heavens make up this memorable ceremony. In 1897, Shoshone Chief Washakie entered into an agreement with the U.S. government to sell a 10-mile (16-kilometer) square of land surrounding the Big Horn Hot Springs (now known as the "Big Spring"). His only proviso was that Indians from Wind River would always be given free access to the spring. Gift of the Waters features many members of the Shoshone and Arapaho nations and also includes traditional dances.

Info: P.O. Box 936, Thermopolis, WY 82443 • 307.864.3192 • http://thermopolis.com/events/gift-of-the-waters-pageant/

SOUTHWEST

Tsikumu is a special mountain to the people of Santa Clara Pueblo, my community of origin. It sits among the Jemez Mountains, which are part of the Rocky Mountains, in north central New Mexico. I remember annual hikes to Tsikumu peak in my youth with my parents and four younger siblings. We hiked there to thank the Spirits for our well-being and to petition for rain to bless our community. Our prayers were always answered. Tsikumu is a divine presence in my memory as old as Creation.

—Dr. Beverly Singer (Tewa/Navajo), Filmmaker, Scholar, Educator

Desert brown and red earth safeguarded by mountain vistas shape this land with volcanic land forms that emerge under brilliant, blue skies that offer an extraordinary supply of cultural and historical sites replete with narratives borne from the land's original inhabitants.

The earlier history of Indigenous peoples in what is known in the Southwest as the Four Corners was home to thousands of Ancestral Puebloan peoples who built a network of settlements and roads throughout the region. They were the first to witness the arrival of Spanish explorers and missionaries in the sixteenth century. By the seventeenth century, when the Spanish began their settlement efforts, the Puebloans resisted in 1680, forcing them to return to Mexico. Many of the Puebloan communities in existence at the time were abandoned, and many were disenfranchised and were never formally recognized but instead were identified as Hispanic communities.

The Southwest is also the homeland of some fifty Native American tribal reservation communities, including Apache and Navajo, or Diné, who are typically associated with the Southwest. Lesser known are the Hualapai, residing near the Grand Canyon, or the Havasupai, who live at the bottom of the canyon, whose ancestors predate the establishment of the state of Arizona. Cocopah and the many communities of Tohono O'odham, Maricopa, and Yaqui in southern Arizona have territories that were separated by the U.S. and Mexico border. Other tribes are in the state as well, along the Colorado River. Ute and Pauite tribes retain their ancestral ties in what became Colorado and Utah. In New Mexico, the nineteen pueblos along the Rio Grande have contributed extensively to the economy of the state through a history of "Indian tourism." In the state of Texas, the Alabama-Coushatta retains its ties to the southeast, while the historic tribes of Kickapoo and Apache had fluid ties with Mexico. Also in Texas, Ysleta del Sur Pueblo survived being displaced after the successful expulsion of Spanish explorers from the region with the 1680 Pueblo Revolt.

All of the tribes in the Southwest have proven resilient and participate in contemporary America today. The venture into casino gaming has brought economic opportunities for tribes in the Southwest, with many located near urban centers, where many Native people now reside in close proximity to their home reservations. The hallmark of the Southwest is the record of Indigenous peoples' presence for thousands of years, whose lives are manifest in ancient settlements, which demonstrate their knowledge, life skills, and determination for living in a desert environment.

ARIZONA

According to the 2010 census, 353,386 American Indian/Alaska Natives live in the state of Arizona. Twenty-two Native governments are in the state of Arizona.

CAMP VERDE
Montezuma Castle National Monument

The original architects and residents of this monument are often called "cliff dwellers," a misleading reference to the Ancestral Puebloans, who lived good lives in this desert landscape and continue to have a presence in locations such as Montezuma Castle, despite having lived here between 1100 and 1425 C.E. It is one of several interrelated Puebloan settlements built during cultural periods, identified as Hohokam and Sinagua by anthropologists. Sierra de Sin Agua in Spanish translates to "mountains without water" and describes this settlement built high up under a cliff with rock masonry. Hohokam is a term derived from a Pima or O'odham word "huhugam" that translates to "all used up" or "those who are gone." Its popular name, Montezuma Castle, draws inference to the Aztec emperor, whose empire had far-reaching influence but collapsed with the Spanish invasion in 1519. From a distance, the five-storied, stone structure with twenty separate rooms resembles a fortress. Significant to Hohokam culture were a division of labor such as stone masonry and the development of trading routes that ranged into Mexico. Montezuma Castle, Montezuma Well, and Tuzigoot are related sites and in close proximity to the Camp Verde Yavapai-Apache Reservation.

Montezuma Castle.

Info: Montezuma Castle, 2800 Montezuma Castle Hwy., Camp Verde, AZ 86322 • 928.567.3322, x.221 • https://www.nps.gov/moca/index.htm

Yavapai-Apache Cultural Center

The Yavapai-Apache Nation welcomes visitors to the Yavapai-Apache Cultural Center where throughout the year, they conduct activities that reinforce their history and culture with programs such as local food preparation, language lessons, and traditional Yavapai-Apache crafts. Annually, they celebrate National American Indian Day in September and open it to the public. The Yavapai originate from Yuman-speaking people known as the Pai. The Apache descend from an Athabascan linguistic culture similar to other Apache groups. The two Indigenous groups coexisted in the region while maintaining their distinct cultures and languages and became one tribal nation in 1934. The Yavapai-Apache Nation owns the Cliff Castle Casino and Hotel located along I-17 in Camp Verde and are within a half-hour drive to Sedona, Prescott, and Jerome. They also operate Distant Drums RV Resort for visitors to Montezuma Castle and local sites.

Info: 2400 W. Datsi St., Camp Verde, AZ 86322 • 928.567.3649 • http://www.yavapai-apache.org

CHANDLER
Huhugam Heritage Center

A modern, architecturally detailed cultural center highlights the ancestral, historic, and current cultures of the Gila River Indian Community, made up of two tribes, the Akimel O'odham and the Pee Posh. The Huhugam Heritage Center was built in 2003, fulfilling their community vision to create a place for community, culture, land, tradition, and spirit: a place to honor and preserve Him-Dak (our way of life). Among the architectural details is a staircase constructed to rise up and out of the desert, and the building silhouettes are designed to blend with the nearby mountain ranges and hills. The center houses a state-of-the-art collections repository for Huhugam, also known by the archaeological name Hohokam. The Gila River Cultural Resources Management Program and the Bureau of Reclamation's Central Arizona Project collection comprise five hundred O'odham baskets, a Pee Posh pottery collection, and memorabilia from Akimel O'odham jazz trombonist Russell Moore. The Blackwater Store and Trading Post and arts and crafts museum collections are also featured. Background provided by the Gila River Indian Community clarifies its cultural history and has been carefully written: "Pima is the common name applied to us, but it is not something we called ourselves prior to European arrival. In our own language, we refer to ourselves as O'odham, which means 'the people.' We are part of a large O'odham population that resides in Arizona and Mexico. To be more specific, we are Akimel O'odham, which means 'River people,' because, unlike our desert-dwelling relatives to the south, we have always resided along and depended upon the rivers that intersect our territory. To be even more precise, we are Onk Akimel O'odham, meaning 'Salt River people,' because that is the specific river along which we reside." The O'odham of Arizona reside on four major reserves: Salt River Pima-Maricopa Indian Community; Gila River Indian Community; Ak-Chin Community; and Tohono O'odham Nation, but they have lived in the area since the beginning. Huhugam is the preferred name and translates to "the rivers no longer flow." The Phoenix metropolitan area has developed around the Salt River Pima-Maricopa Indian Community; they are fully immersed in the contemporary culture of the majority population and still maintain traditional ways.

Info: 21359 S. Maricopa Rd., Chandler, AZ 85226 • 520.796.3500 • http://www.grichhc.org/

Kai Restaurant

Kai means "seed" in the Akimel O'othan language. The Kai Restaurant located at the Wild Horse Pass Sheraton is among the Gila River Indian Community tribal enterprises. The restaurant made history when it became a AAA Five-Diamond/Forbes Five-Star restaurant. Local Akimel O'odham and Pee-Posh ingredients are used to create a distinct Native American menu by well-known non-Native chefs at the restaurant.

Info: 5594 Wild Horse Pass Blvd., Chandler, AZ 85226 • 602.225.0100 • http://www.wildhorsepassresort.com/kai

CHINLE
Canyon de Chelly National Monument

Canyon de Chelly is a visually dramatic, 27-mile (43 kilometer) canyon with two shorter neighboring canyons, Canyon del Muerto at 18 miles (29 kilometers) and Monument Canyon at 10 miles (16 kilometers). They comprise 83,840 acres, or 131 square miles (339 kilometers). The Navajo Nation is the owner of Canyon de Chelly, and in a unique agreement signed in 1931 with the National Park Service, the canyon became a national monument with the understanding that the Navajo Nation would lose no rights of access and had the privilege of furnishing horses and guides to visitors. Since then, the issue of guides and permits for guided tours has been in transition.

The livelihood of forty Diné families has been a fixture in the canyon, and they continue to farm, herd livestock, and plant crops and are sometimes visible by visitors from the canyon rims. Ancient Puebloans first occupied the canyon, noted by pithouse architecture, and later constructed houses in alcoves along the canyon walls to take advantage of the sunlight and natural protection. Due to changing conditions, the Ancient Puebloan peoples left the canyon for better farmland by the mid-1300s. It is suggested that some descendants of those who migrated out of Canyon de Chelly moved toward the Hopi mesas. During this period of out-migration, Navajo people began living in and near the canyon.

The Navajo Nation Reservation was established by treaty with the United States in 1868 that provided over 27,000 square miles (43,452 square kilometers) that included Canyon de Chelly, securing it as Navajo tribal trust land. The Navajo Nation

Canyon de Chelly White House.

Reservation is the largest in the United States; it is nearly the same size as the State of West Virginia. The National Park Service charges no entrance fee. Visitors may drive the North and South rims, paved roads with ten overlooks. The White House Trail is open all year and requires no guide. It starts from the White House Overlook on the South Rim. The town of Chinle is 2 miles (3 kilometers) from the entrance to Canyon de Chelly and is almost entirely populated by Navajo or Diné originally from that area of the Navajo Nation.

Info: Route 7, Chinle, AZ 86503 • 928.674.5500 •
https://www.nps.gov/cach/index.htm

CLARKDALE
Tuzigoot National Monument

Tuzigoot is a large pueblo village built around 1100 and occupied until about 1450. The name is from the Apache Athapascan speakers in the area, who say that Tuzigoot means "crooked water." This large, ancestral site that represents Sinagua culture is located on a hill in northwestern Verde Valley. The farmers who lived here used the river and marshland below the settlement known today as the Verde River and Tavasci Marsh. They also developed extensive trading across the territory based on the studies by the National Park Service Western Archaeological and Conservation Center in Tucson. Conservation work with pottery found at Tuzigoot is on exhibit at the Tuzigoot Visitor Center Museum, which also houses a bookstore run by a nonprofit organization.

Info: 25 Tuzigoot Rd., Clarkdale, AZ 86324 • 928.567.3322, x.227 •
https://www.nps.gov/tuzi/index.htm

COCHISE
Cochise Stronghold Coronado National Forest

The Cochise Stronghold is a desert forest with patchy, rocky peaks in southeastern Arizona managed by the Douglas Ranger District within the Coronado Forest. Cochise Stronghold, named for the Apache headman or leader Cochise, is located to the west of Sunsites, Arizona, in the Dragoon Mountains at an elevation of 5,000 feet (1,524 meters) above the desert. The Arizona woodland area contains granite domes and sheer cliffs. This area was the homeland of one thousand Chiricahua Apache in what became Arizona Territory and later a state. Cochise led the Chiricahua Band of the Apache Tribe during a period of colonial intervention in the West. In 1850, the United States took control over the territory that became the states of Arizona and New Mexico.

Cochise is said to have maintained peace with the Anglo-Americans until 1861, when his people were accused of abducting a child from a ranch. Later, it was proved that the boy was kidnapped by another band of Apache. Cochise and his followers were ordered to be held as hostages by the military, where Cochise escaped by cutting a hole in a tent. Army Lt. George Bascom ordered the hanging of the remaining Apache hostages. Cochise joined forces with Mangas Coloradas, his father-in-law, fighting a resistance struggle against the Army and settlers. In 1863, Cochise led the Apache after the capture and death of Mangas Coloradas. The U.S. Army captured Cochise in 1871, seeking to move the Chiricahua to a reservation hundreds of miles away. Escaping again, he renewed his campaign of resisting the Army and settlers. Cochise was able to negotiate a new treaty with the help of Thomas Jeffords, Army scout, Indian agent, prospector, and superintendent of overland mail in the Arizona Territory. Cochise and his people were allowed to stay in their homeland. Revered for his negotiation and strategic skills and knowledge of the land, he died peacefully on the newly formed Chiricahua Reservation in 1874. His son, Taza, succeeded him as chief. Upon his death, he was secretly buried somewhere in the Dragoon Mountains. The exact location has never been revealed or determined. The town of Cochise, Cochise County, the renowned geological feature known as Cochise's Head in the Chiricahua Mountains, and the Stronghold are all named in tribute to him. The Cochise Stronghold Preserve has a 5-mile (8-kilometer) hiking and equestrian trail.

Info: W. Ironwood Rd., Cochise, AZ 85606 • 520.364.3468 • http://cochisestronghold.com/

COOLIDGE
Casa Grande Ruins National Monument

In the southern Arizona desert between Phoenix and Tuscon is the "huhugam" ancestral settlement of present-day O'odham descendants named Casa Grande by Italian Jesuit priest Eusebio Kino. In the late 1600s, the educated Kino was sent to Mexico as a missionary and traveled through the northern Sonoran Desert region and was impressed by the abandoned massive adobe (mud brick) structure still standing in the desert. Contemporary archaeological studies have revealed the ancient Sonoran

Observation area for the Casa Grande ruins.

Desert people (referred to as belonging to Hohokam culture) as the ancestors of Pima or O'odham peoples, who have formal recognition as the Tohono O'odham Nation. The significant development by the O'odham ancestors was their use of irrigation canals constructed across the desert around 400–500 CE and they continued to use them for the next thousand years. Archaeologists have discovered hundreds of miles of ancient irrigation canals in the Gila River Valley as well as the Salt River Valley of Phoenix, the Santa Cruz River Valley in Tucson, and on the American Indian reservations of southern Arizona. They grew corn and several varieties of beans and squash as well as cotton and tobacco. In addition to their crops, the Hohokam culture made use of indigenous plants such as cactus fruit, pads, and buds, agave hearts (century plant), mesquite beans, and creosote bush. The local game included birds, squirrels, rabbits, snakes, and lizards as well as fish and clams from the rivers and canals. Larger game, such as mule deer and bighorn sheep, were hunted in the mountains. On occasion, descendants of the Casa Grande from the Tohono O'odham Nation offer demonstrations and sell their art at the monument.

Info: 1100 W. Ruins Dr., Coolidge, AZ 85128 • 520.723.3172 • https://www.nps.gov/cagr/index.htm

FLAGSTAFF
Annual Hopi Festival Downtown Flagstaff

The Hopi Festival is an event produced and coordinated by the Hopi Tribe Economic Development office to help Hopi artists sell their work that followed the recession in 2010. The event further helped to reintroduce Hopi life and culture through traditional social dances and food along with the artists who apply to participate. The Hopi Festival is held in late September in downtown Flagstaff and is supported by the Flagstaff City Council as a public education event by way of Hopi arts, traditional social dances, and traditional foods. Lisa Talayumptewa, event coordinator of HTEDC, says: "It is exciting to have our downtown businesses be a part of our festival and hope that our working relationship will only grow stronger."

Info: 5200 E. Cortland Blvd., Suite E200-7, Flagstaff, AZ 86004 • 928.522.8675 • http://www.hopiallnativefestival.com/

Annual Hopi Native Arts and Cultural Festival Museum of Northern Arizona

This is a July Fourth tradition begun in the 1930s by the Museum of Northern Arizona. The Hopi Festival of Arts and Culture features ninety award-winning artists and presenters from the Hopi villages in northern Arizona. In addition to the Hopi contemporary art for sale, the two-day event sponsors invited lectures, artist demonstrations, traditional social dances, and contemporary musical performances.

Info: 3101 N. Ft. Valley Rd., Flagstaff, AZ 86001 • 928.774.5213 • https://musnaz.org/heritage/hopi-festival/

Museum of Northern Arizona

Located in Flagstaff, a city of 74,459 residents, the Museum of Northern Arizona (MNA) says that it has evolved into a regional center of learning and interpreter of the Colorado Plateau. The museum is a private, nonprofit, member-based institution with a 200-acre (0.8 square kilometer) campus at the base of the San Francisco

Peaks. Its collections include some eighteen thousand ethnographic Native American objects, fifty-three thousand archaeological Native American objects, uncataloged archaeological research collections, paleontology, rocks and minerals, botanical and zoological items, fine arts, archives, and seventy-six thousand library titles. The museum has ongoing exhibits, scholarly lectures, and artists-in-residence and youth educational programs and hosts the Hopi Native Arts and Culture Festival over the July 4th weekend. The museum was founded 1928 by Harold S. Colton and Mary-Russell Ferrell Colton and is accredited by the American Alliance of Museums.

Info: 3101 N. Ft. Valley Rd., Flagstaff, AZ 86001 • 928.774.5213 • https://musnaz.org/

Walnut Canyon National Monument

Walnut Canyon, under the stewardship of the National Park Service, is located 10 miles (16 kilometers) southeast of Flagstaff and was occupied by Ancestral Puebloan peoples some seven hundred years ago. Archaeologists identify the settlement as an example of Sinagua culture. The site has multiple deteriorating rock-constructed rooms along the mile long Island Trail at the site, with additional sites visible across the canyon. Walnut Canyon is visually picturesque and abundant, with desert mountain plants used by the Ancestral Puebloan peoples, who grew corn, squash, and beans. During the 1100s, they moved into limestone alcoves below the canyon rim, where they constructed the building remains that are seen today. The Walnut Canyon community thrived for another 150 years before the people moved on.

Walnut Canyon National Monument.

Info: 3 Walnut Canyon Rd., Flagstaff, AZ 86004 • 928.526.3367 • https://www.nps.gov/waca/index.htm

Wupatki National Monument

Wupatki Pueblo is a major ancestral community that was built around 1100. The steward of the site is the National Park Service, and it says, "Wupatki is remembered and cared for, not abandoned. For its time and place, there was no other Pueblo like Wupatki. Less than 800 years ago, it was the tallest, largest, and perhaps the richest and most influential Pueblo around. It was home to 85–100 people, and several thousand more lived within a day's walk. And it was built in one of the lowest, warmest, and driest places on the Colorado Plateau. Human history here spans at least 10,000 years. But only for a time, in the 1100s, was the landscape this densely populated. The eruption of nearby Sunset Crater Volcano a century earlier probably played a part. Families that lost their homes to ash and lava had to move. They discovered that the cinders blanketing lands to the north could hold moisture needed for crops." The agricultural community grew into a few large pueblos, including Wupatki, Wukoki, Lomaki, and other masonry pueblos that emerged from bedrock, with each surrounded by many smaller pueblos and pithouses. Trade networks expanded, bringing turquoise, shell jewelry, copper bells, and parrots from Mexico. Wupatki flourished to about 1250 C.E., when the people moved on.

Info: 6400 U.S. 89, Flagstaff, AZ 86004 • 928.679.2365 • https://www.nps.gov/wupa/index.htm

FOUNTAIN HILLS
Yavapai Nation Orme Dam Victory Days

The Yavapai were not traditionally farmers; they migrated up and down the Verde River, hunting, fishing, and gathering. In 1903, the federal government settled them at Fort

Wukoki Ruins Complex, Wupatki National Monument.

McDowell, a former U.S. Army installation previously used to subdue bands of Apache in Arizona Territory. In 1968, Congress approved the Central Arizona Project (CAP), a plan that called for the construction of Orme Dam at the confluence of the Salt and Verde rivers. The Yavapai fought the project for ten years, and unlike the Gila River tribes, who saw upstream dams nearly destroy their livelihood, they were successful in preventing the dam's construction and also settled rights to water, which they use for profit-production agriculture. Today, one of the biggest celebrations for the Fort Mc-Dowell Yavapai Nation is the Orme Dam Victory Days in early November. The Orme Dam Victory Days includes an all-Indian rodeo, intertribal powwow, parade, and cultural performances and is held at the Fort McDowell Fairgrounds. The Fort McDowell Yavapai Nation is a 950-member Native American tribe that calls central Arizona's upper Sonoran Desert home. Located to the northeast of Phoenix within Maricopa County, Arizona, the 40-square mile (64-square kilometer) reservation is a small part of their ancestral territory in a vast area of Arizona's desert lowlands and mountainous Mogollon Rim Country. The Fort McDowell Yavapai Nation also operates Fort McDowell Casino and two hotel leisure resorts: We-Ko-Pa near Scottsdale and Poco Diablo in Sedona.

Info: Orme Dam Rodeo Grounds, Hwy. 87, 1/4 mi. east of Fort McDowell Rd., Fountain Hills, AZ 85269 • 480.789.7000 • https://www.fmyn.org/

FREDONIA
Kaibab Band of Paiute Indians Sounds of Thunder Mountain Powwow

The Kaibab-Paiute Reservation consists of five villages: Kaibab, Juniper, Redhills, Steamboat, and Six-Mile. It is located in northwestern Arizona in the Kaibab Plateau Basin, just across the Utah–Arizona border from Zion National Park, 50 miles (80 kilometers) northwest of the Grand Canyon. The reservation is accessible by highway from Utah and by back-country roads from the Kaibab Plateau. Fredonia, Arizona, is the tribal headquarters.

The Kaibab-Paiute Band belongs to the larger Southern Paiute Nation, which has historically occupied the region that is now southern Utah, northern Arizona, and the Great Basin of southeastern Nevada. Their language belongs to the Numic branch of the Uto-Aztecan linguistic family. Ancestral Kaibab-Paiute gathered grass seeds, hunted animals, and raised crops near the springs for which Pipe Spring National Monument is named for at least one thousand years. The Sounds of Thunder Mountain Powwow is a community event that offers a free feast and fun-run/walk (registration at 6 A.M.) followed by the Free Fishing Derby, Southern Paiute Hand-Drum Contest, horseshoe tournament, three-on-three basketball tournament, and vendors selling arts and crafts. The powwow events take place in and around the Kaibab Paiute Tribe Park and the community building, near Moccasin.

Info: Kaibab Band of Paiute Indians Tribal Administration, Bldg. #1 N. Pipe Spring Rd., Fredonia, AZ 86022 • 928.643.7245 • http://www.kaibabpaiute-nsn.gov/contact.html

Pipe Spring National Monument and Kaibab Tribal Museum

Pipe Spring National Monument is the least known of the land between Utah's southern boundary and the Grand Canyon known as the "Arizona Strip." The region of Arizona and Utah was originally navigated and used by Paiute Indians in what became Arizona, California, Nevada, and Utah. Dependent on hunting game and gathering roots, seeds, and berries, the Paiute traveled great distances in the region and settled when they began using irrigation to grow corn, which was learned from observing Puebloan farmers and Northern Paiute bands who had always fished. The extended family was the main traditional unit of social organization, with bands led by a headman.

In the late 1700s, immigrant "Mormons," a popular term for those with religious and/or cultural ties to the Church of Jesus Christ of Latter-day Saints, arrived in the region seeking refuge, among them a group of polygamists who sought independence. Pipe Spring was the only water source along a distance of 62 miles (100 kilometers). Historical conflict and violence between Anglo settlers and Paiute ended after U.S. military intervention after the Civil War, when the Paiute were assigned separate reservation lands and many were forced to accept a different way of living. The Kaibab Paiute were formally established under the Indian Reorganization Act of 1934 on a 40-acre 0.16 square kilometers) parcel of land. Pipe Spring National Monument had already been established in 1923 under the U.S. Park Service administration, taking advantage of its location in northwestern Arizona on the road between Zion National Park and the North Rim of the Grand Canyon National Park.

In a unique partnership with the National Park Service initiated in 1998, the Kaibab Band of Paiute Indians Tribal Museum of Culture and History was opened at Pipe Spring National Monument and now draws over fifty thousand visitors a year. The museum focuses on the Kaibab Paiute: their traditions, historical interactions, and contemporary life. The joint venture museum features the Zion Natural History Association Bookstore, a snack bar, and a visitor center and gift shop. The Pipe Spring National Monument is located entirely within reservation boundaries.

Info: 406 Pipe Springs Rd., Fredonia, AZ 86022 • 928.643.7105 • https://www.nps.gov/pisp/learn/photosmultimedia/vc-and-museum-tour.htm

GANADO

Hubbell Trading Post

The start of "Indian" trading posts dates back to first contact between Anglo and Native peoples in North America, who traded raw materials such as animal fur for manufactured goods introduced to Natives. The trading post system was an economic spine of the European westward movement. The oldest continuously operating trading post on the Navajo Nation and in the United States is the Hubbell Trading Post in Ganado. Established in 1878, this mercantile store and other trading posts were developed at the Navajo Reservation by John Lorenzo Hubbell and his family. These posts became an epicenter for trade goods sought by Navajo people following their capture and exile by the U.S. military at Bosque Redondo.

After returning home, the survivors called their imprisonment the "Long Walk of 1864."

Navajo silversmiths and tapestry weavers made blankets and rugs of churro sheep hair, who began trading their culturally distinct, handmade art for groceries and dry goods, often in an unequal exchange that favored the trader. A list of other trading posts include Gap Trading Post in Gap, Arizona; Rough Rock Trading Post in Chinle, Arizona; Tuba City Trading Post in Tuba City, Arizona; Toadlena Trading Post in New-comb, New Mexico; Shonto Trading Post in Shonto, Arizona; Foutz Trading Post in Shiprock, New Mexico; and Tec Nos Pos Trading Post in Tec Nos Pos, Arizona.

The Hubbell Trading Post is the best-known trading post, which was built in 1883 and was acquired by the National Park Service. It is also a National Historic Site, with a visitor center that features a bookstore, exhibits, and rug-weaving demonstrations. Visitors may purchase an entrance fee to visit the Hubbell home and tour the original 160-acre (0.64 kilometers) homestead.

Info: 1/2 AZ-264, Ganado, AZ 86505 • 928.755.3475 • https://www.nps.gov/hutr/index.htm

GLOBE
Besh Ba Gowah Archaeological Park and Museum

The city of Globe began as a copper mining camp for the Old Dominion Mine that opened in 1875. The mine closed in 1931. The city of Globe manages the Besh Ba Gowah Archaeological Park and Museum and offers visitors a chance to explore the site that has a museum featuring a collection of pottery and other artifacts, a botanical garden, and a gift shop. It is open daily 9–4:30 and closed on Thanksgiving, Christmas, and New Year's Day. Summer hours begin July 1 through September 30, and it is closed Mondays and Tuesdays. A small fee is charged.

The story of this place is that five hundred years prior, Besh Ba Gowah was an ancestral settlement constructed by people who identified with the Salado culture period and lived between 1150 and 1450. The name Besh Ba Gowah is an Apache Athabascan word that loosely translates to the "place of metal." The Salado geography was composed of high desert, mountains, and river valleys. The Salt River, after which the Salado were named, is said to be the center of Salado Territory and a major source of water, arable farmland, and trade routes to other tribes in the area. Archaeologists disagree about the basis of Salado culture, which is not included among the three major cultures of the Southwest identified by archaeologists: the Anasazi (Ancestral Puebloan), the Mogollon, and the Hohokam, or the preferred name, huhugham. The Salado have been described as hunters, gatherers, and farmers. The Salado took full advantage of the surrounding desert resources. They gathered desert plants; cultivated cotton, corn, beans, and squash; hunted small game; and obtained water from an ancient spring that still runs today. The Salado culture created elaborate pottery and wove exquisite textiles. Between 1350 and 1450, the region became arid, and they left their small villages and consolidated into larger communities.

Info: 1324 S. Jesse Hayes Rd., Globe, AZ 85501 • 928.425.0320 • http://www.globeaz.gov/visitors/besh-ba-gowah

GRAND CANYON VILLAGE
Tusayan Ruins and Museum

The Grand Canyon has been a site of continued human presence starting from as long as ten thousand years ago through today. The Grand Canyon National Park is the largest National Park Service and receives over five million visitors annually. In 1908, President Theodore Roosevelt declared the Grand Canyon a national monument, placing under federal protection the 10-mile (16 kilometers)-wide, 277-mile (446 kilometers)-long, and one-mile (1.6 kilometer)-deep canyon.

Tusayan was named in Spanish documents in their early explorations in the 1600s and is referred to as the province of Hopi and called Hopiland. Spanish explorers note that during their explorations, they were presented with cotton blankets, some of which were colored and some of which were white, and that the women wore cotton skirts that were embroidered with colored thread. Archaeologists eventually came to identify successive culture periods of Indigenous settlements as Ancestral Puebloan peoples, the first as Basketmaker culture and later the current name Puebloan peoples, that includes Hopi. Also identified in the Grand Canyon are Cinchona, who lived in the canyon area, and Paiute, Cerbat, and Navajo, all of whom

The Tusayan Museum is located on the South Rim of the Grand Canyon.

have ties to the Grand Canyon, and eventually, all surviving Native peoples were forced into reservations by the U.S. government. Therefore, modern-day tribes, including Havasupai, who live in the canyon, Hopi, Hualapai, who live close to the canyon rim, Navajo, Paiute, White Mountain Apache, Yavapai Apache, and Zuni to the east in New Mexico all consider the Grand Canyon their homeland.

Archaeologists estimate that Tusayan Pueblo was built around 1185 and abandoned one hundred years later. Visitors may tour Tusayan by following a paved path located directly east of the Tusayan Museum. Exhibits along the path explain features of the ruin; small, masonry-constructed structures show connected rooms, suggesting extended family living spaces. A connecting gravel trail overlooks the field where Ancestral Puebloan farmers grew their crops. A museum was established to highlight findings of the partially excavated site.

Info: Grand Canyon Village, AZ 86023 • 602.638.2305 • https://www.nps.gov/grca/planyourvisit/visitorcenters.htm

HIDDEN SPRINGS
San Juan Southern Paiute Powwow

The Annual San Juan Southern Paiute Tribal Recognition Powwow is held the second weekend of June in Hidden Springs, Arizona. Southern Paiute lived in northern Arizona and southern Utah for hundreds of years, subsisting as hunter-gatherers, and many Paiute now live in southern Nevada. Paiute boys and men were taken by the Spanish and sold as slaves to work in the mines of central Mexico. Thus disenfranchised, the Southern Paiute lost their land base, and by the 1800s, they had become laborers and craftsmen scattered among other Indian tribes. The San Juan Southern Paiute share a common heritage with the Southern Paiute of northern Arizona, Utah, Nevada, and California while maintaining their unique Native language. The San Juan Southern Paiute have a rich weaving tradition. The Yingup Weavers Association, a tribal organization, has been recognized for excellence by the National Endowment for the Arts.

The San Juan Southern Paiute Tribe was federally recognized in 1989 and is the newest federally recognized Indian nation in the state of Arizona. In the spring of 2000, the tribe signed a treaty agreement with the Navajo Nation, giving the San Juan Southern Paiute Tribe approximately 5,400 acres (22 square kilometers) of land. Most members live in two separate communities, one near Willow Springs and the other near Paiute Canyon and Navajo Mountain. They live within the Navajo Nation and on nine other reservations throughout Arizona, Utah, and Nevada; tribal headquarters are in Tuba City.

Info: Hidden Springs, AZ 93550 • 928.283.5537

MARICOPA
Ak-Chin Him-Dak Community Eco-Museum

At the northern edge of the Sonoran desert, 40 miles (64 kilometers) south of Phoenix, is the Ak-Chin Indian Community. The Ak-Chin Community is composed of Tohono O'odham and the Gila River people. Ak-Chin is an O'odham word translated to mean "mouth of the wash" or "place where the wash loses itself in the sand or ground." The term refers to a type of farming that relies on flood-wash water to grow seasonal food: rains following winter snows and summer rains. The tenets of an "eco-museum" as a place of integral relationships, organisms living in harmony with their past, present, and future environment, this was the first eco-museum recognized in the United States according to the first museum director and tribal member Charles Carlyle in 1992.

The museum hosts the community's annual Thanksgiving dinner, honoring tribal elders, the Him-Dak Anniversary Celebration, and Indian Recognition Day every September. The Ak-Chin tribal enterprises have grown extensively and include the Harrah's Ak-Chin Casino, which opened in 1994, the only tribal casino to have an international management partner; the Ak-Chin Indian Community Farms began in 1962, with cotton as the principal commerce crop in addition to barley, potatoes, alfalfa, and corn grown on 16,000 acres (65 square kilometers) cultivated by Ak-Chin Indian Community Farms; the Vekol Market, opened in 2012, includes a deli, a wide selection of groceries, culturally Indigenous foods, a café, and a patio with space for a farmer's market; they also opened UltraStar Multi-Tainment Center at Ak-Chin Circle, which features a state-of-the-art movie theater, arcade, bowling, and several dining options.

Info: 47685 N. Eco-Museum Rd., Maricopa, AZ 85239 • 520.568.135 • http://www.ak-chin.nsn.us

PAGE
Antelope Canyon

Antelope Canyon is named for the herds of pronghorn antelope who roamed it. It is within the Navajo Nation Reservation, and the Navajo who have lived nearby called it

An inside look at Upper Antelope Canyon.

LeChee, where cattle grazed in winter. Antelope Canyon is highly regarded by the Navajo as a special space akin to entering a cathedral. It is a slot canyon with an Upper and Lower slot, or a narrow-walled canyon formed by water over a million years and marked by layers of woven, sandstone walls of intense, multicolored layers a 1.5-mile (2.4 kilometers) long and 120 feet (37 meters) deep. All tourists visiting either slot canyon are required to do so with a Navajo authorized guide. The Navajo name for Upper Antelope Canyon is Tse' bighanilini, which means "the place where water runs through rocks."

Upper Antelope is at an elevation of about 40,000 feet (12,192 meters), and the canyon walls rise 120 feet above the stream bed. Located next to the LeChee Chapter House of the Navajo Nation is the Lake Powell Navajo Tribal Park Office, where tours are arranged and permits attained. Also in Page is Lake Powell, a man-made reservoir on the Colorado River and a major vacation area in the desert between Arizona and Utah.

Info: Antelope Canyon Lake Powell Navajo Tribal Park Office, Page, AZ 86040 • 928.698.2808 • http://navajonationparks.org/navajo-tribal-parks/lake-powell-navajo-tribal-park/

PARKER
Ahakhav Tribal Preserve

The Ahakhav Tribal Preserve Riparian Zone Restoration was established in 1995 by the Colorado River Indian Tribe and currently consists of 1,253 acres (5 square kilometers) of wilderness area and a 3.5-acre park. The riparian preserve area is the interface between land and a river or stream and the proper nomenclature for one of the fifteen terrestrial biomes of the earth. The Ahakhav Tribal Preserve comprises reconstructed Colorado River backwater, which offers a variety of activities including fishing, canoeing, birding, and swimming. The preserve also maintains a 4.6-mile (7.4 kilometer) fitness trail as well as playground and picnic facilities located in the park, both for recreational purposes and as a learning opportunity for the surrounding community and visitors. The preserve is a revegetation area for endangered and threatened plants and animals native to the Lower Colorado River Basin that had many invasive species. The Ahakhav Preserve is located near the Colorado Indian River Tribal Administration Complex in Parker, Arizona. It is also a bird-watching site with some 350 species of migratory and indigenous birds sighted live around the region or that visit on their annual migrations.

Info: 26600 Mohave Rd., Parker, AZ 85344 • 928.669.9211 • http://www.crit-nsn.gov/crit_contents/tourism/

Colorado River Indian Tribe Museum and River Tourism

The museum is located at the Tribal Government complex in Parker and seeks to provide a comprehensive history of the Colorado River Indian Tribes (CRIT) by providing an overview of CRIT with exhibits and information that date back to before the reservation was established. CRIT reservation lands include almost 270,000 acres (1,093 square kilometers) along both sides of the Colorado River between Parker, Arizona, and Blythe,

California. The largest portion of land is located in La Paz County, Arizona, and 42,696 acres (173 square kilometers) are in San Bernardino and Riverside counties, California.

The CRIT Reservation is home to four tribes. The original inhabitants were the Mohave and the Chemehuevi, who have farmed on the lower Colorado River since the beginning of recorded history. They were later joined by relocated Navajo and Hopi after World War II. Chemehuevi traditionally lived between the Mohave and Quechan, who lived farther to the south. Major traditional crops were corn, melons, pumpkins, Native beans, roots, and mesquite beans. The Colorado River peoples lived in scattered groups, in homes made of brush placed between upright mesquite logs or in houses made of mud and wood, and they traveled the river in reed rafts. Mohave peoples welcomed initial Spanish explorers and soon rejected their advances when they sought to control them.

The Colorado River is a major recreational scenic attraction at the reservation and in the surrounding region. Reservoir Lakes Moovalya and Havasu were formed behind Headgate and Parker dams and provide facilities for swimmers, boaters, and water skiers along 90 miles (145 kilometers) of shoreline. Other historic sites at or near the reservation include the tribally maintained Old Mohave Presbyterian Mission, located 18 miles (29 kilometers) south of Parker. The Poston Memorial Monument and Kiosk, dedicated to Japanese Americans who were incarcerated at Poston during World War II, is located in nearby Poston, Arizona. River fishing for trout, striped bass, catfish, crappie, and bluegill is excellent. Dove, quail, waterfowl, rabbit, and predator hunting are available. Reservation hunting, fishing, and camping permits are required. Lodging is available at the Blue Water Resort and Casino. A marina with a boat launch is available at the resort as well as sandy beaches for swimming. The Blue Water Family Fun Center features a miniature golf course, a video arcade, and the eighteen-hole Emerald Golf Course.

Info: 26600 Mohave Rd., Parker, AZ 85344 • 928.669.9211 • http://www.crit-nsn.gov/crit_contents/tourism/

PAYSON
Tonto Apache Reservation

The Tonto Apache Reservation is located on Highway 87 in central Arizona, 94 miles (151 kilometers) northeast of Phoenix and 94 miles (151 kilometers) southeast of Flagstaff, within the town limits of Payson, Arizona. The reservation was originally named Te-go-suk, or "place of the yellow water." The traditional lands of the Apache Ndeh, which translated means "people," extended from Texas through New Mexico and Arizona into Mexico and California. Over time, the many bands of Apache were forcibly relocated to reservations. The Rio Verde Reserve was established in 1871 for the Tonto and Yavapai Indians. In 1875, the Tonto and Yavapai were forcibly moved to the San Carlos Apache Reservation. Twenty years later, some of the Tonto Tribe returned to the Payson area.

The Tonto Apache Tribe was federally recognized by the Congressional Act of 1972. According to the 2010 decennial census, approximately 120 individuals live on Tonto Apache tribal land in Arizona. They operate the Mazatazal Casino and the Paysonglo Lodge in Payson. The reservation is at the Mogollon Rim and is near the Tonto National Forest and Tonto Natural Bridge and local sites of interest, such as Zane Grey's historic cabin and Strawberry Schoolhouse, the oldest standing schoolhouse in Arizona.

Info: Tonto Apache Reservation 30, Payson, AZ 85541 • 928.474.5000 • http://itcaonline.com/?page_id=1183

Tonto National Forest

Tonto National Forest is the fifth-largest forest in the United States, comprising 3 million acres (12,140 square kilometers) ranging from Saguaro cactus-studded desert to pine-forested mountains beneath the Mogollon Rim. The rim is a topographical and geological feature cutting across the U.S. state of Arizona. It extends approximately 200 miles (322 kilometers), starting in northern Yavapai County, extending east and ending near the New Mexico border. Tonto National Forest is referred to as an "urban" forest, given its approximate boundaries with Phoenix to the south, the Mogollon Rim to the north, and the San Carlos and Fort Apache Indian reservations to the east. Annual visitors to Tonto National Forest match the number of visitors to the Grand Canyon with recreational opportunities throughout the year, given its diversity for recreation.

Info: Payson, AZ 85547 • 928.476.4202 • https://azstateparks.com/tonto/

Tonto Natural Bridge State Park

The Tonto Natural Bridge is the world's largest travertine natural bridge, formed by a small stream flowing through a shady canyon in the wooded foothills of the Mogollon Rim. The bridge can be accessed for sightseeing along several short trails: Gowan Trail, a steep climb; Pine Creek Trail, a longer path with ample view of the bridge; and Waterfall Trail, a short path into the canyon above the bridge. The site became a state park in 1990 and is located 10 miles (16 kilometers) north of the City of Payson on Highway 87.

Info: Highway 87, Pine, AZ 85544-85547 • 928.476.4202 • https://azstateparks.com/tonto/

PEACH SPRINGS
Skywalk at Eagle Point

The Hualapai Tribe in Peach Springs, Arizona, is owner and operator of the Grand Canyon Resort. The Hualapai Reservation, established in 1883, is located on 1 million acres (4,047 square kilometers) of Hualapai ancestral lands within the southern portion of the Colorado Plateau and the Grand Wash Cliffs escarpment. Hualapai or Hwal'bay means "people of the tall pine." The modern northern boundary of the reservation is along the Grand Canyon and the Colorado River and is known as Hakataya, or "the backbone of the river." The ancestors of the Hualapai subsisted primarily through hunting wild game, collecting cactus fruit, gathering roots, seeds,

The Hualapai operate Skywalk, a horseshoe-shaped walkway that protrudes over the Grand Canyon and affords spectacular views.

and berries, and cultivating gardens. A common creation belief among the Pai peoples binds them spiritually to Spirit Mountain, or "Wikahme," along the Colorado River near Bullhead City, Arizona.

Hualapai tribal tourism is considerable and highly developed and is operated through Grand Canyon West Attractions, which offers visitors guided grounds tours, helicopter tours, smooth-water tours, a western town dude ranch, and the Skywalk.

In 2007, the Hualapai opened an extension over the Grand Canyon called the Skywalk at Eagle Point. It is a 10-foot (3-meter)-wide, horseshoe-shaped glass bridge constructed 70 feet (21 meters) beyond the rim of the canyon. The glass platform is 4,000 feet (1,219 meters) above the floor of the canyon below and is said to be strong enough to bear the weight of seventy 747 passenger jets. The Skywalk at Eagle Point, which was named after a natural rock formation that looks like an eagle, has other attractions, including a self-guided tour of a Native village that features local and regional tribal heritage including traditionally built housing, ovens, and sweat lodges. In addition to Native American dances that are performed in an amphitheater, the skywalk includes the Sa' Nyu Wa restaurant and a gift shop.

Info: Eagle Point Rd., Peach Springs, AZ 86434 • 888.868.WEST • http://www.hualapai-nsn.gov and https://www.grandcanyonwest.com/skywalk-eagle-point.htm

Whitewater Rafting on the Colorado River

The Hualapai Tribal Reservation's Hualapai River Runners offers guests a single-day raft trip through the Grand Canyon on the Colorado River. Getting to the site in Peach Springs is almost as exciting as the raft trip itself. The trek involves rough roads and a helicopter ride. In April, the tribe holds a memorial run for those who were force-marched to La Paz in southern Arizona. In May, Route 66 Days draw classic car buffs to Peach Springs. In June, tribal members hold the Sobriety Festival. In July, they celebrate an annual youth powwow. In August, they elect Miss Hualapai. Hualapai Indian Day is on the last Friday in September and is a cultural highlight of the year.

Info: 900 E. Hwy. 66, Peach Springs, AZ 86434 • 928.769.2216 • http://www.hualapai-nsn.gov and https://www.grandcanyonwest.com/

PHOENIX
Heard Museum

The Heard Museum is internationally known for its landmark exhibitions, cultural programs, and events reflecting the culture and artistic achievements of Native peoples, particularly in the Southwest. It has featured exhibits with themes addressing colonial oppression of Natives while also celebrating contemporary Native American art and artists.

The museum was founded in 1929 by *Arizona Republic* newspaper founders Dwight B. and Marie Bartlett Heard, who were avid collectors of "Southwestern Indian artifacts." The museum's collection of Indigenous art from throughout the western hemisphere traverses the presence of Native peoples from 300 C.E. to the present. Among the museum's forty thousand objects in its collection are multiple generations of fine art, weavings, pottery, basketry, sculpture, Katsina dolls, and traditional clothing. It is the largest private museum dedicated to the American Indian experience. The museum is built on an 8-acre (0.03-square-kilometer) campus and has an extensive li-

The "Intertribal Greeting" sculpture by Doug Hyde (Nez Perce) stands outside the internationally famous Heard Museum.

brary and archives with a prized database containing information on twenty-five thousand American Indian artists. The American Indian Veterans National Memorial, the only such monument in the United States, is located at the Heard Museum.

The museum attempts to engage visitors of all ages, especially families, with hands-on activities in its galleries and a focus on art making. The exhibits change throughout the year. They have guided tours throughout the day and special programs such as the Mercado de las Artes in the fall, the World Champion Hoop Dance Competition in February, and the Indian Fair and Market in March, and they began an honors program presenting the Spirit of the Heard Award to an individual who has demonstrated personal excellence either individually or as a community leader.

Info: 2301 N. Central Ave., Phoenix, AZ 85004 • 602.252.8840 • http://heard.org/

Pueblo Grande Museum

Within the city of Phoenix is a fifteen-hundred-year-old archaeological site of an ancestral Hohokam, or huhugam, village located just minutes from downtown, adjacent to Sky Harbor International Airport. It is a National Historic Landmark, and the city of Phoenix has recognized it since 1929. From May through September, the less-than-a-mile trail provides access to the village, featuring a partially excavated platform mound and a ball court similar to those found in ancient sites in Mexico. The museum constructed houses to replicate the ancestral style of architecture. The Pueblo Grande Museum has a main gallery displaying materials made by Hohokam with an interpretation of the history of the Pueblo Grande village site. A children's hands-on gallery and a gift shop features Southwest arts and crafts.

The museum hosts its annual Indian Market in December with performances by Native dancers and one hundred artist booths selling fine and contemporary art, including pottery, jewelry, rock art, and baskets as well as a variety of foods, including fry bread, Navajo tacos, cactus chili, and burgers in food trucks. An entrance fee is charged to attend the market. Of special interest are Ki:him activities and demonstrations sharing pottery, shell necklaces, Native food and seeds, printing, agave fiber weaving, breadwork, arrowhead knapping and atlatl, rock art, hoop dancing, storytelling, weaving, mask carving, gourd painting, piki bread making, and corn grinding.

Info: 4619 E. Washington St., Phoenix, AZ 85034 • 602.495.0901 • https://www.phoenix.gov/parks/arts-culture-history/pueblo-grande

POLACCA
Walpi

Walpi, a village built on the First Mesa in the homeland of the Hopi, has been continuously inhabited for more than eleven hundred years. Walpi was constructed above the valley at 300 feet (91 meters); the view from it offers panoramic vistas. Walpi is at the western edge of First Mesa and shares the mesa with two other villages, Sichomovi and Tewa (Hano), both established in the late 1600s.

Walpi, Hopi First Mesa.

Visitors to First Mesa villages are guided by walking tours provided by the knowledgeable staff of the First Mesa Consolidated Villages' Tourism Program established in 1987. The tour consists of a one-hour walk through the village of Walpi. Check in at the tourism office before going up to the village. The drive up the mesa ascends hundreds of feet quickly and is accessible by passenger vehicles only.

Walpi dates back to about 900 c.e. In 1540, the Spaniard Pedro de Tovar made contact with the Hopi in his search for the seven cities of gold. An estimated two thousand people occupied Walpi at this time. The Spanish began establishing missions in the Southwest seeking to convert the people. In 1680, the Puebloan peoples planned and successfully revolted against Spanish colonists. The Hopi drove the missionaries from their homelands, who returned twelve years later to New Mexico but not to the Hopi.

After the revolt of 1680, two other villages were established on First Mesas Sichomovi and Hano (Tewa). Sichomovi was built by people from Walpi, and Hano was originally a village of Hano people who moved away. Hano was resettled by Tewa from present-day New Mexico in the aftermath of the Pueblo Revolt of 1680. The village of Hano retains the Tewa language and many speak Hopi, but the Hopi do not speak Tewa. Walpi is matrilineal, and the homes are passed through the mother line. The old village of Walpi has no electricity or running water. The First Mesa is known for Hopi polychrome pottery and kachina doll carvings. Artists often sell their work outside their homes, and visitors may purchase directly from them.

Info: Next door to Polacca Post Office, 392 State Route 264, Polacca, AZ 86042 • 928.737.2670 • http://www.experiencehopi.com/walpi-village

ROOSEVELT
Tonto National Monument

Tonto National Monument showcases two Salado-style cliff dwellings. Ceramics or pottery, woven cotton, turquoise jewelry, baskets and cradleboards, bone awls, arrows, and other tools and implements were used by the ancestral peoples living in this region of the northern Sonoran Desert from 1250 to 1450 c.e. The monument museum has a permanent exhibit, and guided tours are offered to the Upper Cliff Dwelling from November through April every Friday, Saturday, Sunday, and Monday.

One of two cliff dwellings at Tonto National Monument.

Info: 26260 N. AZ Hwy. 188, Lot 2, Roosevelt, AZ 85545 • 928.467.2241 • https://www.nps.gov/tont/index.htm

SAN CARLOS
San Carlos Apache Culture Center

The history of Apache is significant in American and Southwest history for their physical resistance to westward settlement. In their language of Athabascan, their name, Ndeh, today constitutes a nation that includes San Carlos, Mescalero, White Mountain, Fort Sill Chiricahua, Chiricahua Nation, Jicarilla, Lipan, Yavapai, Yavapai Apache, and Tonto. All were relocated to the reservations from their traditional homelands extending from Texas through New Mexico and from Arizona into Mexico and California.

The San Carlos Apache Reservation was established on November 9, 1871, and was referred to as a "concentration camp." The San Carlos Apache have a population of over nine thousand from many different ancestral Apache bands of Aravaipa, Chiricahua, Coyotero, Mimbreno, Mogollon, Pinaleño, San Carlos, and Tonto. The culture center serves the San Carlos Apache Reservation, home to over fifteen thousand members of various bands of Apache. A special exhibit, "Window on Apache Culture," describes the Apache's spiritual beginnings and ceremonies, such as the Changing Woman Ceremony. Items for sale in the culture center gift shop include "burden baskets," cradle boards, both ornamental and full size, peridot gem jewelry, paintings, and books about Apache history. The San Carlos Apache celebrate their Independence Day on June 18. The annual All-Indian Rodeo and Fair is in November.

Info: Highway 70, at mile marker 272 on the north side, San Carlos, AZ 85550 • 928.475.2361 • http://www.sancarlosapache.com

San Carlos Apache Gold Casino

The San Carlos Apache Gold Casino employs approximately 450 tribal members and nonmembers from adjacent communities. Opened in November 1996 as a resort complex, it includes 5,000 square feet (1,524 meters) of convention space, an RV park with showers, a swimming pool, phones and satellite TV, a convenience store, two restaurants, and an eighteen-hole championship golf course, Apache Stronghold. Capitalizing on the land's natural beauty while preserving the people's cultural heritage is a hallmark of the facility, where fourteen archaeological sites have been meticulously protected. The Apache Gold Resort complex includes the Pavilion, a state-of-the-art, covered-roof, multipurpose arena where rodeos, car shows, horse shows, concerts, and powwows are held.

Info: 5 Highway 70, San Carlos, AZ 85550 • 928.475.2361 • http://www.sancarlosapache.com

SCOTTSDALE
Huhugam Ki Museum

"Huhugam Ki" is the House of the Ancestors in the Onk Akimel O'odham language that is used to describe the Osborn and Longmore building constructed over fifty years ago by members of the Salt River Indian Community. It was built with adobe to honor their ancestors Akimel O'odham, translated as "river people," and Xalychidom Piipaash, translated as "people who live toward the water." Their ancestral way was to live in harmony with the Salt River and the Sonoran Desert.

The small House of the Ancestors Museum has one exhibit gallery room with emphasis on perpetuating the knowledge and life of the Onk Akimel O'odham and the Xalychidom Piipaash. Guided tours must be scheduled in advance.

The Salt River Reservation was established in 1879. Today, over eight thousand people are members of the community, most of whom are Pima. The Salt River Pima–Maricopa Indian Community (SRPMIC) owns and operates Casino Arizona. Throughout much of the twentieth century, Pima and Maricopa residents of the reservation have continued to farm, relying on irrigation techniques developed over centuries of experience in a desert environment. To assist in the preservation of the O'odham (Pima) and Piipaash (Maricopa) languages, the community initiated the O'odham–Piipaash Language Program and has extensive recordings collected from the elders for use by future generations.

Visitors may also attend many of the tribe's annual events, which include the New Year's Eve Chicken Scratch Dance, the New Year's Basketball Invitational, A'al Tash Rodeo Days, the Valentine Classic Basketball Tournament, the Fall Carnival, the

Red Mountain Eagle Powwow in November, and the Junior Miss and Miss Salt River pageants in March. In addition, the Salt River Pima–Maricopa Indian Community operates several resort properties located on reservation land east of Phoenix in south-central Arizona, adjacent to the cities of Scottsdale, Tempe, Mesa, and Fountain Hills, and it shares a border with the Fort McDowell Indian Nation.

Info: 10005 E. Osborn Rd., Scottsdale, AZ 85256 • 480.850.8000 • http://www.srpmic-nsn.gov/government/culturalresources/hhkm.asp

SECOND MESA
Hopi Cultural Center

The Hopi Tribe is a sovereign nation located in northeastern Arizona approximately 65 miles (105 kilometers) north of Interstate 40, bounded on all sides by the Navajo Indian Reservation. The Hopi Tribe headquarters are located in Kykotsmovi. The reservation occupies part of Coconino and Navajo counties, encompasses more than 1.5 million acres (6,070 square kilometers), and is made up of twelve villages on three mesas.

The Hopi villages are located at First Mesa, Second Mesa, or Third Mesa, situated on or below rocky promontories extending southwest from Black Mesa. They overlook five drainages, or washes: Jeddito, Polacca, Oraibi, Dinnebito, and Moenkopi. The villages of Hanoki (Hano or Tewa), Sitsomovi (Sichomovi), and Waalpi (Walpi) sit atop First Mesa, about 11 miles (18 kilometers) west of Keams Canyon, and the community of Polacca sits below. Second Mesa is home to three villages: Musungnuvi (Mishong-novi), Supawlavi (Shipaulovi), and Songoopavi (Shongopovi). The population on Third Mesa is centered in the communities of Orayvi (Oraibi), Kiqotsmovi (Kykotsmovi), Hoatvela (Hotevilla), and Paaqavi (Bacavi). Munqapi (Moencopi) is also considered a Third Mesa village. Every village is separate and autonomous.

The Hopi maintain their ancestral ties to ceremonial practices associated with growing their crops and following their original teachings. Hopi art is highly evolved and specific to each mesa and is renowned for its symbolism and specific design details and crafting borne from the desert landscape.

The Hopi Cultural Center is located on the Second Mesa and can be a starting point for visitors. It has a lodge and restaurant and information about tours. The cultural center on Second Mesa and the Hopi Silvercraft Cooperative Guild feature Hopi arts, and other galleries at Hopi are Honani Gallery, Dawa's, and Monongya Gallery.

Info: AZ-264, Second Mesa, AZ 86043 • 928.734.2401 • http://www.hopiculturalcenter.com/#intro

SELLS
Tohono Nation Cultural Center and Museum

The Tohono Nation began their cultural center and museum as a place that is working to instill pride by creating a permanent tribal institution to protect and preserve O'odham "jewe c himdag." The building has a main permanent and professionally installed exhibit about Tohono O'odham experiences and other interpretive exhibits, including a story about Tohono O'odham who have served in the U.S. military. Along a glass hallway that faces Baboquivari Mountain is exhibit space as well. Meeting and presentation rooms and a research library are in the building, and a large viewing area looks into the restoration laboratory. Visitors describe the museum as a beautifully situated, "out-of-the-way" place that is quite a hard place to find, with virtually no signage on the main roads.

Info: 85639 Baboquiuari Mt. Rd., Sells, AZ 85634 • 520.383.0200 • http://www.tonation-nsn.gov/

Tohono O'odham Annual Rodeo and Fair

Southern Arizona's longest-running All-Indian Rodeo and Fair Celebration is held in early February at the Eugene P. Tashquinth Sr. Livestock Complex, located three miles (five kilometers) west of Sells, Arizona, along State Route 86. In addition to the powwow, arts and crafts, a Rodeo Queen contest, exhibits, vendors, a waila contest (similar to couples' polka dancing with Mexican musical influence), and a young women's toka (stickball) contest are part of the powwow events.

The Tohono O'odham Nation is comparable in size to the state of Connecticut. Its four noncontiguous segments total more than 2.8 million acres (11,331 square kilometers). Within its land, the nation has established an industrial park that is located near Tucson. Tenants of the industrial park include Caterpillar, the maker of heavy equipment; the Desert Diamond Casino, an enterprise of the nation; and a 23-acre (93,077-square-meter) foreign trade zone. The lands of the nation are located within the Sonoran Desert in south-central Arizona.

The largest community, Sells, functions as the nation's capital. The San Xavier district is known for the San Xavier Mission Del Bac, the White Dove of the Desert. The nation operates the Desert Diamond Casino, located at 7350 S. Old Nogales Highway in Tucson, Arizona.

Info: State Route 86, Sells, AZ 85634 • 520.383.2028 • http://www.tonation-nsn.gov/

SOMERTON
Cocopah Museum and Cultural Center

The Cocopah Museum and Cultural Center is tribally owned and was opened in October 1996. The Cocopah Museum is a recognized federal repository, and its exhibits feature objects and depictions of Cocopah history and culture. One exhibit shows traditional clothing, such as bark skirts and leather sandals, as well as modern beadwork, pottery, traditional tattoo designs, musical instruments, and a Cocopah warriors' display. The museum, which resides on the West Cocopah Reservation, is surrounded by a 1.5-acre (6,070-square-meter) park spotted with luxurious Sonoran trees and plants with a replica of a traditional Cocopah dwelling and Ramada.

The community's traditional tribal dance grounds are used for tribal social events like dances, hand games, annual festivities, and special tribal events, such as the Annual Miss Cocopah Pageant held in February. In April, the people celebrate Land Acquisition Day. A Veterans Day parade and powwow and a community Thanksgiving dinner occur every November. Scenic train excursions from Yuma to the West Cocopah Reservation are provided in cooperation with the Yuma Valley Live Steamers. An early 1800s Cocopah Indian Village has been re-created; Cocopah craftsmen create authentic Cocopah jewelry, and authentic fry bread is made available to guests.

The Cocopah Reservation, established in 1917, is located in southwestern Arizona near the town of Somerton. Three parcels are known as East Cocopah, West Cocopah, and North Cocopah, all lying completely within Yuma County. Tribal administration is located in Somerton in the West Cocopah parcel. The Cocopah Indians are one of the Yuman tribes with a language belonging to the Hokan family, which is spoken by peoples from southern Oregon going south into Mexico. Around 1760, the Yuma, Maricopa, and Cocopah Indians formed one tribe, known as the Coco–Maricopa Tribe, living around the Gulf of California, near the mouth of the Colorado River. They later migrated northward and settled along the Colorado River. The Yuma were traditionally expert farmers of the flatlands of the Colorado River.

Info: 14533 S. Veterans Dr., Somerton, AZ 85350 • 928.627.1992 • https://www.cocopah.com/museum.html

SUPAI
Havasu Falls

For over one thousand years, the village of Supai has been below the rim of the Grand Canyon and is home to the Havasu Baaja, "people of the blue-green waters," who today are the Havasupai Tribe. The limestone aquifer the color of blue-green water has been used to cultivate corn, squash, and beans deep in the Grand Canyon for centuries. The Havasupai Reservation was established in 1880 with an expanded land base in 1975. The isolated location creates both awe and obstacles that pose challenges for the 465 members of the tribe, who allow visitors to Havasu Falls, Mooney Falls, and Beaver Falls. The U.S. Postal Service office in Supai transports all mail in and out of the canyon by mule train. The trail to the bottom of the canyon is 8.7 miles (15 kilometers) long and may be hiked or traveled with the aid of rented horses and mules.

The famous blue-green water draws thousands to remote places in the canyon, where four waterfalls can be seen. Navajo Falls, located 1.5 miles (2.4 kilometers) from the village, is named for a Supai chief. The 100-foot (30.5-meter) Havasu Falls is another half mile downriver. Mooney Falls, the highest, most dramatic waterfall, spills over 200 feet (61-meter) to the canyon floor. Beaver Falls, the farthest away from the village, is the least known; strenuous hiking is required to visit the falls. Visitors can also explore several caves.

Havasu Falls.

Reservations are required before entering the Havasupai Reservation. Visitors can hike down to the lodge and tourist office, then two more miles (three kilometers) to the campground. Camping and a visit to the falls by pack mule down the canyon require payment in advance of a visit. A lodge handles limited sleeping accommodations. Horseback travel is a separate cost. Havasupai Tribal Arts and their tourist enterprise employ tribal members. Although visitation is limited to prevent overcrowding and damage to the delicate canyon ecosystem, more than thirty thousand tourists visit the reservation annually to hike or ride horseback and stay at the Havasupai Lodge or the tribe's simple campgrounds.

In January, the Havasupai celebrate Land Day. A Peach Festival is held the second weekend of August annually, and it includes a rodeo, traditional dancing, and pageantry. Every autumn, the tribe celebrates the Grandmother Canyon Gathering. Reggae music is popular here, and after Bob Marley's death, his band members performed for the Havasupai by their falls.

Info: Havasupai Tribe, P.O. Box 10, Supai, AZ 86435 • 928.448.2731 • http://theofficialhavasupaitribe.com/

TSAILE
Diné College and Ned A. Hatathli Center Museum

Diné College was established in 1968 as the first tribally controlled community college in the United States. In creating an institution of higher education using Navajo architectural design and philosophy of Hozho, which translates to "beauty way," the Navajo Nation sought to serve Navajo people to become educated, contributing members of the Navajo Nation and the world. An eight-member Board of Regents works to carry out the mission that is "rooted in Diné language and culture to advance quality post-secondary student learning and development to ensure the well-being of the Diné people."

As a postsecondary educational institution, Diné College awards associate degrees and certificates in areas important to the economic and social development of the Navajo Nation. Satellite campuses are in Chinle, Arizona; Crownpoint, New Mexico; Shiprock, New Mexico; Tuba City, Arizona; and Window Rock, Arizona, with the main campus in Tsaile, Arizona.

The Ned A. Hatathli Center Museum is located on the campus of Diné College in Tsaile. Most of the collection of almost three thousand Native American arts and artifacts is housed among the museum and various buildings of the Diné College campus. Among the displays are pottery, paintings, weaving, photographs, and documents relating to the rich culture of the Navajo Tribe. The museum hosts a variety of classes in traditional Navajo arts as well as festivals and art shows. The museum has no admission fee, and visitors may find it helpful to call ahead for current hours. A children's interactive section is also one of the new features of the museum. The section will be designated to entertain school-aged children about topics pertaining to the Navajo culture. Navajo artists are a regular feature and invited to present their work. The Navajo phrase "Celebrating Nitsáhákees, Nahat'á, Iiná, Siihasin: From Traditional Aesthetics to Contemporary Navajo Art" is the name of the program.

Info: Ned Hatathli Center, Diné College, 1 Circle Dr., Tsaile, AZ 86556 • 928.724.6653 • http://www.dinecollege.edu/

TUBA CITY
Navajo Interactive Museum

Located in Tuba City, the Explore Navajo Interactive Museum was designed to replicate the four quadrants of Navajo direction represented by four sacred mountains revered by the Navajo that demarcate Navajo homeland. They are Blanca Peak in Colorado to the east, Mount Taylor in New Mexico to the south, San Francisco Peak in Arizona to the west, and Hesperus Peak in Colorado to the north. Visitors walk clockwise through the space, entering at the east, and move to the south, west, and north, where information is given about the land, language, history, culture, and ceremonial life. At over 7,000 square feet (2 square kilometers), the museum also has a traditional Navajo hogan (home), with interpreters who share Navajo culture, traditions, family systems, and more.

Info: 10 Main St., Tuba City, AZ 86045 • 623.412.0297 • http://www.explorenavajo.com/go2/navajo_museum.cfm

TUCSON
San Xavier Mission Del Bac

San Xavier Mission was founded as a Catholic mission by Father Eusebio Kino in 1692 after first visiting the O'odham village of Wa:k. Construction of the current church began in 1783 and was completed in 1797. It is the oldest continuously used European structure in Arizona; the church retains original statuary and mural paintings. The mission continues its original purpose of ministering to the religious needs of its parishioners. Mission San Xavier, which receives two hundred thousand visitors annually from all over the world, has no admission fee.

San Xavier Mission.

The mission was created to serve the needs of the local community here, the village of Wa:k (San Xavier District) on the Tohono O'odham Reservation. It is the policy of the mission staff to only do marriages, baptisms, etc., for the local community. In 1963, San Xavier became a National Historic Landmark.

Info: 1950 San Xavier Rd., Tucson, AZ 85746 • 520.294.2614 • http://www.sanxaviermission.org/

Yaqui Easter Ceremonies

The Pascua Yaqui Reservation, Lios Enchim Aniavu, in southern Arizona is 15 miles (24 kilometers) southwest of Tucson. The traditional territory of the Yaqui people was along the Yaqui River in southern Sonora, Mexico. By 552 c.e., the Yaqui were living in small family clusters along the Yaqui River (Yoem Vatwe), north of the Gila River, where they practiced a hunting and gathering subsistence lifestyle. They also cultivated corn, beans, and squash on small, family plots. The people were traders, traveling widely throughout what is now the south-central United States and northern Mexico, exchanging foods, furs, shells, salt, and other goods with the Shoshone, the Comanche, the Puebloan, the Pima, the Aztec, and the Toltec.

In 1533, when a Spanish military expedition passed through their area, resistance to the Spanish aggression was immediate. Between 1608 and 1610, the Spanish repeatedly attacked. The Yaqui withstood the attacks, and eventually, Jesuit priests came to build missions, which led to the development of eight sacred towns, or "pueblos," around the mission churches. A treaty was signed in 1897 at Ortiz, Sonora, Mexico, between the Yaqui and the Mexican government.

The Old Pascua Village was established in 1903 as Yaqui moved there to escape the violence of the 1910–1920 Mexican Revolution. By 1920, probably more than two thousand Yaqui were in Arizona, but they were often seen as Mexican. Pascua Yaqui are full U.S. citizens, who until recent times have had access to Mexico to visit relatives. The autonomous Yaqui villages in Arizona became larger, and by 1952, they were surrounded by urban communities. In 1964, with the aid of Congressman Morris K. Udall, the Pascua Yaqui received 202 acres (0.8 square kilometers) of desert land to call their own. At first, the State of Arizona was largely uncooperative; officials maintained that these poverty-stricken people should be shipped back to Mexico. The Pascua Yaqui Indian Reservation finally secured federal tribal recognition on September 18, 1978.

Tribal Recognition Day is celebrated annually on September 18. In November 1999, the tribe celebrated the first Harvest Festival just before Thanksgiving, a now annual event in which students and townspeople display and sell handmade arts and crafts items. The event features live entertainment and is open to the public. The Pascua Yaqui operate a radio station, KPYT-LPFM, that began broadcasting in 2005 with thirty volunteers producing and hosting their programs and public service announcements. Easter Ceremonies of the Pascua Yaqui Tribe at Lent welcome visitors who come in a spirit of reverence appropriate for any religious ceremony. Lent is called Hiaki and is held in sacred esteem. Lenten Easter ceremonies are held in New Pascua in South Tucson and in Old Pascua in the Guadalupe Phoenix area. They began around the time of the founding of the now famous San Xavier Mission del Bac.

Info: 7474 S. Camino de Oeste, Tucson, AZ 85746 • 520.883.5000 • http://www.pascuayaqui-nsn.gov

WHITERIVER
Fort Apache Historic Park

The remains of the historic Old Fort Apache, now listed on the National Register of Historic Places, is owned by the White Mountain Apache Tribe. Old Fort Apache is recognized for its association with Geronimo and Cochise, famous leaders from the various Apache bands who were pursued by soldiers from Fort Apache. Located at the foot of the White Mountains, the old site now serves as the focal point for the protection, celebration, and revitalization of the tribe's culture and history. From 1871 until Geronimo's capture in 1886, the fort was a key military base. Later, the fort guarded the White Mountain Agency, while Fort Thomas watched over the San Carlos Agency. Apache grew restless at being hounded by soldiers and faced greater encroachment by settlers and miners, so many left the reservations and resumed traditional hunting, gathering, and raiding, which led to public outcry. After recruiting the scouts, General George Crook organized a Tonto Basin campaign and moved on to Camp Verde.

During the winter of 1872–1873, a number of mobile detachments, using Apache scouts, moved across the Tonto Basin to pursue the Apache and Yavapai. Fort Apache continued as an active post until 1924. The Apache scouts who had been employed by General Crook were transferred to Fort Huachuca in southern Arizona, where they continued to serve. The last three Apache scouts retired in 1947.

When the fort closed, its buildings were turned over to the Bureau of Indian Affairs. Twenty-seven historic buildings make up the core of the 288-acre (1.2-square-kilometer) National Register Historic District. Maps are available at Nohwike' Bágowa and at the White Mountain Apache Cultural Center and Museum, so visitors can explore the district at their own pace. Interpretive signs located throughout the district explain the construction and use of the historic buildings and spaces and allow visitors to immerse themselves in the history of what many consider the best surviving example of an Apache War-era military post. The Fort Apache Cemetery is located 0.25 mile (0.4 kilometers) east of the main fort grounds and is accessible by walking trail or road.

Info: 201 Walnut St., Whiteriver, AZ 85941 • 928.338.4525 • http://www.wmat.nsn.us/wmahistory.shtml

White Mountain Apache Cultural Center Museum, Kinishba Ruins

Within the Fort Apache Historic Park is the White Mountain Apache Cultural Center Museum called Nohwike' Bágowa, House of Our Footprints. The museum exhibits an Apache gowa home at its center, with a multimedia presentation about the ancestors of the Apache through the present time. The cultural center and museum also house an archival collection of manuscripts, photos, arts, music recordings, and other items of cultural and family significance. Ruins are open daily and are included in the admission to Fort Apache Park.

The Kinishba Ruins are a village site originally occupied by Puebloan ancestral peoples around 1400 C.E. by the Hopi and Zuni. The site was excavated in 1930, and recent efforts have been sought to reinforce the old structures. The White Mountain Apache, considered the easternmost group of the western Apache peoples, traditionally lived in an area bounded by the Pinaleño Mountains to the south and the White Mountains to the north. At the time of the Anglo–American occupation of Arizona, the White Mountain Apache represented the largest division of the Western Apache people, with an estimated fourteen hundred to fifteen hundred people. The introduction of the horse greatly increased the range of the Western Apache, allowing them to establish an intricate network of trade and raiding routes. This lifestyle continued, except for a brief time during the Spanish colonial period, until their forced relocation to reservations.

Info: 201 Walnut St., Whiteriver, AZ 85941 • 928.338.4625 • http://wmat.us/fortapachepark.htm

White Mountain Apache Wildlife Activities

The White Mountain Apache Tribe Wildlife and Outdoor Division activities include a hunting program, a rent-by-the-lake program, river running, and canyoneering. Fishing, hunting, backcountry safaris and tours, and other outdoor adventures are a huge draw for visitors. The Hawley Lake Cabins and Resort is available in McNary, Arizona, within walking distance of Hawley Lake and Earl Park Lake. The Sunrise Park Ski Resort, the largest in Arizona, offers downhill skiing with sixty-five runs for skiers at all levels of proficiency, a separate snowboarding area, and cross-country ski trails. Whitewater rafting, canoeing, and kayaking are all possible on the Salt River, which originates on reservation lands. Guided tours are offered between February and June. The Hon-Dah RV Park, next to the casino, has 198 campsites, a recreation room, a covered picnic pavilion, handicap-accessible restrooms and showers, and full utility hookups. The tribe also operates the Hon-Dah Casino, located at 777 Hwy. 260, Pinetop, AZ 85935.

Info: White Mountain Apache Tribe Office of Tourism, 201 Walnut St., Whiteriver, AZ 85941 • 928.338.1230 • http://wmatoutdoor.org/wp_view.html?pageid=7

WINDOW ROCK
Navajo Nation Museum

The Navajo Nation Museum, located in the capital of the Navajo Nation in Window Rock, Arizona, has an extensive repository of art, ethnographic, archaeological, and archival materials. The archives collection includes over forty thousand photographs as well as a wide variety of documents, recordings, motion picture films, and videos. The archives are accessible to authors, researchers, and publishers as a source for historical photographs. Most of the collections are available for on-site study and exhibit loan.

The museum maintains an active and professional exhibition program, most of which is produced in-house. In its new venue, most exhibitions have tended to highlight the work of Navajo artists in various media, including weavings. These art-oriented exhibitions are interspersed with historical and cultural exhibits.

The Navajo Nation extends into the states of Utah, Arizona, and New Mexico and is 27,000 square miles (70,000 square kilometers) in size. Called Diné Bikéyah, or Navajoland, the reservation is larger than ten of the fifty states in the United States. Following a military captivity known as the Long Walk, in which Navajo head-

Navajo Nation Museum.

men agreed to a treaty in 1868 that allowed for resettlement in their homeland, some Navajo escaped capture and remained.

In 1923, a tribal government was established and has evolved into the largest form of American Indian government. The Navajo Nation Council Chambers hosts eighty-eight council delegates representing 110 Navajo Nation chapters. A reorganization occurred in 1991 to form executive, legislative, and judicial government branches. While the council is in session, delegates carry on the tradition of speaking in Navajo, providing a perfect example of how the Navajo Nation retains its valuable cultural heritage while forging ahead with modern progress. When the council is not in session, legislative work is done by twelve standing committees of the council. Inside the circular Council Chambers, the walls are adorned with murals that depict the history of the Navajo people and the Navajo way of life.

Info: Highway 264 and Post Office Loop, Window Rock, AZ 86515 • 928.871.7941 • https://www.navajonationmuseum.org/

YUMA
Fort Yuma Quechan Tribe Museum

Quechan, pronounced Kwatsáan, peoples residing at the Fort Yuma–Quechan Reservation is along both sides of the Colorado River near Yuma, Arizona. The reservation borders the states of Arizona, California, and Baja California, Mexico. Encompassing 45,000 acres (182 square kilometers), the reservation is bisected on the south by Interstate 8. Their language is Hokan, and they have occupied the lands on the banks of the Colorado River since recorded time. The Quechan took advantage of the Colorado River's annual flooding in their farming practices, raising maize, wheat, beans, cantaloupes, watermelons, calabashes, and some cotton and tobacco. Wild seeds, fish, and game supplemented the Quechan's farm produce.

The Quechan people traveled great distances to visit other people, to trade, and to carry on warfare. They ranged as far as Sonora, Needles, and the Pacific Coast in their travels. Friendly relations existed between the Quechan Nation and the Spanish Empire until the 1780s. In late 1780, the Spanish selected Conception, what is now Fort Yuma, as a site for one of two settlements. By 1781, when the pueblo was beginning to take form, Quechan-settler relations began to deteriorate due in great part to the loss and destruction of land and crops.

The Fort Yuma-Quechan Tribe Reservation was established in 1884, and the northwestern portion of the reservation was restored in 1981. The Fort Yuma Quechan Tribe Museum is housed in a small, pink adobe. The Fort Yuma Quechan Museum displays artifacts and photos of the tribe. It is an interesting stop to learn more about the culture of the area. Visitors can purchase handmade crafts at the gift shop. The tribe is an agricultural community and leases land to Indian and non-Indian farmers. The tribe also operates the Paradise Casino and celebrates Annual Indian Days in October, featuring traditional bird singing and dancing.

Info: 350 Picacho Rd., Yuma, AZ 85365 • 760.572.0213 • https://www.quechantribe.com/

COLORADO

Colorado is home to 107,832 American Indian/Alaska Native people, and it contains two Native nations.

BOULDER
Native American Rights Fund Library

The National Indian Law Library (NILL) is a law library established in 1972 that is devoted to American Indian law. It serves both the Native American Rights Fund (NARF) and the public by developing and making accessible a unique and valuable collection of Indian law resources and by providing direct research assistance and delivery of information. NARF has three pillars of service to the public: to provide research assistance and delivery information relating to specific Indian law questions; to provide Indian law updates via the Indian Law Bulletins; and to provide access to tribal law via the Tribal Law Gateway.

The Native American Rights Fund was founded 1970 in Berkeley, California, and incorporated in 1973 in Washington and Alaska. The original NARF Board of Directors developed five priorities that continue into the present: preservation of tribal existence; protection of tribal natural resources; promotion of Native American human rights; accountability of governments to Native Americans; and development of Indian law and educating the public about Indian rights, laws, and issues.

Info: 1522 Broadway, Boulder, CO 80302 • 303.447.8760 • https://www.narf.org/nill/

CHIMNEY ROCK
Chimney Rock National Monument

This remote, archaeological site located at the southern edge of the San Juan Mountains in Southwestern Colorado dates back one thousand years. It is identified as Ancestral Puebloan and linked to Chaco Canyon in present-day New Mexico. Chimney Rock is 7 square miles (18 square kilometers) and contains two hundred ancient structures, some of which have been excavated for viewing and exploration, that includes a Great Kiva, a pithouse, and contiguous living quarters. Chimney Rock is the highest in elevation of all the Chacoan sites, 7,000 feet (2,134 meters) above sea level. The hike to the top is 0.5 mile (805 meters) with 360-degree views. Guided and audio-guided tours are available from May 15 to September 30.

Info: 3179 CO Hwy. 151, Pagosa Springs, CO 81147 • 970.883.5359 • http://www.chimneyrockco.org/

CHIVINGTON
Sand Creek Massacre National Historic Site

The National Park Service, which oversees Sand Creek Massacre National Historic Site, writes the following description: "On November 29, 1864, 675 Colorado volunteer

The Great Kiva at Chimney Rock in Colorado.

soldiers attacked an encampment of approximately 750 people. During the attack, Indians took shelter in the high banks along Sand Creek. As they fled, many were killed and wounded by artillery fire. Well over half of the 230 dead were women and children. Survivors of the attack fled to the north, hoping to reach a larger band of Cheyenne. The massacre profoundly influenced U.S.–Indian relations and the structure of the Cheyenne and Arapaho tribes. Sand Creek Massacre National Historic Site was established in 2007 to preserve and protect the cultural landscape of the massacre, enhance public understanding, and minimize similar incidents in the future." The site is an unofficial nature preserve, and the National Park Service offers ranger programs, talks, and tours.

Info: 910 Wansted, P.O. Box 249, Eads, CO 81036-0249 • 719.438.5916 • https://www.nps.gov/sand/index.htm

CORTEZ
Crow Canyon Archaeological Center

Crow Canyon Archaeological Center is for visitors, especially youth, who really want to learn from the human experience of Ancestral Puebloan cultures who lived in this region over one thousand years ago and left traces of how they lived with each other as family groups and on the land. Unlike the National Park experience, Crow Canyon provides visitors with a personal approach by sharing information and ethical practices of conservation work at monuments and spaces deemed sacred by Native peoples today. The center has a highly trained staff that provides tours and summer programs for different ages, giving guests to this private canyon a way to become familiar with the unfamiliar ways of very old cultures.

Info: 23390 Road K, Cortez, CO 81321 • 800.422.8975 •
http://www.crowcanyon.org/

Hovenweep National Monument

The abandoned villages of Hovenweep were named by photographer William Henry, who adopted the name Hovenweep, meaning "deserted valley" to the Paiute and Ute. Hovenweep National Monument is located in a remote section of the Colorado Plateau, spanning the border of Colorado and Utah. Established in 1923, six Ancestral Puebloan-era villages were built between 1200 and 1300 C.E. Stone brick architecture of square towers, circular towers, kiva spaces, and D-shaped dwellings suggest thoughtful uses of such designs and shapes. The 784-acre (3-square-kilometer) park has 1 mile (1,609-meter) and 0.5 mile (805-kilometer) trail loops around the rim, where visitors may view the sites. Hovenweep Castle is a group of rock towers in Little Ruins Canyon. Desert plants use different strategies to conserve moisture, and wildflowers find moisture niches in which to grow.

Info: McElmo Route, Cortez, CO 81321 • 970.562.4282, x.10 •
https://www.nps.gov/hove/planyourvisit/maps.htm

DENVER
Colorado Indian Market and Southwest Showcase

Every January brings the fun and festive Colorado Indian Market and Southwest Showcase to Denver, featuring three magical days of art, craft, song, dance, and culture. With more than three hundred artists presenting their work, dozens of performers, and dazzling costumes at every turn, the Indian market is a great way to get acquainted with Native American traditions.

Info: 451 E. 58th Ave., Denver, CO 80216 • 303.292.6278 • http://denvermart.com/

Cajon Pueblo, Hovenweep National Monument.

Denver Art Museum

The Denver Art Museum's newly remodeled American Indian art galleries opened on January 30, 2011, with a new focus on artists, their creations, and their inspirations. The American Indian art collection includes more than eighteen thousand art objects representing the heritage of all cultures and tribes across the United States and Canada. Recognized as one of the best of its kind in the United States, the collection spans more than two thousand years of artistic creativity from ancient times to the present.

The collection includes diverse, artistic traditions such as Puebloan ceramics, Navajo textiles, Northwest Coast sculpture, basketry, Plains beadwork, and oil paintings, representing the full range of American Indian art styles. Over the past eighty years, these artworks have been featured both nationally and internationally in scholarly publications, innovative exhibitions, and educational programs. Keep an eye on the museum's events calendar: the Native Arts Department invites Native American artists to exhibit and lecture and sponsors an annual Friendship Powwow in September.

Info: 100 W. 14th Ave. Pkwy., Denver, CO 80204 • 720.865.5000 • http://denverartmuseum.org/

Denver March Powwow

Since 1984, the heritage of American Indians has been celebrated in Denver every March at the Denver March Powwow, one of the largest events of its kind in the country. More than sixteen hundred dancers representing over one hundred tribes

Edgar Heap of Birds' (Cheyenne/Arapaho) steel, porcelain, and stone sculpture, *Wheel,* is on display at the Denver Art Museum, which is famous for its American Indian art collection.

from thirty-eight states and Canadian provinces participate in this three-day event with singing, contest dancing, storytelling, food, and art. Also, more than 170 booths sell a variety of Native American art, Native American fry bread, and Indian tacos. Admission is charged daily at the door, free to six years and under. The pow-wow is at the Denver Coliseum.

Info: Denver Coliseum, 600 Humboldt St., Denver, CO 80216 • 303.934.8045 • http://www.denvermarchpowwow.org/

Indigenous Film and Arts Festival

The International Institute for Indigenous Resource Management (IIIRM) is a law and policy research institute. Although it may seem strange that such an organization would hold a film festival, IIIRM maintains that "film, especially good film, and especially film written, made, and directed by Indigenous peoples, is perhaps the most expressive medium we have for communicating messages about who we were; who we are; and who we are striving to become." The festival provides a forum for the world to see an Indigenous view of the universe plus educate the public on issues affecting Indigenous peoples and their lands and how to resolve contemporary problems.

Info: 444 S. Emerson St., Denver, CO 80209-2216 • 303.744.9686 • http://www.iiirm.org/events/film%20festivals/film_festivals.htm

Tocabe: An American Indian Eatery

Owned and operated by the Jacobs family (Osage), Tocabe is the only American Indian-owned and -operated restaurant in Denver. The menu features Native-inspired foods with a unique twist. Some highlights of Tocabe's affordable menu are bison ribs, Osage hominy, wild rice, and posu bowls.

The restaurant partners with Native and Indigenous producers as well as local vendors who share their food values. Another location is in Greenwood Village.

Info: 3536 W. 44th Ave., Denver, CO 80211 • 720.524.8449 • http://tocabe.com/

DOLORES
Anasazi Heritage Center

The Anasazi Heritage Center is Southwest Colorado's premier archaeological museum, operated by the Bureau of Land Management, which opened in 1988 and continues to interpret the cultures of the Four Corners Southwest region. The center shows films and provides hands-on exhibits that use archaeology to provide background regarding not only the ancestral cultures but also the local history of Puebloan, Ute, and Navajo lifeways. A paved trail provides access to the Escalante and Dominguez Ruins. The Anasazi Heritage Center has over two million artifacts and is 17 miles (27 kilometers) from Mesa Verde National Park.

Info: 27501 Highway 184, Dolores, CO 81323 • 970.882.5600 • https://www.blm.gov/learn/interpretive-centers/anasazi-heritage-center

IGNACIO
Southern Ute Museum

The Southern Ute Museum, operated by the Southern Ute Indian Tribe, says it "is a new building reflecting an old history." The museum is constructed of timber, steel, and glass with a symbolic medicine wheel–designed ceiling with logs forming a circular pattern. The word medicine implies healing, and the symbolic wheel is all-encompassing for the Southern Ute Tribe because it has a unique relationship with the ecosystem of southern Colorado.

After inhabiting and traveling between the mountains and vast areas of Colorado, Utah, Wyoming, eastern Nevada, northern New Mexico, and Arizona, the Southern Ute were forced into a peace agreement in 1849 that was not fully enacted by the United States. The people eventually settled on their reservation in 1873 on a land base that was significantly reduced.

The Ute established routes of travel such as Ute Trail in the Grand Mesa Forest, which was the forerunner of the scenic highway traversing through South Park and Cascade in Colorado. Lake Capote, now reconstructed under the U.S. Department of the Interior's Safety of Dams Program, is a tribal endeavor. The lake has been stocked by the tribe and was recently opened to the general public for trout fishing for a fee. Seven rivers run through the reservation: San Juan, Piedra, Florida, La Plata, Navajo, Animas, and Los Pinos. Three of the rivers, Los Pinos, Piedra, and Animas, are regularly stocked with cutthroat and rainbow trout.

Info: 503 Ouray Dr., Ignacio, CO 81137 • 970.563.9583 • https://www.southernute-nsn.gov/southern-ute-museum/

MESA VERDE
Mesa Verde National Park

Tessie Naranjo from Santa Clara Pueblo says, "The American Southwest is the center of Ancestral Puebloan culture, ancient people have left their traces throughout the area, you can find the evidence all around you in the back country. These are fragile places; learn to visit with respect and care. A thousand years ago these lands were filled with families, their homes and communities. Where did the people go who used to live here? Well for us Pueblo Peoples, We Are Them and that is as certain as I am sitting here, we are Them. We have not gone away. Twenty-five American Indian pueblos and tribes trace their history to the Four Corners region. Whenever I come to old Pueblo sites, it's the beginning of emotions welling up about people my people my ancestors who used to live here and connections with them, there is no past, there is no present, there isn't the divide there that's why when we're here we can greet the people who have not been here for hundreds of years. It's as if they are here and we can talk to them." Mesa Verde National Park is the original homeland of Ancestral Puebloan peoples, who lived here for seven hundred years, from 600 to 1300 C.E.

The National Park Service protects nearly five thousand known archaeological sites, including six hundred cliff dwellings across 40 miles (64 kilometers) of roads

Mesa Verde.

These sites are some of the most notable and best preserved in the United States. The park is open year-round, but some areas are seasonal. Among the most architecturally developed sites is Cliff Palace, apartmentlike, communal buildings made of hand-cut, sandstone layers held up by wood-beamed ceilings that demonstrate the craftsmanship of the Puebloan ancestors, as do many of the other buildings at Mesa Verde. Park rangers are versed in interpreting the buildings, including Balcony House, Long House, Step House, and Spruce Tree House.

The park says that recent archaeological studies reveal that Cliff Palace contained 150 rooms and twenty-three kivas and had a population of approximately one hundred people. Cliff Palace is an exceptionally large dwelling with special significance possibly as the social and administrative location with ceremonial purpose. Mesa top sites are equally as intricate. They include the Badger House Community, the Cedar Tree Tower, the Far View Sites Complex, and the Sun Temple.

Names for all of the Mesa Verde Puebloan Ancestral places were given by non-Native people. Fees are charged for ranger-led tours, vehicles, motorcycles, and bicyclists. On June 29, 1906, President Theodore Roosevelt established Mesa Verde National Park to "preserve the works of man," the first national park of its kind. Today, the continued preservation of both cultural and natural resources is the focus of the park's research and resource management staff. Mesa Verde National Park opened its new visitor and research center in mid-December 2012. The Leadership in Energy and Environmental Design building is located at the park entrance and replaced the old visitor center. It also houses a state-of-the-art research and storage facility for the park's archives and museum collection of over three million objects.

Info: Highway 160, Mesa Verde National Park, CO 81330 • 970.529.4465 • https://www.nps.gov/meve/index.htm

TOWAOC
Ute Mountain Tribal Park

The lesser-known Ute Mountain Tribal Park in Mancos Canyon is a protected area with nearly intact Ancestral Puebloan sites within a 125,000-acre area. Located south of Mesa Verde National Park along both sides of the Mancos River Canyon is a deep canyon with arched sandstone walls where village settlements of Ancestral Puebloans lived between 400–1100 C.E. The Ute Mountain Tribe, whose reservation this area belongs to, while not culturally related to the Puebloan peoples, have taken respectful care of it, and some sites are virtually intact with many inaccessible. Forced out by drought, the Puebloan ancestors moved out of the canyon by 1200 C.E.

One must have a Ute guide to enter the Ute Mountain tribal land, and no self-guided tours are allowed. At the entrance of the park is the tour headquarters with a small exhibit and gifts, books, and refreshments for sale. Overnight stays may be arranged. The Ute Mountain Tribe says: "Our Tribal Park is preserved with many original pictographs and petroglyphs that tell you stories of Ancient Times; Historical and pre-historical sites are preserved in their original state. DO NOT REMOVE pottery shards or any historical elements while visiting."

The Ute Mountain Tribal Park was designated as a Historical District on May 2, 1972. Towaoc, the only town on the reservation, is the site of the Ute Mountain Indian Agency and the residence of most of the people on the reservation. The Ute represent the oldest continuous residents of what is now Colorado. The language of the Ute is Shoshonean, a branch of the greater Uto-Aztecan linguistic family.

In 1911, the Weenuche Band provided acreage for Mesa Verde National Park, where the remains of Anasazi cliff dwellings exist. In exchange for the land provided for the park, the federal government granted the Ute other properties, including most of northern Ute Mountain. In 1938, the federal government returned 30,000 acres (121 square kilometers) of appropriated lands to the tribe. The Ute Mountain Casino Hotel and Resort was opened in 1992. Besides the hotel, the Sleeping Ute RV Park and Campground, opened in April 2004, hosts full-service sites as well as tent and tipi areas.

Info: 3 Weeminuche Dr., Towaoc, CO 81334 • 970.565.9653 • http://www.utemountaintribalpark.info

NEW MEXICO

N ew Mexico has 219,237 Native American or American Indian citizens, and the state has twenty-four Native governments.

ACOMA
Sky City Cultural Center and Haak'u Museum

The Sky City Cultural Center and Haak'u Museum was designed with architectural details and serves as the reception center for visitors to the pueblo of Acoma. Acoma is often referred to as Sky City and remains vital in New Mexico's cultural heritage as the oldest continuously inhabited settlement in North America. Built on top of a mesa, Acoma Pueblo is a federally recognized Indian tribe ,which has a land base covering 431,664 acres (1,118,005 square kilometers). The pueblo is home to forty-eight hundred tribal members with more than 250 dwellings, some of which have electricity, sewer, or water. In 1629, construction began on the massive San Esteban del Rey Mission, a Catholic mission. Both the mission and the pueblo are Registered National Historical Landmarks and are on the National Register of Historic Places.

The Sky City Cultural Center and Haak'u Museum were built to bring to life Acoma traditions while providing insight into the unique history of the Acoma Pueblo. Acoma oral history refers to a time far beyond present imagination, to a time of creation and emergence onto this world they call "Haak'u," a spiritual homeland prepared for their eternal settlement. Recent excavations on Acoma Mesa tend to suggest that Acoma was inhabited before the time of Christ. Archaeologists agree that it has been continuously occupied from at least 1200 C.E. Acoma people believe that they have always lived on the mesa, hospitably receiving other tribes that at one time had plenty of water for farming.

The Sky City Cultural Center offers the guided tour of the mesa top village, and at the museum, visitors are introduced to historical and modern Acoma peoples. The Acoma Pueblo government also operates Sky City Casino, which is off of Interstate 40 and seventy miles from Albuquerque. It is suggested for visitors to dress appropriately for the season and wear comfortable walking shoes, as the tour is 0.75 of a mile (1.2 kilometers) long. Acoma spiritual leaders live on the mesa year-round, and visitors are asked to dress appropriately out of respect for them.

Info: Haaku Rd., Acoma, NM 87034 • 505.552.7861 • http://www.acomaskycity.org/home.html

ALBUQUERQUE
Bien Mur Indian Market

Bien Mur Indian Market Center is the Southwest's largest Native American–owned and–operated trading post. Five different branches are located throughout the pueblo of Sandia Reservation, offering locally made pueblo art. See entry on "Sandia Bison Program," Bernalillo, New Mexico.

Info: 100 Bien Mur Dr. NE, Albuquerque, NM 87113 • 505.821.5400, x.3 • https://www.bienmurindianmarket.com/

Gathering of Nations Powwow

The Gathering of Nations (GON) Powwow is the world's largest Native American cultural event, which features over five hundred Indian tribes participating. The crowning of Miss Indian World and cultural presentations are held at the Kiva Auditorium in downtown Albuquerque on the Thursday evening prior to the start of the GON Powwow. The two-day powwow features thousands of dancers performing different styles from many regions and tribes, hundreds of Native American arts and crafts at

The Gathering of Nations Powwow in Albuquerque is the largest of its type in the world.

the Indian Traders Market, Native American and Southwest food, and lots of dancing. The Grand Entry is the hallmark of the powwow, when thousands of dancers enter the dance floor with all the drum groups taking their turn with an entrance song.

Stage 49 is a separate entertainment venue included in the cost of the powwow admission, featuring contemporary Native music and entertainment with Native and other invited musicians performing in all genres of music: Rock, Blues, Reggae, Hip-Hop, Country, DJs, Jam Bands, World, and Traditional.

The powwow is in Tingley Coliseum, and the other activities take place at Expo New Mexico State Fairgrounds, just outside of Tingley.

Info: 3301 Coors Blvd. NW, Suite R300, Albuquerque, NM 87120 • 505.836.2810 • http://www.gatheringofnations.com

Indian Pueblo Cultural Center

The Indian Pueblo Cultural Center opened on August 28, 1976, by the nineteen Puebloan governors and the tribal councils of New Mexico. The center has become a place that helps preserve and educate visitors from around the world about Puebloan peoples and their living cultures. It is a place to support Puebloan and Native American artists and is built on land once part of the now closed Albuquerque Indian School. The cultural center's semicircular shape was modeled after Pueblo Bonito in Chaco Canyon and has many expansions in which its museum has ongoing exhibits, including "The Pueblo Story." Special events include Native traditional dances, featured artist/scholar lectures, and a Puebloan film festival in November. Visitors may eat in the Pueblo Harvest café, which incorporates a traditional, Puebloan-inspired menu.

Shumakolowa Native Arts is a large gallery featuring Puebloan and Southwestern Native art and artists.

Info: 2401 12th St. NW, Albuquerque, NM 87104 • 505.843.7270 • https://www.indianpueblo.org/

Maxwell Museum of Anthropology

The Maxwell Museum of Anthropology houses anthropological collections from around the world, spanning 2.5 million years of human cultural development. Although its collections emphasize the American Southwest, other strengths include Africa, the Arctic, Australia, Central and South America, India, New Guinea, Oceania, Pakistan, and Southeast Asia.

The museum houses more than one million archaeological and ethnological objects, human skeletal remains, orthodontic records of thousands of individuals, more than one hundred thousand images, and extensive document archives. During its history, the Maxwell Museum has been a leader among university-based anthropology museums. The museum plays a major role in identifying and preserving archaeological sites in New Mexico through the Office of Contract Archaeology. The Maxwell Museum's faculty, staff, and collections provide unique educational and research opportunities for students at the University of New Mexico (UNM) and the public at large.

A recent public program and restoration project at the Maxwell Museum was welcomed by Chief Danial Smith of the Tlowitsis Nation for a blessing and celebration for the recently restored Smith Family Totem Pole. The totem pole originated in 1907 was acquired illegally on Turnour Island, British Columbia; it was created by the artist Charlie Yakuglas James. After a complete review and agreement with the Tlowitsis Nation and the Maxwell Museum, the Smith Family Totem Pole was restored by Kwakwa̱ka'wakw artists Tom Hunt Jr. and Bertram Smith. The pole was moved from the outdoor patio of the Maxwell Museum and raised inside the UNM Hibben Center.

The Maxwell Museum of Anthropology, in cooperation with the Ortiz Center for Intercultural Studies, a public anthropology effort founded by the UNM Department of Anthropology and the Maxwell Museum, promotes collaboration with communities and community scholars to engage in research with museum professionals and anthropology faculty on public programs and new museum initiatives.

Info: 500 University Blvd. NE, Albuquerque, NM 87131-0001 • 505.277.4405 • https://maxwellmuseum.unm.edu/

Petroglyph National Monument

The Petroglyph National Monument protects one of the largest petroglyph sites in North America. Volcanic rocks with carved, symbolic designs dating back seven hundred years, some are identified as the designs of Puebloan peoples, and others are carved by Spanish settlers, who marked some of the rocks four hundred years ago.

Here are some of the many designs one will find on the Rinconada Trail in Petroglyph National Monument, Albuquerque.

The Petroglyph National Monument offers several hiking trails to allow for viewing of natural features and a variety of petroglyphs. The park was divided by a highway, the result of urban expansion and home development in Albuquerque's west side, but it remains a revered place for Native people, who have argued to keep it a protected place. These trails range in difficulty from easy to moderate. Trail guides for each trail system are available at the visitor center.

Info: 6001 Unser Blvd. NW, Albuquerque, NM 87120 • 505.899.0205, x.335 • https://www.nps.gov/petr/index.htm

AZTEC
Aztec Ruins National Monument

Visitors to Aztec Ruins find its location within the town of Aztec highly accessible. The monument features the only reconstructed kiva in the Southwest. Managed by the National Park Service, the Park Service workers say that early settlers mistakenly thought that people from the Aztec Empire in Mexico created these striking buildings. They named the site "Aztec," a misnomer that persisted even after it became clear that the builders were the ancestors of many Southwestern tribes. The people who built at Aztec and other places throughout the Southwest were called "Anasazi" for many years. Archaeologists had adopted that word from the Navajo language, which they understood to mean "ancient ones," then popularized its use. Most Puebloan peoples today prefer that we use the term "Ancestral Puebloans" to refer to their ancestors.

Aztec Ruins was built over a two-hundred-year period and is the largest Ancestral Puebloan community in the Animas River Valley. Concentrated on and below a terrace

Aztec Ruins National Monument.

overlooking the Animas River, the people at Aztec built several multistory buildings called "great houses" and many smaller structures. Associated with each great house was a "great kiva"—a large, circular chamber used for ceremonies. Nearby are three unusual "triwall" structures—aboveground kivas encircled by three concentric walls. In addition, they modified the landscape with dozens of linear swales called "roads," earthen berms, and platforms. In about 1300, the Ancestral Puebloan peoples left the region, migrating southeast to join existing communities along the Rio Grande, south to the Zuni area, or west to join the Hopi villages in Arizona.

Info: 725 Ruins Rd., Aztec, NM 87410 • 505.334.6174, x.0 • https://www.nps.gov/azru/index.htm

BERNALILLO
Pueblo of Sandia

The Sandia peoples have resided at T'uf Shur Tu', "green reed place," since at least 1300 C.E. It has been at its current location since the fourteenth century and comprised over twenty pueblos, with three thousand residing there at the time of the arrival of Coronado in 1539. Mission San Francisco de Sandia was established at Sandia, and the Indigenous people recall abuse and oppression under Spanish occupation, fueling Sandia's participation in the Pueblo Revolt of 1680. The Tiwa name for Sandia Pueblo is Napeya or Nafiat, "at the dusty place," and their village was burned by the Spanish as they left the region, and years later, Governor Antonio de Otermin burned it again during early attempts at reconquest by the Spanish. The people of Sandia sought refuge with the Hopi, and they temporarily settled in the village of Payupki on Second Mesa. The Sandia people were finally permitted to resettle in their traditional territory in 1748 with a Spanish land grant of title.

Sandia Pueblo peoples speak Tiwa and, like other Puebloan peoples, grew corn, beans, and squash. They also grew cotton and tobacco. They hunted deer, mountain lion, bear, antelope, and rabbit. The people also gathered a variety of wild seeds, nuts, berries, and other foods but ate little or no fish.

Fast-forwarding to the present, the pueblo of Sandia has been successful, with entrepreneurs opening a resort and casino and a championship eighteen-hole golf course. The tribe operates the Sandia Lakes Recreation Area, a 70-acre (0.3-square-kilometer) area that includes three fishing lakes stocked with trout and catfish, picnic areas, meeting spaces, a playground, shelters, a bait and tackle shop, and a natural trail along the Rio Grande cottonwoods along the river. The tribe also operates Bien Mur, or "Big Mountain" in the Tiwa, a large retail store of Native arts and crafts near the casino. The Sandia Pueblo celebrate King's Day on January 6 and the Feast of St. Anthony on June 13, and both are open to the public. Families maintain a home in the old village for use during feast days and another home in the newer residential areas.

Info: 481 Sandia Loop, Bernalillo, NM 87004 • 505.867.3317 • http://www.sandiapueblo.nsn.us

Sandia Bison Program

The Lands Bison Program responsibilities include care and feeding the bison herd located in the pueblo's land just off of Tramway Road next to the Bien Mur Indian Market. It has become a valuable educational aide for the younger generation. The 107-acre buffalo preserve was established by the Pueblo of Sandia to promote the resurgence of the American bison. They were all but exterminated during the mass slaughter of the 1800s.

This buffalo preserve, located next to the city of Albuquerque, is a rare sight. The Pueblo of Sandia encourages visitors to experience these magnificent animals in their natural setting while visiting Bien Mur. The westernmost extent of the buffalo

Americans slaughtered bison by the millions, almost making them extinct. The Sandia Bison Program and others have successfully brought them back.

preserve boundary is east of Bien Mur and borders the parking lot. Photography is allowed without any special permits.

Info: Tramway Road next to the Bien Mur Indian Market. Bernalillo, NM 87004 • 505.867.3317 • http://www.sandiapueblo.nsn.us

CHURCH ROCK
Red Rock State Park

Red Rock Park belongs to the City of Gallup parks and recreation department. The park offers a campground with electricity and water, restrooms and showers, a camp store, and a post office. Red cliffs formed over millions of years turned into the site of the five-thousand-seat Red Rock Arena that hosts rodeos and other events, including the hundred-year-old InterTribal Indian Ceremonial in August.

Info: 825 Outlaw Rd., Church Rock, NM 87311 • 505.722.3839 • http://www.gallupnm.gov/207/Red-Park-and-Museum

COCHITI
Cochiti Lake

Cochiti Lake is located within the boundaries of the Pueblo de Cochiti Reservation on the Rio Grande, about 50 miles (80 kilometers) upstream from Albuquerque. Cochiti Dam is one of the ten largest earth-filled dams in the United States, containing more than 65 million cubic yards (59 cubic kilometers) of earth and rock. Cochiti was authorized only for flood and sediment control, and later interests led to fish and wildlife enhancement and other recreation. Congress then modified its authorization for Cochiti Lake to include a 1,200-surface-acre (4.86-square-kilometer) lake for recreation. Water for this lake is imported from the Colorado River Basin to the Rio Grande Basin via the San Juan Diversion Project across the Continental Divide. Construction of Cochiti Lake began in 1965; the main embankment was completed in 1975; and the lake opened to the public in July 1975. In 1976, the Cochiti Recreation area on the west side of the lake was opened to the public, including Cochiti Golf Club Course at Cochiti Lake. Tetilla Peak, another area on the east side of the lake, was opened in 1983. A visitor's center on the west side of the lake, adjacent to the operations building, is available to the public. Recreational facilities include campsites, electrical hookups, picnic sites, group shelters, restrooms/showers, drinking water, dump stations, a universally accessible fishing area, and boat launching ramps. The Pueblo de Cochiti Reservation operates and maintains a small marina.

Info: Pueblo de Cochiti Reservation, P.O. Box 70, Cochiti, NM 87072 • 505.465.2244 • http://www.pueblodecochiti.org/

Cochiti Pueblo Celebrations

The Cochiti speak Eastern Keres, making it one of five New Mexican pueblos who speak Keres and the northernmost Keres speakers. Cochiti ancestors lived at Frijoles Canyon, north of their present pueblo, until a few centuries before the beginning of the Spanish colonial era in the 1590s. Because of the Cochiti's location on the west bank of the Rio Grande, it was not near one of the primary Spanish routes and had fewer outsiders visit until after 1581. In 1680, the Pueblo Revolt resulted in expulsion of the Spanish colonists from the area north of the Rio Grande. The Puebloan Indians maintained their independence, and in 1689, the Spanish Crown established the original pueblo land grant.

The Cochiti Pueblo enjoyed independence until 1821, when the Mexican government gained control over New Mexico and declared the people citizens of Mexico. In 1846, the United States gained control over New Mexico, and the 1848 Treaty of Guadalupe Hidalgo confirmed those traditional Indian land grants. In 1864, Congress patented the original Cochiti land grant from the Spanish Crown.

Today, the people of Cochiti continue to practice traditional cultural elements and speak the Indigenous Keres language. The traditional, patrilineal moiety and matrilineal clan systems remain intact, and the Cochiti are considered a conservative community that continues its traditions and practices. The Pueblo de Cochiti hosts a number of annual festivities and ceremonies, many of which are open to the public, including the pueblo's Annual San Buenaventura Feast Day on July 14 and December 25–29. Social dances are open to the public. The tribe welcomes visitors to the pueblo but expects that all guidelines and restrictions will be adhered to. Visitors may not enter ceremonial buildings, private homes, or other restricted areas. Photos, videos, and other recordings are not permitted without prior permission.

Info: Pueblo de Cochiti Reservation, P.O. Box 70, Cochiti, NM 87072 • 505.761.8787 • https://www.blm.gov/visit/kktr

Kasha-Katuwe Tent Rocks.

Kasha-Katuwe Tent Rocks National Monument

In partnership with the Bureau of Land Management, the Cochiti Pueblo comanages Kasha-Katuwe (Tent Rocks National Monument) on the western edge of the pueblo. The featured geological formations are the result of volcanic eruptions over six million years ago. The site is of cultural significance to the tribe and continues to be used in traditional ceremonies. The Kasha-Katuwe Tent Rocks National Monument is considered an outdoor laboratory, offering an opportunity to observe, study, and experience the geologic processes that shape natural landscapes. The National Monument, on the Pajarito Plateau in north-central New Mexico, includes a national recreation trail and ranges from 5,570 feet (1,698 meters) to 6,760 feet (2,060 meters) above sea level. It is for foot travel only and contains two segments that provide opportunities for hiking, bird watching, geologic observation, and plant identification. While fairly uniform in shape, the tent rock formations vary in height from a few feet up to 90 feet (27 meters).

Info: Pueblo de Cochiti Reservation, P.O. Box 70, Cochiti, NM 87072 • 505.761.8787 • https://www.blm.gov/visit/kktr

CROWNPOINT
Crownpoint Navajo Rug Auction

Founded over fifty years ago, Crownpoint Trading Post in New Mexico was the site of the Crownpoint Rug Auction, a genuine Navajo event featuring contemporary, handmade, all-wool Navajo rugs and the weavers who make them. In 2014, the Navajo Rug Weavers' Association of Crownpoint took over management of the auction and turned it into a prime venue for buyers and weavers of genuine Navajo rugs. The auction takes place once a month (usually on the second Friday) at the Crownpoint Elementary School. Weavers from all over the Navajo Nation bring in their rugs starting at 4:00 p.m., and the rugs are laid out on tables for buyers to inspect. Rug submission/inspection ends at 6:30 p.m., and the auction starts at 7:00 p.m. It can run until 10:00 p.m., or later, if many rugs are to be sold. Rugs sell from less than $50 into the thousands. Buyers can pay for rugs with cash, credit cards, or check.

Info: Crownpoint Elementary School, 1 Codetalker Dr., Crownpoint, NM 87313 • 505.786.2130 • http://crownpointrugauction.com/

DULCE
Jicarilla Apache Territory

The Jicarilla Apache Reservation is 879,917 acres (3,561 square kilometers), located in north-central New Mexico on the eastern edge of the San Juan Basin. The reservation's northern boundary borders the Colorado line. The town of Dulce is the tribal center of government, education, and commerce. The traditional territory of the Jicarilla Apache included portions of Texas, Colorado, and New Mexico. The Jicarilla lived abundantly with hunting, fishing, and agricultural development.

The Apache vehemently resisted encroachment upon their traditional lands by Spanish, Mexican, and American settlers and military forces, but by the mid-1880s, the Apache were consolidated onto various reservations. The Jicarilla were sent to the Mescalero Apache Reservation in southeastern New Mexico. The Jicarilla tribal leadership, stepping outside the bounds of traditional channels, sought to win the support of New Mexico territorial governor Edmund G. Ross in 1886 in an attempt to regain their northern reservation. Ross's influential coalition convinced the president to sign the Executive Order of February 8, 1887, which created the permanent site of the Jicarilla Apache Reservation.

The reservation's natural resources have proven to be the tribe's greatest economic asset. The reservation offers outdoor sightseeing, sports hunting of big game, and fishing opportunities. Five major big game migration corridors cross the reservation. Game includes elk, deer, black bear, mountain lion, turkey, and Canadian goose. In addition, seven of the tribe's fifteen mountain lakes are stocked with rainbow, brown, and cutthroat trout. Fishing is permitted at Dulce, Enbom, Hayden, Horse, La Jara, Mundo, and Stone lakes and at the Navajo River. Tribally issued permits are required and may be secured from the Jicarilla Game and Fish Department. Boaters are also permitted on tribal lakes. The tribe welcomes all visitors but requires that they abide by guidelines and restrictions intended to protect and preserve natural resources. A number of annual tribal celebrations are open to the public, including the Little Beaver Round-Up held the third weekend in July. This event is considered a high point of the midsummer season and includes the Professional Indian Open Rodeo, the Pony Express Race, the 5K Run/Walk, a powwow, a parade, traditional dances, and a carnival. In addition, the Go-Jii-Yah Feast, an annual harvest festival, is held on September 14–15. It has been a part of the Jicarilla culture for hundreds of years. Clan racing, a rodeo, and traditional dances are part of this event.

Info: Jicarilla Fairgrounds, Rodeo Rd., Dulce, NM 87528 • 505.759.3242 • http://www.jicarillaonline.com

ESPANOLA
Puye Cliff Dwellings Welcome Center and Santa Clara Pueblo

Puye Cliff Dwellings is the original village of people from Santa Clara Pueblo, whose Tewa descendants moved closer to the Rio Grande after a severe drought four hundred years ago, and they named their village Kha'p'o Owinge, "Place of Wild Roses." Puye Cliff Dwellings is an elaborate, late-period 1200 C.E. Ancestral Puebloan settlement on top of a mesa plateau named the Pajarito Plateau in what became north-central New Mexico. The people at Puye also built along the side of the cliffs, and into it, multistoried and elaborate homes using volcanic rock. Smaller sites are located near Puye but are not open to the public. The plateau was home to the more than fifteen hundred Puye people who lived, farmed, and hunted game. The first dwellings were caves hollowed in the volcanic tuff cliffs. Archaeologists suggest that the Puye Cliffs were last occupied in about 1680.

Puye Cliff Dwellings.

Puye Cliff Dwellings is a Registered National Historic Landmark in north-central New Mexico. Guided tours are offered, and occasionally, people from the village perform dances and sell their pottery and crafts. It includes a small exhibit about the cultural life when Puye was occupied and remarkably resembles the way people at Santa Clara Pueblo live today. St. Claire of Assisi is the patron saint whose feast is celebrated with corn and harvest dances on August 12 and is open to the public. Other celebrations at the pueblo are Christmas Day, and on June 13, the feast of St. Anthony is also a large celebration that includes dances in the pueblo plaza.

The Santa Clara people have preserved many of their ancient traditions. The clay beds at Santa Clara produced a strong family pottery-making tradition known for highly polished, black-and-red ware with intricate, precise engravings. The technical excellence, innovation, and imagination of Santa Clara potters have helped sustain and promote Puebloan pottery around the world. In addition to pottery, the pueblo members have produced notable sculptors and painters and artists who also create embroidery, beadwork, and weaving.

Santa Clara received its initial land grant from the Spanish and were pronounced citizens of Mexico when that country gained its independence from Spain. Later, the United States recognized the pueblo's tribal rights under the 1848 Treaty of Guadalupe Hidalgo. The United States then confirmed the tribe's land grant in 1858 and became legal in 1909. The reservation features the forested Santa Clara Canyon that was decimated by a wildfire in 2010 that burned over 14,000 acres (57 square kilometers) near Puye.

Puye Cliff Dwellings is located off State Highway 30 southwest of the pueblo, and the entrance fee to the site may be paid at the Santa Clara Travel Center. The Santa Clara Pueblo also owns and operates the Santa Claran Hotel and Casino on land owned by the pueblo in the city of Espanola, which borders the pueblo.

Info: NM 30 and NM 5 (Santa Clara Canyon Rd.), Espanola, NM 87532 • 505.753.7326 • https://www.puyecliffs.com/

FORT SUMNER
Bosque Redondo Memorial

The Bosque Redondo Memorial at Fort Sumner State Monument is in remembrance of the ninety-five hundred Diné Navajo and N'de Mescaleo Apache who were imprisoned there from 1863 to 1868. The memorial statement reads: "The Bosque Redondo Memorial mission is to respectfully interpret the history of two cultures, the Diné and Mescalero Apache, during the United States government's military campaign of ethnic persecution in the 1860s under the orders of General James H. Carleton who enlisted Colonel Christopher 'Kit' Carson to round up the Navajo. Navajo people today recount their history to this time in captivity as 'Hweeldi' also called The Long Walk from what is now Arizona to New Mexico over 300 miles (483 kilometers) from their homeland. During the walk and while imprisoned they faced death, starvation, and physical abuse by the army. Diné people continue to feel the effects of their history as prisoners of the government and upon release in 1868 when they agreed to peace and were assigned a reservation that has expanded to 27,000 acres [110 square kilometers]."

Today, a unique, new museum designed by Navajo architect David Sloan—shaped like a hogan and a tipi—and an interpretive trail provide information about the tragic history of Fort Sumner and Bosque Redondo Indian Reservation.

Info: 3647 Billy the Kid Rd., Fort Sumner, NM 88119 • 575.355.2573 • https://wwwbosqueredondomemorial.com/

ISLETA PUEBLO
Pueblo of Isleta

The Pueblo of Isleta is located in the Middle Rio Grande Valley, 13 miles (21 kilometers) south of Albuquerque, the state's largest city. Its lands are adjacent to and east of the main section of Laguna Pueblo, and the pueblo was built on a knife-shaped reef of lava running across an old Rio Grande channel. The Isleta Pueblo dates to the 1300s and is listed as a Historic District on the National Register of Historic Places. The name Isleta was given by the Spanish and is translated as "Little Island." Because of its location in the direct path of the Spanish explorers, its history with the Spanish and later Anglo settlers has made the pueblo more protective and reserved in sharing with outsiders. The Isleta speak southern Tiwa and have that in common with the Sandia Pueblo north of Albuquerque. St. Augustine Church, built by Isleta people for Francisan missionaries, is located in the village plaza, and an active Catholic community remains at Isleta. Commercial enterprises of the pueblo include the Isleta Casino Resort and Golf Course and Isleta Lake.

Info: Pueblo of Isleta, P.O. Box 1270, Isleta Pueblo, NM 87022 • 505.869.3111 • http://www.isletapueblo.com

JEMEZ
Jemez Historic Site

The Jemez Historic Site at Jemez Springs is the seven-hundred-year-old ancestral Jemez Village of Guisewa, "a place of the boiling waters." Also at the old village is the seventeenth-century Franciscan Mission of San Jose de Los Jemez. The site includes a small museum display and interpretative trail. This site was placed on the National Historic Landmark register on October 16, 2012. The Walatowa Visitors Center promotes the area's attractions by cooperating with the U.S. Forest Service for the Jemez District to distribute literature on the Santa Fe National Forest, the Jemez Mountain Trail, which was designated as a National Scenic and Historic Byway in 1998, the Jemez Mountain National Recreation area, and the Valles Caldera National Preserve. The Pueblo of Jemez is also pursuing the return of its most sacred land, the Valles Caldera, back to tribal ownership.

The Pueblo of Jemez is the only remaining village of Towa-speaking pueblos in New Mexico. Oral history holds that ancestors of the present-day Jemez people originated in a place called "Hua-na-tota." The tribe migrated to the Cañon de San Diego region from the Four Corners area during the late fourteenth century and became one of the largest and most powerful of the pueblo cultures by the time of European contact in 1541. They traditionally relied on hunting, gathering, and farming for subsistence. The pueblo's first contact with Europeans was Francisco Vázquez de Coronado and his exploratory party. Following the Coronado Expedition, the tribe

Jemez Historic Site.

was left in peace for forty years until the next wave of Spanish explorers arrived. During the next eighty years, the Jemez people carried out numerous revolts and uprisings in response to Spanish attempts to forcibly Christianize them that led to the Pueblo Revolt in 1680. Almost two hundred years later, in 1838, the Towa-speaking people from Pecos, a pueblo located just east of Santa Fe, requested to be taken in by Jemez and to resettle there in order to escape harassment by the Spanish and Comanche Indians. In 1936, the two tribes were merged by an act of Congress. Traditional culture remains vital with farming of corn and chili crops. In addition, many tribal members work in the region's timber industry and in the internationally renowned arts and crafts cottage industries. Other members find employment off the reservation at Los Alamos National Laboratory and in Albuquerque or Santa Fe.

Info: 18160 NM-4, Jemez Springs, NM 87025 • 505.829.3530 • http://www.nmhistoricsites.org/jemez

Walatowa Visitors Center

The Pueblo of Jemez is known to its members as Walatowa. It is located in Sandoval County, New Mexico, approximately 55 miles (89 kilometers) northwest of Albuquerque, New Mexico. As one of nineteen New Mexico pueblos, it is a federally recognized tribe. The Pueblo of Jemez has a closed-village policy due to the lack of tourism facilities and out of respect for the privacy of those who live there. The village is therefore open to the public only on its Feast Day in November.

The Walatowa Visitors Center is open year-round and features the pueblo's history museum, a replica of a traditional field house landscaped with Native plants, and a gift shop. The center offers guided tours for visitors interested in the early culture of the Jemez people. It also offers bread-baking demonstrations, artist demonstrations, and traditional dances. The Towa Arts and Crafts Committee, in coordination with the Walatowa Visitors Center, sponsors the annual Jemez Red Rock Arts and Crafts Show.

Info: 7413 NM-4, Jemez Pueblo, NM 87024 • 505.834.7359 • http://www.jemezpueblo.org/

LAGUNA
Laguna Mission

The Pueblo of Laguna is located below the foothills of Mount Taylor, 45 miles (72 kilometers) west of Albuquerque on Interstate 40. The residents of Laguna Pueblo live in six villages: Laguna, Mesita, Paguate, Seama, Paraje, and Encinal.

The largest celebration and tourist attraction at Laguna Pueblo is the Feast of Old Laguna, held annually on September 19 in celebration of St. Joseph. Old Laguna also continues to celebrate the original St. Joseph Feast Day on March 19. Various dances are held throughout the day in front of a shrine specifically erected for the event. Local and regional artisans and craftspeople sell their work, and traditional foods are shared throughout the community. Each of the six villages also celebrates its own feast day, called Grab Days because people with the names of patron saints throw small wares or baked goods from the rooftops of their homes to the people below. St. Joseph's Mission is a National Historic Register site, which Friar Antonio de Miranda, a Franciscan missionary, had Laguna build in 1699. The mission was restored and is open to visitors on weekdays.

Info: 1 Friar Rd., Laguna, NM 87026 • 505.552.6654 • http://www.lagunapueblo-nsn.gov

LOS ALAMOS
Bandelier National Monument

Thirty minutes south of what is now Los Alamos, where the first atomic hydrogen bomb was conceived, is an ancestral pueblo that was built and lived in from 1150 C.E. to 1550 C.E. The people built homes carved from the volcanic tuff, making bricks and building storied blocks. They planted corn, beans, and squash on the mesa; the staple of Ancestral Puebloans was supplemented by hunting deer, rabbit, turkey, and dog. After four hundred years, a severe drought forced them out of Frijoles Canyon, and members of the present-day Cochiti Pueblo are direct descendants.

Some of the numerous cliff dwellings at Bandelier National Monument.

Bandelier National Monument was named after Adolph Bandelier, a Swiss-born archaeologist who immigrated to the United States and established his research in New Mexico. The visitor center, WNPA Bookstore, and Bandelier Trading Company are open daily except on Thanksgiving Day, December 25, and January 1.

Info: 15 Entrance Rd., Los Alamos, NM 87544 • 505.672.3861, x.517 • https://www.nps.gov/band/

MESCALERO
Mescalero Apache Cultural Center and Museum

The name "Mescalero" is a reference to the Mescalero Apache use of the mescal plant, a staple of their diet that sustained them through tumultuous times in their past.

Mescalero and other Apache are known for building temporary brush shelters known as a "wickiup," short, rounded dwellings made of brush twigs, and in winter months, they constructed tipis made of pine poles with elk and buffalo hides. The Mescalero traveled freely throughout the Southwest, including Texas, Arizona, and Chihuahua and Sonora, Mexico, and became known for their hunting and defensive strategies in battles with the Mexican and U.S. militaries. The Mescalero, Lipan, and Chiricahua live at the Mescalero Apache Reservation.

The Mescalero Apache Cultural Center and Museum provides their history and cultural lifeways that made use of stone tools, weapons, and basketry. Advance arrangements can be requested for cultural programs, including dance performances. The Mescalero Apache Reservation, located in the Lincoln National Forest, has operated an extensive parks and recreation program since 1963. Their Ski Apache (1286 Ski Run Rd.) at Sierra Blanca is the state's only ski resort with its own gondola. Accommodations include the Mescalero Cabins, the RVF Park, and the Mountain Gods Inn, Casino, and Resort (287 Carrizo Canyon Rd.).

Info: 181 Chiricahua Plaza, Mescalero, NM 88340 • 505.671.4494 • http://www.mescaleroapachetribe.com

MOUNTAINAIR
Salinas Pueblo Missions National Monument

Salinas Pueblo Missions National Monument is a relatively little-known preserve with fewer visitors than other monuments in the state. The centerpiece of the ruins is a collection of seventeenth-century Spanish Franciscan missions built in the territory and homeland of Tompiro and Tiwa Indians, who left the area around 1677. The northernmost site, and the least visited, is Quarai, in the foothills of the Manzano Mountains, and has a sizeable, red-brick church plus outbuildings and grassy mounds with pueblo foundations. Twelve miles (19 kilometers) south, the Abó ruins receive more visitors as they lie along a main road (U.S. 60) but are similar to Quarai. The desert surrounds the site with views across open plains to the mountains. The third and most extensive site is 20 miles (32 kilometers) further southeast, at Gran Quivira, which is also based around a mission complex, next to a multiroom pueblo village, both rather different in appearance to the red, sandstone buildings further north.

Info: 102 S. Ripley St., Mountainair, NM 87036 • 505.847.2585 • https://www.nps.gov/sapu/index.htm

NAGEEZI
Chaco Canyon National Historic Park

Chaco Canyon is a remote, barely habitable canyon in northwestern New Mexico, where immense construction and buildings have been the subject of heated archaeological debates for decades. Begun more than a thousand years ago and taking twelve generations to complete, Chaco Canyon was thought to be an ancient trading center. Chaco Canyon is a complex network with a highly integrated ceremonial system involving

Chaco Canyon National Historic Park.

the sky, earth, sun, and moon. Chacoan people designed, oriented, and located twelve massive buildings to express a profound knowledge of an order in the universe.

Members of the Zuni, Acoma, and Laguna pueblos are among the present-day Puebloan peoples who are descended from Chaco Canyon and speak of the spiritual significance of Chaco Canyon in pueblo culture today. The National Park Service says, "The massive buildings of the Ancestral Puebloan peoples still testify to the organizational and engineering abilities not seen anywhere else in the American Southwest." The canyon was under construction by Ancestral Puebloans for 250 years and used the sun and moon calendar cycles to develop the buildings found at Chaco between 850 and 1250 C.E.

Chaco has guided tours, hiking and biking trails, campfire talks, and night sky programs. Many people are seriously concerned that Chaco Culture National Historical Park, a World Heritage Site, is being threatened by encroaching oil and gas development with the oil price drop. The momentum of a decades-long energy boom in the San Juan Basin endangers one of this continent's greatest cultural mysteries with fracking development. Before visiting the park, contact park staff; please use written directions to avoid getting lost.

Info: Chaco Canyon National Historic Park, P.O. Box 220, Nageezi, NM 87037 • 505.786.7014 • https://www.nps.gov/chcu/index.htm

OHKAY OWINGEH
Owe'neh Bupingeh Pueblo
Restoring and Rejuvention of the Historic Pueblo

Ohkay Owingeh, previously identified by nonpueblo members as San Juan Pueblo, is a Tewa-speaking pueblo located on the Rio Grande 25 miles (40 kilometers) north of Santa Fe. Puebloan ancestors migrated to the area from southern Colorado around

1200 C.E. The Spanish colonizer Juan de Oñate established the first Spanish capital city in New Mexico, Española, near Ohkay Owingeh Pueblo in 1598.

In 1675, Po'pay and forty-six other Puebloan leaders were convicted of sorcery; he was among those flogged, while others were executed. In 1680, Po'pay from Ohkay Owingeh led the Pueblo Revolt against the Spanish. According to legend, to coordinate the timing of the uprising, he and his followers sent runners to each pueblo with knotted, deerskin strips. One knot was to be untied each day, and the revolt would begin on the day the last one was untied. However, the Spaniards arrested two of the runners, and the pueblos were quickly notified to accelerate the revolt. The attacks began on August 10, two days before the last knot would have been untied. The Spaniards took refuge at Santa Fe; the besieging Indians cut off their water supply but soon permitted them to leave the area. The Pueblo Revolt helped to ensure the survival of the Puebloan culture and shaped the history of the American Southwest. No image of Po'pay exists, but a statue of him is one of two statutes representing the State of New Mexico in Statuary Hall of the Rotunda in Washington, D.C. (See entry on "DC Statuary Hall," Washington, D.C.)

In 2007, San Juan Pueblo officially changed its name to Ohkay Owingeh. The tribe has occupied the site of the pueblo for at least seven hundred years. The original Spanish land grant to the pueblo was confirmed in 1689. The United States reconfirmed this grant in 1858 and patented it in 1864. The Ohkay Owingeh people maintain strong ties to their traditional culture and worldview while living in the twenty-first century. The seven-hundred-year-old historic pueblo and its core plaza is of vital importance to Ohkay Owingeh as the spiritual center where the ceremonial life of the community occurs. In 2010, the Owe'neh Bupingeh Rehabilitation began an entire restoration of the pueblo plaza with the intention of bringing families back to live in the old plaza area.

Ohkay Owingeh has taken a long view of the pueblo's history and heritage and committed itself to revitalizing its spiritual center through community investment in conservation, rehabilitation, and, as appropriate, new construction. Ohkay Owingeh also owns and operates the Best Western Ohkay Casino Resort, located about two miles (three kilometers) north of Española. The San Juan Tribal Lakes offers fishing. The pueblo celebrates with feasting and dances throughout the year; the public is welcome at San Antonio's Feast Day on June 13; San Juan Feast Day on June 23–24; Harvest Dances in September; the Matachines Dance on December 28–29; and the Turtle Dance on December 26.

Info: 220 Popay Ave., Ohkay Owingeh, NM 87566 • 505.852.0189 • http://www.ohkayowingehhousingauthority.org/roob.php

PECOS
Pecos National Historical Park

Southeast of Santa Fe, New Mexico, are the trace remains of the largest Puebloan communities in the Southwest. Pecos Pueblo dominated a major trading route be-

Pecos National Historic Park.

tween the farming Puebloan Indians and the Great Plains hunters. The pueblo was a way station on the Santa Fe Trail. Today, Pecos National Historical Park preserves evidence of the life of Ancestral Puebloan peoples, whose story is directly linked to the story of a region long before the United States was founded. According to the Park Service's stories about Pecos Pueblo trade fairs, the Plains tribes brought slaves, buffalo hides, flint, and shells to trade for pottery, crops, textiles, and turquoise with the river pueblos. By the late Puebloan period, in the last few centuries before the Spaniards arrived in the Southwest, people in this valley had congregated in multistoried towns overlooking the streams and fields that nourished their crops. In the 1400s, these groups gathered into Pecos Pueblo, which became a regional power. The designation as a "historical park" rather than a "national monument" is the way this site was classified from 1965 until 1990. With the acquisition of the Forked Lightning Ranch and Glorieta Battlefield units, Pecos National Monument became Pecos National Historical Park in 1990.

Info: 1 NM-63, Pecos, NM 87552 • 505.757.7241 •
https://www.nps.gov/peco/index.htm

PEÑASCO
Picuris Pueblo

Picuris Pueblo is a northern, Tiwa-speaking community located on the western slope of the Sangre de Cristo Mountains in north-central New Mexico near the town of Peñasco. The Picuris's own name for their pueblo is Pinguiltha, meaning "mountain warrior place" or "mountain pass place." The people of Picurís were influenced by Plains Indian culture, particularly the Apache. The pueblo was visited by the Coronado expedition in 1540, and in 1598, Oñate established the San Lorenzo de Picurís Mission and named the pueblo Pikuria—"those who paint." It is believed that the original church was built soon after 1620, and by 1629, San Lorenzo was an important mission. Tu-pa-tu, the pueblo governor, was heavily involved in helping to organize the Pueblo Revolt of 1680.

Picuris maintains a bison herd that has grown to over fifty, and the pueblo is a member of the Inter-Tribal Bison Cooperative. Bison are both a food source and revered animal. Visitors are welcome to view the herd.

The San Lorenzo Mission located in the community has also been completely restored. Picuris also maintains Pu-na Lake, and visitors may obtain a fishing permit at the Picuris Smoke Shop, located at the intersection of NM Highway 75 and 76.

A museum overlooks the lake that has on exhibit ancient artifacts, photographs, and art. The museum maintains the pueblo ruins, the mission, the scalp house, and several restored kivas within the pueblo. In partnership with the Santa Fe Hospitality Company, Picuris owns a majority of Hotel Santa Fe near downtown Santa Fe, which features a Picuris theme. The Picuris people celebrate and welcome visitors to the Sunset Dance on August 9, the San Lorenzo Feast Day on August 10, the Procession of the Virgin held on Christmas Eve with the Matachines Dance on December 25, and they have their Annual Feast Day on January 25.

Info: Picuris Pueblo, P.O. Box 127, Peñasco, NM 87553 • 505.587.2519 • http://www.picurispueblo.org

PINE HILL
Ramah Navajo Chapter

The Ramah Navajo are known as Tl'ochini Diné'e, "people of the wild onion," who were removed in the Long Walk of 1864 and held in captivity until 1868. Seven families returned to the Ramah area even though it was not part of the new Navajo Reservation set out in the treaty, reuniting with relatives who had avoided removal.

In 1957, the Navajo Tribal Council recognized Ramah Navajo Chapter. However, the chapter perceived itself as being ignored by tribal government and BIA's Navajo Agency. With no voice within the Navajo Nation, the Ramah Chapter was established as a separate agency under the Southwest Region in 1972.

The Navajo language is still spoken by about one-third of the community. The community hosts the Ramah Navajo Fair and Rodeo in August at the Pine Hill Fairgrounds with a parade, a rodeo and livestock events for men and women, a country and western dance, and the Miss Ramah Navajo and Princess Contest.

Info: Ramah Navajo Chapter, 417 BIA, Route 125, Pine Hill, NM 87357 • 505.775.7140 • http://ramahnavajo.org/

SAN FELIPE
Pueblo of San Felipe

The San Felipe Pueblo is a culturally conservative, eastern Keres-speaking village located three miles (five kilometers) north of Albuquerque along the Rio Grande. Katishtya, or the San Felipe Pueblo, was established at its current site in northern

New Mexico in 1706. After they were forced from their original location in the Pajarito Plateau, the people moved to the banks of the Rio Grande. Their identity as a people is very strong, and they consider their privacy integral to maintaining their traditional lifestyle. Ceremonial dances are held throughout the year that follow an older ceremonial structure and practice of traditional rituals. They celebrate their Feast Day on May 1 as hundreds of men, women, and children participate in traditional, green corn dances. San Felipe crafts include shell beads called heshi and turquoise.

The tribe owns and operates San Felipe's Casino Hollywood just east of the pueblo on Interstate 25. The Travel Center, next to the casino, is a twenty-four-hour convenience store, gas station, and restaurant. San Felipe Pueblo hosts an annual arts and crafts show in October.

Info: Pueblo of San Felipe, P.O. Box 4339, San Felipe Pueblo, NM 87001 • 505.867.3381

SAN ILDEFONSO
San Ildefonso Pueblo Museum

Today, San Ildefonso is a pueblo community well known for the black-on-black pottery made famous by Maria and Julian Martinez and highly sought after by art collectors in the twentieth century. San Ildefonso was an agriculture-based society at a time when the pottery style that features highly polished and black matte finishes dramatically revived the economic and cultural life of the pueblo. In addition to pottery, San Ildefonso artists create handcrafted jewelry, moccasins, weavings, carvings, and paintings.

The San Ildefonso Pueblo Museum was created at the pueblo governor's office to feature the arts produced by its members today. San Ildefonso is a Tewa-speaking village that was settled near the site of the present-day pueblo around the year 1300. In 1694, Spanish general Don Diego de Vargas attacked them, and they took refuge atop Black Mesa near their present-day village, where it repelled repeated attacks and withstood captivity. European contact brought diseases that decimated their numbers.

The pueblo is listed on the National Register of Historic Places and is a popular tourist attraction given the traditional-style homes that remain occupied around the village plazas. The tribe takes in revenues from entrance fees from visitors, and they have a fishing lake that is open on a seasonal basis with picnic facilities. The pueblo celebrates feast days throughout the year, including San Ildefonso Feast Day on January 23, St. Anthony's Feast Day in mid-June, the Corn Dance in early September, and the Matachines Dance on December 25, which are open to visitors.

Info: Route 5, San Ildefonso Pueblo, NM 87506 • 505.455.2273 • http://www.sanipueblo.org

SANTA ANA PUEBLO
Tamaya

The Tamaya Indian Pueblo is located in north-central New Mexico along the Rio Grande with people living in three separate locations: Rebahene, Ranchitos, and Chicale. The Pueblo Tribal Council is composed of all the heads of household in the pueblo. Many tribal members are bilingual and speak Keres. The Spanish first encountered the tribe in 1598 in the old Santa Ana village of Tamaya, which remains the location for the tribe's ceremonial activities. It is listed on the National Register of Historic Places.

The people of Santa Ana refer to themselves as Tamayame, with their original settlement along the Rio Jemez moved in the 1500s to its present site. The Santa Ana people engaged in dry farming on the hills behind the village and along the Rio Jemez between Ranchitos and Tamaya. As early as 1350, the tribe was utilizing ditch irrigation. After the arrival of the Spanish, the Tamaya began to raise livestock, extensively raising mostly sheep and cattle. At some point, the region's climate became arid, and farming along the Rio Jemez was less productive. In the late seventeenth century, the Tamayame began farming along the Rio Grande because of their experience in the area and their recognition that the lands along the river valley were more fertile than those along the Rio Jemez.

Most Santa Ana families maintain two houses, one in the old village and one in the farm villages of Chicale, Rebahene, or Ranchitos. Traditional Santa Ana culture manifests itself through tribal theocracy, which continues to play a role in the tribal government, and through the re-emerging tribal arts and crafts community. Tamaya, or the Pueblo of Santa Ana, operates the Santa Ana Golf Club, the Twin Warriors Golf

The Museum of Contemporary Native Arts in Santa Fe.

Club, the Prairie Star Restaurant, a vineyard, the Hyatt Regency Tamaya Resort and Spa, and the Santa Ana Star Casino.

Info: Pueblo of Santa Ana, 2 Dove Rd., Santa Ana Pueblo, NM 87004 • 505.771.6700 • www.santaana-nsn.gov

SANTA FE
IAIA Museum of Contemporary Native Arts

In 1992, the Institute of American Indian Arts (IAIA) relocated its Museum of Contemporary Native Arts (MoCNA) to downtown Santa Fe. It is a national leading exhibition facility for contemporary art by Indigenous artists. MoCNA is a place for advancing the scholarship, discourse, and interpretation of contemporary Native art for regional, national, and international audiences. It stewards the National Collection of Contemporary Native Art, seventy-five hundred artworks in all media created in 1962 or later, which is the only museum in the United States exhibiting, collecting, and interpreting the progressive work of contemporary Native artists.

MoCNA has a breadth of events and programs and has a strong presence in advancing contemporary Native art nationally and internationally. The Institute of American Indian Arts is one of thirty-seven tribal colleges located in the United States. IAIA was established in 1962 during the administration of President John F. Kennedy and opened on the campus of the Indian School in Santa Fe, New Mexico. IAIA became one of three congressionally chartered colleges in the United States in 1986 and was charged with the study, preservation, and dissemination of traditional and contemporary expressions of Native American language, literature, history, oral traditions, and the visual and performing arts. In August 2000, IAIA moved its college to a permanent, 140-acre (0.6-square-kilometer) campus.

Info: 108 Cathedral Pl., Santa Fe, NM 87501 • 888.922.4242 • https://iaia.edu/iaia-museum-of-contemporary-native-arts/

Museum of Indian Arts and Culture

The Museum of Indian Arts and Culture and its exhibit partner, the Laboratory of Anthropology, are located on the Museum Hill campus east of downtown Santa Fe. The museum, part of the New Mexico Division of Cultural Affairs, opened in 1987 to serve as a center of stewardship, knowledge, and understanding of the artistic, cultural, and intellectual achievements of the diverse peoples of the Native Southwest.

In response to unsystematic collecting by eastern museums, anthropologist Edgar Lee Hewett founded the Museum of New Mexico in 1909 with a mission to collect and preserve Southwest Native American material culture. Several years later, in 1927, John D. Rockefeller founded the renowned Laboratory of Anthropology with a mission to study the Southwest's Indigenous cultures. In 1947, the two institutions merged, bringing together the most inclusive and systematically acquired collection of New Mexican and Southwestern anthropological artifacts in the country. The laboratory's collection continued to expand but was largely unavailable to the general public for lack of adequate exhibition facilities. In 1977, the New Mexico legislature appropriated $2.7 million for the design of the new Museum of Indian Arts and Culture.

Info: 710 Camino Lejo, Santa Fe, NM 87505 • 505.476.1269 • http://miaclab.org/index.php

Nambé Falls

The Pueblo of Nambé is home to natural waterfalls in the foothills of the Sangre de Cristo Mountains. Two trails lead to a series of long waterfalls with two tiers at 75 feet (23 meters) and 100 feet (30 meters) tall, respectively. The rates per car are $15 for access. Camping is also available for an additional fee. The lakes may also be fished for another fee, which is collected by the Nambé Pueblo.

Nambé Falls.

One of six Tewa-speaking pueblos in the northern Rio Grande region, the name is a Spanish interpretation of the Tewa word "nanbe," which roughly translates to "earth roundness." Prior to the arrival of Spanish explorers in 1620, the king of Spain ordered the pueblos in what later became the state of New Mexico to choose civil officials by popular vote to work with Spanish civil authorities. Most of the pueblos adopted the new form of government and integrated it into their traditional governing systems. The right of each pueblo to self-govern was subsequently recognized by the Spanish Crown, then by Mexico, and today by the United States.

Info: Nambé Pueblo, Route 1, P.O. Box 117-BB, Santa Fe, NM 87506 • 505.455.2036 • http://nambepueblo.org/

Poeh Cultural Center and Museum

The Pueblo of Pojoaque was established long before the arrival of Spanish explorers seeking gold in the sixteenth century. Pojoaque's Tewa name is P'osuwaegeh, "Water-Drinking Place." Archaeological studies indicate that the community was established by 900 c.e. It was abandoned, however, after the Pueblo Revolt of 1680, with a handful of families resettling in 1706.

During the first half of the 1800s, the population was greatly reduced by non-Indian encroachment. The original land grant and water rights document disappeared;

hence, after the United States took over the region via the 1848 Treaty of Guadalupe Hidalgo, a plea to the surveyor general of the United States to claim title to the original land grant of 13,250 acres (54 square kilometers) was made by those living in Pojoaque. President Abraham Lincoln signed their land grant in 1864. In 1912, the pueblo was in disarray, and tribal lands were being openly used for grazing by non-Indian ranchers. In 1934, owing to a U.S. policy known as the Indian Reorganization Act, the land was retrieved, and in 1946, the Pueblo of Pojoaque was finally recognized as a federal reservation. It is the smallest of the New Mexico pueblos.

The Poeh Cultural Center and Museum was built to tell the pueblo of Pojoaque's story. It has been successful in reintroducing arts programs, exhibits, and the Tewa language to the pueblo.

Within close proximity to Santa Fe, the Cities of Gold Hotel and Casino was established by the pueblo and, later in 2008, they opened the Hilton Santa Fe Buffalo Thunder Resort and Casino, the Hilton Santa Fe Golf Resort and Spa, and Homewood Suites.

Info: 30 Buffalo Thunder Trail, Santa Fe, NM 87506 • 505.819.2276 • http://www.pojoaque.org

Public Art

St. Kateri Tekakwitha permanently resides in front of St. Francis Basilica, her beauty forever captured by sculptor Estella Loretto, Jemez Pueblo.

Info: 131 Cathedral Pl., Santa Fe, NM 87501

Pueblo of Tesuque

The present-day village of Tesuque was established around 1690 along the Tesuque River, just north of Santa Fe. Tesuque is a Spanish variation of the Tewa name Te Tesugeh Oweengeh, meaning the "village of the narrow place of the cottonwood trees." The Tesuque people played an important role in the Pueblo Revolt of 1680, as two of its members served as the messengers who ran by foot carrying the news of the revolt throughout the territory.

Tesuque has a great reverence for its traditions and continues to practice ancient customs despite pressures from other cultures. Farming remains a primary role in the community. The pueblo is another conservative and traditional Tewa-speaking community. Tradition influences tribal governance and all community affairs. Santa Fe growth and popularity has forced the Tesuque to deal with issues over land and water rights resulting from significant numbers of Anglo settlers moving into the Tesuque Valley that stressed the valley's water supply.

Tesuque Pueblo Reservation includes Aspen Ranch and the Vigil Land Grant in the Santa Fe National Forest, and the pueblo is at the foothills of the Sangre de Cristo Mountain Range. The pueblo observes many celebrations and receives many visitors throughout the year. Those open to the public include the Feast of San Diego on November 12, Christmas celebrations in December, and Three Kings Day in January; the Corn Dance is held in June. The pueblo has been listed on the National Register of Historic Places. Tesuque Pueblo is ten minutes north of Santa Fe and the State Capitol and operates the Camel Rock Casino. Camel Rock is actually a place name for a natural sandstone formation that wind and rain eroded into the shape of a camel. Tesuque has many artists who produce pottery, painting, sculpture, and traditional clothing made at the pueblo.

Info: 17486A Highway 84/285, Santa Fe, NM 87506 • 505.983.2667 • http://www.camelrockcasino.com/pueblo-of-tesuque/

Wheelwright Museum of the American Indian

The Wheelwright Museum is a smaller museum with three galleries. The Case Trading Post in the basement is modeled after the Indian Trading Post with Native American art, jewelry, and trade blankets both historic and contemporary for sale. The upstairs gallery focus is Native American art with featured solo artists and less-known genres. The museum was established in 1937 by Mary Cabot Wheelwright, originally from Boston, with help from Hastiin Klah, a Navajo singer and medicine man who designed the building as a Navajo ceremonial hogan.

Info: 704 Camino Lejo, Santa Fe, NM 87505 • 505.982.4636 • https://wheelwright.org

SANTO DOMINGO
Santo Domingo Pueblo

When Don Juan de Onate visited Santo Domingo in 1598, the pueblo was on the north bank of Galisteo Creek, a few miles east of their present village. Galisteo floodwaters washed the village away and survivors established a village near the Rio Grande, but floodwaters struck Santo Domingo in 1692 and again in 1886, flooding the pueblo each time. The present-day pueblo of "Kewa" and the mission church were rebuilt following the flood of 1886.

During much of the Spanish colonial period, Santo Domingo was an important Franciscan mission center and the ecclesiastical capital of New Mexico. A mission church erected before 1607 by Fray Juan de Escalona, it was considered one of the largest and finest in New Mexico. It was washed away in the 1886 flood, but most of the records and religious objects were saved.

Santo Domingo has hosted many visitors during its history, including Zebulon Pike in 1809 and Col. Stephen Watts Kearny in 1846. Santo Domingo Pueblo is a Keres-speaking community with a strong, traditional base that is highly protective. No photography, sketching, or tape-recording is permitted nor is alcohol allowed on the reservation.

Historically, the people of Santo Domingo were extremely successful traders, carrying their jewelry and other crafts as far away as Mexico, the Pacific, and the

Plains. Today, Santo Domingo artists continue to create exquisite, handcrafted, beaded jewelry as well as shell mosaic inlay and silver jewelry, and these distinctive jewelry styles are prized around the world. The traditional pottery of Santo Domingo is also well known with many artists making simple jars of buff clay decorated with black, red, or brown geometric patterns.

The feast day of St. Dominic, patron saint of the pueblo, is celebrated with the Corn Dance, where more than one thousand Santo Domingo residents participate in the dancing. It is the largest pueblo dance ceremony in the Southwest and is a religious observance. Visitors are welcome.

Info: P.O. Box 99, Santo Domingo Pueblo, NM 87052 • 505.465.2214 • http://santodomingotribe.org/

SHIPROCK
Northern Navajo Fair and Rodeo

Every October, the Northern Navajo Fair, which is often called "The World's Largest American Indian Fair," is held at Shiprock. The four-day event features the All-Indian Rodeo, a carnival, Navajo traditional arts and food, a parade, a teen competition, and lots more. It is the oldest of all the Navajo fairs.

The town is named for the storied Shiprock, a monolith rock formation that rises 1,583 feet (482 meters) above the high-desert plain of the Navajo Nation in San Juan County, New Mexico. The formation is the remains of a twenty-seven-million-year-old volcano with a peak elevation of 7,177 feet (2,188 meters). Its Navajo name, Tsé Bit'a'í, is translated as "rock with wings" or "winged rock," which the

Shiprock rock formation, where the Northern Navajo Fair is held.

Navajo say brought them to this place from the North. Revered through this and many other traditional accounts, the Navajo believe it should be treated with respect, and climbing it is banned. Shiprock has a satellite campus of Diné College.

Info: Hwy. 491 and Uranium Blvd., Shiprock, NM 87420 • 505.368.1081 • www.discovernavajo.com

SILVER CITY
Gila Cliff Dwellings National Monument

The Gila Cliff Dwellings National Monument was established in 1907 and is a National Park Service-managed area that is surrounded by the Gila National Forest, managed by the U.S. Forest Service. The surrounding area includes a number of campsites, an interpretive trail, and an educational/visitors center.

The Gila Cliff Dwellings National Monument is especially important as the only unit in the National Park System that contains Mogollon and Mimbres sites, which are rapidly eroding in the Southwest. The Mogollon settled and lived between the late 1270s and 1300. The Mogollon were hunters and gatherers, who also incorporated farming into their daily lives. Their farms were on the mesa tops and along banks of the West Fork of the Gila River. They also produced pottery featuring brown bowls with black interiors and black-on-white vessels. Their clothing and sandals were made of yucca cord, agave leaves, bark, and cotton.

The Mogollon constructed five sites within caves along the cliff made of rock and mortar, which had approximately forty rooms. Trails to the site and ladders along the trail provide additional glimpses of the buildings. The trail is a 1-mile (1.6-kilometer) loop that takes around one hour round-trip to hike. Visitors can obtain information about these trails at the monument's visitor center. The visitor center displays Mogollon artifacts that were found throughout the cliff dwellings and the surrounding area and an exhibit on the Chiricahua Apache, who consider this wilderness area their homeland.

Info: Gila National Forest, Silver City, NM 88061 • 575.536.9461 • https://www.nps.gov/gicl/index.htm

Western New Mexico University Museum

The Western New Mexico University Museum, located in Fleming Hall on the university campus, houses the NAN Ranch Collection, which claims to be the most comprehensive collection of scientifically excavated ancient Mimbres materials from a single Mimbres site. Archaeologists consider Mimbres a subset of the Mogollon culture. Mogollon is one of three major cultures identified in the American Southwest, along with the Anasazi, also referred to as the Ancestral Puebloans, and the Hohokam.

Mimbres, which means "willows" in Spanish, is the name given to a cotton-wood- and willow-lined river in southwestern New Mexico. The ancient pottery found in and around the Mimbres Valley also came to be called Mimbres, and the name was soon applied to the people who made the pottery. Western New Mexico University

Museum has received the NAN Ranch collection of Mimbres pottery that was collected during more than thirty years of scientific excavation on the ranch at a number of archaeological sites.

Info: 1000 W. College Ave., Silver City, NM 88061 • 575.538.6386 • http://museum.wnmu.edu/about/

TAOS
Millicent Rogers Museum

The Millicent Rogers Museum has over seven thousand objects in its collection of art and culture of the Southwest. The museum's collection was begun by its namesake, Millicent Rogers, an heiress who grew up in New York. Millicent's life was transformed after a visit to the Gallup Intertribal Ceremony in 1947, and she was inspired by the jewelry and art made by Native Americans. She moved to Taos and became passionate about both Hispanic and Native America.

The museum has a major collection of pottery by Maria Martinez and her family of San Ildefonso Pueblo. Works of Taos Pueblo artists Albert Looking Elk Martinez, Albert Lujan, Juan Mirabal, and Juanito Concha, and other Puebloan artists are part of the collection. Taos is filled with galleries and museums, having been the home of the Taos art colony founded in the early 1900s by European and American artists attracted by the rich culture and landscape of Taos. The Rio Grande Gorge is located just outside of Taos. The famous long-span bridge over the incredible, six-hundred-foot-deep gorge is a treat along with more than eighty galleries and three museums, located near the Millicent Rogers Museum.

Info: 1504 Millicent Rogers Rd., Taos, NM 87571 • 575.758.2462 • https://www.millicentrogers.org/index.php

Pot Creek Pueblo

Pot Creek Pueblo was formerly home to several hundred Ancestral Puebloan peoples approximately seven hundred years ago. The site consists of at least nine earthen mounds surrounding at least one large plaza area with a great kiva constructed in the mid-thirteenth century. Each room block area surrounds a small plaza. In each of these small plazas, a small kiva—or circular, subterranean structure—was built between 1260 and 1320 C.E. Buried beneath the remains of the adobe rooms are subterranean structures called pithouses, dated between 1100 and 1200 C.E.

Pot Creek Pueblo was abandoned around 1320 C.E., and it is believed that the inhabitants of the site moved to settlements contiguous to the modern settlements at Taos Pueblo and Picuris Pueblo. Pot Creek Pueblo is not open to visitors. It is on private property, owned by Southern Methodist University in Texas. Visitors are welcome to see the Pot Creek cultural site in Taos County.

Info: 208 Cruz Alta Rd., Taos, NM 87571 • 505.587.2255 • https://www.smu.edu/Taos/PotCreek

Taos Pueblo

Taos Pueblo, a National Historic Landmark and UNESCO World Heritage Site, is the most recognizable pueblo, as photographs of the multistory adobe structure appear in all travel destinations. Puebloan peoples still live here. The old village has no electricity. The Tiwa-speaking community of Taos Pueblo dates back to 900 C.E. They are descendants of Ancestral Puebloans, and the architecture of their ancestors is seen at Taos Pueblo today, which consists of two units: Hlauuma is the north house and Hlaukwima is the south house; they were constructed between 1000 and 1450 C.E. Built of adobe brick with wood-beamed vigas (Spanish) and small, conical wood slats called latillas (Spanish) for roofs, each is five stories.

The pueblo welcomes visitors but requests that guests respect the privacy and rights of all residents and adhere to the tribe's policies. Photographs are allowed but only for personal use. Tribal members serve as tour guides within the historic village area.

When the Spanish encountered Taos Pueblo in 1540, it looked much as it does today. Like other pueblo Indians, the Taos Indians were declared citizens of Mexico when that nation gained its independence from Spain. The United States then confirmed the tribe and its land base under the 1848 Treaty of Guadalupe Hidalgo.

Taos Pueblo is said to be the spearhead of the Pueblo Revolt of 1680, uniting the northern pueblos in a successful effort to drive the Spanish out of the area. In 1847, they joined the Mexican settlers in their fight against the U.S. government in Taos and the surrounding region. The present-day San Geronimo Chapel at Taos Pueblo was constructed in 1850 to replace the church that the U.S. Army destroyed during the Mexican–American War in 1847. The original church, built in 1619, had been destroyed during the Pueblo Revolt of 1680. It was rebuilt on the same site, and the ruins are evident on the west side of the village.

Taos Pueblo.

San Geronimo is the pueblo's patron saint, and a large celebration is held each September on his feast day. The tribe hosts a number of ceremonial and celebratory dances year-round, many of which are open to the public. The tribe also hosts the annual Taos Pueblo Powwow.

Taos Pueblo's history also involves a landmark court case involving the lake of reverence known as Blue Lake that was taken by the federal government and incorporated into the Carson National Forest in 1906. The tribe took the federal government to court seeking the return of Blue Lake, and in 1970, the lake was restored to the Taos people. This marked the first time that land instead of money was returned to an American Indian tribe upon completion of a land claims case.

Info: 120 Veterans Hwy., Taos, NM 87571 • 505.758.8626 •
http://taospueblo.com/home/

ZIA PUEBLO
Zia Pueblo Cultural Center

Zia Pueblo traces its ancestry to the Ancestral Puebloan settlement of Chaco Canyon in western New Mexico prior to 400 c.e. At the end of the twelfth century, migrations out of Chaco Canyon began after extended years of drought. Zia people settled in their present location. In 1540, Spanish records described Zia Pueblo as having one thousand well-kept two- and three-story houses. Spanish interference with the pueblo's spiritual traditions led Zia to join in the Pueblo Revolt of 1680. The once large pueblo was destroyed after a bloody assault in 1688 in the Spanish reconquest of what became New Mexico Territory. In 1692, Zia people accepted Catholic baptisms, which, they say, "did not erase our old ways."

A source of debate is about the State of New Mexico's adoption and use of the Zia symbol of four hatches with a circle in the center, resembling a cross design on both the flag and license plates. The symbol originated with the Indians of Zia Pueblo, which reflects their tribal philosophy and teachings as the basic harmony of all things in the universe.

Zia Pueblo is listed on the National Register of Historic Places. They opened the Zia Pueblo Cultural Center in 1992. Zia Pueblo, a Keres-speaking community, celebrates its Feast Day with their corn dance on August 15.

Info: 135 Capitol Square Dr., Zia Pueblo, NM 87053 • 505.867.3304 •
http://zia.com/home/zia_info.html

ZUNI
A:shiwi A:wan Museum and Heritage Center

Established by a small group of Zuni tribal members in 1992, the A:shiwi A:wan Museum and Heritage Center is dedicated to serving the Zuni community with programs and exhibitions reflecting their past and importance to the present and future. It is a tribal museum and heritage center for the Zuni people and by the Zuni people to provide learning experiences that emphasize A:shiwi ways of knowing as well as exploring modern concepts of knowledge and the transfer of knowledge.

As an ecomuseum, it retains harmony with the Zuni's environmental values and is dedicated to honoring, cultivating, and nurturing dynamic Zuni culture. As part of its vision, the AAMHC promotes, facilitates, and conducts collaborative initiatives with several museums and collecting institutions located both in the United States and abroad. One of the main purposes of these collaborations is to "set the record straight," to correct inadequate, inaccurate, and/or wrong representations of Zuni collections housed at satellite museums and archives. The collections acquired by the A:shiwi A:wah have been identified through long-term collaborations with major institutions that have films, sound recordings, and other cultural objects made and used by Zuni people.

Groups and individuals are invited to schedule an appointment to view particular films in the collection.

The Zuni and their ancestors occupied the Zuni and Little Colorado river valleys for more than two thousand years. Zuni Pueblo or Halona Idiwan'a, translated to "Our Middle Place," is a large, Zuni-speaking community, and it is the only pueblo that speaks Zuni. It is located the farthest west of the nineteen New Mexico Indian pueblos. The present-day reservation lies on the site of Halona, one of the Seven Cities of Cibola. Zuni Pueblo, the community's principal town, was founded around 1350. The main body of the reservation was established by an executive order in 1877. An act of Congress put the pueblo's land into trust in 1978.

Info: 02E Ojo Caliente Rd., Zuni, NM 87327 • 505.782.4403 • http://www.ashiwi.org

TEXAS

The American Indian/Alaska Native population of Texas identified in the 2010 Census was 315,264, and Texas has twelve Native nations.

ALTO
Caddo Mounds State Historic Site

Caddo Mounds, a state park until around 1995, had a large Caddo grass house at the site, but the structure became unstable and was removed. The USDA and Texas Parks and Wildlife are constructing a new Caddo grass house and creating new land-management projects to restore Native prairie, create pollinator habitats, form a turkey co-op for the reintroduction of wild turkeys, and develop an interpretive garden.

Twelve hundred years ago, a group of Caddo Indians known as the Hasinai built a village 26 miles (42 kilometers) west of present-day Nacogdoches. The site was the southwesternmost ceremonial center for the great mound-building culture. Today, three mounds are visible in the Pineywoods landscape. The Hasinai Caddo groups continued to live through the 1830s in their traditional east Texas homeland in the Neches and Angelina River valleys, but by the early 1840s, all Caddo groups had moved to the Brazos River area to remove themselves from Anglo-American repressive measures and colonization efforts. They remained there until the U.S. government placed them on the Brazos Indian Reservation in 1855 and then in 1859, the Caddo were removed to the Washita River in Indian Territory, now western Oklahoma. The Caddo continue to live in western Oklahoma, primarily near the Caddo Nation Headquarters outside Binger, Oklahoma.

Info: 649 State Hwy. 21 W., Alto, TX 75925 • 936.858.3218 • http://www.thc.texas.gov/historic-sites/caddo-mounds-state-historic-site

AUSTIN
Austin Powwow and American Indian Heritage Festival

This one-day, annual powwow is held in the city of Austin in November and has been celebrated for almost thirty years. Great Promise for American Indians, a local American Indian organization, hosts the event. The organization also supports programs that preserve the traditions, heritage, health, education, and culture of American Indian peoples in the Austin area. The powwow is at the Travis Exposition Center at 7311 Decker Lane in Austin.

Info: Great Promise for American Indians, 3710 Cedar St. #19, Austin, TX 78705 • 512.371.0628 • http://www.austinpowwow.net/mission/

COMSTOCK
Seminole Canyon State Park and Historic Site

More than two hundred pictograph sites can be seen on guided tours. The art ranges from single paintings to caves with panels of art hundreds of feet long. Numerous figures or motifs repeat in different places. The visitor center displays artifacts found in the area and dioramas depicting the lives of these early people.

Hikers in Seminole Canyon.

Info: U.S. Hwy. 90, Comstock, TX 78837 • 432.292.4464 • https://tpwd.texas.gov/state-parks/seminole-canyon

EAGLE PASS
Kickapoo Empire

The Kickapoo Traditional Tribe of Texas, like other Kickapoo bands, speaks an Algonquian language closely related to the Mesquakie-Sauk language. Prior to first contact, the Kickapoo lived in fixed villages throughout the lower Great Lakes region of the Midwest. European expansion and intertribal conflicts led to migrations and dispersal widely throughout Indiana, Illinois, Missouri, and Texas.

As early as 1775, the Kickapoo were granted land by the king of Spain in the northern part of the Spanish Territory of what was then Mexico. This part of Mexico later became Texas. In the early 1800s, one group migrated to Mexico. By 1865, the only large concentration of Kickapoo in the United States was in Kansas.

Until recently, those Kickapoo who chose dual residency did not have clear legal status in either the United States or Mexico and received only limited assistance and government services from either country. In 1979, they asked the U.S. government to clarify their American citizenship status; they entered into negotiations with the interior and state departments, the Mexican government, and the Inter-American Indian Institute with legal assistance from the Native American Rights Fund and support from the Kickapoo in Oklahoma and Kansas. These negotiations resulted in the passage of the Texas Band of Kickapoo Act in 1977, paving the way for federal recognition in January 1983. The tribe was federally recognized as the Kickapoo Traditional Tribe of Texas, a distinct, self-governing subgroup of the Kickapoo Tribe of Oklahoma. On November 21, 1985, 145 members of the 650-member band became American citizens. In 1989, the Kickapoo Traditional Tribe of Texas developed a constitution and submitted it to the secretary of the interior, requesting federal recognition as a separate and distinct tribe.

In 1984, the Kickapoo Trust Land Acquisition Committee purchased 125 acres (0.5 square kilometers) along the Rio Grande River in Maverick County, Texas, about 8 miles (13 kilometers) south of Eagle Pass. In the absence of a land base of their own, most tribal members have historically lived just across the Rio Grande in a village, El Nacimiento Rancheria, since the late 1860s. They continue to live in traditional houses made of reed mats on 17,290 acres (70 square kilometers) granted them by the Mexican government. The village is located in the State of Coahuila, 25 miles (40 kilometers) northwest of Muzquis, approximately 125 miles (201 kilometers) southwest of Eagle Pass, Texas.

The Kickapoo's aboriginal religion revolves around a seasonal ceremonial cycle, beginning in early spring, with a series of major ceremonies that continue for several weeks. Many ceremonies take place in Nacimiento, and a large number of Oklahoma Kickapoo travel to Mexico to join with their kin in a traditional Kickapoo environment. Tribal members in Texas and Oklahoma preserve the Kickapoo language. In 1996, the tribe first built the 15,000-square-foot (1,400-square-meter) Kickapoo Lucky Eagle Casino on land purchased near Eagle Pass, Texas.

Info: 2212 Rosita Valley Rd., Eagle Pass, TX 78852 • 830.773.2105 •
https://kickapootexas.org/

EL PASO
Tigua Indian Cultural Center

The Tigua Indian Cultural Center shares five centuries of rich Ancestral Puebloan history and ongoing tradition at the center's museum and entrance to the Alderette-Candelaria House, an adobe home believed to have been built, with the help of Tigua Indians, for Benigno Alderete in the 1870s. Alderete served as a Texas ranger, county commissioner, and town mayor.

Wall art painted on the Ysleta del Sur Pueblo at the Tigua Indian Cultural Center celebrates three centuries of history.

The cultural center and pueblo social dances are held in the plaza area, and Tigua youth are often the tour guides. Ysleta del Sur Pueblo is in close proximity to the cities of El Paso and Socorro, Texas, just north of the Mexico border along the Rio Grande. The primary reservation community is 1 mile (1.6 kilometers) northeast of the Zaragoza international border between the United States and Mexico.

Ysleta del Sur Pueblo ("the pueblo") is a U.S. federally recognized Native American tribe and sovereign nation. The tribal community known as "Tigua" established Ysleta del Sur in 1682. After leaving the homelands of Quarai Pueblo due to drought, the Tigua sought refuge at Isleta Pueblo and were captured by the Spanish during the 1680 Pueblo Revolt and forced to walk 400 miles (644 kilometers) south. The Tigua resettled and built their pueblo, Ysleta del Sur Pueblo, constructing an acequia (water canal) system that sustained a thriving, agriculturally based community.

Today, the pueblo leadership have as their mission to promote self-sufficiency, improve the quality of life, and preserve the cultural identity for the pueblo. Ysleta del Sur Pueblo is the gateway to El Paso's Mission Valley that includes the historic communities of Ysleta, Socorro, and San Elizario. These scenic villages include historic missions, old adobe buildings, informative museums and cultural centers, fine restaurants, and alluring boutiques and attractive shops with original arts and crafts.

Info: 305 Yaya Ln., El Paso, TX 79907 • 915.859.8053 • http://www.ysletadelsurpueblo.org

HOUSTON
American Indian Genocide Museum

Currently, this is primarily a traveling museum with exhibits that tell the multifaceted story of American Indian genocide and oppression.

Info: P.O. Box #230452, Houston, TX 77223 • 281.841.3028 • http://www.aigenom.org/

Native American Indian Championship Powwow Traders Village

The Annual Native American Indian Championship Powwow Traders Village is a two-day event with a dance competition for prize money, arts and crafts, and honoring ceremonies. Sponsored by the DW Inter-Tribal Association, many different nations are represented, including the Kiowa, Pawnee/Otoe, and Navajo.

Info: 7979 N. Eldridge Rd., Houston, TX 77041 • 281.890.5500 • http://www.crazycrow.com/site/event/native-american-indian-championship-pow-wow-traders-village-houston

LIVINGSTON
Museum of the Alabama and Coushatta

The Alabama and Coushatta Tribe operates a visitor and information center as well as the Museum of the Alabama and Coushatta, which includes the "Living Indian Village" exhibit featuring live demonstrations of basket making, weaving, beadwork, arrowhead making, and food preparation, and visitors can also take a guided walking tour.

The Alabama-Coushatta Reservation is Texas's oldest reservation, located approximately 70 miles (113 kilometers) northeast of Houston. Established in 1854 by Sam Houston, the reservation borders the Big Thicket National Preserve. The Alabama and Coushatta Tribe is part of a Muskogean linguistic group, and its members are descendants of the southeastern mound-building peoples whose subsistence was based on agriculture, hunting, and gathering.

Following Euro-American colonial expansion, the Coushatta moved east to Texas in the late 1800s and supported Texas's independence from Mexico. Living in small villages, the Coushatta moved and joined the Alabama-Coushatta Reservation in 1906 and did not become federally recognized until August 1987. Tribal members continue to value their ancestral teachings.

Recreational opportunities on the reservation include tours of the Big Thicket Wilderness Preserve, featuring educational, open-air bus rides, and the Big Chief Train ride, a twenty-minute excursion into the preserve. Lake Tombigbee, a 26-acre (0.1-square-kilometer) reservoir, offers water-based recreation with campsites, full RV hookups, and nature trails, receiving more than two hundred thousand visitors annually.

Info: 571 State Park Rd. 56, Livingston, TX 77351 • 936.563.1100 • http://www.alabama-coushatta.com/

MCALLEN
Lipan Tribal Museum and Cultural Center

The Lipan Apache Tribe was officially recognized by the State of Texas's Senate and House of Representatives in March 2009. The Lipan Apache Tribe of Texas is the continuation of the historical Lipan Apache Tribe, whose territorial homelands are in the southern Great Plains, the Mapimi Basin in northern Mexico, and the Gulf of Mexico. The Lipan people functioned as a confederation of different bands of Plains Apache living independently yet allied with each other for mutual aid and the common defense of homelands.

Larger communities of present-day Lipan live mostly throughout the U.S. Southwest, with clusters at the San Carlos Apache Indian Reservation in Arizona and on the Mescalero Reservation in New Mexico.

The Tribal Museum and Culture Center is located in McAllen, Texas, and housed in the Native cultural center with the tribe's central office. Visits to the cultural center are by appointment only.

Info: Lipan Apache Tribe of Texas, P.O. Box 5218, McAllen, TX 78502 • 956.648.9336 • http://www.lipanapache.org/Communitypages.html

SAN ANTONIO
UTSA Institute of Texan Cultures

Research, exhibits, and collections at the Institute of Texan Cultures share and interpret the rich cultural tapestry that makes this state what it is today. Long-term

The Institute of Texan Cultures.

and rotating exhibits present stories of Texans past and present, with an emphasis on the heritage of the many different peoples who chose to make this their home. Artifacts, both on exhibit and those in the collection, provide tangible links to these stories and allow us to share experiences across time and space. The Texan culture collections make use of an experimental weblog designed to make the collections of the Institute of Texan Cultures more accessible to all audiences: source communities, students, the general public, educators, and research scholars.

Info: 801 E. César E. Chávez Blvd., San Antonio, TX 78205-3296 • 210.458.2300 • http://www.texancultures.com/

UTAH

The 2010 Census identified the state of Utah as having a population of 50,064 American Indian/Alaska Natives, and five Native nations are in Utah.

CEDAR CITY
Paiute Tribe of Utah

The Pauite Indian Tribe of Utah, or "PITU" as it is often called, was created on April 3, 1980, by an act of Congress and resulted in the restoration of the tribe. The tribe consists of five bands: Cedar, Indian Peaks, Kanosh, Koosharem, and Shivwit, each with independent stories and identities. After the invasion of European settlers and Mormon pioneers, only the Cedar Band of Paiute received a separate reservation.

In 1954, a policy of termination of all federal responsibility over Indian tribes was carried out in Utah, and the Shivwit, Kanosh, Koorsharem, and Indian Peaks Paiute were terminated. Repudiation of this termination policy began in 1970, leading to the restoration of the federal trust relationship of the five bands reorganized as the Paiute Indian Tribe of Utah. The PITU community today is only in its second generation of existence. The PITU is actually a confederation of constituent Paiute communities that have been independent for many generations.

The PITU Reservation consists of ten separate land parcels located in four southwestern Utah counties.

The Southern Paiute had many social gatherings. They gathered together in a large group called a "big time." Some reasons for getting together were piñon harvests, round dances, or funerals. The Southern Paiute had many gatherings/events that in today's society would be considered a holiday, but they were for celebrating the different times of seasons. Today, a "big time" usually refers to a memorial cry or mourning ceremony called yaxape. Spring and summer were always favorites for celebrations; people would gather from all around and meet near lakes and mountains, with an abundance of food. They would hunt, fish, and have games such as horse racing, foot racing, dancing, an archery contest, gambling, and numerous other events. Spring was also the time for the Bear Dance, when the bears would come out of hibernation. This dance brought people from all around, with food and fun for everyone. The Paiute Tribe hosts the Annual Restoration Gathering and Powwow in recognition of their restored place as a reservation-based federal Indian tribe.

Info: 440 N. Paiute Dr., Cedar City, UT 84721 • 435.586.1112 • http://www.utahpaiutes.org/

FORT DUCHESNE
Northern Ute Indian Tribe of the Unitah and Ouray Ute Reservation

The Uintah and Oray Ute Reservation is located in northeastern Utah at Fort Duchesne, approximately 150 miles (241 kilometers) east of Salt Lake City, Utah, on U.S. Highway 40. The reservation is located within a three-county area known as the Uintah Basin. It is the second-largest Indian reservation in the United States and covers over 4.5 million acres (18,211 square kilometers). Utah and Nootuvweek, or Ute Indian Country, are said to be the land of the Noochew, "the people." The tribal government oversees approximately 1.3 million acres (5,261 square kilometers) of trust land.

The tribe's Fish and Wildlife Department manages eight major reservoirs and six rivers/streams along the south slope of the Uintah Mountain Range for fly-fishing and other angling. Both seasonal and day permits are available, and sport fishing is a popular tourist draw to the reservation. Outdoor recreation sites near these rivers and reservoirs, such as those at Bottle Hollow, are managed by the Parks and Outdoor Facilities office within the Fish and Wildlife Department. The Ute Tribe Outfitting and Guide Service offers four annual big game hunts for trophy elk, Bighorn sheep, cougar, and buffalo. Permits for other hunting, such as bear, goose, pheasant, and duck, are also available. The program provides a guide and a horse or vehicle to properly permitted hunters, provide taxidermy services, and assist in transporting the meat to a meat plant in Arcadia for cutting, wrapping, and freezing.

The Dinosaur Diamond Prehistoric Highway, a two-state but national scenic byway that passes through the reservation in eastern Utah and western Colorado, is in close proximity to the Dinosaur National Monument and the Carnegie Dinosaur Quarry. Many geographic natural attractions and historical museums lie along the course of this 512-mile (824-kilometer) loop, such as the Colorado National Monument, the Arches National Monument, the Duchesne Starvation State Park, the Flaming Gorge (on the Green River), and Fort Duchesne, a former army post.

Info: Northern Ute Indian Tribe of the Unitah and Ouray Ute Reservation, P.O. Box 190, Fort Duchesne, UT 84026 • 435.722.5141 • http://www.utetribe.com

IBAPAH
Confederated Tribes of the Goshute Reservation

The Confederated Tribes of the Goshute Reservation (CTGR) lands straddle the east-central Nevada border with the western Utah state line. Tribal headquarters are located in Ibapah, Utah, and are accessible by a paved road.

The name "Goshute" comes from the Native word Ku'tsip or Gu'tship, meaning "ashes," "desert," or "dry earth and people." The Shoshonean-speaking people maintained aboriginal territory in the Great Basin extending from the Great Salt Lake to the Steptoe Range in Nevada and south to Simpson Spring.

Historically, they wintered in Deep Creek Valley in dugouts built of willow poles and earth. Native food resources included some eighty-one species of wild vegetable food, including seeds, berries, roots, and greens. Important to the Goshute are pinon pine nuts, and these are gathered annually.

The Goshute have remained active in traditional arts that include weaving willow baskets, carving cradleboards, beading jewelry, and tanning deerskin for trade. The Goshute Tribe holds an annual powwow and hand game tournaments in August. The Lincoln Highway, the first intercontinental road in the United States, crosses the reservation lands following the paths taken by Pony Express and Overland Stage routes. The Ibapah Valley Ramble is a long-distance bicycle trail ride that covers local historic sites, and information for that nontribal event is at http://www.cycling utah.com/issues/2011/june-2011/ibapah-valley-ramble/.

Info: 195 Tribal Center Rd., HC 61, P.O. Box 6104, Ibapah, UT 84034 • 435.234.1138 • https://utahindians.org/archives/ctgr.html

MONUMENT VALLEY
Monument Valley Tribal Park and Visitors Center

The character and setting for the American West lives on in Hollywood movies through the prevailing landscape at Monument Valley with red, sandstone buttes that form natural monuments out of the desert floor. It is best to visit either at sunrise or sunset, when the colors are at their most intense. The Navajo Nation Parks and Recreation operates a visitor center 4 miles (6.4 kilometers) southeast of the park entrance from U.S. 163 in Utah. Horseback and four-wheel-drive tours of the valley can be arranged at the Monument Valley Lodge at Goulding's Lodge. The lodge

Monument Valley.

is in Utah, but a majority of the tribal park is situated in Arizona. Temperatures range from an average low of 25 degrees Fahrenheit (–4 degrees Celsius) in the winter to an average high of 90 degrees Fahrenheit (32 degrees Celsius) in the summer.

Info: Oljato-Monument Valley, UT 84536 • 435.727.5870 • http://www.discover-navajo.com/parks.aspx

THE WEST COAST

The Makah Tribe has called the spectacular Neah Bay, Washington area home since time immemorial. The name Makah was attributed to the Tribe by the neighboring tribes, meaning "people generous with food" in the Salish language. The meaning still applies today, as we invite you to visit our community to enjoy the natural beauty and learn about our culture and history.

—Makah Tribal Council, Neah Bay, Washington

Airlines offer a special package called the Pacific Rim, allowing passengers to make several stops to countries bordering the Pacific Ocean for one flat fare. Did you know that you could stay entirely within the United States and Canada and travel to Indigenous sites and communities located within the Pacific Rim, or West Coast? The province of British Columbia plus its outer islands, the states of Alaska, California, Oregon, Washington, all are homelands of ancient peoples who still survive, although colonization has impacted their territories, their economic systems, their religious beliefs, their health, their governments, their education, and their self-determination.

These communities are often strategically located in the struggles between powerful nations and have been invaded, exploited, and ruled by warring countries that have had little respect or consideration for the rightful owners. Traditional homelands located on the country's western coasts have often been devastated by U.S military operations. During World War II, the entire Unangan (Aleutian) community was removed to mainland relocation camps in abandoned canneries. Several died of cold and hunger. They were not allowed to return home until long after the war was over, and when they were allowed back on their islands, they found their homes, buildings, and churches destroyed. Other usurped western homelands have been turned into agribusiness locations, housing tracts, and expensive resorts.

Most Pacific Indigenous lands are located in the horseshoe-shaped "Ring of Fire," a string of volcanoes and sites of seismic activity—earthquakes. Roughly 90 percent of all earthquakes occur along the Ring of Fire, and the ring is dotted with 75 percent of all active volcanoes on Earth. The eastern edge of this great ring is defined on the east by the Cascade Range, Sierra Nevada, Mojave Desert, and Aleutian Islands. The climate differs from Mediterranean to Arctic to temperate. Some areas have only two seasons: winter and summer.

The West Coast has lots of vacation and travel opportunities. Some vacation resorts are owned by Native peoples; other venues have pushed out the Native population, who may live in poverty while visitors enjoy the best beaches, which are often ceremonial sites for original peoples. From California's tony Palm Springs to Alaska's iconic Totem Bight Park, the West Coast is a supermarket of Indigenous landmarks, recreation, art, adventures, and education. But it is important to remember that these vacation lands are the homelands of First Nations, a fact often ignored by travel agencies.

ALASKA

A laska's Native citizens number around 139,700. Eleven major cultural groups are in the state.

ANCHORAGE
Alaska Native Heritage Center

The Alaska Native Heritage Center (ANHC), which opened in 1999, is a cultural center sharing the rich heritage of Alaska's eleven major cultural groups. A tour of the

Benjamin Schleifman was a featured artist at the Alaska Native Heritage Center for Contemporary Native Arts Day, 2010.

center allows people to see and hear living Alaska Native cultures. Performances, such as storytelling, dance, music, and game demonstrations, take place in the Gathering Place, a large, circular hall. The Hall of Cultures houses pictures and artifacts that portray the life and environment of the eleven distinct cultural groups. Studio workshops demonstrate various crafts. The theater hosts a variety of movies all day, including the Heritage Center-produced film *Stories Given, Stories Shared*.

Guests can stroll through authentic, life-size Native dwellings situated in a wooded area around Lake Tiulana, where they are introduced to the traditional structures and lifeways of the Athabascan, Inupiaq St. Lawrence Island Yupik, Yup'ik/Cup'ik, Aleut, Alutiiq, Eyak, Tlingit, Haida, and Tsimshian peoples.

The Heritage Café offers samples of Native fare, such as the Alaska Reindeer Hot Dog and the Salmon Burger. The gift shop features authentic Alaska Native arts and crafts.

Info: 8800 Heritage Center Dr., Anchorage, AK 99504 • 907.330.8000 • http://www.alaskanative.net/

Anchorage Museum at Rasmuson Center

The Anchorage Museum, whose former name was the Anchorage Museum of History and Art, first opened in 1968, and a major expansion in 2010 added the Smithsonian Arctic Studies Center, a museum-within-a-museum. The Smithsonian Center's main exhibition is titled "Living Our Culture, Sharing Our Heritage: The First Peoples of Alaska." It features more than six hundred Alaska Native objects that were selected and interpreted with help from Alaska Native advisors. Visitors can view short films

Anchorage Museum at Rasmuson Center.

and photographs and listen to recordings of Alaska Native storytellers that show and tell what being Alaska Native means today and how traditions are being carried into the future.

Notable in the gallery is the Dena'ina tribute wall, giving thanks to the first people who lived on the land where the museum sits today.

Besides the museum's Alaskan history exhibits and many art galleries, it contains an excellent collection of contemporary Alaska Native art.

Info: 625 C St., Anchorage, AK 99501 • 907.929.9200 • https://www.anchoragemuseum.org

Fur Rendezvous

Known locally as "Rondy," this local winter festival began as a sports tournament in 1935, when Anchorage was a tiny town of three thousand residents. The three-day event took place at the time when miners and trappers came to town with their yield. The Emporium of Alaska Native Art is a regular part of Rondy and features more than 150 Alaska Native artisans selling and demonstrating their art: basket weaving, dolls, beading, carving, and more. Festival activities include a traditional Native blanket toss (used in historic times to spot whales), a dogsled race, snow sculptures, a fur auction, running of the reindeer, and different sports events.

Info: 800 E. Diamond Blvd., Anchorage, AK 99515 • 907.274.1177 • http://www.furrondy.net/

Indigenous World Film Festval

The Alaska Native Heritage Center hosts an annual two-day Indigenous World Film Festival, one of its winter events, free and open to the public. The festival features Indigenous films from Alaska, the lower forty-eight First Nations, Canada, Greenland, and New Zealand. Guest filmmakers and actors speak at question-and-answer sessions.

Info: 8800 Heritage Center Dr., Anchorage, AK 99504 • 907.330.8000 • http://www.alaskanative.net/

BARROW
The Iñupiat Heritage Center

The Iñupiat Heritage Center was dedicated in February 1999 and houses exhibits, artifact collections, a library, a gift shop, and a traditional room where people can demonstrate and teach traditional crafts. The North Slope Borough owns and manages the heritage center on behalf of the whaling villages of the North Slope.

The Iñupiat Heritage Center (IHC) brings people together to promote and perpetuate Iñupiat history, language, and culture. This dynamic interaction between the Iñupiat and their environment fosters the awareness, understanding, and appreciation of the Iñupiat way of life from generation to generation.

The heritage center is one of several partners, associated through New Bedford Whaling National Historical Park legislation, who participate in telling the story of commercial whaling in the United States. Park partners operate independently but collaborate in a variety of educational and interpretive programs.

Info: 5421 North Star St., Barrow, AK 99723 • 907.852.0422 • https://www.nps.gov/inup/details.htm

BETHEL
Yupiit Piciryarait Museum

With over five thousand objects, the tribally owned and operated Yup'ik museum houses priceless and one-of-a-kind objects that showcase the Yup'ik people of the Yukon-Kuskokwim delta region. The gallery houses two permanent exhibits and one temporary exhibit that changes every three months. The museum goal is to sustain the Yup'ik culture, history, language, and arts via the transmission of knowledge from this generation of elders into the future.

Info: 101 Main St., P.O. Box 219, Bethel, AK 99559 • 907.543.7335

CHUGIAK
Eklutna Historical Park

Dating back to 1650, Eklutna is the oldest continually inhabited Athabascan site in the state. The Athabascan used the site as a fishing camp. A tour of the park provides a chance to experience an Alaska Native and Russian Orthodox cultural experience. Visit the historic St. Nicholas Russian Orthodox Church and walk around many "spirit houses" that adorn ancestral graves of some of the Athabascan.

Info: Eklutna Village Rd., Chugiak, AK 99567 • 907.764.7233 • http://www.eklutnahistoricalpark.org/

CORDOVA
Ilanka Cultural Center

In 2004, the Ilanka Cultural Center opened its doors to foster the well-being of our Native cultures in the face of modern times. The center shares its heritage: food and languages, art and regalia, and songs and dances with visitors. The center honors the heritage and culture of the Eyak, Alutiiq, Ahtna, and Tlingit peoples.

The center museum preserves and exhibits a collection of ancient, historic, and contemporary tribal artifacts from the Prince Sound and Copper River Delta. The center hosts annual traveling exhibits.

In July 2000, an Orca whale became stranded and died at Hartney Bay in Cordova. A community effort salvaged his bones. A group of people, scientists, and the Cordova community rearticulated the complete skeleton, which hangs in Ilanka's lobby, one of five in the world on display.

Info: 100 Nicholoff Way, Cordova, AK 99574 • 907.424.7738 • http://eyak-nsn.gov/ilanka-cultural-center/

FAIRBANKS
Midnight Sun Intertribal Powwow

A highlight of this annual July powwow is the release of a rehabilitated eagle from the Bird Treatment and Learning Center. Native dancers and musicians from around the state join in for the three-day celebration with potato and hoop dancing, arts, demonstrations, and camaraderie.

Info: 2010 2nd Ave., Fairbanks, AK 99701 • 907.456.2245 • http://www.midnightsunintertribalpowwow.com/

University of Alaska Museum of the North

Discover fascinating stories about Alaska's people, places, and wildlife in the University of Alaska Museum of the North's exhibit galleries. The centerpiece of the expanded museum, the Rose Berry Alaska Art Gallery, shows many treasures once in storage but now in public view. The gallery presents the full spectrum of Alaska art, from ancient Eskimo ivory carvings to contemporary paintings and sculpture, both Native and non-Native.

In the Gallery of Alaska, exhibits are grouped thematically to represent Alaska's major ecological and cultural regions. Highlights include Alaska's largest gold display, extensive displays of Alaska Native art, and artifacts. Watch videos on a whale hunt and Alaska Native dances.

The university also sponsors the annual, three-day Festival of Native Arts, a major celebration of Native Alaskan arts for almost fifty years. Not only do the spectacular performances demonstrate the diversity and beauty of the state's First Peoples, but art workshops are offered in everything from photography from a Native perspective to agutak making (traditional ice cream). https://fna.community.uaf.edu/

Two contestants in an Ear Pull Match at the 2008 World Eskimo Indian Olympics.

Info: UAF Campus, 1962 Yukon Dr., Fairbanks, AK 99775 • 907.474.7505 • http://www.alaska.org/detail/ua-museum-of-the-north

World Eskimo Indian Olympics

The first World Eskimo Olympics, held in Fairbanks in 1961, drew contestants and dance teams from Barrow, Unalakleet, Tanana, Fort Yukon, Noorvik, and Nome. The event was a big success and has been held annually ever since in July.

Not only do athletes compete for top honors in more than a dozen physical events, but visitors can also view stunning dance performances and buy intricate arts and crafts works. It is a chance for Alaska's communities to come together and share their culture with each other and the world.

The games that are played today display the preparation one needed for survival hundreds of years ago and even today. They require skill as well as strength, agility, and endurance. Hundreds of years ago, the games were played to teach children that they had to be tough to make it on their own not just in one area but in all areas. The games leave no part of the body untested. Today, the WEIO games continue to be the high point of the year for athletes.

Info: Carlson Center, 2010 2nd Ave., Fairbanks, AK 99701 • 907.452.6646 • http://www.weio.org/

HAINES
Alaska Indian Arts

Alaska Indian Arts is a nonprofit corporation dedicated to the preservation and continuation of traditional Native craft and culture of the Northwest Coast Native Tribes.

The former Fort William Seward, a U.S. Army post hospital, houses Alaska Indian Arts, where visitors have the rare opportunity to observe Native American craftsmen at work in a unique, historic setting: weavers, silversmiths, and totem pole carvers. The world's largest totem pole, exhibited at the Osaka World's Fair of 1970, was carved here.

Info: P.O. Box 271, Haines, AK 99827 • 907.766.2160 • http://www.alaskaindianarts.com/

Chilkat Center for the Arts

Traditional Tlingit dances are performed at the Chilkat Center, a former cannery that was moved to Fort William Seward in 1919 and turned into a recreation hall. The dance troupe has toured the world, and its members are famed for their dexterity; their fringed and vividly colored shawls are made by local Native people. The fort's parade ground has been turned into a typical Indian village of the nineteenth century with a replica of a traditional house and several totem poles. Owned by the Haines Borough, the Chilkat Center for the Arts is a multipurpose facility available for conventions, concerts, plays, dance, film showings, meetings, workshops, community gatherings, exercise classes, radio and television production, and more.

Info: 122 Second Ave., Haines, AK 99827 • 907.766.6418 •
https://www.visithaines.com/chilkat-center-arts

Sheldon Museum and Cultural Center

The Sheldon Museum and Cultural Center showcases the art and culture of the Haines community. It houses over four thousand artifacts from Chilkat blankets to the Eldred Rock lighthouse lens, twelve thousand cataloged photographs, and slides of images from the nineteenth century until today.

Info: 11 Main St., Haines, AK 99827 • 907.766.2366 •
http://www.sheldonmuseum.org/

HOONAH
Icy Strait Point

Icy Strait Point is a destination that offers access to adventure, wilderness, wildlife, and genuine Native Tlingit hospitality. It is Alaska Native–owned and –operated and generates income for the Hoonah community, Alaska's largest Native Tlingit village. Icy Strait Point features over twenty tours, a restored 1912 Alaska salmon cannery and museum, nature trails, restaurants, 100 percent Alaskan-owned retail shops, and even a beach! Eagles soar overhead, and whales are regularly seen from the shore.

Info: 108 Cannery Rd., Hoonah, AK 99829 • 907.789.8600 •
http://icystraitpoint.com/

JUNEAU
Alaska State Museum

The collections of the Alaska state museums (Alaska State Museum and Sheldon Jackson Museum) represent the diverse cultures and rich historical record of a large geographic area. The museums' broad mandate is to collect, preserve, and interpret

Entrance to the Alaska State Museum.

the state's human and natural history—it owns more than thirty-two thousand cataloged objects.

Alaska Native material dominates the collection and includes items from the Alaskan Yup'ik and the Inupiat, Athabascan, Aleut, and Northwest Coast groups that represent both daily and religious life. The Northwest Coast and Eskimo basket collection is among the most comprehensive in existence and includes fragments of three recently discovered baskets that have been dated to 5000 B.C.E., the oldest ever recovered in Alaska or the Northwest Coast. The Eskimo-carved ivory collection is comprehensive, ranging from ancient to historic to twentieth century. The museum also maintains an outstanding collection of work by contemporary Native artists.

Info: 395 Whittier St., Juneau, AK 99801 • 907.465.2901 • http://museums.alaska.gov/about_collections.html

Celebration

For four days every other June, the streets of Juneau fill with Native people of all ages dressed in the signature regalia of clans from throughout Southeast Alaska and beyond. The celebration has traditional song and dance, arts and crafts, and food. Local Native languages are spoken at this biennial festival of Tlingit, Haida, and Tsimshian cultures.

A Haida woman with her niece at Celebration in Juneau.

Celebration is one of the largest gatherings of Southeast Alaska Native peoples and is the second-largest event sponsored by Alaska Natives in the state of Alaska. The event draws about five thousand people, including more than two thousand dancers.

Info: 105 S. Seward St., Suite 201, Juneau, AK 99801 • 907.463.4844 • http://www.sealaskaheritage.org/institute/celebration

Sealaska Heritage

In May 2015, the Sealaska Heritage Institute dedicated the Walter Soboleff Building in downtown Juneau. It is a special place for Southeast Alaskan Natives and a place where everyone—Native and non-Native alike—can feel welcome and learn something about their heritage.

The Soboleff Building is designed to be like an enormous, traditional bentwood box in that it holds our at.óowu—our treasures. Administrative offices share space with archives, classrooms, the Sealaska Heritage Store, and a true Southeast experience. A work of art in its own right, the building contains space for art demonstrations and exhibits as well as a traditional clan house clad in hand-adzed cedar. The clan house was given the name Shuká Hít ("ancestors' house") during the grand opening ceremony.

At Sealaska Heritage Institute's Walter Soboleff Building, visitors will see monumental art made by some of the most acclaimed artists—Tlingit, Haida, and Tsimshian—which are represented in the large installations.

Info: 105 S. Steward St., Juneau, AK 99801 • 907.586.9114 • http://www.sealaskaheritagecenter.com/

KETCHIKAN
Saxman Village Totem Park

Saxman Village's Totem Park includes twenty-five totems that are authentic replicas of original poles that were left in abandoned villages as Native Alaskans moved into more populated cities. Visitors can take an organized, guided tour and learn more about each pole's story. The Cape Fox Dance Group welcomes guests by song and dance in the Beaver Clan House. Native carvers are commissioned worldwide to create poles; visitors can watch the artists at work using traditional tools and techniques in the carving shed.

Info: 2706 S. Tongass Hwy., Ketchican, AK 99901 • 907.225.4846 • http://www.alaska.org/detail/saxman-totem-park

Tongass Historical Society Museum

This downtown facility is a private, nonprofit corporation whose purpose is to discover, preserve, and disseminate knowledge of the history of Ketchikan and Southeast Alaska for present and future generations. Established in 1961, the society brings together people of all ages who share an interest in Ketchikan's rich and colorful heritage.

The museum features displays on the historic crafts of Native peoples. Prominently featured are bentwood boxes, made of a single piece of cedar bent three or four times to form a container, brilliantly colored, intricately patterned Chilkat blankets, and several examples of wood carving. The museum emphasizes the changing culture of the local peoples.

Info: 629 Dock St., Ketchikan, AK 99901 • 907.225.5600 • http://www.tongasshistory.org/contact/

Totem Bight State Historical Park

Totem Bight State Historical Park, an 11-acre (0.04-square-kilometer) park, is packed with restored and recarved totems. Totem Bight is best known for its spectacular

This reproduction at Totem Bight State Historical Park, built by Native Alaskan craftsmen working for the CCC in the 1930s and early 1940s, is on the National Register of Historic Places.

setting on a cove overlooking Tongass Narrows. It contains a reproduction of a community longhouse.

Info: 9883 N. Tongass Hwy., Ketchikan, AK 99901 • 907.247.8574 • http://dnr.alaska.gov/parks/aspunits/southeast/totembigshp.htm

Totem Heritage Center

The Totem Heritage Center houses several rooms of unrestored, nineteenth-century poles from deserted Tlingit and Haida villages. Photos and information about the old village sites help one imagine these poles as they stood originally. Native artifacts such as baskets, masks, button vests, and regalia give additional insight into the artistry and cultural heritage of the Tlingit, Haida, and Tsimshian. Exhibit cases

Three totem poles at the Totem Heritage Center.

surrounding the standing totem poles show Native arts and crafts, carving tools, and other artifacts.

Info: 601 Deermount St., Ketchikan, AK 99901 • 907.225.5900 • http://www.alaska.org/detail/totem-heritage-center

KLUKWAN
Jilkaat Kwaan Cultural Heritage and Bald Eagle Preserve Visitor Center

The center opened in 2016 nearly a century after the idea of putting a cultural museum in the small Tlingit village 22 miles (35 kilometers) north of Haines was first discussed. The center displays famed Chilkat weaving: intricately patterned blankets and robes and the tribe's house posts and carved screens, hundreds of years old, which depict the ravens, eagles, and killer whales that help define the identity of the Tlingit people.

Plans are underway to display other treasured artworks in the village as well as those that are currently stored in other museum facilities. Among these are several artifacts that have been returned to Klukwan through the Native American Graves and Repatriation Act (NAGPRA), various works of art, and historically significant pieces that have been designated by families and clans.

An eagle-viewing corridor will be located along the Chilkat River within easy viewing range of abundant eagle activity.

A hospitality center offers gifts and food. Within the building itself will be space for carvers and weavers to work and room for cultural classes of all kinds in addition to the museum.

Info: 9 Chilkat Ave., Klukwan, AK 99827 • 907.767.5485 • http://jilkaatkwaanheritagecenter.org/

KODIAK
Alutiiq Museum and Archaeological Repository

The Alutiiq Museum's work involves a deep commitment to the Kodiak Archipelago—the museum's home and the geographic center of the Alutiiq world. The museum cares for more than 250,000 items reflecting the culture and history of the Alutiiq people. The holdings include archaeological materials, photographs, ethnographic objects, archival items, film and audio recordings, and natural history specimens that reach beyond written records to reveal details from all eras of Alutiiq history—from ancient traditions to the daily lives of contemporary Alutiiq people. The collections are used to illustrate exhibits and education programs, provide information for research, and inspire the world to know more about the Alutiiq's remarkable heritage.

Info: 215 Mission Rd., First Floor, Kodiak, AK 99615 • 844.425.8844 • https://alutiiqmuseum.org/

METLAKATLA
Duncan Cottage Museum

The Duncan Cottage Museum was built in 1891, the same year that the island became the Annette Island Indian Reserve through an act of Congress. It is the oldest building in the community and the only building that has National Historic Site status. It has displays relating to the Tsimshian culture.

The museum was the home of the late missionary William Duncan, who was originally sent to work among the Tsimshian of British Columbia by the Church Missionary Society of England. He worked among the people for sixty-one years before his death in 1918.

Info: 501 Tait St., P.O. Box 8, Metlakatla, AK 99926 • 907.886.4868 • https://wdcmuseum.weebly.com/

SITKA
Sheldon Jackson Museum

The Sheldon Jackson Museum includes objects from each of the Native groups in Alaska: Tlingit, Haida, Tsimshian, Aleut, Alutiiq, Yup'ik, Inupiat, and Athabascan. The collections strongly reflect the collecting done by founder Sheldon Jackson from 1887 through about 1898 during his tenure as general agent of education for Alaska. Other objects were subsequently added to the collection, but in 1984, when the museum was purchased by the State of Alaska, the decision was made to add only Alaska Native materials made prior to the early 1930s.

Info: 104 College Dr., Sitka, AK 99835 • 907.465.2151 • http://museums.alaska.gov/about_collections.html

Sitka National Historical Park

Alaska's oldest national park was established in 1910 to commemorate the 1804 Battle of Sitka. Sitka National Historical Park preserves the site of a battle between invading Russian traders and the Indigenous Kiks.ádi Tlingit in 1804. All that remains

One of the many totem poles on display at Sitka National Historical Park.

of this last major conflict between Europeans and Alaska Natives is the site of the Tlingit Fort and battlefield.

Southeast Alaska totem poles and a temperate rain forest setting combine to provide spectacular scenery along the park's coastal trail. The park is also home to the Russian Bishop's House, one of the last surviving examples of Russian colonial architecture in North America.

Info: 103 Monastery St., Sitka, AK 99835 • 907.747.0110 • https://www.nps.gov/sitk/index.htm

Southeast Alaska Indian Cultural Center

The Southeast Alaska Indian Cultural Center (SEAICC) helps visitors learn the history and understand the culture of the Native Sitka Tlingit community. On-site is an artist studio in which Tlingit artists can learn and practice traditional crafts.

The cultural center is housed in the Sitka National Park Visitor Center but is a completely independent, Native, nonprofit organization. It was established in 1969, just a few years after the national park opened the visitor center.

A tremendous amount of history is contained in the cultural center—the many exhibits, collections, and informational placards all work together to illustrate the strife between the Russians and the Tlingit and how the Tlingit have struggled to retain their identity and culture.

Info: 456 Katlian St., Sitka, AK 99835-7505 • 907.747.8061 • http://www.wild strawberrylodge.com/about-sitka/southeast-alaska-indian-cultural-center/

UNALASKA
Museum of the Aleutians

The Museum of the Aleutians is the state-of-the art cultural center of the Aleutian Islands and the community of Unalaska. The museum opened its doors in 1999 with the mission to collect, preserve, and research the ethnography and history of the Aleutian Islands region. Through actively growing ethnographic, Russian/American, WWII, and artwork collections, the museum provides stimulating permanent and changing exhibits as well as a home to researchers and community events.

The museum presents the history and culture of the Unangan (Aleut) people, who have lived on the island continually for nine thousand years. Collections and exhibits showcase archaeology, history, ethnography, and masterpieces of Unangan artistry, especially basketry. A museum shop sells books and educational products.

Info: 14 Salmon Way, Unalaska, AK 99685 • 907.581.5150 • http://www.aleutians.org/

WRANGELL
Petroglyph Beach State Park and Wrangell Visitor Center

Petroglyph Beach has the highest concentration of petroglyphs in Southeast Alaska. An accessible boardwalk to a deck overlooks Petroglyph Beach, the Stikine River,

Petroglyph Beach State Historic Park.

and Zimovia Straits. Replicas of several designs are displayed on the deck for visitors to make rubbings. Access to the beach is provided directly from the deck overlook.

The petroglyphs that remain on the beach are found on the boulders and bedrock outcrops on the shore just below and above mean high tide. It is thought that they were created by members of the Tlingit Tribe, and most of the petroglyphs can be found close to places of importance such as salmon streams and sites of habitation. They depict whales, salmon, and faces of the community. Petroglyphs are under the protection of federal laws and the State of Alaska Antiquities Law.

Info: 293 Campbell Dr., Wrangell, AK 99929 • 800.367.9745 •
http://www.wrangell.com/visitorservices/petroglyph-beach-state-historic-park

YAKUTAT
The Yakutat Tern Festival

This annual festival is a collaboration among the Yakutat Tlingit Tribe, the Yakutat Chamber of Commerce, the U.S. Forest Service, the National Park Service, and the Yakutat City and Borough. The events highlight the extraordinary natural and cultural resources of Yakutat by celebrating Aleutian and Arctic terns; little is known about these birds. This area is one of their largest and southernmost known breeding colonies and is at the forefront of Aleutian tern research. Participants of the festival will enjoy birding activities, natural history field trips, art exhibits, educational events for kids and adults, and Native cultural presentations.

Info: P.O. Box 510, Yakutat, AK 99689 •
http://www.yakutatalaska.com/events.html

CALIFORNIA

The 2010 U.S. census identified 362,801 people who identify as American Indian or Alaska Native living in California. Many Native nations are in California.

BANNING
Malki Museum of the Morongo Reservation

The Malki Museum is California's first museum founded by Native Americans indigenous to the state. In February 1965, Malki officially opened its doors and was dedicated in a traditional ceremony where nearly one thousand Native and non-Natives gathered. The museum began as the result of a dream that Jane K. Penn, a Wanikik Cahuilla, with the help of others, translated into a reality. Through the years, Malki has remained dedicated to its goals of preservation and education of Cahuilla culture. After Penn's death in 1982, Dr. Katherine Siva Saubel, a Mountain Cahuilla of the Los Coyotes Reservation near Warner Springs, related to Penn by marriage, continued the dream until her death in 2011.

Since 1965, much growth has occurred: the construction of a permanent, adobe-brick museum; the redesign of the Temalpakh Ethnobotanical Garden, which grows plants used by the Cahuilla for food, housing, and medicine; several educational projects; and annual events. The Fall Gathering features Native arts, crafts, and games as well as Cahuilla harvest foods such as wewish (acorn mush), a time-consuming, but staple, dish.

The Morongo Reservation is located in inland southern California. Its residents are primarily members of the Cahuilla Tribe; the Serrano, Cupeño, and Chemehuevi tribes make up the remainder of the population. In the long period of reconstruction as a sovereign, self-governing tribe in California, their experience with the Spanish Mission system provided inspiration to overcome the disease and oppression suffered into the early twentieth century. To that end, the Morongo Tribe has successfully challenged their history and is now owner and operator of the Morongo Casino, Resort, and Spa, which opened in 2004.

Info: 11795 Malki Rd., Banning, CA 92220 • 951.849.7289 • http://malkimuseum.org/

BISHOP
Owens Valley Paiute and Shoshone Cultural Center and Museum

The Owens Valley Paiute and Shoshone Cultural Center and Museum's use of educational displays relate the history of the Paiute and Shoshone tribes in Owens Valley. Exhibits feature the art and lifeways of the Nuumu, or Paiute, and Newe, or Shoshone; their language family is Uto-Aztecan. The museum's memorial hall is a tribute to Native American veterans and their families, the environment, objects and artifacts, and historical archives.

The Native Garden and Walking Trail runs through the tribe's COSA (Conservation Open Space Area). In 1912, 67,000 acres (271 square kilometers) of land were to be provided for the Bishop Colony and Big Pine Colony as reservations, but in 1937, the Bureau of Indian Affairs exchanged these lands for an area owned by the City of Los Angeles in Inyo and Mono counties for 875 acres (3.5 square kilometers) that constitute the present-day Bishop Reservation. The Owens Valley is known as the deepest valley in America because it lies between two of the country's highest mountain ranges with the Sierra Nevada on the west and the White Mountains on the east.

The Owens Valley Paiute and Shoshone Tribe hosts an annual, three-day Indian Days Celebration and Pabanamanina Powwow in September. The tribe operates the Paiute Palace Casino. Owens Valley is home to numerous outdoor attractions, including Bishop Creek Canyon, South Lake, Buttermilk Country, North Lake, Rock Creek Canyon, Ancient Bristlecone Pine Forest, and the Mount Whitney State Fish Hatchery. Within and surrounding the Bishop Reservation are over one hundred thousand petroglyphs known as the Coso petroglyphs that were left by Indigenous ancestors, and in 2001, they were incorporated into a larger National Historic Landmark District, which was called the Coso Rock Art District. The Maturango Museum in Ridgecrest, California, offers tours and does not collaborate with the Owen Valley Paiute and Shoshone Cultural Center.

Info: 2300 W. Line St., Bishop, CA 93514 • 760.873.3584 • http://www.bishoppaiutetribe.com/cultural-center.html

COVELO
Round Valley Indian Tribes California Indian Days Celebration

Known as the "gateway to northern California's wilderness," the Round Valley Indian tribes operate the Hidden Oaks Recreation Center, which includes rodeo grounds, baseball diamonds, a campground, and an RV park. The California Indian Days Celebration is held the last week in September at the Hidden Oaks Recreational Park. A combined baseball tournament and powwow, the celebration also features arts and crafts, hand games, and a parade. The Round Valley Indian Reservation is located in the northeastern part of Mendocino County, the second-largest federal Indian reservation in California.

Yuki ancestors have lived in Round Valley for thousands of years. The larger Nome Lackee Reservation was established in 1854 on the eastern foothills of the Coast Range, but many other Indigenous peoples living around Central Valley were forced to relocate. When Euro-American settlers claimed their land in 1863, the Yuki and others were sent to Round Valley.

Info: 77826 Covelo Rd., Covelo, CA 95428 • 707.983.6126 • https://www.rvit.org/

DAVIS
C. N. Gorman Museum

The C. N. Gorman Museum was founded in 1973 by the University of California–Davis's Department of Native American Studies in honor of retired faculty member Carl Nelson Gorman, Navajo or Diné artist, WWII code talker, and Native American advocate. The museum, located on the campus of the University of California–Davis, has become for over forty years a destination for exhibition of works by living Indigenous artists that are curated by Native Americans.

Info: 1316 Hart Hall, One Shields Ave., Davis, CA 95616-8667 • 530.752.6567 • http://gormanmuseum.ucdavis.edu

FREMONT
Tuibun Ohlone Village Site at Coyote Hills Regional Park

Regional Park is a two-thousand-year-old Tuibun Ohlone Village site. The Coyote Hills Regional Park offers guided tours of an Ohlone home, sweathouse, and outdoor arbor used for shade. Public access to the site is by reservation only by calling Coyote Hills Regional Park at 510.544.3220. Ancestral Ohlone life has been described as a series of ripenings and harvestings that divided the year into different periods, giving Ohlone life a characteristic rhythm moving from one harvest to the next. Ohlone peoples were the first peoples in what is now known as the San Francisco Bay area. The Muwekma Ohlone Tribe of the San Francisco Bay Area is composed of all of the known surviving lineages aboriginal to the Bay Area who trace their ancestry through the Missions Dolores, Santa Clara, and San Jose and were members of the historic, federally recognized Verona Band of Alameda County.

Info: 8000 Patterson Ranch Rd., Fremont, CA 94555 • 510.544.3220 • http://ebparks.org/parks/coyote_hills

HOOPA
Hoopa Tribal Museum

The Hoopa Valley Tribal Museum is adjacent to the Tsewenaldin Inn, which is inside the Lucky Bear Casino operated by the Hoopa Valley Tribe. The museum collections include Hoopa, Yurok, and Karuk material culture objects such as Hoopa dance regalia and basketry on loan from tribal members. The reservation spans approximately 144 square miles (232 square kilometers) in northeast Humboldt County along the Trinity River. In 1988, after a long history of changing status and land theft, the Hoopa/Yurok Act created the largest reservation in the state of California.

For centuries, the Trinity River was abundant with Chinook salmon and steelhead and was the center of Hoopa culture. At the heart of the valley is the ancient village of Takimildin, "the center of the world" for the Hoopa people, known as "the place where the trails return." The tribe sponsors an annual Sovereign Day Celebration in honor of the original treaty that established the reservation and the month when Congress recognized the tribe's ownership of the lands. Festivities include a parade, vendors, dancers, music, games, fireworks, a softball tournament, Indian cards, the Hoopa cultural Stick Tournament, and the All-Indian Rodeo over a three-day weekend in a theme chosen by the Sovereign Day's planners.

Info: Hwy. 96, North of Willow Creek, Hoopa, CA 95546 • 530.625.4110 • https://www.visitredwoods.com/listing/hoopa-tribal-museum/3/

INDIO
Cabazon Cultural Museum

The Cabazon Band of Mission Indians is a band of Cahuilla whose tribal name is that of Chief Cabazon, a leader of the Desert Cahuilla during the mid-1830s. The Cabazon Reservation spans 1,706 acres (7 square kilometers) in southern California and was established as an Indian reservation in 1877. Operated by the Cabazon Nation in collaboration with the University of California–Riverside, the museum features culture and history exhibit displays. Each November, the tribe hosts the Indio Powwow in the special events center at the casino and is free and open to the general public as a way to foster a sense of community among Native Americans as well as to provide others with the opportunity to celebrate their culture with them. The Cabazon Tribe also owns and operates the Fantasy Springs Resort Hotel and Casino in Indio.

Info: 84245 Indio Springs Pkwy., Indio, CA 92203 • 760.238.5770 • https://visitgreaterpalmsprings.com/visit/listing/cabazon-cultural-museum/

KLAMATH
Yurok Tribe Salmon Festival

The Yurok Tribe provides this background about themselves: "At one time our people lived in over fifty villages throughout our ancestral territory. The laws, health and spirituality of our people were untouched by non-Indians. Culturally, our people are known as great fishermen, eelers, basket weavers, canoe makers, storytellers, singers, dancers, healers and strong medicine people. Before we were given the name 'Yurok' we referred to ourselves as 'Oohl', meaning Indian people."

The Klamath-Trinity River is the lifeline of Yurok people because the majority of the food supply, like *ney-puy* (salmon), *kaa-ka* (sturgeon), and *kwor-ror* (candle-fish), are offered to them from these rivers. Also, important to people are the foods that are offered from the ocean and inland areas such as *pee-ee* (mussels), *chey-gel'* (seaweed), *woo-mehl* (acorns), *puuek* (deer), *mey-weehl* (elk), *ley-chehl* (berries), and *wey-yok-seep* (teas). These foods are essential to people's health, wellness, and religious ceremonies. The Yurok way was never to overharvest and to always ensure sustainability of the food supply for future generations.

The federal government established the Yurok Reservation in 1855 and immediately confined the Yurok people to the area. They are the largest tribe in California with more than five thousand enrolled members.

The tribe provides numerous services to the local community and membership. The tribe's major initiatives include: the Hoopa-Yurok Settlement Act, dam removal, natural resources protection, sustainable economic development enterprises, and land acquisition. They also operate the Redwood Casino and Hotel. It is the only casino located within the Redwood National and State Park's boundaries. The annual Salmon Festival, which draws almost four thousand guests, provides an opportunity for the whole community to come together and celebrate the Klamath River.

Info: 190 Klamath Blvd., Klamath, CA 95548 • 707.482.1350 •
http://www.yuroktribe.org/

LAKESIDE
Barona Cultural Center and Museum

The Barona Cultural Center and Museum opened in 2000 as the first museum in San Diego County dedicated solely to the area's Indigenous populations. Today, the museum collections total nearly twenty-two thousand pieces that focus on the history and perspectives of the Barona Band of Mission Indians, southern California's Native American community members.

After ten years of developing the collection, the Barona Cultural Center and Museum is one of the largest repositories of ancestral and contemporary southern and Baja California Native American material. The collections include archival records, paintings, sculpture, photography, textiles, basketry, ceramics, and gaming pieces. Traditional classes are offered exclusively to tribal members and include basket weaving, pottery, stories, and the construction of a Kumeyaay-style house, an 'ewaa.

The museum works closely with the Head Start program and childcare center and has created an annual Thanksgiving event with the Barona Indian School. The Barona Reservation is located 30 miles (48 kilometers) northeast of San Diego in the traditional Kumeyaay/Diegueño territory, home to descendants of Hokan-speaking peoples who lived in this region, and into southern Mexico. The tribe also operates the Barona Ranch Resort and Casino. They are one of twelve bands of the Kumeyaay/Diegueño Tribe. Archaeologists have identified middens, or refuse heaps, along the coastal country and the Salton Sea margins that date back some twenty thousand years.

Info: 1095 Barona Rd., Lakeside, CA 92040 • 619.443.6612 •
http://malkimuseum.org/

LOS ANGELES
Autry Museum of the American West

The Autry's Southwest Museum of the American Indian's collection of Native American art is one of the most significant of its kind in the United States, second only to the Smithsonian Institution's National Museum of the American Indian. The 238,000-piece collection includes fourteen thousand baskets, ten thousand ceramic items, sixty-three hundred textiles and weavings, and more than eleven hundred pieces of jewelry. It represents work by Indigenous peoples from Alaska to South America with an emphasis on the cultures of California and the Southwestern United States. The regional exhibit associated with the tribes of the Southwest desert is said to be the largest in the United States. The collections also contain Mesoamerican and South American classic pottery and textiles and Hispanic folk and decorative arts.

The four main exhibit halls focus on the Native people of the Southwest, California, the Great Plains, and the Northwest Coast. Changing shows highlight the cultures of various Native groups. The museum has as its mission to remain as inclusive

The Autry Museum of the American West.

as possible about the stories, culture, art, and peoples of the American West, past and present. Changing exhibits have included: "La Raza"; "Harry Gamboa, Jr., Chicano Male Unbounded"; "Play"; "Standing Rock Art and Solidarity"; "California Continued"; "Art of the West"; "Cowboy Gallery"; "Ted and Marian Carver Imagination Gallery"; "Western Frontiers Stories of Fact and Fiction"; and "Four Centuries of Pueblo Pottery." The Southwest Museum opened to the public in 1914; it is the oldest museum in Los Angeles and a National Historic Landmark.

Info: 4700 Western Heritage Way, Griffith Park, Los Angeles, CA 90027 • 323.667.2000 • https://theautry.org/

Historic Southwest Museum, Mount Washington Campus

The Historic Southwest Museum, Mount Washington Campus was originally the Southwest Museum of the American Indian, founded by Charles F. Lummis and the Southwest Society in 1907. It was the project of the western branch of the Archaeological Institute of America. The Autry Museum acquired and merged the collections of the Southwest Museum with the Autry Museum. The Southwest Museum of the American Indian collection was the second-largest collection of Native American objects in the United States. Some of the earliest pieces in the collection include archaeological materials from museum-sponsored excavations. From 2004 to 2016, the Autry focused on completing its extensive multiyear, multimillion-dollar work to preserve the significant collections of art, archives, and cultural materials that had been housed at the 103-year-old Southwest Museum site. The combined collections of the museums, numbering more than five hundred thousand, are now at the Resources Center of the Autry in Burbank. Since the merger, the Autry has exhibited thousands of objects from the Southwest Museum collection, primarily at its Griffith Park campus, helping to present a more complete story of the American West for students, researchers, and the general public.

Info: 234 Museum Dr., Los Angeles, CA 90065 • 323.221.2164 • https://theautry.org/visit/mt-washington-campus

Red Nation Film Festival

The Red Nation Film Festival strives to break down the barrier of racism by replacing American Indian stereotypes and propelling American Indian filmmakers to the forefront of the entertainment industry. Its November annual film festival introduces the public to Native-produced films and champions both Native women and Native youth to enter into film and television careers.

Info: 9420 Reseda Blvd., Suite 352, Northridge, CA 91324 • 818.665.5753 • http://www.rednationff.com

NAPA
Napa Valley Aloha Festival

The Manaleo Hawaiian Cultural Foundation sponsors this annual festival, held the third Saturday in September. Performers and vendors from the Hawaiian and Polynesian communities present authentic foods, music, dance, arts, crafts, clothing, and wares. Participants are from the mainland and Hawaii. Many activities are interactive, like lei making.

Info: 575 Third St., Napa, CA 94559-2701 • 707.418.8588 • manaleohcf.org/aloha-festival

NORTH FORK
Sierra Mono Museum

The Sierra Mono Museum, which is operated by the North Fork Rancheria, was established in 1971 after receiving land from the local school district for a museum. It serves as an important source of cultural identity and practices for the region's Western Mono people. Located in North Fork, the preservation of the Nium language spoken by the Western Mono is an ongoing focus for the museum. The museum has the largest display of Mono Indian basketry in California. Many of the exhibits on display are donated and on loan by members of the Mono Tribe. Other collections include weapons, traditional games, ceremonial items, tools, beaded crafts, and dioramas of the Tettelton Wildlife Collection.

The museum is located in the geographical center of California along the Sierra Vista National Scenic Byway. The North Fork Rancheria Tribe's status as a federally recognized Indian tribe was restored in 1983 under a court-approved settlement after 132 years of disenfranchisement and broken-treaty agreements with the federal government. The lands reserved in these treaties were quickly overrun by Anglo settlers, ranchers, miners, and, later, farmers, leaving only a series of small "Indian farms" operating over a large area.

In 1903, a Presbyterian mission was established in the town of North Fork. Native parents began sending their children to be educated and sheltered at the mission while continuing their migratory patterns by working as wage laborers on farms and logging operations in the San Joaquin Valley. In 1916, the federal government purchased the 80-acre (0.3-square-kilometer) North Fork Rancheria next to the mission where children were attending.

In 1961, the federal government terminated the tribe's federally recognized status and transferred the Rancheria land to the lone resident then living on the Rancheria. The tribe's status as a federally recognized Indian tribe was restored in 1983 under a court-approved settlement. Four years later, the lands within the Rancheria boundaries were restored as "Indian Country." The tribe subsequently elected a governing body and later adopted a constitution in 1996. Today, the tribe is the largest restored tribe in California with nearly eighteen hundred tribal citizens whose ancestors have always lived here.

Info: 33103 Road 228, North Fork, CA 93643 • 559.877.2115 • https://sierramonomuseum.org/

NOVATO
Marin Museum of the American Indian

Located in Miwok Park, the museum is devoted to Native American culture and is the only one of its kind in the Bay Area. It also serves as an educational center to over four thousand elementary children each year. The Native American artifacts and reference materials are irreplaceable and provide a unique opportunity to learn about the local Native lifeways.

The museum was founded in 1967 in response to the rapid development of Marin County. Construction activity in the county unearthed masses of archaeological objects related to the original inhabitants of the region, the Coast Miwok people. The museum was originally designed to serve as a repository for these materials. Today, the museum still houses a large collection of Coast Miwok artifacts; however, the scope has broadened considerably, and its programs and collections represent Native American cultures from across the entire continent. Artifacts on display include Navajo textiles, Eskimo carvings, Plains beadwork, birch bark baskets, and northwest coast masks. Visitors learn to appreciate the diversity and beauty of Native American art and culture.

Educational programs include a summer program for six- to twelve-year-olds, lectures, traditional storytelling by Native elders, professional exhibitions that explore traditional art forms, and annual, public events such as the Trade Feast. The Coast Miwok Indians' approximately six hundred village sites, many thousands of years old, have been identified in the area along with remains of their integrate basketry, flint knapping, and clamshell bead making. Coast Miwok lands covered present-day Novato, Marshall, Tomales, San Rafael, Petaluma, and Bodega. The Southern Pomo people are from the Sebastopol area. Many of the Coast Miwok and Southern Pomo people still live within their ancestral territories. In 2000, the Coast Miwok and Southern Pomo tribes were restored to federally recognized status as the Federated Indians of Graton Rancheria.

Info: 2200 Novato Blvd., Novato, CA 94947 • 415.897.4064 • http://www.marinindian.com/about.html

OROVILLE (CHEROKEE)
Cherokee Heritage

Little more than a wide spot along the road is the byway called Cherokee Road off State Highway 70 in Butte County. Once a gold mine boom town with a population of over a thousand, today Cherokee (close by the larger town of Oroville, which is used as the mailing address) has about a dozen residents. The former boarding house is now the present-day Cherokee Museum with displays of a miner's cabin; photos and artwork; petrified mammoth bones and other mineral specimens from the spectacular hydraulic diggings; local "Indian relics," to use their words; and a curious "coffin rock" with undecipherable ancient inscriptions. The museum is open on weekends, weather permitting.

Cherokee history in California is about a group of Cherokee from Oklahoma following the Gold Rush of 1849. The Cherokee Diamond Mine opened in 1873, but the stones were of industrial quality, and the mine quickly expired. In a few years, the town was abandoned, and today, it may well be the only Native American mining ghost town in the West. The territory was originally that of the Maidu Indians.

Info: 4041-4219 Cherokee Rd., Oroville, CA 95965 • https://www.atlasobscura.com/places/cherokee

PALM SPRINGS
Agua Caliente Cultural Museum

The Agua Caliente Band of Cahuilla Indians has plans to relocate its museum to a new, 5.8-acre (23,472-square-meter) cultural center in the heart of Palm Springs. The current museum is a very active center of exhibitions and learning opportunities on-site with classes, demonstrations, and outdoor explorations for adults and children. They feature guided cultural hikes in the Indian Canyons, which are located in the Coachella Valley. They host multiple special events at the museum and at off-site locations that range from collaborative exhibits, performances of Native storytelling, and traditional bird singing and dancing, at their own annual Holiday Open House. Nine Cahuilla bands are in California, each with their own reservation. These reservations are: Agua Caliente, Augustine, Cabazon, Cahuilla, Los Coyotes, Morongo, Ramona, Santa Rosa, and Torres-Martinez.

The Agua Caliente Indian Reservation is named for the hot spring in downtown Palm Springs. This reservation comprises approximately 32,000 acres (130 square kilo-

Agua Caliente Cultural Museum.

meters) in three townships. The reservation was set aside for the use and occupancy of the Agua Caliente people during the administrations of President Ulysses S. Grant in 1876 and President Rutherford B. Hayes in 1877. It is not a contiguous reservation but a checkerboard of alternate and even-numbered sections in the cities of Palm Springs, Cathedral City, Rancho Mirage, and unincorporated Riverside County. The Agua Caliente Band of Cahuilla Indians evolved into a strong tribal presence in the southern California desert and operates the Agua Caliente Casino in Rancho Mirage.

Info: 219 S. Palm Canyon Dr., Palm Springs, CA 92262 • 760.778.1079 • http://www.accmuseum.org/Welcome-to-the-Museum

Tahquitz Canyon Visitor Center

Tahquitz Canyon is in the homeland territory of the Agua Caliente Band of Cahuilla located in the Coachella Valley near Palm Springs. The canyon has a seasonal, 60-foot (18-meter) waterfall, rock art, ancient irrigation systems, indigenous wildlife, and plants. Located at the entrance to the canyon, the Tahquitz Canyon Visitor Center offers educational and cultural exhibits including an array of artifacts, an observation deck, and a theater room for viewing the legend of Tahquitz Canyon. The Cahuilla tell different stories about the canyon's significance and regard it as a place to be respected. A hiking trail and a 2-mile (3.2-kilometer) loop lead to Tahquitz Falls.

Info: 500 W. Mesquite Ave., Palm Springs, Greater Palm Springs, CA 92264-8391 • 760.416.7044 • http://www.indian-canyons.com/

PINE GROVE
Chaw'se Indian Grinding Rock State Historic Park and Museum

The Chaw'se Indian Grinding Rock State Historic Park is a California state park, pre-serving more than one thousand marbleized limestone mortar holes. This is the largest collection of bedrock mortars in North America and was used by the Miwok, who gathered acorns from large valley oaks in the area. The Chaw'se Museum has been designed to reflect the architecture of the traditional roundhouse. As a regional museum, the collection at Chaw'se includes northern, central, and southern Miwok, Maidu, Konkow, Monache, Nisenan, Tubatulabal, Washo, and Foothill Yokut. Examples of basketry, feather regalia, jewelry, arrowpoints, and other tools are on display.

Some of the bedrock mortars at Chaw'se Indian Grinding Rock State Historic Park.

The Chaw'se Celebration is on the last weekend of September and has become a major observance among the California tribes with representatives from most of them participating in the dances and craft booths.

Info: 14881 Pine Grove–Volcano Rd., Pine Grove, CA 95665 • 209.296.7488 • http://www.parks.ca.gov/?page_id=553

POWAY
Kumeyaay-Ipai Interpretive Center

The Kumeyaay-Ipai Interpretive Center of Pauwai provides this background about the center, calling it a "5-acre site rich in Kumeyaay-Ipai local history. The Native Americans lived primarily on the east side of the hill that blocked the prevailing winds. The land had thousands of oak trees along Poway Creek, large sycamore trees and a year-round stream. Game was plentiful, and vegetation produced enough food to sustain a large tribe. The site also had the highest vantage point in the Pauwai Valley which allowed them to look out for game and predators. The large boulders provided shelter and it was also thought that the boulders and rock peak had a religious significance, although this theory has not been substantiated. The City of Poway began acquiring the various parcels which comprise the Center beginning in 1987 to preserve the site as a significant American Indian cultural site."

The Kumeyaay-Ipai, also known as Diegueno, are represented today by the Barona Band of Mission Indians in Lakeside, California, who operate the Barona Cultural Center and Museum; see Lakeside listing. The Kumeyaay-Ipai Interpretive Center has docents who offer interpretive tours for the public in the heritage practices of the ancient Kumeyaay.

Info: 13104 Ipai Waaypuk Trail, Poway, CA 92064 • 858.668.1292 • http://poway.org/372/Tours

SAN DIEGO
Chamorro Cultural Festival

The annual festival brings together Chamorro people from California and other states plus Guam and the Mariana Islands. San Diego is home to the largest population of Chamorro outside of the Northern Mariana Islands. The festival includes traditional food, music, dance, and activities.

Info: http://www.chelusd.org/

SAN FRANCISCO
Annual American Indian Film Festival (AIFI)

For over forty years, AIFI has been the major Native American media and cultural art event in California, and its festival is the world's oldest and best-known exposition dedicated to Native Americans in cinema. The November festival is completely produced by Indigenous Americans and features film screenings and a catalog, panel discussions, workshops, an awards ceremony, and networking events. In addition, their Tribal Touring Program introduces media training to tribal youth; many of these works are featured at the festival.

Info: 2940 16th St., Suite 304, San Francisco, CA 94103 • 415.554.0525 • https://www.aifisf.com/

SANTA MONICA
Garifuna International Indigenous Film Festival

Founded by Freda Sideroff, Garifuna, this annual festival features films that support the world's Indigenous cultures. Although the organization is based in Santa Monica, festival screenings are usually in Los Angeles. The Garifuna are descendants of West African, Central African, Island Carib, European, and Arawak peoples, who formed blended cultures and are originally from Honduras, Belize, Guatemala, Nicaragua, St. Vincent, and the Grenadines. The U.S. Garifuna population is more than two hundred thousand.

Info: 1245 16th St., Suite 210, Santa Monica, CA 90404 • ttp://garifunafilmfestival.com/

SMITH RIVER
Rowdy Creek Park

The Smith River has no dams, making it the largest undeveloped wild and scenic river in the continental United States. Famous for salmon and steelhead fishing, the Smith River area includes sites such as St. George's Reef and Battery Point Lighthouses. Smith River is also the Easter lily capital of the world. The Pacific Ocean beaches and redwood national and state parks are major attractions. Visitors can access many area boat ramps and have a choice of trails for hiking deeper into the natural environment with opportunities for fishing, boating, biking, camping, RV camping, golfing, kite flying, crabbing, beach combing, river walks, and bird watching.

The Tolowa Dee-ni' Nation operates the Lucky 7 Casino and Rowdy Creek Park, which is along Rowdy Creek. Shaa-xu'-xat, pronounced "shaw-hoot-hot," is a 7-acre (0.03-square-kilometer) camping park with amenities for campers and day picnicking. Reservations are required. The Tolowa Dee-ni' Nation is a federally recognized Indian tribe of Tolowa Indians 3 miles (5 kilometers) south of the Oregon–California border in Northwest California.

Info: 140 Rowdy Creek Rd., Smith River, CA 95567 • 707.487.9255 • http://www.tolowa-nsn.gov

TRINIDAD
Su-Meg Village at Patrick's Point State Park

Su-Meg Village is a re-created Yurok seasonal village consisting of traditional-style family houses, a sweathouse, changing houses, a redwood canoe, and a dance house. The 1-square-mile (1.6-square-kilometer) Patrick's Point State Park sits on a lushly forested promontory beside the Pacific Ocean and features tide pools, seals, sea lions, and migrating whales. In the park's interior is a visitor center, a Native plant garden, and a reconstructed Yurok plankhouse village. Summer walks at the park are led by a docent or professional naturalist.

Info: 4150 Patrick's Point Dr., Trinidad, CA 95570 • 707.667.3570 • https://www.parks.ca.gov/?page_id=417

TUOLUMNE
Acorn Festival

Members of the Tuolumne Rancheria descend from the northern, southern, and central groups of the Sierra Me-Wuk Tribe. Traditional homelands of the northern Me-Wuk surround much of the Central Sierra region and include present-day Amador and Calaveras counties. The central Me-Wuk homelands were in southern Calaveras and Tuolumne in the Sierra Nevada, and the southern Me-Wuk homelands included territory between Mariposa County and Yosemite National Park.

The Tuolumne Rancheria is one of two federally recognized Miwok (or Me-Wuk) reservations. The traditional territory of the Sierra Me-Wuk was the setting for the California gold rush; the fabled mother lode was discovered there in 1848. Contact with Euro-Americans reduced their numbers from a population of eight thousand to less than seven hundred by 1910. Foreign diseases and genocidal practices account for this decline. Once the gold rush had run its course, logging of the dense forests in the region became a major industry, one in which many area residents found employment. Today, few tribal elders under the age of sixty speak the Me-Wuk language largely because of the historic insistence by government Indian schools that students not speak their Native languages. Traditional Me-Wuk culture remains alive on the rancheria, however.

The main cultural event of the year is the Acorn Festival, celebrated during the second week of September. This weekend of dance honors the acorn crop, as the black acorn was once a food staple of the Me-Wuk.

Info: 19595 Miwuk St., Tuolumne, CA 95379 • 209.928.5300 • http://www.mewuk.com

VALLEY CENTER
Wasxayam Pomki Museum

Wasxayam Pomki is the name of the Rincon Band of Luiseño Indians' Tribal Museum and associated Rincon Cultural Resources Center. The collections include works of aesthetic, religious, and historical significance as well as articles produced for everyday use, and the stories shared are about traditional lifestyle, ceremonies, and their basketry. The museum provides an opportunity for community members to submit ideas for exhibits, such as one about the Sherman Indian School located in Riverside, where many Luiseño were forced to attend as part of the federal policy of boarding school education.

The Luiseño, or Payómkawichum, translated as "people of the west," at the time of the first contact with the Spanish in the sixteenth century inhabited coastal areas of southern California. The Rincon Band of Luiseño was established in 1875 and is recognized by the U.S. Constitution, Congress, court precedent, and federal policy. The Rincon Reservation is in the northeastern corner of San Diego County, California.

Info: 1 W. Tribal Rd., Valley Center, CA 92082 • 760.297.2635 • https://www.rincontribe.org/culture-history

OREGON

The Native population in Oregon is 40,130 per the 2010 U.S. Census, and ten Native nations are in the state.

ASTORIA
Lewis and Clark National Historical Park

The Lewis and Clark Expedition is a turning point in the history of the United States. When Lewis and Clark reached the northwest tip of what is now Oregon in 1805, they found some four hundred Clatsop living in several villages on the southern side of the Columbia River and south down the Pacific Coast to Tillamook Head. Their neighbors, the Chinook, lived on the northern banks of the Columbia and on the Pacific Coast, while the Nehalem, the northernmost band of the Tillamook, lived on the Oregon coast at Tillamook Head south to Kilchis Point. Per the National Park Service description offered by Lewis and Clark, these tribal peoples were "wealthy and shrewd traders, masterful canoe builders, with few enemies, and they treated Lewis and Clark with "extraordinary friendship." The park contains a Fort Clatsop replica, and during peak visitor season, rangers in buckskins offer demonstrations such as flintlock gun shooting, hide tanning, and candle making. Astoria is a port city near the mouth of the Columbia River, where it meets the Pacific Ocean.

Info: 92343 Fort Clatsop Rd., Astoria, OR 97103 • 503.861.2471 • https://www.nps.gov/lewi/index.htm

BEND
High Desert Museum

The High Desert Museum Wildlife and Living History opened in 1982. Its mission is to bring regional wildlife, culture, art, and natural resources together to promote an understanding of the natural and cultural heritage of this region. The museum uses indoor and outdoor exhibits, wildlife in natural-like habitats, and living-history demonstrations. The Henry J. Casey Hall of Plateau Indians is a permanent exhibit with specific emphasis on local culture, natural resources, wildlife, and art. Also, an exhibit of Native American horse tack is used for the Pendleton Round-Up.

Info: 59800 Highway 97, Bend, OR 97702 • 541.382.4754 • https://www.highdesertmuseum.org

JOSEPH
Nez Perce National Historical Park:
Idaho, Montana, Oregon, Washington, and the Grave of Old Chief Joseph

At the base of Lake Wallowa in Joseph, Oregon, is the grave of Old Chief Joseph, the father of young Chief Joseph, one of the Nez Perce leaders in the events of 1877. In 1926, the National Park Service states that "2,500 people lined up to see the remains of t?wi•te q?s or Old Chief Joseph interned at a new gravesite at the base of Lake Wallowa, overlooking the lands he once called home."

The Nimiipuu, or Nez Perce, homeland is located in eastern Oregon. Tt?wi•te q ?s was born between 1785 and 1790 and led the Nimiipuu living in the Wallowas. He signed the Treaty of 1855 but refused to put his mark on the Treaty of 1863. He died in 1871, telling his son to hold fast and defend his homeland and people. Following the threat of being evicted by the U.S. Army, Young Joseph left the Wallowas in the spring of 1877 for the Nez Perce Reservation in Idaho. They have been gone for over a century, yet the grave of Old Chief Joseph is a tangible link to a place that is still special to the Nez Perce, whose reservation is in Idaho. The Nez Perce National Historical Park is spread across four states and hundreds of miles of highway, which explains why the headquarters of the Nez Perce National Historical Park is in Idaho.

Info: 39063 U.S. Hwy. 95, Lapwai, ID 83540-9715 • 208.843.7009 • https://www.nps.gov/nepe/learn/historyculture/old-chief-joseph-gravesite.htm

PENDLETON
Pendleton Roundup

The first Pendleton Round-Up was to be "a frontier exhibition of picturesque pastimes, Indian and military spectacles, cowboy racing and bronco busting for the championship of the Northwest." It turned out to be a success and has continued since its inception in 1910. The group of corporations founded it was originally named the Northwestern Frontier Exhibition Association. The Umatilla Reservation lies just to the east of this site, and Native Americans have actively participated in this town's famous western celebration from the start.

One of the first winners of the all-around cowboy award was Jackson Sundown, a nephew of Chief Joseph, whose wife was a member of the Umatilla Tribe. The Pendleton Round-Up promotes Native culture through dance, a tipi village, and a tribal market as part of the celebration. The Umatilla have worked to turn their reservation into a prime recreational attraction, with good fishing, hunting, and camping opportunities in the foothills of the Blue Mountains. The Emigrant Pendleton overlook, located on Interstate 84 on the reservation, is a famous viewpoint with vistas over vast wheatlands to the Cascades in the distance. On clear days, the snowy cone of Mount Hood, 100 miles (161 kilometers) to the west, is visible.

Info: 1205 SW Court Ave., Pendleton, OR 97801 • 800.524.2984 • http://www.pendletonroundup.com

Tamátslikt Cultural Institute

The Tamástslikt Cultural Institute is a museum and research institute located on the Umatilla Indian Reservation, the only Native American museum along the Oregon Trail. It is dedicated to the culture of the Cayuse, Umatilla, and Walla Walla tribes

The front gate of the famous Pendleton Round-Up.

with its permanent exhibition featuring all three and the reservation itself. Sacred artifacts, photographs, and other archives are expertly preserved.

The institute participated in the national celebration of the Lewis and Clark Bicentennial Commemoration and oversaw production of five thousand beaded, buckskin pouches to be sold to the U.S. Mint for the 2004 Commemorative Dollar. The museum produced the Cayuse, Umatilla, and Walla Walla Homeland Heritage Corridor map, distributed through the Oregon Bureau of Tourism. It sponsors the annual Salmon Walk and raises funds for local schools' natural resources curricula.

Info: 47106 Wildhorse Blvd., Pendleton, OR 97801 • 541.429.7700 • http://www.tamastslikt.org/

PORTLAND
Portland Art Museum

The Portland Art Museum's collection of Native American art is housed in the Confederated Tribes of Grand Ronde Center for Native American Art, located in the museum's main building. It is remarkable for both its depth and diversity, consisting of more than five thousand ancient and more recent objects created by some two hundred cultural groups from throughout North America. Included are outstanding works by Native American masters such as Allan Houser, Charles Edenshaw, and Maria Martinez in addition to regional, contemporary artists such as Lillian Pitt, Joe Feddersen, Pat Courtney Gold, Rick Bartow, and James Lavadour. Each gallery is devoted to art from a specific cultural region. The center is named in honor of the Confederated Tribes of Grand Ronde and the Spirit Mountain.

Info: 1219 SW Park Ave., Portland, OR 97205 • 503.226.2811 • https://portlandartmuseum.org/

Portland Art Museum.

Rock Art and the Columbia River Gorge

American Indian rock art is found from southeastern Oregon to the Pacific Coast along canyons and riverbeds and in forests and the central high desert. The greatest concentration is found along the Columbia River area. Archaeologists date sites back three thousand years between the Dalles in Oregon and the Tri-Cities in Washington. Known as a busy trade route for the ancestral Indigenous who fished for salmon in the region, the art or pictographic and petrogyphic images are not directly linked to present-day tribes. However, stylistic features provide some reference. The Oregon Archaeological Society has documented and developed reference materials that people can read about. Visiting any archaeological site in Oregon or the Pacific Northwest is protected by the State Historic Preservation Office.

Indian rock art by Horsethief Lake in the Columbia River Gorge area.

Info: Oregon Archaeological Society, P.O. Box 13292, Portland, OR 97213 • 503.727.3507 • http://www.oregonarchaeological.org

WARM SPRINGS
Museum of Warm Springs

Founded in 1993, the museum at Warm Springs preserves the culture, history, and traditions of the Wasco, Warm Springs, and Paiute, who comprise the Confederated Tribes of Warm Springs. It is the first tribal museum in the state and is designed to provide a visual welcome to the public as well as a safe conservatory for the traditional treasures of the tribes. The 25,000-square-foot (7,620-square-meter) building features the stories of the three Confederated Tribes, each speaking separate languages but sharing the same colonial westward settler history through videos, recordings, and life-size dioramas using artifacts, photos, and historical documents.

The tribes host numerous cultural events that are open to the public. The Pi Ume Sha/Treaty Days Celebration in June offers drumming, dancing, vendors, games, the Fry Bread Golf Tournament, and an all-Indian rodeo. The tribe also sponsors Lincoln's Powwow, the Hawaiian and Local Boys Golf Tournament, the First Catch Salmon Feast, a Fourth of July celebration, and the Root Feast in early April.

Info: 2189 Highway 26, Warm Springs, OR 97761 • 541.553.3331 •
http://www.museumatwarmsprings.org/

WASHINGTON

In the 2010 U.S. Census, the number of people who identified as American Indian/Alaska Native in the state of Washington was 103,869. The state is home to twenty-nine federally recognized Indian tribes.

BELLINGHAM
Lummi Stommish and Reserve

Lhaq'temish are the Lummi people who are the original inhabitants of Washington's northernmost coast and southern British Columbia. For thousands of years, they fished, hunted, gathered, and harvested the abundance on the shores and waters of Puget Sound. The Lummi Reservation consists of a peninsula bounded by Lummi Bay on the west and Bellingham Bay on the east, a smaller peninsula, and a 1,000-acre (4-square-kilometer) island off the tip of the main peninsula, Portage Island.

The Point Elliot Treaty of 1855 marked the creation of the Lummi Reservation. Certain portions of the treaty boundaries were redrawn in 1873 by executive order, altering the size of the reservation. The Lummi Indian Nation during the twentieth century was inexorably tied to its fishing-centered economy and treaty fishing-rights issues. After the 1855 treaty, the federal government expected the tribe to adopt agriculture as its primary means of subsistence. The Lummi continue to travel to off-reservation sites for fishing and gathering, particularly to their traditional reef net locations.

The Lummi Stommish Water Festival is held in June and began in 1946 to honor and welcome home Lummi military veterans. The highlight of activities includes traditional war canoe races and Shal Hal bone games. It is based on the traditional potlatches of the Northwest, gatherings at which tribes met for a communal feast and exchange of gifts. The Lummi operate a charter boat, manned by tribal members, for cruises through the local waters. A gift shop carries wool sweaters, baskets, and carvings, which are characteristic Lummi crafts.

Info: 2665 Kwina Rd., Bellingham, WA 98226 • 360.312.2000 •
https://www.lummi-nsn.gov/

COULEE DAM
Colville Tribal Museum

This museum is located in a renovated church, where the top floor is the museum, and the bottom floor is an art gallery and gift shop. The interpretive displays give collective and individual histories of each of the twelve tribes that comprise the Confederate Tribes of the Colville Reservation: Colville; Wenatchee; Entiate; Chelan; Methow; Okanogan; Nespelem; San Poil; Lakes; Moses-Columbia; and Palus bands, who traditionally occupied territories in eastern Washington State; the twelfth band, the Nez Perce, originated in northeastern Oregon.

The Colville Indian Reservation was established in 1872, but the tribe's original land base was in flux with losses and later additions of the Chief Moses and Chief Joseph bands, among others. They helped to create a reservation that was unparalleled in cultural and political complexity, which was in part due to different languages spoken by the Confederated Tribes. In 1938, the federal government engineered the Grand Coulee Dam, which flooded the tribes' salmon-spawning areas and ruined orchard and agricultural lands, dramatically changing the tribes' economic opportunities. The Native people won a case against the government for mismanagement of tribal resources that were decimated by federal hydroelectric projects like the Grand Coulee Dam.

Info: 512 Mead Way, Coulee Dam, WA 99116 • 509.633.0751 • https://www.colvilletribes.com/

DALLESPORT
Columbia Hills Historical State Park

Columbia Hills is home to Horsethief Butte, which is known to climbing enthusiasts. It is also the site of pictographs and petroglyphs that can be seen on guided tours. Among them is the world-famous Tsagaglalal ("she who watches").

Info: 85 Highway 14, Dallesport, WA 98617 • 509.439.9032 • https://parks.state.wa.us/489/Columbia-Hills

MARYSVILLE
St. Anne's Church and Tulalip Reserve

The Treaty of Point Elliott was not ratified until 1859. It was not until December 23, 1873, that the Tulalip Indian Reservation was officially established. The Tulalip were expected to become farmers after the reservation was established even though they were fishermen, not farmers, and the heavily timbered land was not suited for agriculture.

Before a government school could be established, a traveling missionary named Reverend E. C. Chirouse came down the Snohomish and Snoqualmie rivers to establish a school by the French Roman Catholic Oblates of Mary Immaculate Church. By 1857, he had built a log church on a reservation beach, adorning it with a bell and a statue of St. Anne that had traveled with him from France. Chirouse wrote Snohomish-language books and taught religion, wood carving, and farming. He cared for tribal members through a devastating smallpox epidemic, although he called traditional Native religious observances "the devil's work." The Sisters of Providence arrived in 1868, and until 1901, they operated the Tulalip Mission School of St. Anne, which was the first Indian contract school in the United States. Originally for girls, the school was located below today's mission cemetery on the southern bank of Tulalip Bay. In 1878, the pope transferred Chirouse, and the Sisters of Providence took charge of the male students under Chirouse's separate care.

In the 1880s, the U.S. government began what it felt would be a productive assimilation, and the Indian Boarding School was born, forcing children to leave their homes on the reservations to live at the government-assisted school. In 1934, Congress enacted the Indian Reorganization Act to encourage tribes to strengthen and revitalize their tribal governments. After much deliberation, the members of the Snohomish, Snoqualmie, and Skykomish tribes at Tulalip voted to form a single reservation governmental structure, the Tulalip Tribes of Washington. The federal government nevertheless continued to recognize and deal with the Snohomish, Snoqualmie, and Skykomish as the three integral tribes that formed the Tulalip Tribes.

Info: 7321 Totem Beach Rd., Marysville, WA 98271 • 360.653.9400 • http://stmary-stanne.weconnect.com/

NEAH BAY
Makah Cultural and Research Center and Makah Museum

Neah Bay is located at the extreme northwestern corner of the continental United States. An account of the region was published in England and served as a guide to Captain James Cook when he explored the area in 1778. Cook called the headland here Cape Flattery because, he wrote, "it flattered us with hopes of finding a harbor," but it did not.

In 1791, a Mexican expedition tried to set up a colony at Neah Bay. It was abandoned after just five months, and for the next sixty years, the area was absent of outsiders. The Makah, who lived in the region's coastal villages around the cape, hunted whale and seal in cedar canoes with eight-man crews. The Makah voluntarily stopped whaling in the 1920s when commercial whaling had decimated gray whale populations. In 1999, they harvested a whale and were met with protests by animal rights groups. Meanwhile, the International Whaling Commission, which governs global whaling, continues to support the tribe's current approved quota of harvesting up to five eastern north Pacific gray whales a year through 2018.

The Makah Cultural Resource Center and Museum was built to care for and interpret the objects found at the Ancestral Makah Village of Ozette south of their current settlement. Makah oral history told of a "great slide," which buried a portion of Ozette long ago. Archaeologists collaborated with the tribe to prove this oral history correct. Radiocarbon dates demonstrated that a slide some five hundred (give or take fifty) years BP (before present) buried six longhouses and their respective contents, locking the precontact, wooden and wood-based artifacts in a shroud of mud. The eleven-year excavation produced over fifty-five thousand artifacts, which the Makah kept on the reservation.

Info: 1880 Bayview Ave., Neah Bay, WA 98357 • 360.645.2711 • http://makahmuseum.com/

PASCO
Sacajawea Historical State Park

Sacajawea Historical State Park is a 257-acre (1-square-kilometer) park at the confluence of the Snake and Columbia rivers and marks the place where Lewis and Clark

Expedition first saw the Columbia River, the final passageway on their voyage from St. Louis, Missouri, to the sea. On October 16, 1805, the Corps of Discovery arrived here, where they camped for two nights near the Native settlements of Yakama and Wanapam, which later became Sacajawea State Park.

Historical marker erected by the Washington State Historical Society in Sacajawea State Park.

Sacagawea was a Shoshone woman who traveled with the Lewis and Clark Expedition as navigator, interpreter, and emissary for them. Recent scholarly research and study of the original journals both indicate that the preferred spelling of this historical figure's name is "Sacagawea" and that her name is spoken with a hard "g" sound, but because the park has been known as Sacajawea for many decades, the "j" spelling is retained. Elsewhere in brochures, exhibits, and programs, the "g" is used. Sacajawea Historical State Park is a 284-acre (1.1-square-kilometer) marine and day-use park, sporting 9,100 feet (2,774 meters) of freshwater shoreline, a big sky, and excellent views of the two rivers. The interpretive center on-site features the Lewis and Clark Room, retelling the story of these early explorers and the role of Sacagawea.

Info: 2503 Sacajawea Park Rd., Pasco, WA 99301 • 509.545.2361 • https://parks.state.wa.us/575/Sacajawea

SEATTLE
Burke Museum

The Burke Museum of Natural History and Culture is home to the Bill Holm Center for the Study of Northwest Native Art, a premier center for the study of Native arts of the Northwest. The center facilitates education about Northwest Native art and supports research about and access to the Native art collections at the Burke. Bill Holm, professor emeritus of art history and curator emeritus of Northwest Coast Indian art at the Burke Museum, is recognized internationally as one of the most knowledgeable experts in the field of Northwest Coast Native art history. Holm advanced the study of Native arts with the idea that artists in non-Western societies could be seen as individuals, but very little had been written on the subject, and many people, some art historians among them, were still viewing tribal arts as generic works whose makers were not only anonymous but faceless and indistinguishable.

Reproduction of "A Dzunukwa Holds Tináa" (copper shields) outside the Burke Museum.

Info: 1413 NE 45th St., Seattle, WA 98105 • 206.543.7907 • http://www.burkemuseum.org/

Daybreak Star Indian Cultural Center at Seattle's Discovery Park

Established in 1977, The Daybreak Star Indian Cultural Center is located in Seattle's Discovery Park. The building is an impressive piece of modern architecture incorporating many elements of traditional Northwest Native architecture. The center grew out of United Indians of All Tribes, an organization founded by Colville Confederated Tribes activist Bernie Whitebear (1937–2000) to provide an urban base for Native Americans in the Seattle area.

The Daybreak Star Indian Cultural Center has use of 20 acres (0.08 square kilometers) in Seattle's Discovery Park in the Magnolia neighborhood. Following a nonviolent militant takeover and occupation of land where the Fort Lawton military base had been declared surplus by the U.S. Department of Defense, the United Indians of All Tribes successfully retained the land to develop a Native American center that has become a hub of activity for Native peoples and their supporters locally, nationally, and internationally hosting social, educational, and cultural programs and operating the Daybreak Gallery of Native American Art. The Seattle Indian Days Powwow is held annually on the third weekend in July in conjunction with the Seattle Seafair.

Info: 5011 Bernie Whitebear Way, Seattle, WA 98199 • 206.285.4425 • http://www.unitedindians.org/daybreakstarcenter

Public Art

Andrew Morrison (Apache/Haida) painted all of the murals at the Wilson Pacific School, formerly the Indian Heritage High School from 2001 to 2013, using spray paint. In 2013, the school was slated for demolition, and it was to be replaced with two new schools. A Memorandum of Understanding (MOU) between Morrison and Seattle Public Schools was created to preserve, protect, remove, and relocate the existing Native American murals into both the new Robert Eagle Staff Middle School and Cascadia Elementary School buildings.

The sculptures of Lawrence Beck (Yup'ik) can be seen on the grounds of Highline Community College in Midway, Washington; King County International Airport; and Golden Garden Park in Seattle as well as in other cities in the country.

Info: 1330 N. 90th St., Seattle, WA 98103 • http://andrewmorrison.org/

SHELTON
Squaxin Island Tribe Museum Library and Research Center

The Squaxin Island Tribe are known as "people of the water." They are descendants of the maritime people who lived and prospered along these shores for untold centuries. The Squaxin Island Reservation occupies most of Squaxin Island, located at the southern end of Puget Sound in the state of Washington. The island itself is unoccupied; the tribal community and tribal headquarters are in Kamilche between Little Skookum and Totten Inlets near Shelton, where over the years, the tribe has purchased land for housing and tribal offices.

Over the centuries, Squaxin Island has been a gathering place for the people of the region, a centrally located stopping point for trade and for social or spiritual gatherings. In Lushootseed, or Lushutseed, a variant of the wider Salish language traditionally utilized by many coastal tribes, Squawksin meant "in between" or "piece of land to cross over to another bay." The people of Squaxin Island are closely related to the Nisqually Tribe, with similar cultural traditions, through intermarriage and language. They are, along with the Puyallup Tribe and the Nisqually, fellow signatories to the Treaty of Medicine Creek of 1854, wherein the tribes ceded 2,560,000 acres (10,360 square kilometers) of aboriginal territory to the federal government. On display in the museum are artifacts excavated from an ancient Squaxin site, Mud Bay Village, now located on private property on South Puget Sound. The tribe continues many traditional practices of cultural and spiritual value, such as the First Salmon Ceremony honoring the first salmon run of the season, each year in August.

Info: Squaxin Island Museum, 150 SE K'WUH-DEEGS-ALTXW, Shelton, WA 98584 • 360.432.3839 • http://squaxinislandmuseum.org/

SUQUAMISH
Suquamish Museum and Chief Sealth (Seattle) Gravesite

The new, 9,000-square-foot (2,743-square-meter) Suquamish Museum is a tribute to the Suquamish Tribe and culture. It's a snapshot of the tribe, which details its past and present and looks to the future of the Suquamish Nation. It is filled with artifacts with a permanent gallery, another exhibit gallery, and a fifty-seat auditorium.

Chief Sealth's grave is nearby. He is the namesake of the city of Seattle. Sealth was a Suquamish chief who negotiated and befriended early white settlers in the 1800s. The Suquamish were part of a confederacy of Native peoples who occupied the land around what is known today as Puget Sound and Lake Washington. Sealth offered friendship toward whites and sought allies against raids. Seattle realized that the number of white settlers was growing. He signed on to the Port Elliott

Treaty of 1855, which ceded lands in return for reservation lands. As was the custom on many parts of the frontier, white settlers named their new town in honor of the displaced chief, hoping it would preserve a spirit of amity with the Indians.

A widely circulated speech attributed to Seattle poetically summarizes the passing of his time and people from the land. Unfortunately, it may have been fabricated despite having a vision of an Indian presence and vanished glory. Another place of interest in the Suquamish area is the Old-Man House, the birthplace of Chief Seattle, which was given to the Suquamish Tribe in 2004 by the Washington State Parks Commission, who could no longer afford the 1-acre (4,047-square-meter) park, which includes a shell-strewn beach that is sacred to the tribe. It was the site of their "mother village" and of Chief Seattle's longhouse.

Chief Sealth (Chief Seattle), well-known Suquamish leader (1786-1866).

Nearby is a cedar longhouse belonging to the Dwamish Confederacy; the archaeological evidence identified it as 520 feet (159 meters) long and covering an area of 1.25 acres (5,059 square meters). The crossbeams supporting the roof were sixty-five feet long and up to 22 inches (56 centimeters) in diameter. The house was built on the beach, and its shape followed the contours of the shore. Only a trace remains from more than a century ago, but its outline and some of its stakes are still visible.

The Port Madison Indian Reservation is the homeland of the Suquamish Tribe. The reservation, located in northern Kitsap County, is divided into two separate parcels by Miller Bay. The towns of Suquamish and Indianola are both within the reservation.

The Suquamish Museum is in the heart of Suquamish Village on the Port Madison Indian Reservation located on the breathtaking Kitsap Peninsula, named after Suquamish Chief Kitsap. The county boasts over 250 miles (402 kilometers) of saltwater shoreline, miles and miles of hiking and biking trails, and many vibrant communities. At the corner of Suquamish Way and Division Street, the new Suquamish Museum facility has a natural and environmental footprint. The location requires taking the Bainbridge Island Ferry from Seattle or the Edmonds Kingston Ferry.

Info: Suquamish Museum, 861 NE South St., P.O. Box 498, Suquamish, WA 98392 • 360.394.8499 • http://www.suquamishmuseum.org/

TOPPENISH
Yakama Nation Museum and Cultural Center

The Yakama Reservation is located in a rural, isolated area in south-central Washington 200 miles (322 kilometers) from the urban centers of Seattle and Spokane. The reservation lies along the eastern slopes of the Cascade Mountains. In the Native language, the origin of their name is "E-yak-ma," meaning "a growing family." Traditionally, they were trappers, fishers, and gatherers. They built lodgepole houses and lived in extended families.

The Yakama Reservation was established by the Port Elliot Treaty of 1855, confederating fourteen tribes and bands who were removed to a reservation after ceding over 10 million acres (40,469 square kilometers) of ancestral homeland to the U.S. government. The bands reserved their right to hunt, fish, access, and use traditional cultural sites and gather traditional foods and medicine in all of their "usual and accustomed places" within this ceded area. White settlers violated the treaty terms, including fishing rights.

Yakama Chief Kamiakin called upon the tribes to oppose outsiders, and thereafter, a series of raids, counter-raids, and reciprocal atrocities began, which was known as the Yakima War. The war continued until 1859, when the last phase, known as the Coeur d'Alene War, ended. Federal Indian agents took control of the reservation. The Port Elliott Treaty of 1855 relegated the Native peoples in the region to inferior lands while opening up the fertile portions of eastern Washington to white settlement.

The Yakama Museum and Cultural Center holds classes in the Yakama language for residents of the reservation and also promotes the observance of rituals, a major result of that renewal. The facility is housed in a structure meant to resemble a winter lodge, with a central, 76-foot (23-meter) -high, beamed hall. The tribe's history and crafts are chronicled in the displays.

Info: Yakama Nation Museum, P.O. Box 151, Toppenish, WA 98948 • 509.865.2800 • http://www.yakamamuseum.com

TULALIP
The Hibulb Cultural Center and Natural History Preserve

In 2011, the Hibulb Cultural Center and Natural History Preserve was opened to revive, restore, protect, interpret, collect, and enhance the history, traditional cultural values, and spiritual beliefs of the Tulalip tribes that include the Snohomish, Snoqualmie, Skagit, Suiattle, Samish, and Stillaguamish tribes. The center is approximately 23,000 square feet (7,010 square meters), with a 50-acre (0.2-square-kilometer) natural history preserve. The interactive cultural center features a main exhibit, a temporary exhibit, two classrooms, a longhouse, a research library, and a gift shop. It also features a fully certified collections and archaeological repository. It is certified by the State of Washington.

The Tulalip Reservation is located west of the city of Marysville in Tulalip, Washington, about 40 miles (64 kilometers) north of Seattle. It sits directly on Puget Sound. Approximately 2,600 acres (10.5 square kilometers) of forest land in various parcels were purchased recently with the intention of using them for preservation and reclamation of reservation land.

The Tulalip Tribes of the Tulalip Reservation, a federally recognized tribal entity, was established via the Treaty of Point Elliot on January 22, 1855, with certain land, fishing, education, and health care rights. The reservation boundaries were formally defined in 1873. Tulalip means "small mouthed bay," which refers to a particular part of Puget Sound.

The Hibulb Cultural Center is one of many tribal developments, including the Tulalip Resort and Casino and the Bernie Kai-Kai Gobin Hatchery, which produces over ten million salmon, including summer chinook, coho, and chum. The reservation's location on Puget Sound also makes commercial and recreational fishing activities quite viable and productive.

Info: The Hibulb Cultural Center, 6410 23rd Ave. NE, Tulalip, WA 98271 • 360.716.2600 • http://www.hibulbculturalcenter.org

WALLA WALLA
Whitman Mission National Historic Site

Whitman Mission National Historic Site was established to focus on the continuing relevance of the history and impact of Marcus and Narcissa Whitman's religious mission to the Cayuse Nation in the early nineteenth century. This Cayuse mission was sponsored by the American Board of Commissioners for Foreign Missions (ABCFM), a Boston group responsible for Protestant mission operations around the world. The National Park Service, which administers the Whitman Mission National Historic Site, describes the Whitman story. It features activities at the mission, including the Indian crafts that were carried on there, such as weaving, mat assembly, and cooking.

Cayuse Indians were an influential tribe because of the superiority they gained as accomplished horsemen. Their horses were known as cayuse throughout the West. They were feared as adversaries even by other tribes that far outnumbered them.

Cayuse ceremonial life involved treating illness, and they were deeply aligned with ritual practices. These factors led to the tragic events that have become known as the Whitman Massacre. Narcissa Whitman was one of the first white women to reach the West along the Oregon Trail. She and her husband, Marcus, arrived in 1836 to open a mission along the Walla Walla River at Waiilatpu. The Whitmans were successful in gaining trust and winning converts, but prolonged drought in the 1840s and illness led to the spiritual leaders' belief that only the presence of the mission could explain such catastrophes. In November 1847, the mission was attacked, and all thirteen of its occupants were slain. Two years later, the Cayuse surrendered the five Cayuse men, who were hanged.

The Cayuse, Umatilla, and Walla Walla tribes are all members of the Confederated Tribes of the Umatilla Reservation. These tribes traditionally resided in the areas of northeastern Oregon and southeastern Washington. After the introduction of the horse, they became more mobile and often joined the Nez Perce and other bands to hunt bison on the western plains.

Through partnering with the Confederated Tribes of the Umatilla Indian Reservation, the National Park Service seeks to present the continuing story of the Cayuse Nation and the impact of this early interaction with foreign immigrants. The Whitman Mission Site has summer and winter hours.

Info: Whitman Mission National Historic Site, 328 Whitman Mission Rd., Walla Walla, WA 99362 • 509.522.6360 • https://www.nps.gov/whmi/index.htm

U.S. ISLANDS

Hawaii—the word, the vision, the sound in the mind—is the fragrance and feel of soft kindness. Above all, Hawaii is "she," the Western image of the Native "female" in her magical allure. And if luck prevails, some of "her" will rub off on you, the visitor. Tourists flock to my native land for escape, but they are escaping into a state of mind while participating in the destruction of a host people in a native place.

—Haunani Kay-Trask (Kanaka Maoli)

Hawaii was a great monarchy until it was seized by the Americans and made into a territory. Decades later, most Indigenous Hawaiians resisted statehood. But Hawaii was made into a state anyway in 1959, changing its territorial status.

The United States still has sovereignty over fourteen territories. Five of them (American Samoa, Guam, the Northern Mariana Islands, Puerto Rico, and the U.S. Virgin Islands) have a permanent, nonmilitary population, while nine of them do not. Navassa Island, Puerto Rico, and the U.S. Virgin Islands are located in the Caribbean, all other territories are in the Pacific. Citizens of American territories are subject to U.S. laws but do not have voting power in Congress or federal elections. All residents of these territories are U.S. citizens and free to come to the mainland; they are not considered immigrants.

Guam is the largest in size (214 square miles [344 square kilometers]), the most populated, and the southernmost of the Mariana Archipelago, which is made up of fifteen islands. American Samoa comprises five islands and two atolls for a total of 77 square miles (199 square kilometers) and has about 50,000 residents, 90 percent of whom are Samoans. Meanwhile, in the Caribbean Sea, Puerto Rico, covers 3,515 square miles (9,104 square kilometers) and is the third largest island in the United States and the 82nd largest island in the world.

AMERICAN SAMOA

Settled around 1000 B.C.E. by Polynesian navigators, Samoa, like Guam, has been the victim of international rivalries beginning in the nineteenth century and resolved by an 1899 treaty in which Germany (later Britain) and the United States divided the Samoan archipelago. The United States formally occupied its portion, a smaller group of eastern islands with the excellent harbor of Pago Pago, the following year. Although it is U.S.-occupied, American Samoa operates by a traditional village political system common to all of the Samoa Islands, the *Fa'amatai*, and the *Fa'asamoa* interacts across the current international boundaries. The *Fa'asamoa* represents language and customs, and the *Fa'amatai* determines the protocols of the *Fono* (council) and the chief system. The *Fa'amatai* and the *Fono* take place at all levels of the Samoan government from the family to the village and include regional and national issues. There are over 50,000 Samoan people. When visiting, make sure to respect the Samoans and follow protocol: https://www.nps.gov/npsa/learn/historyculture/faasamoa.htm.

PAGO PAGO
Jean P. Haydon Museum

Originally a naval commissary during World War II, this building is now a small museum with a remarkable collection of Samoan artifacts and art, including canoes.

Info: Fagatogo, Pago Pago, Tutuila 96799-1540, AS • 684.633.4347 • http://www.ashpo.org/walktour/15.html

National Park of American Samoa

This park is the only one operated by the American National Park Service south of the equator. Spread across three separate islands—Tutuila, Ofu, and Ta'ū—the park preserves and protects coral reefs, tropical rain forests, fruit bats, and the Samoan culture.

Info: Pago Pago, AS 96799 • 684.633.7082 • https://www.nps.gov/npsa/index.htm

GUAM

Guam is the largest and southernmost of the Mariana Islands chain and is known to most Americans as a strategic military and economic position between Asia and North America. However, Guam has a complex cultural heritage and has been inhabited for thousands of years by the Chamorro, whose ancestors were seafaring people probably from Southeast Asia.

Guam's Indigenous peoples have been subjected to three colonial powers in the last four hundred years: Spain, Japan, and the United States. During World War II, Japan invaded and ruled until 1944, when the Americans reclaimed "their" territory. The Chamorro people have been victimized by each country, including the oppressive U.S. Naval Administration. The Indigenous spirit, language, and culture of the Chamorro is strong today in spite of their long colonial history, and people all over the world come to visit. Chamorro festivals and cultural events occur in California, where many live. Sixty-five thousand Chamorro people live in Guam.

HAGATNA
Guam Museum

Chamorro architect Andrew T. Laguaña designed the stunning museum building to represent the great seal of Guam, which is in the shape of the Chamorro slingstone, a weapon made of basalt and coral. Inside is a visual and audio bazaar of all the history and culture of the Chamorro people and of Guam. A community effort, the Chamorro and others had been collecting and preserving stories and objects long before a building existed to house the treasures; the result is the creation of a museum that reflects the diversity, creativity, and resilience of Guam and the Mariana Islands. The museum offers many events, like the annual Guam International Film Festival, which features films made by regional artists as well as from around the world.

Info: 193 Chalan Santo Papa, Juan Pablo Dos., Hagatna, GU 96910 •
671.989.4455 • http://guammuseum.org/

Latte Stone Park

Latte stones are pillars on which ancient Chamorro houses were constructed as early as 500 B.C.E. and can only be found in Guam and the Northern Marianas Islands. They were composed of two pieces: a supporting column (halagi) that was made from coral limestone and a capstone (tasa) made from coral heads, which were usually carried several miles from the quarry site or reef to the house. They are treated with great reverence and untouched. Many ruins are in northern Guam. The ones found in this park were transferred from their original location in Me'pu in Guam's southern interior.

Info: West O'Brien Dr., Hagåtña, GU 96910 •
http://theguamguide.com/latte-stone-park/

UMATAC
Chamorro Heritage Month

Every March, a grand celebration of Chamorro culture takes place during Chamorro Heritage Month and Heritage Day. The festival lasts for two weeks and includes a plethora of activities, including the Humatak Heritage Walking Tour, which was designed to promote young people's role in safeguarding traditional culture and raising awareness. Young Chamorro lead tour groups and provide detailed explanations of the history, culture, and heritage of the Chamorro. This festival features performances, panels, and workshops with the intent of preserving the Chamorro heritage and language.

Info: https://www.facebook.com/Guam-History-Chamorro-Heritage-Day-Festival-323599644416015/

HAWAII

The Hawaiian Archipelago, or Ka Pae 'Aina O Hawai'i Nei in the Hawaiian language, is made up of 132 islands, reefs, and shoals, extending 1,523 miles (2,451 kilometers) southeast to northwest. "Hawaii" (probably the Native Hawaiian word *Owhyhee*, meaning "homeland") has 6,500 square miles of (10,461 square kilometers) land, with eight big islands, seven of which are inhabited: Hawai'i: The Big Island; Maui: The Valley Isle; Kaho'olawe: The Target Isle; Lāna'i: The Pineapple Isle; Moloka'i: The Friendly Isle; O'ahu: The Gathering Place; Kaua'i: The Garden Isle; and Ni'ihau: The Forbidden Isle. Now an American state, Hawaii was a great kingdom until 1893 with a palace that rivaled the White House, a state department with embassies abroad, a navy, and legendary kings and queens, who traveled the world. Although today Hawaii is often treated as America's private vacation destination, Indigenous Hawaiians make up almost three hundred thousand of the 1.429 million people who live in Hawaii. People are asked to respect the lands and waters when visiting, as Hawaii is considered the "endangered species capital of the world"; often called a "paradise" by tourism advertisers, the paradise is at risk.

King Kamehameha Celebration

A statewide holiday on June 11, the King Kamehameha Celebration is observed through various events and festivals on different islands. A great warrior, diplomat, and leader, King Kamehameha I united the Hawaiian Islands into one royal kingdom in 1810 after years of conflict. Hawaiian legend prophesized that a light in the sky with feathers like a bird would signal the birth of a great chief; Kamehameha was born in 1758, the year Halley's comet passed over Hawaii. His storied life and many challenges rival any accounts of world heroes. By uniting the warring factions in the Hawaiian homelands, he probably saved the islands from being torn apart by competing western interests. Among the great king's accomplishments were the establishment of trade with foreign countries and the development of the sandalwood industry. He was known as a just ruler, introducing the Law of the Splintered Paddle, which protected the weak from the strong and insured that every man, woman, and child had the right to "lie down to sleep by the roadside without fear of harm." The law is a part of today's Hawaiian state law. In his later years, King Kamehameha was recognized as a great statesman.

Info: http://ags.hawaii.gov/kamehameha/

HILO (OAHU)
Merrie Monarch Hula Festival

This weeklong April festival, founded in 1964, is not the hula offered by Hawaii's resorts but a celebration of the sacred art of Hawaii's Indigenous heritage. It also honors King David Kalākaua (1836–1891), who inspired the perpetuation of Hawaiian traditions, language, and art in spite of objections by white missionaries and was nicknamed the Merrie Monarch. Attendees are treated to hula shows of miraculous synchronicity, dazzling outfits, and daring dance moves as well as a Miss Hula pageant, Hawaiian arts fair, and a grand parade through Hilo town. The world's premier forum for people of all ages to display their skills and knowledge of the art of ancient and modern hula, the Merrie Monarch Festival is a renaissance of the Hawaiian culture that is being passed on from generation to generation.

A dancer participates in the Merrie Monarch Hula Festival.

Info: 865 Piilani St., Hilo, HI 96720 • 808.935.9168 • http://www.merriemonarch.com

HŌNAUNAU (THE BIG ISLAND)
Pu'uhonua o Hōnaunau National Historical Park

Hawaiians lived by a code of laws called Kapu, which governed every aspect of their society. Breaking Kapu (law/constitution/tenets/vows) had serious penalties—sometimes violators were even executed—but this sacred place, the Pu'uhonua, was a place of refuge for the kapu breaker, defeated warriors, and civilians during war times. Those within the boundaries of the Pu'uhonua were protected from any physical harm or punishment. A great wall marks the sanctuary, which includes many ki'i (carved, wooden images) and the Hale o Keawe temple, burial site of chiefs. It remains a sacred place, and activities are restricted.

Info: State Hwy. 160, Hōnaunau, HI 96726 • 808.328.2326 • https://www.nps.gov/puho/index.htm

A Replica of the *Holokai*.

HONOLULU (OAHU)
Bishop Museum

Established in 1889, this is the state's largest museum and houses an unparalleled collection of Hawaii cultural artifacts. It also publishes materials, sponsors research, and hosts many festivals and events. It is funded through the trust of Bernice Pauahi Bishop (1831–1884), a philanthropist/Ali'i, who was a princess and descendant of King Kamehameha but chose to not ascend the throne. Bishop's estate was the largest private land ownership in the Kingdom of Hawai'i, made up of about 9 percent of Hawaii's total area. Her concern was for her Hawaiian people, and she left her vast holdings in trust, which funds the Kamehameha schools and other charities for Indigenous Hawaiians. Her husband, Charles Reed Bishop, founded the Bernice P. Bishop Museum to memorialize her.

The history of the Polynesian Voyaging Society (PVS) is exhibited in the "Holo Moana: Generations of Voyaging—O'ahu" installation. PVS was founded in 1973 to carry out an experiment that would help answer the questions of how Polynesians settled the far-flung islands of the mid-Pacific. Was it an accident or by design? An exact replica of an outrigger canoe was constructed and sailed successfully using traditional navigation techniques, proving that, indeed, the ancient Polynesians were a scientific and goal-oriented people. PVS grew into an educational organization that seeks to perpetuate and preserve the spirit, art, and culture of ocean exploration as well as protecting the ecosystems of the world's seas and islands. Currently, the PVS flagstaff vessel, the *Holokai*, is sailing the world, visiting communities across the planet. By tracking the monumental journey, people can visit the *Holokai* when it docks for a celebration of Hawaiian culture. http://www.hokulea.com/

Info: 1525 Bernice St., Honolulu, HI 96817 • 808.847.3511 • http://www.bishopmuseum.org/

Duke Kahanamoku Statue

This 9-foot (2.7-meter) statue of the "Father of Modern Surfing" adorns Waikiki Beach, one of the world's most famous surfing sites. Duke Paoa Kahinu Mokoe Hulikohola Kahanamoku (1890–1968), who grew up near Waikiki, earned gold and silver medals for swimming in three different Olympics. Duke was the first person to be inducted into both the Surfing Hall of Fame and the Swimming Hall of Fame.

Info: Kalakaua Ave., Honolulu, HI 96815 • http://www.publicartinpublicplaces.info/duke-paoa-kahanamoku-1990-by-jan-gordon-fisher

Hawaii International Film Festival

The annual festival is known for showing feature films, documentaries, and shorts made about the Pacific by Pacific Islanders and films made by Hawai'i filmmakers that present Hawai'i in a culturally accurate way. It is held in various venues in Honolulu and other cities.

Info: 680 Iwilei Rd., Suite 100, Honolulu, HI 96817 • 808.792.1577 • https://www.hiff.org/

Hawai'i State Art Museum

Artworks in the collection, which are displayed in many Hawaiian public buildings, are primarily contemporary works by artists with a connection to Hawai'i, not just Native Hawaiians.

Info: 250 S. Hotel St., Honolulu, HI 96813 • 808.586.0300 • http://sfca.hawaii.gov/

Iolani Palace

The palace was the official residence of the Hawaiian monarchs, where they held state functions and entertained dignitaries from around the world. Ahead of its time when it was built in 1882, it had electric lights, indoor plumbing, and telephones before the White House. Although the last reigning Hawaiian monarch, Queen Liliuokalani, lived nearby in Washington Place, she was tried at Iolani Palace by the conspirators, who, with the help of the U.S. Navy, illegally overthrew her government in 1893. The queen was sentenced to five years of hard labor, but that was overturned, and she was imprisoned in the one bedroom of the palace for almost a year. In 1993, President Bill Clinton apologized for the U.S. overthrow of the Hawaiian monarchy, but by this time, the Hawaiian Kingdom had been turned into a state, and the monarchy was never restored.

Iolani Palace.

Iolani's unique architecture is known as American Florentine and is seen nowhere else in the world. On the first floor, a grand hall faces a staircase of koa wood; ornamental plaster decorates the interior. The blue room features a koa wood piano, where Lili'uokalani played her own compositions for guests. A tour of the house and grounds includes a film, *Iolani Palace*.

Info: 364 S. King St., Honolulu, HI 96813 • 808.522.0822 • http://www.iolanipalace.org/

'Ōiwi Film Festival

This annual spring film festival held at the Honolulu Museum of Art showcases new work directed by Indigenous Hawaiian filmmakers. Films focus on Hawaiian culture and storytelling.

Info: 900 S. Beretania St., Honolulu, HI 96814 • 808.532.8700 • https://honolulumuseum.org/

Prince Kūhiō Festival

Held in various venues in Honolulu, this month-long festival honors Prince Jonah Kūhiō Kalaniana'ole, an activist and founder of the Hawaiian Civic Club movement. He was a prince of the reigning House of Kal kaua when the government of Queen Lili'uokalani was illegally overthrown in 1893. Later, Prince Kūhiō became a delegate representing the territory of Hawai'i in the U.S. Congress, where he was a proponent of the Hawaiian Homestead Act of 1920 and the Hawaiian Homes Commission Act of 1921.

Info: 808.221.0991 • http://princekuhiofestival.org/

Queen Emma Summer Palace

This museum was once the summer home of Queen Emma (1836–1885), wife of King Kamehameha IV, and houses her belongings, furnishings, and artifacts. She led a fascinating life and was at times the center of controversy. She was also a philanthropist and established the Queen's Hospital, where she visited patients almost daily whenever she was in Honolulu. It is now called the Queen's Medical Center. The Queen Emma Summer Palace sits on a 2.16-acre (8,741-square-meter) plot owned by the Queen Emma Estate and maintained by the Daughters of Hawaii. The grounds are extensively landscaped, with many plants native to the Hawaiian Islands.

Info: 2913 Pali Hwy., Honolulu, HI 96817 • 808.595.3167 • http://daughtersofhawaii.org/

Washington Place

Built by American sea captain John Dominis for his family, the manor eventually became the royal residence for Queen Lili'uokalani after she married the captain's son in 1862. This was the place where she was arrested and the Hawaiian Kingdom was overthrown by the American Navy and wealthy American landowners. She lived here until her death in 1917. Today, it is the official Hawaii Governor's Residence and a National Historic Landmark with a museum of the queen's collections and a weekly guided tour.

Info: 320 S. Beretania St., Honolulu, HI 96813 • 808.536.8040 • http://www.washingtonplacefoundation.org/

KA LAE (THE BIG ISLAND)
Ka Lae (South Point)

This National Historical Landmark is one of the most important landmarks in Hawaii. The rocky outcrop marks the most southern location in Hawaii and all of the United States. Home to ruins of heiau (temples), fishing shrines, and other cultural vestiges, Ka Lae is also a favorite fishing spot for locals and tourists. It is believed that the first Polynesians to arrive in the Hawaiian Islands landed here somewhere between 400 and 800 C.E. The beautiful coastal scenery contrasts with giant wind turbines on modern wind farms.

Info: http://tps.cr.nps.gov/nhl/detail.cfm?ResourceId=182&ResourceType=District

KAILUA-KONA (THE BIG ISLAND)
Hulihee Palace

Built during the early nineteenth century out of local lava rock, Hulihee Palace was once used by Hawaiian royalty as a vacation home, and today, it is a museum. Exhibits of memorabilia chronicle the lives of its regal residents, including King Kalakaua, who gave the palace the new title of Hikulani Hale after himself, a literal translation of "house of the seventh leader."

Info: 75-5718 Alii Dr., Kailua-Kona, HI 96740 • 808.329.1877 • http://daughter-sofhawaii.org/2017/05/01/hulihe'e-palace/

Iolani Luahine Hula Festival

Iolani Luahine (1915–1978), considered the high priestess of the ancient hula, was a kuma hula, dancer, chanter, and teacher. The annual January festival, established in her memory, awards an annual scholarship to a hula student and features hula performances by men, women, and children.

Info: Festival location is at the Sheraton, 78-128 Ehukai St., Kailua-Kona, HI 96740 • http://www.iolaniluahinefestival.org/

KANEOHE (OAHU)
Pali Lookout

The Pali (cliff in Hawaiian) Lookout is of deep historical significance, as it was the site of the 1795 Battle of Nuuanu that determined a great victory for King Kamehameha I in his struggle to unite Oahu under his rule. This fierce battle claimed hundreds of soldiers' lives, who plummeted to the bottom of Pali's sheer cliffs. Known for its strong and howling winds, Pali is one of Oahu's best scenic points for breathtaking views of the island's lush Windward Coast.

Info: Nuuanu Pali Dr., Kaneohe, HI 96744 • https://www.gohawaii.com/islands/oahu/regions/windward-coast/nuuanu-pali-lookout

KEKAHA (KAUAI)
Kōke'e Museum and State Park

Colorful canyons, sparkling waterfalls, a unique, dry forest, and a panoramic view of the Island of Niihau are treats for hikers through this state park. The museum offers a cultural and natural history of the area.

Info: Kekaha, HI 96752 • 808.335.9975 • http://www.kokee.org/

Pali Lookout.

KONA (BIG ISLAND)
Kaloko Honokohau National Historical Park

This coastal park illustrates the successful Hawaiian lifeways in ancient times on the rugged Kona coast: four different ahupuaa (traditional, mountain-to-sea land divisions) as well as heiau (sacred temples) and kii pohaku (petroglyphs). Two incredible fish ponds depict the engineering feats of these ancient peoples, who possessed knowledge of the location of precious fresh water (wai) that flows into the many brackish pools throughout the park. Local wildlife includes honu (Hawaiian green sea turtles), birds, Hawaiian monk seals, and others. The visitor center offers special programs and guided tours.

Info: 73-4786 Kanalani St. #14, Kailua-Kona, HI 96740 • 808.329.6881 • https://www.nps.gov/kaho/index.htm

LAHAINA (MAUI)
Lahaina Heritage Museum

This museum offers a comprehensive, interactive look at the complex history of Lahaina from ancient Hawai'i to the Monarchy era, including the missionary and whaling period, and from the Plantation era to early tourism. Lahaina Village itself played a significant role in the development of the Hawaiian Kingdom, Republic, Territory, and State of Hawai'i. The natural history and current status of the environment is also explored.

Info: 120 Dickenson St., Lahaina, HI 96761 • 808.661.3262 • http://lahainarestoration.org/lahaina-heritage-museum/

Performers do a traditional Hawaiian dance at the Polynesian Cultural Center. The center also educates visitors about other Polynesian peoples.

LAIE (OAHU)
Polynesian Cultural Center

Founded in 1963 by the Latter-Day Saints, the center was designed to provide employment for students at Brigham Young University while preserving Polynesian cultures. Eight simulated villages are staffed by cultural interpreters who demonstrate various art from Hawaiian, Samoan, Tahitian, and Māori cultures.

Info: 55-370 Kamehameha Hwy., Laie, HI 96762 • 800.367.7060 • http://www.polynesia.com/

LANAI (LANAI)
Kaunolu Village Site

A visit to this site, the largest of the Hawaiian ruins, is not an easy trip. This ancient fishing community, occupied since at least the 1400s, was composed of different towns featuring almost ninety residences, several religious structures, priests' houses, and isolated petroglyphs. It was a pu'uhonua (place of refuge; see above), where Hawaiian rulers and important leaders visited when the Hawaiian Islands were a unified and independent kingdom. The well-preserved compound gives visitors a glimpse of almost every aspect of Hawaiian culture. House platforms range from one to three stories; many have terraces, an inner area, and stone papamu "boards" for konane, a game resembling checkers. Located on the cliffs above the ocean, one needs a car with four-wheel drive to navigate the rocky, winding roads. The Kaunolu Village Site is a sacred place, but guided tours and a 3.5-mile (5,633-meter)-long, self-guided interpretive hike are available.

Info: Kaupili Rd., Lanai, HI 96763 • 808.565.7600 • https://www.nps.gov/nr/travel/asian_american_and_pacific_islander_heritage/Kaunolu-Village-Site.htm

Walls of Temple (Heiau).

Maui Nei Native Expeditions

Native Hawaiian cultural specialists take visitors on a cultural immersion excursion of Lahaina's historic sites, including Moku'ula and Mokuhinia. Educational workshops and presentations are offered at the Moku'ula restoration site, home to great Maui chiefs since the sixteenth century. Along with traditional accounts of Hawaiian heritage, participants learn to process taro and play traditional instruments.

Info: 505 Front St., Lahaina, HI 96761 • 808.283.4201 • https://mauinei.com/

LIHU'E (KAUAI)
Kaua'i Museum

The Kauai Museum is chock full of island history, exhibited in two buildings. Charts, artifacts, works of art, and fully restored boats help visitors understand the ancient and contemporary heritage of Hawaii. Special events occur at the museum, too.

Info: 4428 Rice St., Lihu'e, HI 96766 • 808.245.6931 • http://www.kauaimuseum .org/

UALAPUE (MOLOKA'I)
Hokukano-Ualapue Complex

A National Historic Landmark, this archaeological site includes seven heiaus (temples) and two fish ponds designed by early people for intensive fish production and cultivation. Considered to be one of the most important collections of Native Hawaiian precontact places, it is home to 'Ili'ili'ōpae, the largest heiau on Molokai and the second largest in all of Hawaii. 'Ili'ili'ōpae is a towering four tiers, rising to a stone platform measuring 287 feet (87 meters) by 87 feet (27 meters). According to legend, 'Ili'ili'ōpae Heiau was constructed in a single night with boulders passed from hand to hand along a chain of menehune, a race of forest-dwelling creatures.

Volcano Art Center.

Info: Hawaii Route 450, Ualapue, Moloka'i, HI 96748 • 800.553.5221 • https://www.nps.gov/nr/travel/asian_american_and_pacific_islander_heritage/ Hokukano-Ualapue-Complex.htm

VOLCANO (BIG ISLAND)
Volcano Art Center

Performances and workshops in a variety of Native Hawaiian cultural areas are featured in this facility located in Hawaii Volcanoes National Park. Tours of the Niaulani Rain Forest with ethnobotanists are offered; participants can help out with forest restoration activities, too.

Info: 19-4074 Old Volcano Rd., Volcano, HI 96785 • 808.967.7565 • http://volcanoartcenter.org/

WAILEA (MAUI)
Young Kamehameha Statue

Said to be the most accurate representation of Kamehameha the Great, this 1990 monumental, bronze statue was sculpted by Hawaiian cultural traditionalist and artist Herb Kawainui Kane (1928–2011). This formidable sculpture, along with other magnificent statues and paintings by Kane, who was elected a Living Treasure of Hawai'i in 1984, are on display at the Grand Wailea Resort.

Info: 3850 Wailea Alanui Dr., Wailea, HI 96753 • 808.875.1234 • https://www.grandwailea.com/gallery/art/

WAILUKU (MAUI)
Iao Valley State Park

This serene, 4,000-acre (16-square kilometer), 10-mile (16-kilometer) -long park is home to one of Maui's most memorable landmarks—the 1,200-foot (366-meter) Iao

Iao Valley State Park.

Needle. The green-mantled rock outcropping overlooks the Iao Stream and is part of the natural tropical and sacred Iao Valley, which was where the Battle of Kepaniwai took place in 1790. King Kamehameha I's victory over Maui's army changed the course of Hawaiian history as the kingdom was united under one ruler.

A pedestrian path meanders from the parking lot to Iao Needle; the ridgetop lookout provides panoramic views of the valley. The Hawaii Nature Center, which is also located within Iao Valley, has interactive exhibits and a botanical garden that shows the history of the plants brought to the islands by the ancient Hawaiians.

Info: 54 S. High St., Wailuku, Maui, HI 96793-2102 • 808.587.0300 • https://hawaiistateparks.org/parks/maui/'iao-valley-state-monument/

NORTHERN MARIANA ISLANDS

Almost twenty thousand Chamorro still live on the fourteen islands that make up their homeland. The total land area is approximately 179 square miles (464 square kilometers). During World War I, they were used by the Japanese and were used for the same purpose by U.S. forces during World War II. Eventually, the islands became a territory of the United States. Guam is also part of the island chain but has not been reunited with the Northern Mariana Islands because of their very different colonial experiences.

TINIAN
House of Taga

The ancient latte stone pillars (also called taga stones) at the House of Taga stood 15 feet (4.6 meters) high and were quarried about 4,000 feet (1,219 meters) south

Only one of the original latte stone pillars remains standing at the House of Taga.

of the site. Originally, probably twelve megaliths existed, but only one remains. According to Chamorro history, Taga, a giant with incredible strength, was born to the maga'låhi, or chief, of Ritidian Village, Guam. After feuding with his father, he moved to Rota and challenged the leading maga'låhi to a series of contests. He won them all, married a local Chamorro woman, and had a daughter, but both eventually died, and he felt responsible. Taga first appeared in European records in 1638 when he rescued sailors from the wreck of the ship, *Nuestra Señora de la Concepción*. Taga paddled through rough waters to save them and took them to Taga House, where they recuperated. Tinian is thought to be the first place where humans settled in Oceana.

Info: San Jose, Tinian 96952, CNMI •
https://www.atlasobscura.com/places/house-of-taga

PUERTO RICO

According to the 2010 U.S. Census, 35,753 people in Puerto Rico identified themselves as "American Indian and Alaska Native." Tribal organizations exist as well as a push to get Taino people formally recognized.

JAYUYA
Cemi Museum

This quirky little museum is itself a giant Cemi, which are usually small stone carvings of religious significance to the Taino. The Cemi Museum features the area's artifacts as well as examples of Taino influences on contemporary culture. Displays and films are in Spanish and English.

Entrance to the Cemi Museum.

Info: PR-144, Jayuya, PR 00664 • 787.828.4618 •
http://www.puertoricodaytrips.com/cemi-museum/

PONCE
Centro Ceremonial Indigena

Considered to be one of the premier archaeological sites in the Caribbean, Centro Ceremonial Indigena features many stone-lined courts/plazas shaded by Native trees. The on-site museum offers artifacts, films, and information in Spanish and English. After the museum visit, a tour guide heads an excursion of the rest of the site and points out flora and fauna and how the Taino used it for food and home and canoe construction. A re-creation of a Taino town, ball fields, and ceremonial plazas is also shown.

Info: Route 503, Km. 2.2, Tibes Ponce, PR 00730 • 787.840.2255 •
https://www.nps.gov/nr/travel/prvi/pr15.htm

UTUADO
Caguana Indigenous Ceremonial Park and Museum

The Caguana Ceremonial Ball Courts Site was constructed in stages from 1200 to 1500 c.e. and was still in use at the time of Spanish contact. More than just a sport, the game was part of the Taino religion, and the outcome often influenced important decisions for the Nation. Played by two teams, players were only allowed to use certain parts of their bodies, like knees, elbows, shoulders, and heads. It is thought that the batey game, played throughout the Caribbean, had its origins in Mesoamerica. Caguana, which is Taino for "between the mountains," is the largest ball court that has been found in the islands. Cobblestone paths border thirteen bateyes of

Petroglyphs at Centro Ceremonial Indigena.

varying sizes—some may have been for children. Stone monoliths, several featuring petroglyphs, surround some of the courts. La Mujer de Caguana, an extremely rare petroglyph, is depicted with a large headdress and frog legs—she is a fertility figure and one of the most significant images in the park. The majestic *ceiba* (Taino word) trees seem to rise to the sacred mountain in the distance, which can be viewed at every vantage point on the area. The ceiba is the national tree of Puerto Rico.

The on-site museum exhibits archaeological finds and displays chronicling the history of food crops, like corn, *yautïa*, sweet potatoes, and *cassava*. Information is in both Spanish and English. The artifacts and discoveries that were made here may be the most important in the history of Puerto Rico, as they tell the story of the ancestors of modern-day Puerto Ricans. It was and still is, for many people of Taino descent, a very spiritual place. Indeed, visitors feel a sense of peace and awe walking the beautiful grounds.

Info: Route 111, Km. 12.4, Utuado, PR 00641 • 787.894.7325 • https://www.nps.gov/nr/travel/prvi/pr25.htm

Canada

CANADA

The form of the proposed monument was developed to represent the Mi'kmaq people and their history in the Kejimkujik area in as meaningful a way as possible. For this reason, each image used for the monument's features is drawn from the Mi'kmaq petroglyphs located within the park.

> —Mi'kmaw traditionalist Muin'iskw,
> designer of the Kejimkujik Park Commemorative Monument

The Atlantic Region in the far east of Canada, sometimes called the Maritimes, is organized into four provinces: New Brunswick, Newfoundland and Labrador, Nova Scotia, and Prince Edward Island. Located northeast of the U.S. state of Maine, the region extends almost as far east as Greenland and does not have large and sparsely populated northern regions like the rest of Canada. The provinces are a small collection of islands and peninsulas connected to Quebec's eastern border and form the crescent-shaped Gulf of St. Lawrence, the country's busiest eastern port. Newfoundland, an island surrounded by the Atlantic Ocean, and Labrador, a large land mass connected to mainland Canada, are two separate geographical areas but together form one province. The Atlantic Canadian landscape is fringed with pine forests, hills, and dangerous, rocky cliffs dotted with lighthouses that provide safe harbors for marine traffic. Coastal areas are usually cool, wet, and foggy with cold, stormy winters and mild, pleasant summers. Inland areas are drier and are known for some of Canada's largest snowfalls. The Innu, Mi'kmaq, Maliseet, and Passamaquoddy people are indigenous to the region and still maintain a strong presence. Unlike the rest of Canada, each Atlantic province can be crossed in a two-hour drive.

NEW BRUNSWICK

More than ten thousand First Nations citizens, mostly Mi'kmaq and Maliseet, live in New Brunswick. The Passamaquoddy maintain a land claim on St. Andrews and are historically from the area but have no Canadian official status as aboriginal and no reserves.

ELSIPOGTOG FIRST NATION
Elsipogtog First Nation Powwow

The Jingle, the Fancy Shawl, and the Grass Dance Competition make this Mi'kmaw annual September powwow a festive celebration.

Info: 373 Big Cove Rd., Elsipogtog First Nation, NB E4W 2S3 • 506.876.2431 • https://www.tourismnewbrunswick.ca/Products/A/AnnualElsipogtogFirstNation Powwow.aspx

RED BANK
Metepenagiag Heritage Park

Metepenagiag Heritage Park views the ancestral home of the Metepenagiag Mi'kmaq First Nation. It is also the location of two of the most significant aboriginal heritage archaeological sites in eastern Canada: the Augustine Mound National Historic Site, which exhibits artifacts from twenty-five hundred years ago, and Oxbow National Historic Site, the still flourishing Mi'kmaq community that has endured for three thousand years. It is the oldest continually occupied village in New Brunswick. The park includes interpretive walking tours and a shop offering Mi'kmaq-made arts.

Info: 2156 Micmac Rd., Red Bank, NB E9E 2P2 • 506.836.6118 • http://www .metpark.ca/

ST. JOHN
New Brunswick Museum

This 60,000-square-foot (18-square-kilometer) museum has displays of Beothuk and other maritime historic Indian artifacts plus offers special events. The exhibit "Koluskap: Stories from Wolastoqiyik" features over nine hundred artifacts plus recent aboriginal history.

Info: 1 Market Sq., St. John, NB E2L 4Z6 • 506.643.2300 • http://website.nbm-mnb.ca/Koluskap/English/Gallery/index.php

NEWFOUNDLAND AND LABRADOR

Almost 70 percent of reserve residents speak their Indigenous language, Innu/Montagnais being the best known. The province is home to 35,800 First Nations, Inuit, and Métis people.

BOYD'S COVE
Beothuk Interpretation Centre

The Beothuk people were one of the original owners of the area now called Newfoundland. Although some historians consider them extinct and maintain that the last Beothuk died in the 1800s, many Mi'kmaq refute that theory. According to Chief Mi'sel Joe of the Miawpukek First Nation, the Beothuk fled to the mainland and integrated with other First Nations. They resisted European contact and culture and retreated to the central part of the island away from the ocean, their main source of food. At that time, few land animals were in the region, and freshwater fish were scarce. Because of the climate, farming was difficult. Malnutrition and European diseases had a fatal effect on the Beothuk, although many believe that the Europeans did their best to exterminate them. The center is located on the site of a traditional Beothuk town and features exhibits and trails dedicated to them. In addition, the center maintains a connection with contemporary aboriginal communities and collaborates with them to showcase Native arts, cultures, and history. The site's Spirit Garden provides a quiet place for reflection of European impact on Native peoples with the intent that healing and reconciliation can happen.

A diorama of Beothuk people at the Beothuk Interpretation Centre.

Info: Boyd's Cove, NL A0G 1G0 • 709.656.3114 • http://www.seethesites.ca/the-sites/beothuk-interpretation-centre.aspx

CONNE RIVER
Miawpukek First Nation Powwow

The Mi'kmaq have been the main residents of the area for at least ten thousand years and, like other Indigenous peoples, were skilled at building their lives around the environment. Their northern regions were too cold for regular agriculture, so the economy and culture centered around the sea and waterways. During winters, communities moved inland and hunted and trapped moose, beaver, and caribou. As any successful culture, theirs was dynamic and changed over the years; eventually they created seven districts, which became the Mi'kmaw nation.

It is thought that they, along with the Beothuk, were the first North American Indigenous peoples to have regular contact with Europeans starting in the eleventh century with the Vikings or possibly Basque fishermen. Their prophecies had chronicled European arrival, so although John Cabot is credited with being the first European in Mi'kmaq lands (1497), he was definitely not. Cabot took three Mi'kmaq to England, and upon his return to North America, he disappeared from the same area; many thought it was revenge for taking Mi'kmaq citizens against their will. In 1501, Basque, Spanish, French, British, and Irish fishing boats made regular summer trips to the Grand Banks and, after a few years, began to trade for furs. As hard as they tried to establish permanent towns, Europeans could not survive the winters, but their presence spread foreign diseases that began to decimate the Native population.

The Mi'kmaq developed amicable relations with the French and their Catholic missionaries, which led to an alliance against the British until the 1760s. The empire expanding designs of France and England created intolerable conditions for the Indigenous peoples, and in 1749, the British governor placed a "scalp" bounty on those Mi'kmaq he considered to be rebels. After centuries of conflict, the Mi'kmaq and British created an alliance that brought some peace to the region. The eight-pointed star design was created as a symbol depicting the Mi'kmaw seven districts and their relations from other islands.

Today, Newfoundland only has one reserve; it is the site of the July Miawpuket First Nation Powwow. Traditionalists from across the Mi'kmaq Nation celebrate dance, art, music, and lifeways. Vendor booths and exhibits present the prized quill and birch bark art for which the people are known. The stunning views of the province's south coast are an added treat.

Info: 50 Miawpukek Dr., Conne River, NL A0H 1J0 • 709.882.2470 • http://www.mfngov.ca/powwow/

FLAT BAY
Abadak Wilderness Adventures, Inc.

The Sunrise Ceremony begins this adventure on Mi'kmaq traditional lands in southwest Newfoundland. Experienced guides of the Flat Bay Band teach adventurers how to fish for salmon and hunt for moose, caribou, and bear in a respectful way and using traditional techniques. Guests are treated to traditional stories and cultural events; activities are centered around Tia'mui'sit ("moose call"), a remote lodge nestled in the Long Range Mountains above the Victoria Lake watershed.

Info: Victoria Lake W., Flat Bay, NL A0N 1Z0 • 709.647.3478 • http://www.abadakwildernessadventures.ca

NORTH WEST RIVER
Labrador Heritage Society

Displays of Native Canadian cultures are open to the public. The Labrador Heritage Festival is held in July.

Info: River Rd., North West River, NL A0P 1M0 • 709.497.8282 • http://www.labradorheritagemuseum.ca/home/

PORT AU CHOIX
Port Au Choix National Historic Site

Archaeological finds of over fifty-five hundred years of habitation on this site are on display in the Interpretive Center. Visitors can trace the changes in aboriginal communities over the years. The area is a treasure trove of history of the maritime First Peoples from many eras, including the present.

Info: Point Riche Rd., Port au Choix, NL A0K 4C0 • 709.861.3522 • http://pc.gc.ca/en/lhn-nhs/nl/portauchoix

ST. GEORGE
K'Taqmkuk Mi'kmaw Cultural Historic Museum

To celebrate the rich and ancient culture of the Mi'kmaq people, the St. George Mi'kmaq community renovated a historic building into the only official Mi'kmaw cultural historic museum for Newfoundland. It is located in "Seal Rocks," what was the largest and principal Mi'kmaq settlement on the west coast of Newfoundland. Events include Cultural Sharing Days and Sharing Circles.

Info: 183 Main St., St. George, NL A0N 1B0 • 709.647.3293 • http://www.sgibnl.ca/ktaqmkuk-mikmaw-cultural-historic-museum-newfoundland/

ST. JOHN'S
Newfoundland Museum

This is a provincial museum with First Nations displays. Workshops for children are offered.

Info: 285 Duckworth St., St. John's, NL A1B 3P9 • 709.729.6007 • http://attractions.worldweb.com/1-12647-Newfoundland_Museum.html

TWILLINGATE
The Twillingate Museum and Craft Shop

This local collection features some items from the Beothuk peoples.

Info: 1 St. Peters Church Rd., Twillingate, NL A0G 4M0 • 709.884.2825 • http://www.tmacs.ca/index.shtml

NOVA SCOTIA

The Mi'kmaq are the original owners of the lands now called Nova Scotia and remain the predominant aboriginal group within the province. When Europeans arrived in the sixteenth century, Mi'kmaq Territory stretched from the southern portions of the Gaspé Peninsula eastward to most of modern-day New Brunswick and all of Nova Scotia and Prince Edward Island. Today, 16,245 registered Indians live in Nova Scotia; 5,877 live on the reserve. They are represented by thirteen band councils and two tribal councils, the Confederacy of Mainland Mi'kmaq, and the Union of Nova Scotia Indians. In addition, the Mi'kmaq Grand Council is the traditional and spiritual government for the Mi'kmaw nation.

BEAR RIVER
Bear River Heritage Museum

Museum artifacts and exhibits focus on Mi'kmaq history.

Info: Oakdene Centre, 1913 Clementsvale Rd., Bear River, NS B0S 1B0 • 902.467.1211 • https://bearrivermuseum.wordpress.com/heritage-museum/

Enjoying the ancient game of Waltes.

ESKASONI
Eskasoni Cultural Journeys

Mi'kmaq cultural interpreters guide guests along a scenic trail on Goat Island by the picturesque Bras d'Or Lake, a UNESCO biosphere reserve. On the trail, hikers visit several villages to join in a variety of activities: making four cents cake over an open fire; creating baskets; playing the ancient game of Waltes; joining in traditional dances; and learning lots of other aspects of both historical and contemporary Mi'kmaq lifeways. Eskasoni First Nation is the largest Mi'kmaw community in the world.

Info: 63 Mini Mall Dr., Eskasoni, NS B1W 1A1 • 902.322.2279 • http://eskasoniculturaljourneys.ca/index.html

HALIFAX
Museum of Natural History

This natural history museum contains all that one expects and also features the archaeology and anthropology of the original owners of the area, the Mi'kmaq.

Info: 1747 Summer St., Halifax, NS B3H 3A6 • 902.424.7353 • https://naturalhistory.novascotia.ca/

LIVERPOOL
Sipuke'l Gallery

Operated by Acadia First Nation, this spectacular gallery showcases contemporary art shows, workshops, and demonstrations by Mi'kmaw artisans. In addition, it holds a museum displaying historic items found in 2004 when the local Mersey River was drained to upgrade power dams and unearthed thousands of artifacts.

Info: 219 Main St., Liverpool, NS B0T 1K0 • 902.354.5501 • https://www.facebook.com/pg/sipukelgallery/

MAITLAND BRIDGE
Kejimkujik National Park and National Historic Site

Kejimkujik, established as a national park in 1968, is known for its old growth forest, rare wildlife, and traditional Mi'kmaq waterways. It is named for Kejimkujik Lake, a Mi'kmaq phrase for "the little people," for the beings that lived in the area. It was also called Fairy Lake. For millennia, the Mi'kmaq used it to travel from the Bay of Fundy to the Atlantic Coast. They marked their treks by creating petroglyphs along the shore; the 450 ancient carvings are a record of Mi'kmaq history and can be viewed on a guided tour. The protected area is one of the seven traditional districts of the Mi'kmaq and incorporates almost forty traditional sites. Today, the Mi'kmaq still have a strong presence in the park on their homelands. Tribal traditionalist Kaqtukwasisip Muin'iskw (1961–2011) designed the commemorative monument that marks the area's history and honors the original Indigenous artists of centuries ago. The entire site is a cultural landscape of the Mi'kmaq.

Info: 3005 Kejimkujik Main Pkwy., Maitland Bridge, NS B0T 1B0 • 902.682.2772 • http://www.pc.gc.ca/eng/pn-np/ns/kejimkujik/index.aspx

MEMBERTOU
Membertou Heritage Park

The 5-acre (20,234-square-meter) site features a living history of the Mi'kmaq people of Membertou through indoor exhibits and engaging programs. The flourishing com-

Jean Augustine-McIsaac (Mi'kmaw), designer of the Kejimkujik Park Commemorative Monument.

munity has been located in this special place on Cape Breton for centuries, long before Europeans came to the area. The center honors the cultural intrepidness and spiritual strength of these unique peoples by treating visitors to walking tours plus interactive and educational experiences that share how Mi'kmaw heritage is preserved. The Petroglyph Shop is a supermarket of Mi'kmaw arts and crafts created locally in Atlantic Canada. The park is an ever-expanding cultural landscape.

Info: 35 Su'n Awti, Membertou, NS B1S 0A5 • 902.567.5333 • http://www.membertouheritagepark.com/

MILLBROOK
Millbrook Cultural and Heritage Centre

Glooscap, memorialized in a gigantic monument, towers above the tree line and keeps watch over the Millbrook Cultural and Heritage Centre. Many different accounts exist of the culture hero, but most agree that he is the creator of the Wabanaki peoples. The center itself offers a gigantic slice of Mi'kmaw history and culture through innovative multimedia presentations, exhibits of ancient artifacts, presentations of contemporary arts, and workshops on an array of subjects. It is the heart of the Truro Power Centre, a successful real estate venture of the Millbrook First Nation.

Info: 65 Treaty Trail, Millbrook, NS B6L 1W3 • 902.843.3493 • http://www.millbrookheritage.ca/

PRINCE EDWARD ISLAND

The aboriginal population of the province is around 2,250; most people live in Charlottetown. PEI has the smallest number of Native peoples in Canada. Although both of the reserves are Mi'kmaq, the Métis and the Inuit also live in the province.

CHARLOTTETOWN
Mi'kmaq Confederacy Annual Powwow

A community feast highlights this August festival. The prime minister has dropped by in the past to join the Mi'kmaw celebration, located on the waterfront.

Info: Confederation Landing Park, Charlottetown, PE • 902.626.2882 • http://www.mcpei.ca/

LENNOX ISLAND
The Lennox Island Mi'kmaq Cultural Center

The center's interpretive displays highlight Mi'kmaq culture from historical times until today as well as workshops, educational sessions, and powwows. It offers the Path of Our Forefathers Guide Tour in July and August; visitors can choose between a 3- and 6-mile (5- and 10-kilometer) trail hike to learn about traditional forest use, local history, or local ecology. Self-guided hikers also have interpretative

A dancer at the Mi'kmaq Confederacy Annual Powwow.

signs at key sections of the trail. Indian Art and Crafts of North America is a store that stocks Mi'kmaq art.

Info: 8 Eagle Feather Trail, Lennox Island, PE C0B 1P0 • 902.831.3109 • http://www.lennoxisland.com/

CENTRAL CANADA

Working in your community, showing what you have, your culture, your past, talking about the art and craft that you learned from your great-grandfather that you're still recreating today—it's pride.

—Aboriginal Tourism site

The region called Central Canada is composed of Ontario and Quebec, the country's largest and most populous provinces. Both are part of the enormous Canadian Shield, named for its distinctive shape. The massive Hudson Bay is the northern border, while the South is bounded by four of the Great Lakes: Superior, Huron, Erie, and Ontario. Most of the area features a green landscape of grassy fields, rolling hills, and deciduous forests, except for the far north, where it is rocky with sparse vegetation. Thousands of small lakes and rivers are located in moist wetlands, home to moose and beaver, Canada's most iconic animals. Most human residents are located in the Great Lakes–St. Lawrence Lowlands, an area of fertile farmlands surrounding Lake Ontario and the majestic St. Lawrence River.

ONTARIO

Almost a quarter of a million people in Canada identify as First Nations, representing 133 communities. Urban arts and activities also reflect the cultures of First Nations; two-thirds live in the province's cities. Others live in small, remote towns and have maintained a deep connection with their ancestral environment. About three thousand Inuit share the area's city neighborhoods, too. The Métis in Ontario have a unique culture that has changed over time to embody the blending of their Native and European roots. Métis communities were established during the fur trade; their territory includes the waterways of Ontario, surrounds the Great Lakes, and spans across the historic Northwest. Today, most Métis are represented by the Métis Nation of Ontario, with offices in Ottawa.

Joseph Brant Monument.

BRANTFORD
Brant County Museum

The museum has a fine collection of Six Nations items, many belonging to Joseph Brant (see entry on "Her Majesty's Royal Chapel of the Mohawks," Brantford, Ontario) and the poetess Pauline Johnson. Born a few miles from Brantford on the Six Nations Reserve, Johnson, the daughter of a Mohawk chief, was one of the first published Native literary voices in Canada. She caused a sensation in Toronto in 1893 when she recited her works while dressed in traditional Mohawk clothing. Johnson's most famous poem, "The Song My Paddle Sings," led to a national tour as well as readings in Great Britain, where she was greatly admired. Her volumes sold out quickly in Canada in the early twentieth century. Johnson died in 1913 and forty-eight years later became the first Native Canadian to be depicted on a commemorative postage stamp.

Info: 57 Charlotte St., Brantford, ON N3T 2W6 • 519.752.2483 • http://brantmuseum.ca/home/

Her Majesty's Royal Chapel of the Mohawks

Joseph Brant (1742–1807), a Mohawk scholar, leader, and military tactician, was among the most contradictory and compelling personalities in the American Revolution. His Mohawk name was Thayendanegea ("he who places two bets" or "two sticks bound together for strength"). An adept strategist, he served the needs of his people amid the revolutionary storm that was sweeping across North America and earned the respect of his community, who appointed him as a chief. In combat, he was a skilled soldier and was involved in some of the bloodiest encounters in the war. Brant fought with the British as a teenager in the French and Indian War and again allied himself with them in the war against Pontiac, the Ottawa chief who led the 1763 Great Lakes nations rebellion. By his midtwenties, Brant was recognized as a prominent leader of the Haudenosaunee (Iroquois Confederacy); he chose to side with the British during the American Revolution and was commissioned as a colonel. His actions split the confederacy, which had vowed to remain neutral; the Mohawk, Seneca, Cayuga, and Onondaga fought on the British side, while the Tuscarora and Oneida supported the Americans. When peace came, American colonists seized Iroquois lands, and Brant and his followers were forced to relocate along the Grand River of Ontario. The new community was named after him. In 1785, Brant built Her Majesty's Chapel of the Mohawks, now the oldest Protestant church in Ontario; it is the only religious edifice in the world designated as a Royal Indian Chapel. Six stunning, stained-glass windows depicting the history of the Iroquois are worth the visit. Brant's tomb is adjacent to the chapel.

Info: 301 Mohawk St., Brantford, ON N3S 7V1 • 519.756.0240 • http://mohawkchapel.ca/

Her Majesty's Royal Chapel of the Mohawks.

Reconstructed Mohawk Longhouse and Palisade.

Kana:ta Village

Kana:ta means "village" in Mohawk, and the center was designed to be a learning and tourist destination for all things Mohawk as well as the diverse cultures of the Six Nations and Turtle Island. On-site is a reconstructed longhouse with outbuildings and a walled barrier, along with a giant maze of cedar trees in the shape of a turtle and a large building that houses a myriad of activities: Native artisan fairs; feasts; dances; performances; and classes. Interactive sessions offered on the property are archery, lacrosse, and other traditional games and nature trail walks. In 1779, the British government awarded the Mohawk of the Grand River almost 1 million acres (4,047 square kilometers) as wartime reparations for loss of their lands in the United States after the nation sided with the British during the Revolutionary War. The pledge was strengthened in the Haldimand Proclamation of 1784. However, over the years as Canada became independent and land became more valuable, the Mohawk lost more and more of their land in fraudulent deals. Kana:ta Village is a reminder to the Mohawk visitors and neighbors that this land has never been sold and never will be sold.

Info: 440 Mohawk St., Brantford, ON N3S 0H2 • 519.774.6721 • http://www.kanatavillage.org/

Woodland Indian Cultural Education Centre

The center celebrates the culture of Ontario's southern Native peoples, concentrating on the heritage of the Haudenosaunee—the original residents plus those who arrived with Joseph Brant. The cultural center's museum is home to a collection of over

Woodland Cultural Centre.

thirty-five thousand artifacts, and a permanent exhibit showcases an Iroquois and Algonquian timeline from the beginnings to today. Temporary exhibits feature a broad array of subjects. The center's library is a repository of books, journals, magazines, and curriculum materials about the local Native community. The art gallery hosts the First Nations Art (FNA), one of the longest-running annual shows of both established and emerging Indigenous artists, which runs from mid-May to early June, offering gallery talks, live performances, artist lectures, films, and demonstrations.

On-site is the former Mohawk Institute Indian Residential School (1828–1970), which has been preserved to teach visitors about the Canadian government's brutal policy of forcing First Nations children to assimilate into European Christian society. For a century and a half, children were ripped from their Indigenous communities and sent away to boarding schools, where thousands were victimized by staff and forbidden to speak their languages, see their families, or engage in cultural activities. On this site, staff forced children to dig holes for apple trees when, in fact, they were digging graves for their classmates. In January 1998, the government made a Statement of Reconciliation—including an apology to those people who were sexually or physically abused while attending residential schools—and established the Aboriginal Healing Foundation (AHF). AHF has the task of funding community-based healing projects addressing the legacy of physical and sexual abuse. For over four decades, visitors to the Mohawk Institute Indian Residential School have gained in-depth and historically significant insight into the destructive Residential School System.

Info: 184 Mohawk St., Brantford, ON N3S 2X2 • 519.759.2650 •
http://woodlandculturalcentre.ca/

BURLINGTON
Joseph Brant Home

The Joseph Brant Home is a reconstruction of Wellington Square, the home Joseph Brant built in 1800 at the head of Lake Ontario (see entry on "Her Majesty's Royal Chapel of the Mohawks," Brantford, Ontario) and lived in for the last seven years of his life. Brant's landholdings became the city of Burlington; his house was rebuilt at its original location in 1939. In addition to displays of Brant's personal memorabilia—including the medal presented to him by King George III—the museum contains displays on local Native culture.

A portrait of Joseph Brant painted by artist George Romney when the Mohawk leader was in his early thirties.

Info: 1240 N. Shore Blvd., Burlington, ON L7S 1C5 • 905.634.3556 • https://museumsofburlington.ca/joseph-brant

CORNWALL
Akwesasne International Powwow

An annual, two-day event held on the shores of the beautiful St. Lawrence River on the weekend after Labor Day, this powwow enables visitors to enjoy drummers and dancers from the area as well as from different parts of Canada and the United States. The cultural experience showcases a variety of Native artisans and features the famous Iroquois Smoke Dance, "the fastest dance on two feet." This exciting and intricate dance derives its name from when people would use rapid foot movements to create air circulation to help get fires started.

Info: A'Nowara'Ko Wa Arena, Cornwall, ON K6H 5T3 • akwesasnepowwow@yahoo.com • http://www.akwesasnepowwow.com/

Native North American Traveling College (NNATC)

For decades, the NNATC has traveled the world to share the teachings of the Mohawk people. Its cultural center publishes books, pamphlets, and posters, produces audiovisual materials, hosts Native craft classes, and offers a group of traveling presenters who can visit universities, museums, festivals, and the like, to teach Native history and culture. Native crafted items are for sale in the art gallery, and many events take place in the amphitheater. They also have a U.S. address, as the Akwesasne Reservation is divided by the U.S./Canada border.

Info: 1 Ronathahon:ni Ln., Akwesasne Territory, Cornwall, ON K6H 5R7 • 613.932.9452 • http://www.nnatc.org/

CURVE LAKE
Whetung Ojibwa Centre

The Whetung family has successfully operated a market for fellow band members to sell Ojibwa items, which have been produced in a cottage industry for decades. The 10,000-square-foot (3,048-square-meter) building also houses a museum filled with objects from across Indigenous Canada.

Info: 875 Mississauga St., Curve Lake, ON K0L 1R0 • 705.657.3661 • https://www.whetung.com/

KENORA
Lake of the Woods Museum

At the core of the collections in this small museum is the collection of over three hundred Native artifacts from former Kenora Indian agent Captain Frank Edwards, who served from 1920 until 1945. Beadwork, pipes, baskets, and other objects are representative of the Ojibway and other First Nations in the area.

Info: 300 Main St. S., Kenora, ON P9N 3X5 • 807.467.2105 • https://www.lakeofthewoodsmuseum.ca/

Lake of the Woods Ojibway Cultural Centre

A research resource, the center has a fine repository of books and audiovisual materials on First Nations and Inuit heritage. A section of the craft store houses several artifacts.

Info: 237 Airport Rd., Kenora, ON P9N 0A2 • 807.548.5744 • http://www.ojibwayculturalcentre.com/

LONDON
Museum of Ontario Archaeology

Committed to the study and preservation of over eleven thousand years of regional history, the museum offers gallery space, a theater, a classroom, and a children's activity area as well as tours of the reconstructed village of the Attawandaron people. Within the village are remains of longhouses, middens, and pits. Over five hundred thousand artifacts have been recovered from the site, providing insight into the daily lives of the original inhabitants. They were skilled agronomists and farmed vast fields surrounding the village, which boasted corn, beans, and squash (called the Three Sisters) as well as tobacco, which they also used for trade. The Attawandaron disappeared; some were absorbed by the Huron, others by the Iroquois. The annual Harvest Festival and Powwow is held in September.

Info: 1600 Attawandaron Rd., London, ON N6G 3M6 • 519.473.1360 • http://archaeologymuseum.ca/

M'CHIGEENG
Great Spirit Circle Trail

An aboriginal enterprise, the Great Spirit Circle Trail offers a unique nature-based and culturally competent opportunity to tour stunning, magnificent Manitoulin Island and the Sagamok region of Northeastern Ontario, Canada. A variety of packages include adventures to wilderness eco-adventures, retracing ancient canoe routes, and educational interpretive tours. To enhance the experience, First Nations guides recount the accurate history and culture of the region and its original inhabitants: the Ojibwe, Odawa, and Pottawatomi peoples. Tourists can choose a relaxing day trip or a longer stay in a variety of accommodations. Tasty, traditional regional cuisine is on the menu, and shops and galleries are overflowing with traditional and contemporary art. In addition, instructive activities help visitors appreciate the area's natural beauty. "The warmth of the people, the serenity of the forests and waters and the vibrant culture of the Anishnawbek people are yours to discover as you 'Experience the past' and 'Enjoy the present.'"

Info: Manitoulin Island–Sagamok Region, 5905 Hwy. 540, P.O. Box 469, M'Chigeeng, ON P0P 1G0 • 705.377.4404 • https://www.circletrail.com/

MIDLAND
Huronia Museum

Stepping back centuries before European contact, visitors find themselves in a reconstructed full-scale Huron/Ouendat village, which includes a lookout tower, a wigwam, and a full-size longhouse. The exhibit gallery features thousands of artifacts and photographs.

Info: 549 Little Lake Park, Midland, ON L4R 4P4 • 705.526.2844 • https://huronia museum.com/

"Big House" interior in the Huron Ouendat Village.

Huron Christian altar in a reconstructed chapel.

Sainte-Marie among the Huron

While the English colonies clung to a few isolated settlements along the Atlantic seaboard, French Jesuits had reached the Canadian shore of Lake Huron and, by 1639, had built a mission within the territory of the Huron Wendat Nation. As part of their colonial policy, the French aligned themselves with the Huron Wendat, as they controlled water routes that had direct access to the fur trade. Farther east, the Haudenosaunee were vehemently opposed to French ambitions. The French strategy, however, doomed the Huron-Wendat. The Iroquois were determined to quash their European enemies and saw that they were most vulnerable at this exposed point in the West. By 1642, they had begun to infiltrate the perimeter of the Huron country, attacking fur shipments that passed their way. By 1647, the Iroquois were victorious, as they had captured one village after another and driven out the French priests. The Huron Wendat, knowing the situation to be hopeless, burned down Sainte-Marie and retreated to nearby islands for safety, then they completely abandoned their former homeland and dispersed in Quebec and the western lakes area. The location of Sainte-Marie was lost for centuries. This reconstructed site illustrates the interaction between the French and Wendat nations. Longhouses built in Huron style housed visiting Native Huron, while the chapel reflected Huron design and attracted Christian Huron. Visitors can tour the Interpretive Museum and dine in the Restaurant Sainte-Marie. On National Aboriginal Day (June 21), the cultures of Canada's Indigenous peoples are celebrated at Sainte-Marie with music, dance, crafts, waterway and lacrosse demonstrations, and many more cultural events. The Restaurant Sainte-Marie cooks up a special menu of tasty Indigenous dishes of original recipes, like "Three Sisters Soup."

Info: 16164 Highway 12 E., Midland, ON L4R 5E3 • 705.526.7838 • http://www.saintemarieamongthehurons.on.ca/sm/en/Home/

MOUNT BRYDGES
Ska-Nah-Doht

Ska-Nah-Doht means "a village stands again" in the Oneida language. This village is a reconstruction of a typical walled farming community of Iroquoian people from around a thousand years ago. Eighteen outdoor exhibits, including longhouses and a palisade maze, are constructed to mystify and slow down unwelcome intruders. Artifacts unearthed at the site are on display, and an educational program is available.

Info: 8348 Longwoods Rd. (County Road 2), Mount Brydges, ON N0L 1W0 • 519.264.2420 • http://www.ltvca.ca

OHSWEKEN
Chiefswood National Historic Site

Built on the Grand River in 1856, this culturally integrated mansion was the birthplace and home of Pauline Johnson, honored Mohawk poetess (see entry on "Brant County Museum," Brantford, Ontario). The two front doors symbolize Johnson's Native heritage as well as her English ancestry as one faces the river to welcome the Mohawk who arrived by canoe; the other opens to the road for the English who visited by buggy. The grounds boast rare grassland prairies, Carolinian forests, and swamplands, plus the Grand River itself. Six Nations members celebrate Aboriginal Day in June and the Champion of Champions Powwow in July.

The home of Pauline Johnson.

Info: 1037 Highway 54, Six Nations of the Grand River Territory, Ohsweken, ON N0A 1M0 • 519.752.5005 • http://www.sixnationstourism.ca/chiefswood-national-historic-site/

Grand River "Champion of Champions" Powwow

This two-day, annual event attracts tourists and participants from all over Canada and the United States as well as the world. Dancers and singers, representing almost every North American cultural group, vie for cash prizes displaying fancy footwork and spectacular regalia. The venue site is on the former estate of esteemed Mohawk poetess E. Pauline Johnson at the Six Nations of the Grand River, the largest First Nations reserve in Canada, with a total of 25,660 members. It is the only reserve in

North America that is home to members from all six Haudenosaunee nations: Mohawk, Cayuga, Onondaga, Oneida, Seneca, and Tuscarora. Some Delaware are also living in the territory.

Info: Chiefswood Park, Six Nations of the Grand River, Brant Country Road 254, Ohsweken, ON N0A 1M0 • 866.393.3001 • http://www.grpowwow.ca/

Six Nations Fair

For over a century and a half, the Six Nations Agricultural Society has been staging a fair every fall, making it the oldest Native fair in Canada. The four-day event highlights include the Baby Show, the Demolition Derby, a midway, entertainment, food vendors, exhibits, a singing competition, the Pet Show, amateur harness racing, the Petting Zoo, the Classic Car Show, and the Tractor Pull, which makes it similar to other country fairs, but this one also features the Miss Six Nations Pageant, aboriginal arts, a ball tournament, and other Six Nations expositions, plus the Smoke Dance Competition.

Info: Six Nations Fairgrounds, 1738 Fourth Line Rd., Ohsweken, ON N0A 1M0 • 519.758.5444 • https://www.snfallfair.com/

OTTAWA
Asinabka Film and Media Arts Festival

This annual August festival showcases film and media regarding Indigenous peoples. Held in the capital city of Ottawa, also traditional Algonquian territory, it provides a venue for Indigenous peoples to tell their stories and a public forum for Indigenous issues.

Info: 51B Young St., Ottawa, ON K1S 3H6 • 613.889.9559 • http://www.asinabkafestival.org/Home.html

Canadian Museum of Nature

Located within the museum's Canada Goose Arctic Gallery is the Northern Voices Gallery, a kaleidoscope of temporary exhibits designed with Indigenous groups to share their own perspectives of their relationships with the lands of the Arctic.

Info: 240 McLeod St., Ottawa, ON K2P 2R1 • 613.566.4700 • http://nature.ca/en/plan-your-visit/what-see-do/our-exhibitions/arctic-gallery/arctic-northern-voices-gallery

Indigenous Walks

Jaime Koebel, Apeetagosan/Nehiyaw (Métis/Cree), offers walking/talking tours of Indigenous Ottawa. The landscape, architecture, art, and monuments of the city are explored through an Indigenous perspective.

Info: http://Indigenouswalks.com/

National Aboriginal Veterans Monument

The bronze monument (unveiled in 2001) commemorates the service of all aboriginal peoples in war and peacekeeping operations from World War I to the present. Designed by Saskatchewan sculptor Lloyd Pinay of the Peepeekisis First Nation, the monument depicts a golden eagle (symbolic as both the creator and the spirit of Indigenous peoples) as the messenger between the Creator and man. Four human figures, facing the four cardinal points, represent First Nations Inuit and Métis. Female figures honor the role of women; the human depictions hold both war and spiritual items. Each of the four animal figures, one on each corner, symbolize a special attribute: a wolf (family values), a buffalo (tenacity), an elk (wariness), and a bear (healing powers).

The National Aboriginal Veterans Monument was designed by sculptor Lloyd Pinay, Peepeekisis First Nations.

Info: 100 Elgin St., Ottawa, ON K1P 5K8 • http://www.veterans.gc.ca/eng/ remembrance/memorials/canada/national-aboriginal-veterans-monument

National Gallery of Canada

Indigenous art on display includes works from aboriginal peoples of Canada and Indigenous works from around the globe as well. The gallery includes creations from some of the best-known aboriginal artists in Canada: Carl Beam, Brian Jungen, Faye HeavyShield, Shelley Niro, Jeffrey Thomas, and Lawrence Paul Yuxweluptun.

Info: 380 Sussex Dr., Ottawa, ON K1N 9N4 • 613.990.1985 • https://www.gallery.ca/collection/collecting-areas/Indigenous-art

PETERBOROUGH
The Canadian Canoe Museum

More than six hundred canoes and kayaks illustrate the history of Canada through the glorious multipassenger dugouts of the Pacific Northwest to the singular bark canoes of Newfoundland's Beothuk culture to the skin-on-frame kayaks of Nunavat's Inuit mariners. From coast to coast and as far away as the Amazon, this unique museum explores water travel. Special events include workshops and paddle adventures.

Info: 910 Monaghan Rd., Peterborough, ON K9J 5K4 • 705.748.9153 • https://www.canoemuseum.ca/

A display at the Canadian Canoe Museum.

STRATTON
Kay-Nah-Chi-Wah-Nung Historical Centre

Long before Europeans illegally and forcibly created their own countries where sovereign countries already existed, Indigenous nations had distinct cultural, regional, historical, and political characteristics that defined any sovereign nation. European-devised country borders (and later state and province designations) dissected original nations dividing communities and hindering the economy and health of First Nations. A clear example of this devastation and usurping of the original governments can be seen in the remains now protected by the Kay-Nah-Chi-Wah-Nung Historical Centre. Just 40 miles (64 kilometers) from the headwaters of the Mississippi River, the site was the hub of a lively continent-wide trading network. The "place of the long rapids" (Ojibway) was where people came from many areas to fish, process sturgeon, and trade for thousands of years. Later, it also became a location for collective sharing, ceremony, and burial. Today, the Rainy River First Nation stewards this national historic site and welcomes others to honor the legacy of the history and burial mounds. Kay-Nah-Chi-Wah-Nung encompasses 2 miles (3.2 kilometers) of Rainy River shoreline, extending inland 1 mile (1.6 kilometers) or more, and has at least thirty villages and temporary sites and seventeen burial mounds. It was home to the Ojibway people in the past century and was the Long Sault Reserve from 1873 until 1916. It contains evidence of house structures, trails, gardens, and associated activities. It is a massive area of almost 223 acres (0.9 kilometers). The visitor center is well appointed with interpretive galleries and a gift shop.

Info: 341 Ross Rd., Stratton, ON P0W 1N0 • 807.483.1163 • http://manitoumounds.com/

THUNDER BAY
Thunder Bay National Exhibition Centre and Centre for Indian Art

The center is one of the few public art galleries in Canada (or the United States) that champions the collection, preservation, and exhibition of contemporary Native art and treats the art with the same respect and dignity afforded to the works of great European artists. Visitors are regaled by a great variety of styles created by Roy Thomas, Carl Beam, Daphne Odjig, Edward Poitras, Joane Cardinal Schubert, Norval Morrisseau, Arthur Shilling, Shelley Niro, Allen Sapp, Benjamin Chee Chee, and other contemporary masters. The center has earned both national and international recognition as a leader in the art world and for propelling Native art into the mainstream, successfully advocating for the right of Native artists and their art to merit a contemporary presence instead of always being relegated to anthropologic or ethnographic status. Although the collections do include some artifacts, the displays debunk the stereotype that Indian art is lost to the "past." Besides paintings, many varieties of art forms are on display, including pottery, quilts, photography, and sculpture from bands all across North America.

Info: 1080 Keewatin St., Thunder Bay, ON P7B 6T7 • 807.577.6427 • http://theag.ca/about/

Woodview

Some of the rock carvings found in the secluded Petroglyphs Provincial Park were made about a thousand years ago by Algonquian people in this area. The petroglyphs were not found, however, until 1954, and in 1981, they were designated a World Heritage Site. A huge structure has been built around them for protection from further weather erosion.

An ancient rock carving of a boat in Woodview, Ontario.

Info: 2249 Northeys Bay Rd., Woodview, ON K0L 3E0 • 705.877.2552 • https://www.ontarioparks.com/park/petroglyphs

TORONTO
ImagineNATIVE Film & Media Arts Festival

ImagineNATIVE is the world's largest festival of Indigenous films and is recognized locally, nationally, and internationally for excellence and innovative programs. The annual fall festival fosters understanding of Indigenous cultures and peoples through the presentation of contemporary, Indigenous-created media arts (film, video, audio, and digital media). Based in Toronto and Indigenous operated, imagineNATIVE is an award-winning organization that celebrates the indigeneity of the city and of Canada and spans across the globe telling the story of the world's First Peoples and present-day communities. Besides the festival, imagineNATIVE provides public education and helps debunk stereotypes through professional development workshops and panels, public education initiatives, research projects, and curriculum/educators' packages for secondary schools created from Indigenous teaching strategies.

Info: 401 Richmond St. W., Suite 446, Toronto, ON M5V 3A8 • 416.585.2333 • http://www.imaginenative.org/

Louis Riel Day

Events are held in Métis communities every November 16 to honor the great Métis leader Louis Riel (see entries in Manitoba). He is always commemorated in a special ceremony held on the lawn of the Provincial Legislature at Queen's Park in Toronto, the location of the Northwest Rebellion Monument near the seat of the very legislature that put a price on his head. The monument honors Canadian soldiers whose mission was to quell the rebellion (see entry on "Riel House National Historic Site," Winnipeg, Manitoba) and capture the esteemed revolutionary, but on Louis Riel Day, the monument is reverentially draped with Métis symbols, including a portrait of Riel.

Info: 111 Wellesley St. W., Toronto, ON M7A 1A2 • 613.798.1488 • http://www.metisnation.org/news-media/louis-riel-day/

QUEBEC

Eleven distinct ethnic groups represent Quebec's ten First Nations and Inuit communities. Around 142,000 aboriginal peoples live in the province's cities and on reserves.

GATINEAU
Canadian Museum of History

The museum's First Peoples Hall celebrates the diversity, creativity, resourcefulness, and intrepidness of Canada's First Nations, Métis, and Inuit peoples from historical times to today. On display are objects from antiquity to contemporary along with images and documents. One of the oldest representations of the human face is featured as are the lives and achievements of modern aboriginal peoples from many

The Canadian Museum of History.

different backgrounds and professions: athletes, authors, artists, military personnel, teachers, leaders, etc. On display is a magnificent, 18.5-foot (5.6-meter), ocean-going canoe created by master builder Todd Labrador, Mi'kwaw, from Acadia First Nation in Nova Scotia. Located directly across the river from the national capital in Ottawa, the museum also offers special events.

Info: 100 Laurier St., Gatineau, QC K1A 0M8 • 1.800.555.5621 • http://www.historymuseum.ca/

INUKJUAK
Daniel Weetaluktuk Museum

Inukjuak, on the eastern shore of the Hudson Bay, is the home of the Daniel Weetaluktuk Museum, named for the first Inuit archaeologist in Nunavik. A circular room houses the "Takunnatauninga ilirsusivut takunnagusitigut/Our Culture as We See it" display. Cleverly combining both old and new Inuit items, treasures include soapstone sculptures, drawings, traditional clothing, handcrafted figurines, tools, and more. Activities include cultural workshops.

Info: Inukjuak, QC J0M 1M0 • 819.254.8277 • http://www.avataq.qc.ca

KAHNAWAKE
Kahnawake Powwow

Every summer, the Mohawk community of Kahnawake hosts a two-day powwow on their reserve, just a short drive north of Montréal. One of the eight communities that comprise the Mohawk (Kanien:keha'ka) Nation, they have historic, political, and cultural ties to the Oneida, Seneca, Onondaga, Cayuga, and Tuscarora Nations of the Haudenosaunee. The Tsi Niionkwarihò:ten Tsitewaháhara'n Center, located on the reserve, holds educational and cultural events throughout the year.

Info: Kahnawake, QC J0L 1B0 • 450.632.8667 • http://kahnawakepowwow.com/

Kanien'kehá:ka Onkwawén:na Raotitióhkwa
Language and Cultural Center Museum

Along with exhibits chronicling the rich heritage and history of the Kanien'kehá:ka from the origins of the Haudenosaunee Confederacy to the 1990 Oka Crisis, local artists are featured in thematic exhibits. Events and guided tours of the community are offered.

Info: 969 Cemetery Rd., Kahnawake, QC J0L 1B0 • 450.638.0880 • http://korkahnawake.org/museum-welcoming-centre/

The Shrine of St. Kateri Tekakwitha

Kateri Tekakwitha (1656–1680), from the Mohawk community of Kahnawake, was the first Native woman to be canonized a saint (October 12, 2012). It is fitting that her shrine be located in the main church of the St. Francis Xavier Mission on the Kahnawake reserve. Her memory has always been respected by the Mohawk community, where many regard her as a strong woman, a saint, or an ancestor. Many First Nations peoples as well as the Mohawk revere and pray to her. Her shrine displays historic artifacts and gifts from Native peoples, Canadians, and Europeans dating from the seventeenth to twentieth centuries. Kateri's statue is topped by a beaded crown donated by a community member for her intercession. Ivory crucifixes and many paintings and drawings of St. Kateri Tekakwitha, including the earliest known oil painting (1690) by Father Claude Chauchetiere S.J., manuscripts, carvings, old vestments, arrowheads, flints, corn mashers, and traditional beadwork are on display along with a replica of the U.S. World Trade Center fashioned by Mohawk ironworkers, who built the Trade Towers and helped clean up after 9/11.

Info: 1 River Rd., Kahnawake, QC J0L 1B0 • 450.632.6030 • http://kateritekakwitha.net/shrine/

MASHTEUIATSH
Mashteuiatsh Indian Museum

The Mashteuiatsh Indian Museum preserves the history and culture of the Pekuakami-ulnuatsh (Innu of Lac-Saint-Jean). The Innu are not as well known as other Indigenous peoples of the area, but, in fact, they were some of the first to meet up with the Norse and, later, the Portuguese, Basque, French, Dutch, and British. For most of the year, they lived deep in the interior of Quebec-Labrador and made infrequent trips to the coast. This lifestyle not only lessened their contact with early Europeans, but it may have helped protect their culture as well. In the 1700s, they made more trips to the coast to interact with the European fishermen, which eventually led to the establishment of coastal villages in the twentieth century. By that time, European loggers and trappers, both Native and non-Native, had a negative impact on Innu traditional life and health. In the 1950s, mines began dotting western Labrador while newly established game laws restricted Innu subsistence hunting, favoring non-Innu sports hunters. To hasten the decline of a once healthy community, Innu hunting territory was flooded by the Churchill Falls Dam in 1969. No warning was given; many hunters lost all of their equipment and livelihoods. The next few decades brought another kind of devastation to the Innu as the military began using their airspace for deafening, low-level military training. Today, the Innu Nation is involved in land claims negotiations as they try to protect their land from industrial development. The Mashteuiatsh Indian Museum recounts both ancient history and contemporary issues. Located on the western shores of Lake Saint-Jean, also known as Pointe-Bleue, the museum offers guided tours, activities, and archives of audiovisual materials. Although the population of the reserve is small, the July powwow attracts more than ten thousand people across the country and planet.

Mashteuiatsh Monument.

Info: 1787 Amishk St., Mashteuiatsh, QC G0W 2H0 • 418.275.4842 • http://cultureilnu.ca/

MONTRÉAL
Canadian Guild of Crafts

The Art of the First Nations Collection (late nineteenth century to mid-twentieth century) highlights Indigenous artwork created from hides, bark, porcupine quills, and cedar roots in different eras. The Inuit Art Collection (1900 to today) features works fashioned from ivory, soapstone, fur, and bone and their evolution over the years. Each year, temporary exhibitions celebrate contemporary, recognized, or emerging Inuit and First Nations artists and artisans.

Info: 1460 Sherbrooke St. W., Suite B, Montréal, QC H3G 1K4 • 514.849.6091 • http://www.canadianguildofcrafts.com

Maison Nivard-De Saint-Dizier, Museum and Archaeological Site

Located on the largest archaeological site in Montréal, this museum displays treasures unearthed during on-site excavations. From ancient times until today, this was a popular spot for Native peoples. To appreciate the archaeology process, visitors can participate in a dig.

Inukshuk sculpture by Jusipi Naluturuk, Inuit, at the McCord Museum.

Info: 7244 Boulevard LaSalle, Montréal, QC H4H 1R4 • 514.765.7284 •
http://www.maisonnivard-de-saint-dizier.com

McCord Museum

Founded in 1921, the museum exhibits showcase the social history of Montréal from historic times until today. Plus, it has one of the largest historical collections of First Peoples objects, clothing and textiles, photographs, decorative and visual artworks, prints, and textual archives—more than 1.4 million artifacts!

Info: 690 Sherbrooke St., West Montréal, QC H3A 1E9 • 515.398.7100 •
http://www.mccord-museum.qc.ca

Montréal Botanical Garden

This is North America's largest garden devoted to the First Nations and Inuit peoples. Native guides lead visitors through a variety of indigenous plants and structures. Although located in a big city, one takes a step back in time in these peaceful gardens. A variety of events are offered in each season.

Info: 4101 Rue Sherbrooke E, Montréal, QC H1X 2B2 • 514.872.1400 •
http://www.espacepourlavie.ca/en/botanical-garden

Montréal First Peoples Festival

The annual festival begins with a parade that opens the August celebration of music, art, and cinema created by Indigenous and aboriginal people from all over Canada

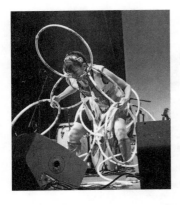

Hoop dancer Barbara Diabo (Mohawk Nation) performs at the Montréal First Peoples Festival.

and sometimes the world. As beautiful as the event is, it is also educational and features the stories and struggles of First Peoples and the renewal and reconciliation of their cultures.

Info: 5445 Avenue de Gaspé, Bureau 508, Montréal, QC H2T 3B2 • 514.278.4040 • http://www.presenceautochtone.ca/en

Montréal Museum of Fine Arts

The Inuit art collection illustrating Inuit identity and culture fills the entire fourth level of the Claire and Marc Bourgie Pavilion of Quebec and Canadian Art. Level three focuses on early and contemporary aboriginal art highlighting First Nations artistic interpretations of their history, cultures, and interactions with Europeans. In addition, the museum offers family workshops and other cultural activities based on the collections.

Info: 1380 Sherbrooke St. W., Montréal, QC H3G 1J5 • 514.285.2000 • http://www.mbam.qc.ca/en

Pointe-à-Callière, The Montréal Archaeology and History Complex

Recounting history from the first aboriginal owners of the Montréal area to the present-day Native peoples and their history with Euro-Canadians, the museum has twists and turns that make the visit exciting.

Info: 350 Place Royale, Old Montréal, QC H2Y 3Y5 • 514.872.9150 • http://www.pacmusee.qc.ca

MONT-SAINT-HILAIRE
La Maison Amerindienne

This museum approaches the First Peoples culture through gastronomic activities. Raising awareness of Native cultures through exhibits, workshops, interpretation trails, guided tours, and discourse, events are organized by season. The most popular events are in the sugaring season, highlighted by aboriginal-style meals.

Info: 510 Montée des Trente, Mont-Saint-Hilaire, QC J3H 2R8 • 450.464.2500 • http://www.maisonamerindienne.com/

ODANAK
Musée des Abénakis

Founded in 1965, the Abenaki Museum was the first aboriginal museum in Quebec and is located in the former Catholic school on the Abenaki Odanak Reserve. Odanak is the Abenaki phrase for "in the village." The Abenaki are one of five nations that are part of the Wabenanki Confederacy, the dominant power in northern New England at the time of European arrival (see entry on "Penobscot Island and Museum," Old Town, Maine). The Abenaki quickly became involved in the colonial competition between France and England, with the majority becoming allied with France. As Britain extended its rule northward toward the end of the seventeenth century, most Abenaki fled into Quebec for protection. The museum exhibits historical material relating to the Abenaki and their lives in Quebec. Displays include clothing from the turn of the century until today, basketwork, vintage photographs of families and events, drums, and other items. Films give a glimpse into Native art and the Abenaki language. The museum is located in a beautiful spot on the St. Francis River.

Info: 108 Rue Waban-Aki, Odanak, QC J0G 1H0 • 450.568.2600 • http://museedesabenakis.ca/data/

OUJÉ-BOUGOUMOU
Aanischaaukamikw Cree Cultural Institute

The Cree community came together to ensure that its culture, history, and language survive and are preserved for future generations. They created an extraordinary museum and cultural institution that showcases the history of the James Bay Cree. Over seven thousand years of their relationship and reverence with the land are expressed in the pictures, events, and objects housed in this building.

Info: 205 Opemiska Meskino, Oujé-Bougoumou, QC G0W 3C0 • 418.745.2444 • http://creeculturalinstitute.ca/

VAL-D'OR
Kinawit

Deep in Anicinabek Territory, visitors can learn to identify and gather medicine plants, participate in cultural workshops, take guided tours into the forest, and sleep in a tipi. The unique travel opportunity gives tourists insight into this ancient and vibrant culture.

Info: 255 Chemin des Scouts, Val-d'Or QC JP9 7A8 • 819.825.6856 • http://www.quebecaboriginal.com/port/kinawit/

WENDAKE
Kwahiatonhk! The First Nation Book Fair

This annual event, held in late fall or early winter, celebrates aboriginal authors and invites visitors to join them in poetry breakfasts, round table talks, and literary evenings on both the Huron-Wendat Reserve and in neighboring Quebec City with activities for young people, too.

The Prairie Provinces

Info: Location changes, but it is always in Wendake and Quebec City • 418.407.4578 • https://www.facebook.com/salonlivrepn

Musée Huron-Wendat

The Huron-Wendat Museum is a short trip from Quebec City and presents various themes, including history and medicine. Displays are interactive; culturally competent guides are available. The outside space boasts a medicinal plant garden, waterfall, and brook. Exhibits and information detail Native memories and knowledge. The on-site boutique hotel is another Huron-Wendat cultural treat.

Info: 15 Place de la Rencontre, Wendake, QC G0A 4V0 • 418.847.2260 • http://www.museehuronwendat.ca/

Onhoüa Chetek8e Huron Traditional Site

Located on the Huron-Wendat Indian Reserve, the Huron Traditional Site offers a tour by a tribal member in traditional dress. Visitors get a glimpse of the past through reconstructed Huron buildings and cultural presentations of historic times. Time-honored transportation modes are discussed, and tourists are treated to an explanation of canoe manufacturing while sitting in one. The tour, available in French, Spanish, and English, is topped off with an overview of contemporary Huron life. A restaurant offering traditional fare is on-site.

Info: 575 Rue Chef Stanislas Koska, Wendake, QC G0A 4V0 • 418.842.4308 • http://www.huron-wendat.qc.ca/

THE PRAIRIE PROVINCES

With a lot of my work, I try to create this dialogue between the settler culture and First Nations culture because we've been living together for hundreds of years now and we've been exchanging ideas and our cultures have been influencing each other. When I look at the art history...there's not much evidence of that because the art history as told and perpetuated in our museums is still very one sided.

—Kent Monkman, Cree mixed media artist

Located in the center of Canada, Manitoba, Alberta, and Saskatchewan are called the prairie provinces, bordered by Ontario on the east, the Rocky Mountains on the west, the Northern Territories on the north, and the U.S. states of Idaho, Montana, North Dakota, and Minnesota on the south. Known as having some of the most fertile farmland in the world, the region is often wrongly thought of as being only grasslands, yet it is an area of widely diverse ecosystems from the flat, treeless prairies in the South to the more diverse landscape of low hills and sporadic aspen parkland forests in the center to the vast and sparsely inhabited boreal forests in the North. Conifers, rivers, and myriad lakes envelop the rocky outcrops of the Canadian Shield; polar bears, caribou, and bison represent some of the wildlife. Its widely varied landscape is spread over 250,900 square miles (403,784 kilometers).

ALBERTA

Alberta's varied landscape is composed of mountains, glaciers, foothills, lakes, rivers, forests, badlands, and wetlands and is mostly open plain. Ninety percent of Alberta is part of North America's interior plain, with heavily forested areas and peat lands in the North, grasslands in the South, and parkland in the east and central areas. The badlands are home to some of world's greatest paleontological finds unearthed in what is now Dinosaur Provincial Park, a UNESCO World Heritage Site. A landlocked province, Alberta is bordered by the Northwest Territories, the U.S. state of Montana, and British Columbia. Almost 117,000 people are members of forty-eight First Nations or "bands" in Alberta, belonging to nine different ethnic groups.

BANFF
Buffalo Nations Luxton Museum

Nestled among towering pines on the Bow River, this museum is dedicated to the appreciation, interpretation, demonstration, and display of the cultures, traditions, and values of the First Nations of North America. With an emphasis on the Cree, Blackfoot, Blood, and Stoney peoples, information not only shows the ancient history of the people but celebrates their survival after European contact. Events have included a buffalo-inspired fashion show, cross-cultural powwow, and Indigenous market.

Buffalo Nations Luxton Museum.

Info: 1 Birch Ave., Banff, AB TOL OCO • 403.762.2388 • http://www.buffalonationsmuseum.com/home

CALGARY
Calgary Stampede

Every July, this ten-day event is a multicultural celebration. Members of the Treaty 7 nations host visitors in the Indian village, featuring twenty-six tipis representing

Participants in the Calgary Stampede.

the five Treaty 7 nations: Kainai, Tsuut'ina, Stoney Nakoda, Siksika, and Piikani. Treaty 7 is one of eleven numbered treaties signed between many First Nations and the British Crown between 1871 and 1921 and involved mostly the Blackfoot band governments in what is today southern Alberta. The treaty established a much-reduced land base (reserves) for tribes, promised annual payments from the queen, and secured continued hunting and trapping rights on the "tract surrendered." The First Nations were forced to cede their traditional territories. At the annual Stampede festival, each tipi is embellished with unique designs, and inside, cultural objects and artifacts are on display. Aboriginal dance competitions, storytelling, games, traditional food, and other activities are enjoyed by visitors. First Nations members also participate in other Stampede events, like the rodeo.

Info: 1410 Olympic Way SE, Calgary, AB T2G 2W1 • 403.261.0101 • https://www.calgarystampede.com/stampede

Glenbow Museum

One of the largest museums in western Canada, the Glenbow prides itself on being a repository of cultural history and contemporary life of the region. The museum houses a significant collection of First Nations artifacts and material culture. For over twenty years, the Blackfoot people worked with the museum to repatriate sacred medicine bundles to the Blackfoot Nation.

Info: 130 9th Ave. SE, Calgary, AB T2G 0P3 • 403.268.4100 • http://www.glenbow.org/

The Glenbow Museum.

Nickle Galleries

Part of the University of Calgary, the galleries feature contemporary art in western Canada as well as fascinating art and artifacts from the university's extensive collection.

Info: 410 University Ct. NW, Calgary, AB T2N 1N4 • 403.210.6201 • https://nickle.ucalgary.ca/

CANMORE
Mahikan Trails

An aboriginal company offering tours by First Nations and Métis guides, activities include learning traditional skills of tracking and herbology. Excursions are conducted during all seasons, include night hikes, and feature snowshoe tours, historical accounts, traditional stories, ice walks, pictograph interpretation, and cosmology.

Info: 82 Grotto Way, Canmore, AB T1W 1K3 • 403.679.8379 • http://www.mahikan.ca/about.html

EDMONTON
Dreamspeakers Film Festival

When a Dene filmmaker returned to his Northwest Territories community, there was no Dene word for film. People called it dream talking, and today, the art is showcased during the annual September film festival celebrating Indigenous filmmakers, performers, and artists from around the globe who share a common bond: "a linkage with a natural world whose harmonies and rhythms are being forgotten by those that came later."

Info: 8726 112 Ave., Edmonton, AB T5B 0G6 • 780.378.9609 • http://dreamspeakers.org

FORT MACLEOD
Head-Smashed-In Buffalo Jump

A UNESCO heritage site for its cultural and historic significance, the Head-Smashed-In Buffalo Jump is one of the oldest and best-preserved spots that demonstrates

Head-Smashed-In Buffalo Jump.

communal hunting methods and lifeways of the Northern Plains people, whose lives revolved around the vast herds of bison for thousands of years. Because of their in-depth knowledge of topography and bison behavior, they were able to hunt bison by stampeding them over a cliff—thousands of the big animals' skeletons are in the area. The five-level interpretive center with informative displays is constructed inside a hill. Visitors end up at the top, where the buffalo jump cliffs are located with an incredible panorama of the Rocky Mountains, prairies, and the Oldman River.

Info: P.O. Box 1977, Fort Macleod, AB T0L 0Z0 • 403.553.2731 • ttp://www.history.alberta.ca/headsmashedin/

FORT SASKATCHEWAN
Elk Island National Park

In the park's recorded 227 Native sites, cultural history spans from the receding of the glaciers until the 1900s. It is thought that the original inhabitants were the Sarcee, who were later forced out by the Cree. Called the Beaver Hill people, the Cree operated a lucrative fur-trading business with the Europeans. They also hunted bison, but with the depletion of the herds and other game and fur animals, they eventually left. Today, an important refuge for bison, elk, and more than 250 bird species, it conserves wildlife that was once almost extinct. In fact, the park has partnered with Indigenous nations to repatriate the buffalo to original homelands in both the United States and Canada. The events are called the Bison Homecoming.

Info: 1 - 54401 Range Road 203, Fort Saskatchewan, AB T8L 0V3 • 780.922.5790 • http://www.pc.gc.ca/eng/pn-np/ab/elkisland/natcul/beaverhills.aspx

Bison roam free along with elk and hundreds of bird species on Elk Island National Park.

LETHBRIDGE
International Peace Powwow

This two-day February powwow, held at the Enmax Centre in Lethbridge, is sponsored by the Blackfoot Canadian Cultural Society. The society also holds an Aboriginal Artists Award Ceremony and hosts the Miss Blackfoot Canada Pageant and AbFest, a multidisciplinary arts festival and gala. It also manages the Blackfoot Art Gallery, located in Lethbridge Centre.

Info: 2510 Scenic Drive S., Lethbridge, AB T1K 1N2 • 403.329.7328 • http://www.downtownlethbridge.com/profile.asp?bPageID=2423

Lethbridge Indian Battle Park

Original Cree homelands ranged over a vast region of northern woodlands between the shores of Hudson Bay and Lake Superior. Organized into several bands, their contact with French traders set into motion a series of culture shocks, resulting in the Cree's two-hundred-year migration to the Southwest. By the beginning of the nineteenth century, the lead groups in the movement had acquired horses and reached the northern bank of the Missouri River in Montana. There, they clashed with the powerful Blackfoot Confederacy, whose lands extended from the High Plains to the Rockies. A series of wars between the two nations lasted for half a century, culminating in the 1850s. With both sides nearing exhaustion through war, disease, and steady reduction of the buffalo herds on which they depended, the final battle between them was fought near present-day Lethbridge. The park is situated in a beautiful area along the Oldman River, and although commercialized, one can trace battle sites believed to be the last major war between the Indigenous people of North

America. The beauty of the area belies its war-torn past. Although this book stays away from battlegrounds, this area illustrates the disastrous results of Native nations being displaced by European conquest and fighting each other for territory.

Info: 200 Indian Battle Rd. S., Lethbridge, AB T1K • 403.320.3076 • http://www.lethbridge.ca/Things-To-Do/Parks/Pages/Indian-Battle-Park.aspx

LONGVIEW
The Lost American Art Gallery and Museum

Exhibits feature late 1800s saddle bridles and chaps as well as jewelry, pottery, and baskets from many aboriginal groups. The gift shop carries mainly art from the Southwestern U.S. Indigenous peoples.

Info: 122 Morrison Rd., Longview, AB T0L 1H0 • 403.558.3693 • http://www.thelostamericanartgallery.com/

MILK RIVER
Writing-on-Stone Provincial Park

Writing-on-Stone Provincial Park contains the greatest concentration of rock art on the Great Plains: more than fifty rock art sites with thousands of figures, some over three thousand years old. Over the centuries, the Blackfoot and the Shoshone used the rock as a communications center: the bands left each other messages on the towering sandstone along the Milk River. Early archaeological sites show a pictorial record of the lives of a society that followed bison herds on foot. Later rock art depicts how the introduction of horses, guns, and metal impacted Northern Plains cultures. Some of the pictographs were painted with red ochre (iron ore and

Writing-on-Stone Provincial Park.

Blackfoot Crossing Interpretive Centre.

water), while others were drawn with markers fashioned from limestone. Most of the petroglyphs were carved with antlers and bones; later, they were carved with metal tools. The animal and human figures, engaged in daily activities, provide an account of history through the ages; other art is a mystery and is thought to represent the sacred.

Info: NW 36 TW1 range 13, Milk River, AB T0K 1M0 • 403.647.2364 • https://www.albertaparks.ca/writing-on-stone.aspx

SIKSIKA
Blackfoot Crossing Interpretive Centre

The architecture of the stunning building itself is symbolic of Blackfoot culture, its sacred icons, and the everyday life of the Siksika people. Sculptures and designs depict a sacred eagle feather fan, winter count, tipi, buffalo, and many other references to the Siksika heritage. The Seven Sacred Society Tipis on the roof represent an ancient encampment; the spectacular nighttime view glows like lanterns created by ancient cooking fires. Everything from floor tiles to paint colors chronicles the history of the people who designed this magnificent center. Programs include interactive exhibits, a gallery, a library, performances, films, lectures, guided tours, and an overnight stay in an authentic tipi in part of an authentic tipi village.

Info: Hwy. 842, Siksika, AB T0J 3W0 • 403.734.5171 • http://www.blackfootcrossing.ca/index.html

MANITOBA

Abutting Hudson Bay on the northeast, Manitoba has more than 110,000 lakes, including Lake Winnipeg, the tenth-largest freshwater lake in the world. Some traditional Native lands and boreal forest on Lake Winnipeg's east side are a proposed UNESCO World Heritage Site. Sixty-three different First Nations are in Manitoba, as well as Métis, with almost two hundred thousand members.

CHURCHILL
Eskimo Museum

The Eskimo Museum has one of the best and oldest collections of Inuit carvings and artifacts in the world, dating from Pre-Dorset (1700 B.C.E.) through Dorset, Thule, and modern Inuit times. The gift shop's focus is on regional books, Canadian Inuit art, and local preserves.

Info: 242 Laverendrye av, Churchill, MB R0B 0E0 • 204.675.2030 • https://www.travelmanitoba.com/listings/eskimo-museum/555/

Wapuska Adventures

Located in the tundra town of Churchill, which is nicknamed the polar bear capital of the world, Wapuska Adventures, a Métis-owned company, provides visitors an authentic dog-sledding tour through a boreal forest. No roads lead into Churchill; train or plane are the only ways to get there. However, the community has an open-car-door policy: cars must remain unlocked in case a pedestrian meets up with a polar bear and needs to get shelter fast! People just jump in the nearest car and sound the horn to scare off the animal and alert others of the situation.

Info: 321 Kelsey Blvd., P.O. Box 728, Churchill, MB R0B 0E0 • 204.675.2887 • http://wapuskadventures.com/

WINNIPEG
Canadian Museum for Human Rights

First Nations, Métis, and Inuit peoples share similar concepts of rights and responsibilities in which everyone and everything are interrelated. This museum presents these worldviews in a 360-degree film as told by four different generations. The striking theater space also houses original contemporary art.

Info: 85 Israel Asper Way, Winnipeg, MB R3C 0L5 • 204.289.2000 • https://humanrights.ca/

Eastside Aboriginal Sustainable Tourism, Inc. (E.A.S.T., Inc.)

E.A.S.T., Inc., offers visitors an opportunity to share firsthand the Anishinabe culture of Manitoba. Guides lead tourists on a journey to participate in Indigenous festivals, explore traditional lands/waters and landmarks like the Brokenhead Wetland Interpretative Trail, interact with Indigenous cultural interpreters, enjoy Indigenous foods, relax in Native-owned resorts like the Bloodvein River Lodge, and experience aboriginal dance and music performances.

Info: 211-428 Portage Ave., Winnipeg, MB R3C 0E2 (Urban Office) • 204.949.1041 • http://eastinc.ca/

Manito Ahbee Festival

Manito Ahbee means "where the Creator sits" and refers to a sacred site located in what is now Manitoba's Whiteshell Provincial Park. Traditionally, it was a gathering

Canadian Museum for Human Rights.

place where First Nations shared teachings and socialized. Today, Manito Ahbee Festival is an annual spring celebration of Indigenous arts, culture, and music promoting traditional principles to "unite the spirits of all people, honor the Creator and the seven sacred teachings: love, respect, courage, honesty, wisdom, humility, and truth." The festival features the Indigenous Music Awards, the Indigenous Music Conference, the International Powwow, and the Indigenous Marketplace and Trade Show. Other events include: a square dance competition, "Getting Jiggy with It"; an art expo with categories in beadwork, quillwork, ribbon work, and star blanket; an art challenge where contemporary artists create a painting in only thirty minutes; and the MTS Future First Youth Education Day.

Info: 472 Madison St., Winnipeg, MB R3J 1J1 • 204.956.1849 • https://www.manitoahbee.com/

Manitoba Indigenous Cultural Education Centre, Inc.

The center contains the beautiful and airy People's Library, a collection of over eleven thousand books, artwork, periodicals, vertical files, music, DVDs, and educational kits about Indigenous peoples and cultures. A diverse list of workshops offers traditional arts instruction and history and current issues, and several are open to the public. Cultural events include dance and music performances and language preservation classes. One of the main highlights of this urban oasis for Indigenous people is the Annual Indigenous Minor Hockey Tournament featuring six divisions: Squirt, Novice, Atom, Peewee, Bantam, and Midget, which has been held every spring for over thirty years. This spectacular competition showcases young and talented Native athletes from all over the province.

Info: 119 Sutherland Ave., Winnipeg, MB R2W 3C9 • 204.942.0228 • https://www.micec.com/

Neechi Commons

Located on a 50,000-square-foot (15-square-kilometer) lot in Winnipeg's North End neighborhood, Neechi Commons is a major focal point for commerce and development. The business complex houses an aboriginal worker-owned and -operated supermarket, art store, bookstore, and bakery as well as other enterprises. Traditional foods like freshly baked bannock bread, wild rice, and locally grown produce and fresh fish are available in the markets and restaurant. A seasonal farmers market features a variety of crops raised by urban Indigenous youth and shares retail space with clothing, arts, books, and crafts created by over two hundred Indigenous artists and authors. This wonderful market and cultural oasis functions on traditional Native values and is Winnipeg's largest commercial employer of First Nations and Métis people. Customers are treated to many live performances and literary events. The Neechi Supermarket has won awards for promoting healthy lifestyles and was the first Winnipeg store to NOT sell cigarettes.

Info: 865 Main St. (at Euclid Ave.), Winnipeg, MB R2W 3N9 • 204.949.1338 • https://neechi.ca/

Riel House National Historic Site

The story of the Métis entwines all the cultural strands that still shape Canada. French traders intermarried with the Cree people, and after several generations, these blended families established their own identities as Métis. Some continued to live a traditional existence well into the nineteenth century following the buffalo herds on their seasonal migrations across the prairies. Others preferred urban life in St. Boniface, a French-speaking community that is now part of Winnipeg. The Red River

Canadian politician and Métis leader Louis Riel led two rebellions against the Canadian government and was briefly the president of the provisional government of Saskatchewan.

area, known as Assiniboia, was governed by the Hudson's Bay Company, but in 1869, it was turned over as a territory to the new Canadian government. Until then, the Métis and the English-speaking settlers from the East had had a polite understanding: the traditional ways were respected, and the two peoples lived in a strict sort of friendship. When the government sent surveying teams into the area and started laying out sections that cut across the French-style ribbon farms of the Métis, the

Métis began fearing that their rights would be swept away. These fears were justified by what had happened when white settlers poured onto the prairies of the United States, displacing Native peoples. Activist Louis Riel (1844–1885), descended from an old Métis family, identified strongly with his Cree heritage. A fiery and inspirational speaker, he had been educated in Quebec and returned to Assiniboia at age twenty-five. He quickly rose to an influential position among the Métis and was named to head a provisional government that opposed confederation with Canada. The Canadian government hurriedly made Manitoba a province while dispatching troops to stifle any opposition. Later, Riel was elected to Parliament from Manitoba, but he was expelled in 1875 for his perseverance protecting Métis rights. Twice in the next few years, he was hospitalized in Quebec for mental duress. Riel moved to Montana and taught school.

In 1885, the Canadian Pacific Railroad was making its way across the country, touching off a boom in Saskatchewan. Native peoples were displaced as their lands were illegally sold. The Métis in the area were on the edge of rebellion. Seeing the chance to unify the interests of both the French and the Cree, Riel returned to Canada. Appealing to both sides for support, he took control of the revolt. For three months, the Métis defied the Canadian government, but when troops finally reached the scene, the rebellion collapsed. Riel surrendered and was tried for treason and hanged at Regina in November. His body lay in state in his house, which was built in 1881. After his death, he became a martyr to both the French and Native causes, issues that still figure prominently in Canadian society. Before the Riel Rebellion, railroad proponents were having a difficult time garnering public support; money ran out and the work stalled, but when the public saw how quickly the troops arrived by rail to quell the rebellion, people were swayed to approve funding. The Riel house in the St. Boniface district is now a memorial to the leader and his failed rebellion with displays on the history of the Métis and their struggle and many personal items belonging to the Riel family.

Info: 330 River Rd. (St. Vital), Winnipeg, MB R2M 3Z8 • 204.983.6757 • http://www.pc.gc.ca/eng/lhn-nhs/mb/riel/index.aspx

Winnipeg Aboriginal Film Festival

Although this annual November festival celebrates the finest Canadian Indigenous films, it also features Indigenous media arts from around the world.

Info: 101 - 478 River Ave., Winnipeg, MB R3L 0B3 • 204.774.1375 • http://www.waff.ca/waff/

SASKATCHEWAN

About 145,000 people belong to seventy First Nations in Saskatchewan. Tourists are treated to a cherished past as well as contemporary stories of the province's Indigenous communities. These are the homelands of legendary leaders Poundmaker,

Big Bear, Louis Riel, and Gabriel Dumont, with opportunities to visit a plethora of heritage sites, galleries, museums, and events. In 1992, the federal and provincial governments signed a historic land claim agreement with Saskatchewan First Nations, which resulted in First Nations having the resources to buy land. Today, around 761,000 acres have been turned into reserve land, while many First Nations acquire properties in urban areas.

DUCK LAKE
Duck Lake Regional Interpretive Centre

From late May to early September, this site is open to view artifacts pertaining to the Northwest Resistance, First Nation and Métis Pioneer society of 1870–1905. Unique artwork is on display in the gift shop, and visitors are treated to a 24-mile (38.6-kilometer) viewing tower, theater, and bilingual tours.

Info: 5 Anderson Ave., adjacent to Hwy. 11, Duck Lake, SK S0K 1J0 • 866.467.2057 • http://www.ducklakemuseum.ca

PUNNICHY
Touchwood Agency Annual Powwow

The Touchwood Hills people are composed of four bands under the leadership of Kawacatoose ("poor man" or "lean man"), Kaneonuskatew ("one that walks on four claws" or "George Gordon"), Muscowequan ("hard quill"), and Kisecawchuck ("daystar"). Today they are known as the Kawacatoose, Gordon, Muskowekwan, and Daystar bands and are collectively part of the Touchwood Agency Tribal Chiefs (TATC),

Duck Lake Regional Interpretive Centre.

including the Fishing Lake Band. They sponsor an annual powwow, which rotates among the four different communities.

Info: P.O. Box 280, Punnichy, SK S0A 3C0 • 306.835.2937 • http://touchwoodagency.ca/events/tatcannualpow-wow

REGINA
Civic Museum of Regina

Métis culture and Plains Indian exhibits are on display.

Info: 1231 Broad St., Regina, SK S4R 1Y2 • 306.780.9435 • http://www.civicmuseumofregina.com/

First Nations University of Canada Powwow

The First Nations University of Canada offers students of all nations to learn in an environment of First Nations cultures and values. Each year, it holds a powwow to celebrate the diverse cultures of aboriginal Canada.

Info: 1 First Nations Way, Regina, SK S4S 7K2 • 306.790.5950 • http://fnuniv.ca/powwow

SASKATOON
Saskatchewan Indigenous Cultural Centre (SICC)

The Saskatchewan Indian Cultural Centre (SICC) celebrates the cultural identity of First Nations cultures of what is now known as Saskatchewan: Plains Cree, Swampy Cree, Woodlands Cree, Dene, Saulteaux, Dakota, Nakota, and Lakota. The center offers many cultural events, including powwows and workshops, plus maintains video, photo, and audio archives. At the forefront of preserving sacred sites in the province, their current project is finding a home for the Buffalo Child Stone, an ancient, massive, stone icon that was dynamited by the provincial government a half century ago and recently discovered at the bottom of a lake.

Info: SICC, 305 - 2555 Grasswood Rd. E., Saskatoon, SK S7T 0K1 • 306.244.1146 • http://www.sicc.sk.ca/index.html

Wanuskewin Heritage Park

This international site interprets over six thousand years of Northern Plains Indian culture through walking trails, a medicine wheel, tipi rings, a buffalo pound, and

Wanuskewin Heritage Park.

costumed docents. The visitor center contains an art gallery, a conference facility, a gift shop, and a restaurant. Overnight and camping adventures include tipi sleep-overs, archaeological digs, and day camps. In the winter, visitors can snowshoe and participate in workshops like moccasin and drum making instruction.

Info: RR 4, Penner Rd., Saskatoon, SK S7K 3J7 • 306.931.6767 • https://wanuskewin.com/

WAKAW
Batoche National Historic Park

Batoche was a village on the Saskatchewan River, the site that marked the end of the Riel Rebellion of 1885 (see entry on "Riel House National Historic Site," Winnipeg, Manitoba). This area had become a center of Métis settlement after they were driven from Manitoba by white expansion. After a fifteen-year interval, the conflict between the Métis and Anglo settlers began again here; Louis Riel returned to Canada from Montana to lead a resistance of the Métis, the French-speaking westerners, and the Cree, but after three months, Riel's troops were overwhelmed by eight thousand soldiers in a decisive battle that forced their surrender. Visitors may tour the various sections of the battlefield as well as the ruins of the Métis town. Displays, an audiovisual presentation in the park museum, and guides explain the history of the Métis and their resistance. On the last weekend of July, descendants of the Métis gather for Batoche Days, a cultural celebration of music, dances, and games reflecting their blended French–Native American heritage.

Info: RR#1, P.O. Box 1040, Wakaw, SK S0K 4P0 • 306.423.6227 • http://www.pc.gc.ca/en/lhn-nhs/sk/batoche

THE FAR NORTH

There was a time when many of my generation did not have pride in our Inuit identity and were not sure if they wanted to be Canadian citizens. Today, there is a resurgence of Inuit pride and we have become loyal Canadians. Even though our people have encountered racial discrimination in the past, we want reconciliation and we want all to feel welcome in our homeland. Our patience and our willingness to share continue to be cornerstones of our society.

—John Amagoalik, Inuit and called the "Father of Nunavut"

North America is capped by Canada's vast North, composed of Nunavut on the east, Northwest Territories in the center, and the Yukon on the west. The area is one-third of the country's land mass but its population is only one hundred thousand. Often called "Land of the Midnight Sun," daylight can last up to twenty-four hours during the summers, which are short and cool. Winters are the opposite: dark, long, and frigid. Much of the region is a tundra atop an immense, Arctic plain; the soil is permanently frozen, where few trees grow. The very northern areas are part of the Canadian Arctic Archipelago. Many residents earn a living by hunting, fishing, and trapping, while others mine gold, lead, copper, zinc, and diamonds. The Indigenous peoples and the environment are in danger from the developing oil and gas industry. Inuit art created in these far North homelands is sought-after around the world and is also a source of income for Indigenous people.

NORTHWEST TERRITORIES

The Northwest Territories, in the center of the North, features a boreal forest (taiga) and boasts the deepest body of water in North America, Great Slave Lake, as well as Great Bear Lake, the largest lake located entirely within Canada. The Nahanni National Park Reserve is a UNESCO World Heritage Site. The Northwest Territories is one of two Canadian jurisdictions (Nunavut is the other) where the majority of the population is aboriginal. It has more official languages than any other place in the Americas: Chipewyan, Cree, English, French, Gwich'in, Inuinnaqtun, Inuktitut, Inuvialuktun, North Slavey, South Slavey, and Tłįchǫ. In Inuktitut, the Northwest Territories are referred to as ᓄᓇᑦᓯᐊᖅ (Nunatsiaq), "beautiful land." Around twenty-one thousand Indigenous people live in the Northwest Territories.

FORT SMITH
Northern Life Museum and Cultural Centre

Over seventeen thousand artifacts, including traditional work of the Inuit, Inuvialuit, Dene, and Métis, are on display, along with a hands-on exhibit depicting the fur trade. A replication of an aboriginal village is part of a guided tour. Beautiful beadwork, clothing, a birch bark canoe, and other cultural objects share space with a natural history exhibit of wildlife indigenous to the area.

Info: 110 King St., P.O. Box 420, Fort Smith, NT X0E 0P0 • 867.872.2859 • http://www.nlmcc.ca/the-museum/

GRIZZLY BEAR MOUNTAIN AND SCENTED GRASS HILLS
Saoyú-ʔehdacho National Historic Site

Saoyú-ʔehdacho has great cultural and spiritual meaning for the Sahtu people and is a prominent part of their history. In the Slavey language, Saoyú means "belonging to the bear" and ʔehdacho means "big point." About 2,157 square miles (5,587 square kilometers) in size, it is made up of two peninsulas: Saoyú (Grizzly Bear Mountain) and ʔehdacho (Scented Grass Hills). Archaeological finds date human occupation to be over five thousand years. It is a remarkable area of flat summits and raised beaches. It is also remarkable as being the first Canadian National Historic Site both designated and acquired on the basis of consultation with aboriginal peoples; the first National Historic Site jointly managed by Parks Canada and an aboriginal group; and the first cultural landscape in northern Canada commemorated by Canada.

Info: Location: Grizzly Bear Mountain and Scented Grass Hills, NT; Contact: Western Arctic Field Unit, Parks Canada Agency, P.O. Box 164, Délįne, NT X0E 0G0 • 867.589.3130

INUVIK
Annual Reindeer Crossing

Every year in the early spring, crowds gather to watch almost four thousand reindeer being herded from their winter home near Jimmy Lake to their calving grounds on Richards Island near Tuktoyaktuk. Tundra "cowboys" guide the animals on snowmobiles. In the early 1900s, the Inuvialuit were facing famine as the caribou herds were severely impacted and diminished by climate warming and depletion of natural resources by overdevelopment. The government imported Scandinavian reindeer along with Indigenous Sami reindeer herders to prevent a crisis. Today, Canada's only free-ranging reindeer are jointly owned by the Inuvialuit of the Mackenzie Delta and local descendants of the Sami, who helped bring the herd to the Northwest Territories.

The only mammals who can see ultraviolet light, reindeer navigate well in the Arctic's blinding white landscape. Their multipurpose hooves are perfectly adapted to polar survival. They are large and broad and function as snowshoes carrying them atop drifts; the hooves also act as chisels for digging out food beneath the ice and operate as paddles so the animals can swim easily. Able to run at almost 50 miles (80 kilometers) an hour, the herd seems to slow down so tourists can have time to photograph and enjoy this annual journey.

Info: 185 Mackenzie Rd., P.O. Box 2785, Inuvik, NT X0E 0T0 • 800.420.9652 • http://tundranorthtours.com/

Muskrat Jamboree

Coinciding with the Annual Reindeer Crossing is this annual, four-day festival where participants can learn ice chiseling or harpoon throwing. The end-of-winter event features jigging, dog races, community feasts, drumming, dancing, and other highlights of Inuvialuit culture.

Info: Town of Inuvik, 2 Firth St., P.O. Box 1160, Inuvik, NT X0E 0T0 • 867.777.8600 • http://www.inuvik.ca/en/getting-active/Muskrat-Jamboree.asp

YELLOWKNIFE
Dene Culture Journey

An opportunity to tour the different Dene communities of Yellowknife, Dettah, and N'dilo, participants can explore the cultural significance of the Dene lands' traditions. Visitors join in Dene hand games and learn about the environment from a Native perspective.

Info: P.O. Box 2397, Yellowknife, NT X1A 2P8 • 867.444.0451 • http://www.bdene.com/

Prince of Wales Northern Heritage Centre.

National Aboriginal Day

Celebrated throughout the region as well as in other parts of Canada every June 21, the Yellowknife First Nations present a variety of events during National Aboriginal Day. The North Slave Métis Alliance holds a free fish fry with music, artists, and a tipi-building contest. The Yellowknife Dene First Nation conducts a giant mine-healing ceremony, followed by a fish fry and drum dance. Other First Nations contribute for the weeklong celebration of the Solstice and the longest day of the year in this Arctic environment.

Prince of Wales Northern Heritage Centre

Showcasing history, language, and culture through artifacts, clothing, oral history, and photographs of the NWT's diverse Indigenous groups, this museum also investigates contemporary issues, like how Arctic coastal communities are coping with climate change.

Info: 4750 48th St., P.O. Box 1320, Yellowknife, NT X1A 2L9 • 867.767.9347 • http://www.pwnhc.ca/about/#14/62.4562/-114.3804

NUNAVUT

Nunavut ("our land" in Inuktitut) was established in 1999 to be separate from the eastern part of the Northwest Territories. It is the first Indigenous self-governing territory in the Americas since European colonization and the successful outcome of the largest aboriginal land claims agreement between the Canadian government and the Inuit. Its capital, Iqaluit, sits on vast Baffin Island, known for its ice-capped mountains and tundra valleys. Near the city, Sylvia Grinnell Territorial Park is home to caribou and Arctic foxes. Qaummaarviit Territorial Park, on a tiny island near the city, contains archaeological remains of the ancient Thule people. Around thirty-six thousand Inuit citizens live in Nunavut, making up 85 percent of the population; Inuktitut is an official language and the first language in schools. Inuit means "the people who are alive at this time" in Inuktitut; the term "Eskimo" is considered derogatory and is not used in Nunavut.

ARCTIC BAY
Arctic Bay Adventures

The excitement of the dogs is infectious as they carry tourists by traditional qamutiq sleds to the very edge of the Arctic Ocean sea ice to view narwhals, called the unicorns of the sea, great white polar bears, and other amazing creatures in this far north land. Guests partake of winter solstice celebrations and ring in the New Year with this traditional Inuit community when it comes together to play centuries-old games, sing, dance, and celebrate life in this magical ice land. Summer travelers are regaled by a kaleidoscope of wildflower colors on the tundra and learn about survival in this harsh climate.

Info: Arctic Bay, NU X0A 0A0 • 867.439.8888 • http://arcticbayadventures.com/

IGLOOLIK
Rockin' Walrus Arts Festival

Summertime in the Arctic is an explosion of music, dance, and acrobatic and theatrical performances at the annual Rockin' Walrus Arts Festival. The little hamlet of Igloolik is also home to Artcirq, the only Inuit circus troupe in the world! The troupe performed at the opening of the 2010 Olympics. It is also the home of renowned Igloolik film director Zacharias Kunuk, who directed the epic movie *Atanarjuat: The Fast Runner* (based on an ancient Inuit legend) that won the prestigious Caméra d'Or Award at the 2001 Cannes Film Festival.

Info: http://www.isuma.tv/en/igloolik-bands/rockin-walrus-arts-festival-13

IQALUIT
Alianait Arts Festival

The world's largest circumpolar stage presents the Alianait Arts Festival every June. Inuit and other circumpolar artists take the lead while sharing performance space with world-class musicians, circus acrobats, dancers, storytellers, actors, filmmakers, and visual artists who travel to this exciting venue from every place on the planet. The Alianait Entertainment Group holds concerts throughout the year as well; the organization's mission is to build a healthier Nunavut through the arts and facilitate mentoring between Native artists and Native students.

Info: Alianait Entertainment Group, 166 Umiaq Crescent, Iqaluit, NU X0A 0H0 • 867.979.6000 • https://alianait.ca/

Nunatta Sunakkutaangit Museum

The museum's building is an old Hudson Bay Company warehouse that has gone through several renovations, including a move. Its large collection of local and re-

Nattinnak Centre.

gional Inuit artifacts and fine art, along with interpretive displays and traveling exhibits, makes this a special place to visit.

Info: 212 Sinaa, Iqaluit, NU X0A 0H0 • 867.979.5537 • http://www.canada-travel .ca/nunavut/iqaluit/nunatta-sunakkutaangit-museum_1188

Toonik Tyme Festival

For over half a century, this weeklong festival every April has welcomed the Arctic spring. Ancient traditional Inuit games and activities, such as igloo building, dogsled races, and seal skinning contests, share the event with newer Inuit traditions, like snowmobile racing. Plenty of food and music round out festival offerings.

Info: 901 Nunavut, Iqaluit, NU X0A 0H0 • 867.979.5600 • http://www.tooniktyme .com

POND INLET
The Nattinnak Centre

The center was constructed to look like an iceberg and fits right into the environment. Inside is a cultural feast of drum-dancing and throat-singing performances. Visitors are invited to take an Inuktitut class or learn to play the traditional qilaut (drum).

Info: Pond Inlet, NU X0A 0S0 • 867.899.8225 •
http://www.pondinlethotel.com/pond-inlet-traditions.htm

THE YUKON

The westernmost and smallest territory is the mountainous and heavily forested Yukon, celebrated in books and films for its Gold Rush history. It shares a border with Alaska. Most of the more than eight thousand aboriginal peoples belong to the Athabascan- or Tlingit-language families. Two-thirds of Yukon's residents live in its capital and only big city, Whitehorse.

BURWASH LANDING
Kluane Museum of Natural History

On display are the Southern Tutchone people's clothing, tools, and weapons. Locally made crafts, including moccasins, are available in the gift shop.

Info: Burwash Landing, YT Y0B 1V0 • 867.841.5561 • http://kluanemuseum.ca/

HAINES JUNCTION
Shakat Tun Wilderness Camp

Wildlife, Indigenous knowledge, and aboriginal hospitality are on the agenda at this family-run camp. Shakat Tun means "summer hunting trails" in the Southern Tutchone language, and visitors are introduced to wolf, coyote, bear, gopher, hare, moose, caribou, raven, eagle, and many more wild critters of this remarkable land of extremes a few hours north of Whitehorse. The Allen family shares their family history of successful living in the wild and respect for all living things. Traditional medicine walks, drum making, and Indigenous methods of harvesting and preparing for winter are served up high in the Yukon mountains located next to Kluane National Park and Reserve (a UNESCO World Heritage Site), home to North America's largest ice field and Mount Logan, the continent's second-highest mountain. One can celebrate National Aboriginal Day in this historic and ecofriendly location with the Southern Tutchone Dancers playing hand games and Indian bingo.

Info: Haines Junction, YT Y0B 1L0 • 867.332.2604 • http://www.shakattunadventures.com

TESLIN
Teslin Tlingit Heritage Centre

The Teslin Tlingit Heritage Centre is a stunning building that houses the Great Hall, the Clan Governance for the Teslin Tlingit, and interpretive displays that illustrate two centuries of Tlingit history and the culture of the Inland Tlingit people. A gift shop features striking Tlingit art.

In the summer of odd years, the Ha Kus Teyea Celebration is hosted at the center by the Inland Tlingit nations, the Teslin Tlingit Council, the Carcross/Tagish First Na-

Teslin Tlingit Dancers.

tion, and the Taku River Tlingit First Nation. Members of Tlingit nations in Alaska and elsewhere attend the joyous event, which reconnects Inland and Coastal Tlingit peoples. A traditional lake crossing and arrival in a Tlingit canoe is followed by a greeting ceremony and lighting of the Celebration Fire. The Grand Entrance Parade is also held on the first day with pageantry, flags, and people dressed in traditional Tlingit clothing. For seven days, guests are treated to public art workshops, cultural demonstrations, storytelling, canoe rides, First Nation and contemporary performers, the Artists' Market, the Kids Zone, hand game demonstrations, Tlingit language lessons, and many more special events. An evening public feast is followed by cultural performances.

Info: Alaska Hwy., Teslin, YT Y0A 1B0 • 867.390.2532 • http://www.ttc-teslin.com/heritage-centre.html

WHITEHORSE
Kwanlin Dün Cultural Centre

The Kwanlin Dün First Nation became one of the first in the country to have urban land repatriated. Today, the nation is self-governing with a chief and council elected every three years. They are comprised mainly of the Tutchone, Tagish, and Tlingit peoples, speak the Tlingit language, and practice potlatch ceremonials. Potlatch comes from the Nuu-chah-nulth word *pachitle*, meaning "to give," and is celebrated by many Northwest Coast peoples. The center's scenic location on the Yukon River is a welcoming place for exhibits, events, and the annual, world-class Adäka Cultural Festival, which celebrates the creative spirit of Yukon First Nations people. Every summer, the festival reconfirms the artistic and cultural heritage of the region in a weeklong gala that features dozens of performances, workshops, lectures, and demonstrations.

Info: 1171 Front St., Whitehorse, YT Y1A 0G9 • 867.456.5322 • http://www.kwanlinunculturalcentre.com/

Kwanlin Dün Cultural Centre.

MacBride Museum of Yukon History

The museum has an exhibit on Indigenous artifacts from the area and is located on the Yukon River.

Info: 1124 Front St., Whitehorse, YT Y1A 1A4 • 867.667.2709 • http://www.macbridemuseum.com/index.html

Skookum Jim Friendship Centre

Skookum Jim (James Mason; 1856–1916), Tagish of the Dak l'a Weidi Clan, discovered gold on Bonanza Creek in 1897. His find led to the great Klondike Gold Rush. Highly respected by his people, Skookum Jim's fortune was put into trust, and according to the terms of his will, the money generated from the interest was to fund health and education for Indian people of the Yukon. The trust fund still exists and provides monies for the Skookum Jim Friendship Centre and its programs, which help Native people adjust to urban life in Whitehorse. It is the oldest Indigenous organization in the Yukon and gave birth to several other Native organizations: the Yukon Native Brotherhood, the Yukon Association of Non-Status Indians; the Yukon Native Youth, the Yukon Native Women; the Yukon Native Court Workers, and the Yukon Indian Women's Association. For almost fifty years, they have held the annual Skookum Jim Folklore Show in February, headlining Indigenous performers from the region like the Teslin Tlingit Dancers and the Tr'ondek Hwech'in Han Singers.

Skookum Jim.

Info: 3159 3rd Ave., Whitehorse, YT Y1A 1G1 • 867.633.7680 • https://skookumjim.com/

THE WEST COAST

I consider myself one of the most fortunate of men, to have lived at a time when some of the old Haidas and their peers among the Northwest Coast peoples were still alive, and to have had the privilege of knowing them.

—Bill Reid, Haida Artist

BRITISH COLUMBIA

The westernmost Canadian province, British Columbia is bordered by the Yukon and Northwest Territories, U.S. states of Alaska, Washington, Idaho, and Montana, Alberta, and the Pacific Ocean. The province features the greatest diversity of landforms and life-forms in the country from the island-dotted Pacific coast to the towering Rocky Mountains to the hot, dry grasslands to the moist and grand coastal forests. Not surprisingly, British Columbia has the largest representation of distinct First Nations in Canada, with more than fifty First Nations based in over two hundred communities, whose lifeways are as varied as the geography (or topography). Seven of Canada's eleven unique language families are located exclusively in British Columbia—more than 60 percent of the country's First Nations languages. The province is home to more than 260,000 First Nations, Métis, and Inuit residents. The variety of cultures and ecosystems make travel in British Columbia a unique experience.

ALERT BAY
U'Mista Cultural Society

Founded in 1980 to house potlatch artifacts seized by the government in earlier Kwakwaka'wakw First Nations history, the museum sparked the movement to repatriate cultural objects and is one of the most successful of its kind in British Columbia. Besides exhibits, museum operations include an extensive art gallery and gift shop, group tours, and cultural presentations. In addition, U'Mista hosts international scholars and supports researchers in a range of disciplines. The tallest totem

U'Mista Cultural Center.

pole (173 feet [53 meters]) in the world towers over the 'Namgis Traditional Big House, which is also home to the T'sasala Cultural Group dance performances.

Info: #1 Front St., P.O. Box 253, Alert Bay, BC V0N 1A0 • 250.974.5403 • http://www.umista.ca/

CAMPBELL RIVER
Adventures Village Island

Owned by the Mamalilikulla-Qwe'Qwa'Sot'Em (an amalgamation of separate West Coast First Nations), Adventures Village Island offers visitors an exceptional experience to kayak, fish, whale watch, tour the pristine environment (see bears, eagles, and other wildlife), and lodge in a cabin decorated with Native art. The business is not only Native run and Native staffed, but it is a fine example of environmental stewardship and ecotourism.

Info: 1441 B16th Ave., Campbell River, BC V9W 2E4 • 250.287.2955 • http://www.kayakadventuresvillage.com/

Museum of Campbell River

Visitors are greeted by "Raven Transforming," a contemporary sculpture by Laich-wiltach artist Max Chickite, that sets the mood for an exploration into the cultures of Northwest Coast First Nations. Besides being a repository of both historic and

A totem shelter on Quadra Island.

contemporary art, the museum features a look out onto the Discovery Passage, a waterway filled with marine traffic and killer whales.

Info: 470 Island Hwy., Campbell River, BC V9W 4Z9 • 250.287.3103 • http://www.crmuseum.ca/home

CAPE MUDGE
Nuyumbalees Cultural Centre

Canada's first facility designed specifically to both house a repatriated collection and to be located on a First Nation reserve, the center also promotes cultural and artistic activities of the Kwakwaka'wakw people like carving and dance. It features an archive of historical documents and knowledge. On display are a few petroglyphs carved into the huge boulders of Quadra Island, moved to the site for conservation.

Info: 34 Weway Rd., Cape Mudge, BC V0P 1N0 • 250.285.3733 • http://www.museumatcapemudge.com/

HAZELTON
'Ksan Indian Village and Museum

This replication of a historical Gitksan village is located on the same site that was a transportation hub for the Gitksan people for thousands of years. Built to illustrate the many different periods of their history, it is a living museum where artisans and cultural interpreters showcase the community's arts and culture. Towering totem poles, visible from the nearby Skeena River, stand in front of richly decorated houses.

Info: 1450 Ksan Rd., Hazelton, BC V0J 1Y0 • 250.842.5544 • https://ksan.org/

KELOWNA
Kelowna Museums Society

The museum collections contain traditional, earth-covered, semisubterranean Indian homes as well as other Native exhibits.

'Ksan Indian Village.

Info: 470 Queensway Ave., Kelowna, BC V1Y 6S7 • 250.763.2417 • https://www.kelownamuseums.ca/museums/

LUND
I'hos Cultural Tours

This Tla'amin-owned enterprise presents tours of different parts of the beautiful homelands of the Tla'amin people and their cultural practices. Tourists help paddle a traditional, 35-foot (11-meter), Salish-style-type canoe and cultural interpreters share songs and stories of the Salish people while on the waters of the Kwoo Kwahk Thys, also known as the Copeland Islands.

Info: 5245 Highway 101, Lund, BC V0N 2G0 • 604.483.1308 • http://ihostours.com/

NANAIMO
Nanaimo Museum

The Snunéymuxw First Nation's collection is held in trust by the museum, with whom they work closely to interpret their story. Often, a First Nation elder is in residence, who also advises the museum's board of directors.

Info: 100 Museum Way, Nanaimo, BC V9R 5J8 • 250.753.1821 • http://nanaimomuseum.ca/

OSOYOOS
Nk'Mip Desert Cultural Centre

The center is located in a desertlike region that extends into Washington State and is on the Osoyoos Indian Band Reserve, around 3 miles (4.8 kilometers) north of the U.S. border. Part of the Okanagan Nation Alliance, the reserve boasts a four-star resort and the first Native-owned vineyard and winery in North America. The building that houses the Nk'Mip Desert Cultural Centre reflects the peoples' commitment to

Nk'Mip Desert Cultural Centre.

conserve Canada's only desert and was constructed using ancient architectural techniques of rammed earth, "green" roofs, and walls made of young trees killed by beetle infestation, a by-product of global warming that has had a devastating effect on the vast forests of British Columbia. Visitors learn about the citizens' efforts to preserve the desert lands, one of Canada's three most endangered ecosystems. Osoyoos members have developed programs to save the habitat of many endangered plant and animal species, like the rattlesnake research and tagging project. The center provides on-site cultural tours, programs, self-guided nature trails, interpretive displays, Native sculptures, and cultural events that highlight the distinctive and contemporary experience of the rich desert heritage of the Okanagan people.

Info: 1000 Rancher Creek Rd., Osoyoos, BC V0H 1V6 • 1.888.495.8555 • http://www.nkmipdesert.com/

PORT ALBERNI
Alberni Valley Museum

On display are Northwest Coast peoples' cultural items. Events include dance performances by Nootka Indians. Port Alberni is located within the traditional territories of the Hupacasath and Tseshaht First Nations.

Info: 4255 Wallace St., Port Alberni, BC V9Y 3Y6 • 250.720.2863 • https://www.portalberni.ca/alberni-valley-museum-0

PRINCE RUPERT
Museum of Northern British Columbia

Honoring the cultures of the northwest coast, the museum is located within a northwest coast longhouse overlooking the harbor with splendid displays of the arts, past

Museum of Northern British Columbia.

and present, of the northwest coast Indigenous peoples. The beautiful venue also hosts events and special programs like the Winter Feast Tour and Performance, which delights visitors with a trek through museum exhibits and ends with an invitation to the feast house for a performance of music, dance, and storytelling.

Info: 100 First Ave. W., Prince Rupert, BC V8J 3S1 • 250.624.3207 • http://museumofnorthernbc.com/

SKIDEGATE
Haida Heritage Centre at Ḵay Llnagaay

An award-winning aboriginal tourism attraction, the center celebrates the thriving culture of the Haida through language, art, and performances that affirm the Haida relationship with the land and sea. The center, located on the site of an ancient seaside Haida community, features a museum, the Bill Reid Teaching Centre, the Carving House, the Canoe House, the Ḵay Bistro Eating House, and the Performance House, which is built like a traditional dugout longhouse.

Info: #2 Second Beach Rd., Skidegate, BC V0T 1S1 • 250.559.7885 • http://haidaheritagecentre.com/

TLELL
Haida House at Tllaal and Ocean House at Stads K'uns Gawga

Owned and operated by the Haida First Nation, the two resorts offer all-inclusive tours and authentic Haida experiences and adventures. Visitors enjoy first-class accommodations in a natural setting that provides a home base for treks into Gwaii Haanas National Park and the Haida Protected Area, named the best national park in North America, as well as other sites in Haida land.

Info: 2087 Beitush Rd., Tlell, BC V0T 1Y0 • 1.855.557.4600 • http://www.haidahouse.com/

VANCOUVER
Bill Reid Gallery of Northwest Coast Art

Downtown Vancouver is home to the only public art gallery in the country dedicated to Northwest contemporary Indigenous arts. Named for the celebrated Haida artist Bill Reid (1920–1998), the gallery highlights his monumental bronze and stone sculptures as well as magnificent pieces from a diverse group of regional Indigenous artists.

Info: 639 Hornby St., Vancouver, BC V6C 2G3 • 604.682.3455 • http://www.billreidgallery.ca/

Sea to Sky Highway

Cruising along one of the world's most beautiful routes is an awe-inspiring drive through the cultural legacy of the Squamish First Nation. Beginning in Vancouver and ending in Whistler, the 70-mile (113-kilometer) trek snakes around the curves of bays up and down the Coastal Range Mountains and past huge boulders with signs carved in Squamish and English. At seven different sites, Native cedar-hat-shaped kiosks emerge from the stunning scenery. Each kiosk offers history about First Peoples as well as Native insight into place names, animals, geological wonders, and traditional

The Bill Reid Gallery.

A totem pole display at the University of British Columbia Museum of Anthropology.

accounts of the area. Travelers can have a bite in one of several Squamish restaurants along the road. The route ends at the Squamish Lil'wat Cultural Center in Whistler.

Info: BC Highway #99 • https://www.tourismvancouver.com/activities/itineraries/sea-sky-highway-weekend/

University of British Columbia Museum of Anthropology

A superb collection of material relating to the arts and cultures of the Native peoples of the Pacific Northwest is housed in a striking glass and concrete structure on cliffs overlooking the ocean. Visitors are greeted by enormous totem poles, dugout canoes, and exceptionally fine, carved masks and jewelry of argillite, a black stone found in this region. The museum includes displays of other Pacific cultures, but the Native section is the centerpiece.

Info: 6393 NW Marine Dr., Vancouver, BC V6T 1Z2 • 604.822.5087 • http://moa.ubc.ca/

VICTORIA
Royal British Columbia Museum

The museum's First Nations collections showcase thousands of stunning photographs, films, recordings, and objects spanning a history of over ten thousand years. On display in Totem Hall are monumental carvings from the Kwakwaka'wakw, Heiltsuk, Nux-

Thunderbird Park is adjacent to the Royal British Columbia Museum.

alk, Gitxsan, Haida, and Nuu-chah-nulth communities juxtaposed with contemporary works by Kwakwaka'wakw, Heiltsuk, Nuxalk, Haida, Tsimshian, Gitxsan, Nisga'a, Nuu-chah-nulth, and Salish master carvers. This museum is unique in that it presents both historic and modern creations as art, not as material culture. Exhibits celebrate the diversity and resilience of Indigenous peoples whose roots are in British Columbia.

Info: 675 Belleville St., Victoria, BC V8W 9W2 • 250.356.7226 • http://royal bcmuseum.bc.ca/about/explore/featured-collections/first-nations-collections

WHISTLER
Audain Art Museum

This breathtakingly beautiful destination is a chance to experience the traditional and historical art of British Columbia's First Peoples.

Info: 4350 Blackcomb Way, Whistler, BC V0N 1B4 • 604.962.0413 • http://audainartmuseum.com/

The Squamish Lil'wat Cultural Centre

Rising from the Pacific Northwest forest, this stunning building features a spectacular view of Blackcomb Mountain. The center is a collaboration between the Squamish and Lil'wat First Nations and showcases both heritages through tours, music, interactive indoor and outdoor exhibits, aboriginal art, food, and film. They were awarded the 2015 BC Cultural Centre of the Year.

Info: 4584 Blackcomb Way, Whistler, BC V0N 1B4 • 604.964.0990 • https://slcc.ca/

FURTHER READING

BOOKS ABOUT LANDMARKS

Birmingham, Robert A., and Amy L. Rosebrough. *Indian Mounds of Wisconsin*. 2nd edition. Madison: University of Wisconsin Press, 2017.

Dennis, Yvonne Wakim, Arlene Hirschfelder, and Shannon Rothenberger Flynn. *Native American Almanac: More Than 50,000 Years of the Cultures and Histories of Indigenous Peoples*. Detroit: Visible Ink Press, 2016.

Erickson, Patricia Pierce. *Voices of a Thousand People: The Makah Cultural and Research Center*. Lincoln: University of Nebraska Press, 2002.

Hirschfelder, Arlene, and Paulette Molin. *The Extraordinary Book of Native American Lists*. Lanham, MD: Scarecrow Press, 2012.

Kennedy, Frances H., ed. *American Indian Places: A Historical Guidebook*. Boston: Houghton Mifflin, 2008.

Kosik, Fran. *Native Roads: The Complete Motoring Guide to the Navajo and Hopi Nations*. 3rd edition. Tucson: Rio Nuevo Publishers, 2013.

Lawlor, Mary. *Public Native America: Tribal Self-Representation in Casinos, Museums, and Powwows*. New Brunswick, NJ: Rutgers University Press, 2006.

Little, Gregory L. *Native American Mounds in Alabama: An Illustrated Guide to Public Sites*. 2nd edition. Memphis, TN: Archetype Books, 2017.

Pauketat, Timothy R. *Cahokia: Ancient America's Great City on the Mississippi*. New York: Viking, 2009.

Thomas, David Hurst. *Exploring Ancient Native America: An Archaeological Guide*. New York: Macmillan, 1994.

GENERAL RESOURCES

AAA
Members of AAA have access to free maps and planning tools for visiting Indigenous landmarks and communities.

American Indian Alaska Native Tourism Association (AIANTA)
AIANTA provides a guide to Indigenous travel destinations and events. They also supply First Nations with training in sustainable tourism and preservation.
https://nativeamerica.travel/
https://www.aianta.org/

American Indians and Route 66
Route 66 snakes east to west or west to east (depending on where one begins), from Chicago, Illinois, to Santa Monica, California. An officially commissioned highway from 1926 to 1985, the iconic 2,400-mile (3,850-kilometer) route touches twenty-five Native nations and produced a plethora of roadside attractions from metal tipis to concrete wigwams. Most of these tourist sites perpetuated stereotypes and misrepresented the cultures they supposedly represented. The highway created many problems for Indian people, including the theft of land to build it on. Today, the highway has been reinvented under the tutelage of Native consultants. Motorists can tour contemporary and historical Native cultures as they wind their way from one end to the other. A companion guide designed by AIANTA (see above) is available through its website.
http://www.americanindiansandroute66.com/

Go Native America
Featuring Native guides to a variety of Indigenous sites and events, this organization is sponsored by National Geographic.
https://www.gonativeamerica.com/

The Hawaiian Survival Handbook
Brother Noland is an acclaimed ki ho'alu (slack key) guitarist, singer and composer and considered a Hawaiian Legacy. He grew up with and has studied with Native practitioners around the world and is a stellar tracker and outdoorsman. *The Hawaiian Survival Hand-*

book (Honolulu: Watermark Publishing, 2014) provides island visitors with invaluable Hawaiian cultural skills, including outdoor survival techniques such as tracking, avoiding a wild pig attack, fire-making, net-throwing, exploring ancient sites, and more.

Indian Country Today

A digital online newspaper, this publication has a wealth of information about Indigenous cultures, issues, and events.

https://newsmaven.io/indiancountrytoday/

Indigenous Canada

Created in partnership with the Indigenous Tourism Association of Canada, this organization offers quite a variety of vacations and getaways set on Native lands.

https://Indigenouscanada.travel/

Indigenous Tourism Association of Canada (ITAC)

The Indigenous Tourism Association of Canada (ITAC) is a nonprofit organization committed to developing and promoting sustainable, culturally appropriate Indigenous tourism businesses in Canada. Organized by regions, this resource is essential for anyone traveling to Indigenous sites and events across Canada. There are links to tourism boards for each province.

https://Indigenoustourism.ca/en/

National Museum of the American Indian Magazine

Available online, this quarterly magazine features articles and information about landmarks, festivals, and other events in Indian country. It is published by the Smithsonian NMAI.

https://www.americanindianmagazine.org/

National Park Service

Several different destinations under the National Park Service administration are sprinkled throughout the book; this is the NPS general website for American Indian landmarks.

https://www.nps.gov/subjects/travelamericancultures/amindsites.htm

Native Guide Hawaii

Owned by Native culture practitioner Warren Costa of Hawaii, who is also a naturalist and archeologist, the company provides a myriad of experiences like visiting ruins, lava flows, and tidal pools. It is a stellar experience for those interested in an Indigenous perspective of Hawaii. Tours are enhanced by the telling of Native history.

http://www.nativeguidehawaii.com/

Native Hoop Magazine

This online magazine offers several different articles about Native events.

https://nativehoopmagazine.weebly.com/

Tribal Maps

Aaron Carpanella has produced accurate and compelling maps of pre-contact and contemporary Indigenous North America, including Mexico and the Caribbean.
http://www.tribalnationsmaps.com/

FESTIVALS AND POWWOWS

First American Indian Art Magazine

This is a very extensive calendar of Indigenous arts events.
http://firstamericanartmagazine.com/calendar/

The Hawaiian Tourism Society

This organization produces a weighty calendar of events with links to various Hawaiian organizations and activities.
https://www.gohawaii.com/cultural-events-in-hawaii

Indigenous Music Awards

This annual event held in Winnipeg, Manitoba, celebrates luminary Indigenous musicians.
https://www.Indigenousmusicawards.com/

MAMo: Maoli Arts Month

The PA'I Foundation, with partner Bishop Museum, sponsors a month-long celebration of Native Hawaiian arts, artists, and cultural practitioners every April. Programming features exhibitions, arts markets, trunk shows, and the extraordinary MAMo Wearable Art Show. MAMo can be experienced on the Hawai'i Island, Kaua'i, and Maui, nationally in Alaska, Minnesota, New York, Oregon, and Texas, and internationally in Austria, Germany, and Japan.
https://www.paifoundation.org/

Native American Festivals

From the National Indian Taco Championship in Pahuska, Oklahoma, to the Catawba Indian Nation Fall Craft Fair in Rock Hill, South Carolina, one can find a smorgasbord of Native festivals on this calendar.
https://www.everfest.com/cultural/native-american-festivals

Native American Music Awards (NAMA)

For over twenty years, NAMA has been held an annual celebration of Native music and performers.
https://www.nativeamericanmusicawards.com/home

Powwow Locator

Not only does this online resource provide an exhaustive calendar of powwows, but one can get live notices of powwow highlights on social media by just signing up. Articles and craft instructions are also featured.
http://www.powwows.com/

World Hoop Dancing Competition

The annual World Hoop Dancing Competition held in Phoenix, Arizona, showcases dancers from across the United States and Canada as they vie for the prestigious title of World Champion Hoop Dancer. Contestants are judged on five skills: precision, timing/rhythm, showmanship, creativeness, and speed.

http://heard.org/

SPORTS

Aboriginal Sport and Wellness Council of Ontario (ASWCO)

ASWCO sponsors the annual Masters Indigenous Games, a cultural feast for both participants and spectators alike. Traditional and nontraditional games offer adults an opportunity to compete in this exciting event. A key part of the gathering is a festival showcasing Indigenous artists, performers, storytellers, and vendors, as well as the Embody the Spirit Powwow.

http://mastersIndigenousgames.ca/about/about-the-games/

All Indian Rodeo Cowboys Association (AIRCA)

This is the oldest Indian Rodeo organization and sponsors competitions mainly in the Southwest.

http://www.aircarodeo.com/

Arctic Winter Games

This biannual competition attracts Indigenous northern and arctic athletes.

http://www.arcticwintergames.org/index.html

Duke's Ocean Fest

This August festival, held on the shores of Waikiki, commemorates Olympian Duke Kahanamoku's life, athletic contributions, and his "aloha" spirit. A variety of the Duke's beloved sports are featured: longboard surfing, paddleboard racing, swimming, tandem surfing, and stand-up paddling.

http://dukesoceanfest.com/

Ganondagan Native American Winter Games

Hosted annually by the Seneca in upstate New York, this event features games of snow snake, snow boat, and snow shoeing, along with craft workshops and traditional dancing.

http://ganondagan.org/Events-Programs/Native-American-Winter-Games-Sports

Indian Nationals Finals Rodeo

Rodeos are features throughout the United States and Canada, with the Nationals held in Las Vegas, Nevada.

https://www.infr.org/

Indian Relay Races

For almost two decades, Indian relay teams representing the "Horse Nations" across the northern Rockies and High Plains located in Idaho, Montana, North Dakota, South Dakota, Washington, Wyoming, and Canada have regaled fans across the country with this thrilling, dangerous sport.

The rules of Indian relay seem simple. Teams consist of one rider, one mugger, two holders, and three horses. There are no saddles or protective equipment. The rider speeds through the half-mile track of three laps, changing horses at the beginning of each lap, while the holders calm and ready the waiting horses. The mugger catches the arriving horse of the incoming rider as he dismounts and hops on the new horse. The races are anything but simple as the rider makes a perilous and rapid exchange of horses, bouncing from one horse to another. Paying tribute to their reverence for horses, horsemanship, and bravery, teams of men, women, and even children from seven different nations display their superb horsemanship and daring as they battle it out on the racetrack amid a throng of rearing horses and excited riders.

http://www.horsenationsrelay.com/

Lori Piestewa National Native American Games

Part of the Arizona Grand Canyon State Games, the Lori Piestewa National Native American Games is an intergenerational competition in seven different sports. Named for Piestewa (Hopi), the first Native woman to die in the military (Iraq 2003), participants vie for medals in basketball, baseball, cross country, softball, track & field, volleyball, and wrestling.

http://www.gcsg.org/events/nativegames/

Louis Tewanima Footrace

The Louis Tewanima Memorial Footrace is held annually on the Hopi reservation (Arizona) in honor of silver medalist Louis Tewanima, the first and only Hopi Olympian to represent the United States in the 1908 and 1912 Olympic Games. He set an American record for the 10,000-meter race in the 1912 Games that stood until broken by Billy Mills (Lakota) in 1964.

http://www.tewanimafootrace.org/

Native American Basketball Invitational (NABI)

This annual Basketball Tournament for Native youth, usually held in Arizona, is the largest of its kind. Along with seeing some stellar Native athletes, visitors are treated to Indian cultural events.

http://www.nabifoundation.org/

Native Youth Olympics

Every spring, hundreds of youth gather to compete in this three-day Olympian contest of Native games. It is held in Anchorage, Alaska, and although the events are

Indigenous to Alaska, junior and senior high competitors from all backgrounds can participate.
https://www.anchorage.net/winter/events/nyo-games/

NDN Sports

This online magazine, which is chocked full of all kinds of information and schedules about Indians in sports, was founded by Bert Cahwee (Pawnee/Euchee) and John Harjo (Muskogee Creek). Great resource for following favorite athletes and games.
http://www.ndnsports.com/

North American Indigenous Games

This multisport contest for youth and adults draws thousands of Native athletes who compete in sixteen summer sports events. Location and dates change.
http://www.naigcouncil.com/

Queen Liliuokalani Long Distance Canoe Races

For five days around Labor Day, these races have been held in Hawaii since 1971 and are the longest long-distance canoe race in the world. The women's and men's 18-mile (29-kilometer) races follow a historically and culturally significant course running between Kamakahonu Beach in Kailua Bay and Puuhonua O Honaunau National Historic Park. Double-hull canoe races, SUP races, OC1 and OC2 races, and teen long-distance races, accompany an interpretative walk through Kailua Village, International Paddlers Night, Paddling Talk Story, the Torch Light Parade, award ceremonies, and a traditional Hawaiian Luau.
https://www.qlcanoerace.com/

World Indian-Eskimo Olympics (WEIO)

WIEO preserves and promotes traditional Alaska Native cultures by holding this event every summer in Fairbanks, Alaska. In historic times, a variety of games were played to help hone skills needed to navigate the cold Arctic seas on fishing expeditions. Captains often attended these gaming events to scout for their crews. They selected those who were coordinated, agile, strong, and had remarkable endurance as they competed in events like the ear pull, knuckle hop, one-foot high-kick, and kneel jump. Today, WEIO features those contests and others, plus drumming, dancing, and singing.
https://www.weio.org/

NATIVE-OWNED MUSEUMS IN THE UNITED STATES

Abenaki Tribal Museum and Cultural Center

100 Grand Ave., Swanton, VT 05488
Accohannock Museum and Village
Accohannock Indian Tribe, Inc.
28380 Crisfield Marion Rd., Marion Station, MD 21838
http://www.indianwatertrails.com/village.html

Agua Caliente Cultural Museum
219 S. Palm Canyon Dr., Palm Springs, CA 92262
http://www.accmuseum.org/

Ah-Tah-Thi-Ki Museum
34725 West Boundary Rd., Big Cypress Seminole Indian Reservation, Clewiston, FL 33440
http://www.ahtahthiki.com/

Ak-Chin Him-Dak Eco Museum & Archives
47685 N. Eco-Museum Rd., Maricopa, AZ 85239
http://www.azcama.com/museums/akchin

Akwesasne Museum
321 State Route 37, Hogansburg, NY 13655-3114
http://www.akwesasneculturalcenter.org

Alutiiq Museum & Archaeological Repository
215 Mission Rd., #101, Kodiak, AK 99615
https://alutiiqmuseum.org/

Angel Decora Memorial Museum/Research Center
Winnebago Tribe of Nebraska
100 Bluff St., Winnebago, NE 68071
http://www.winnebagotribe.com/cultural_center.html

Aquinnah Wampanoag Indian Museum (operated by the Aquinnah Cultural Center)
35 Aquinnah Circle, Aquinnah, MA 02535
http://wampanoagtribe.net/Pages/Wampanoag_ACC/index

Arvid E. Miller Memorial Library Museum
N8510 Moh-He-Con-Nuck Rd., Bowler, WI 54416
http://mohican-nsn.gov/Departments/Library-Museum/

A:shiwi A:wan Museum & Heritage Center
Pueblo of Zuni
02 E Ojo Caliente Rd., Zuni, NM 87327
http://ggsc.wnmu.edu/mcf/museums/ashiwi.html

Ataloa Lodge Museum/Bacone College
2299 Old Bacone Rd., Muskogee, OK 74403
http://ataloa.bacone.edu/

Barona Cultural Center and Museum
1095 Barona Rd., Lakeside, CA 92040
http://www.baronamuseum.org/

Bernice Pauahi Bishop Museum
1525 Bernice St.
Honolulu, HI 96817
http://www.bishopmuseum.org/

Bois Forte Heritage Center
1500 Bois Forte Rd., Tower, MN 55790
http://www.boisforte.com/divisions/heritage_center.htm

Cabazon Cultural Museum
84245 Indio Springs Pkwy., Indio, CA 92203
http://www.fantasyspringsresort.com/prod/cbmi

Catawba Cultural Preservation Project
1536 Tom Stevens Rd., Rock Hill, SC 29730
http://www.ccppcrafts.com/

Cherokee Heritage Center
21192 S. Keeler Dr., Park Hill, OK 74451
http://www.cherokeeheritage.org/

Cheyenne Cultural Center, Inc.
22724 Route 66 N, Clinton, OK 73601

Cheyenne Indian Museum
1000 Tongue River Rd., Ashland, MT 59003
http://www.stlabre.org/

The Chickasaw Cultural Center
867 Cooper Memorial Dr., Sulphur, OK 73086
http://chickasawculturalcenter.com/

Chitimacha Museum
155 Chitimacha Loop, Charenton, LA 70523
http://www.chitimacha.gov

Chugach Museum & Institute of History & Art
560 E. 34th Ave., Anchorage, AK 99503-4196
www.chugachmuseum.org

The Citizen Potawatomi Nation Cultural Heritage Center
1899 S. Gordon Cooper Dr., Shawnee, OK 74801
http://www.potawatomi.org/culture/cultural-heritage-center

Colville Tribal Museum
512 Mead Way, Coulee Dam, WA 99116
http://www.colvilletribes.com/colville_tribal_museum.php

Comanche National Museum and Cultural Center
701 NW Ferris Ave. (behind McMahon Auditorium), Lawton, OK 73507
http://www.comanchemuseum.com/

Fond du Lac Cultural Center & Museum
1720 Big Lake Rd., Cloquet, MN 55720
http://www.fdlrez.com/%5C/Museum/index.htm

Fort Belknap Museum
269 Blackfeet Ave., Harlem, MT 59526

Garifuna Museum
1523 W. 48th St., Los Angeles, CA 90062
http://www.garifunamuseum.com/index.php

George W. Brown, Jr. Ojibwe Museum & Cultural Center
603 Peace Pipe Rd., Lac du Flambeau, WI 54538
http://www.ldfmuseum.com/

George W. Ogden Cultural Museum
Iowa Tribe of Kansas & Nebraska
3345 B Thrasher Rd., White Cloud, KS 66094

Hana Cultural Center & Museum
4974 Uakea Rd., Hana, HI 96713
http://hanaculturalcenter.org/

Harry V. Johnston, Jr. Lakota Cultural Center
Cheyenne River Sioux Tribe
2001 Main St., Eagle Butte, SD 57625
http://www.sioux.org

Hoo-hoogam Ki Museum
10005 E. Osborn Rd., Scottsdale, AZ 85256
http://www.srpmic-nsn.gov/history_culture/kimuseum.htm

Hoopa Valley Tribal Museum
CA-96, Hoopa, CA 95546
http://online.sfsu.edu/cals/hupa/Hoopa.HTM

Hopi Museum (Hopi Cultural Center, Inc.)
AZ-264, Second Mesa, AZ 86043
http://www.hopiculturalcenter.com/

Huhugam Heritage Center
4759 N. Maricopa Rd., Chandler, AZ 85226
http://www.huhugam.com

Huna Heritage Foundation
9301 Glacier Hwy., Juneau, AK 99801-9306
http://www.hunaheritage.org

The Indian Pueblo Cultural Center, Inc.
2401 12th St. NW, Albuquerque, NM
www.indianpueblo.org/

Inupiat Heritage Center
5421 North Star St., Barrow, AK 99723
http://inupiat.areaparks.com/

Ioloni Palace
364 S. King St., Honolulu, HI 96813
http://www.iolanipalace.org/

Kanza Museum
698 Grandview Dr., Kaw City, OK 74641
http://kawnation.com/?page_id=4188

Lenape Nation of Pennsylvania Cultural Center
342 Northampton St., Easton, PA 18042
https://sigalmuseum.org/tag/lenape-nation-of-pennsylvania-cultural-center/

Lummi Records & Archives Center & Museum
2665 Kwina Rd., Bellingham, WA 98226
http://www.lummi-nsn.org/website/dept_pages/culture/archives.shtml

The Makah Cultural & Research Center
Neah Bay, WA 98357
http://www.makah.com/mcrchome.htm

Mashantucket Pequot Museum & Research Center
110 Pequot Trail, Mashantucket, CT 06338-3180
http://www.pequotmuseum.org/MuseumInfo.aspx

Mashpee Wampanoag Indian Museum
414 Main St., Mashpee, MA 02649
http://www.mashpeewampanoagtribe.com/museum

Mille Lacs Indian Museum & Trading Post
43411 Oodena Dr., Onamia, MN 56359
http://www.mnhs.og/places/sites/mlim/

Monacan Ancestral Museum
2009 Kenmore Rd., Amherst, VA 24521
http://www.monacannation.com/museum.shtml

The Museum at Warm Springs
Native Paths Cultural Heritage Museum
3300 Beloved Path, Pensacola, FL 32507
http://www.perdidobaytribe.org/about/native-paths-heritage-museum-jones-swamp

The Museum of the Cherokee Indian
589 Tsali Blvd, Cherokee, NC 28719
https://www.cherokeemuseum.org/

Museum of Contemporary Native Arts
108 Cathedral Pl., Santa Fe, NM 87508
http://www.iaia.edu/museum/

Museum of the Plains Indian
124 2nd Ave. NW, Browning, MT 59417
http://www.browningmontana.com/museum.html

Navajo Nation Museum
Highway 264 and Loop Rd., Window Rock, AZ 86515
http://www.navajonationmuseum.org/

Nohwike' Bagowa-White Mountain Apache Cultural Center & Museum
Fort Apache, AZ 85926
http://www.wmat.nsn.us/wmaculture.html

Nottoway Indian Tribe of Virginia Community House & Interpretive Center
23186 Main St., Capron, VA
http://nottowayindians.org/interpretivecenter.html

Oneida Nation Museum
W892 County Highway EE, De Pere, WI 54155
http://www.oneidanation.org/museum/

Osage Tribal Museum
819 Grandview Ave., Pawhuska, OK 74056
http://www.osagetribalmuseum.com/

Pamunkey Indian Tribe Museum
175 Lay Landing Rd., King William, VA 23086
http://www.pamunkey.net/museum.html

Penobscot Indian Nation
12 Downstreet St., Indian Island, ME 04468
http://www.penobscotnation.org/museum/Index.htm

The People's Center
53253 Highway 93 W, Pablo, MT 59855
http://www.peoplescenter.org/

Poeh Museum and Cultural Center
78 Cities of Gold Rd., Santa Fe, NM 87506
poehcenter.org/

Ponca Tribal Museum
2548 Park Ave, Niobrara, NE 68760
http://www.poncatribe-ne.org/Museum

Potawatomi Cultural Center and Museum
1899 S. Gordon Cooper Dr., Shawnee, OK 74801
https://www.fcpotawatomi.com/culture-and-history/

Pueblo of Acoma Historic Preservation Office
Sky City Cultural Center
1-40, Exit 102, Acoma, NM 87034
http://www.puebloofacoma.org/Historic_Preservation.aspx

Quechan Tribal Museum
350 Picacho Rd., Winterhaven, CA 92283

Sac & Fox Nation of Missouri Tribal Museum
305 North Main St., Reserve, KS 66434
http://www.sacandfoxcasino.com/tribal-museum.html

San Carlos Apache Cultural Center
US-70 @ Milepost 272, Peridot, AZ 85542
http://www.sancarlosapache.com/San_Carlos_Culture_Center.htm

Seneca-Iroquois National Museum
814 Broad St., Salamanca, NY 14779
https://www.senecamuseum.org/Default.aspx

Shakes Island
Wrangell Cooperative Association
104 Lynch St., Wrangell, AK, 99929-1941
http://www.shakesisland.com/

Sheet'ka Kwaan Naa Kahidi Tribal Community House
456 Katlian St., Sitka, AK 99835
http://www.sitkatours.com/

Shinnecock Nation Cultural Center & Museum
100 Montauk Hwy., Southampton, NY 11968
http://www.shinnecockmuseum.com/

Shoshone Cultural Center
90 Ethete Rd., Fort Washakie, WY 82514
https://www.wyomingtourism.org/things-to-do/detail/Shoshone-Tribal-Cultural-Cen
ter/8475

Shoshone-Bannock Tribal Museum
I-15 Exit 80, Simplot Rd., Fort Hall ID, 83203

Sierra Mono Museum
33103 Road 228, North Fork, CA 93643
http://www.sierramonomuseum.org/

Simon Paneak Memorial Museum
Anaktuvuk Pass, AK 99721
http://www.north-slope.org/departments/inupiat-history-language-and-culture/
simon-paneak-memorial-museum/our-museum

Six Nations Indian Museum
1462 County Route 60, Onchiota, NY 12989
http://www.sixnationsindianmuseum.com

Skokomish Indian Tribe
80 N. Tribal Center Rd., Skokomish, WA 98584
http://www.skokomish.org/culture-and-history/

Southeast Alaska Indian Cultural Center, Inc.
8800 Heritage Center Dr., Anchorage, AK 99504
http://www.alaskanative.net/

Southern Ute Museum Cultural Center
77 Co. Rd. 517, Ignacio, CO 81137
http://www.succm.org/

Suquamish Museum
6861 NE South St., Suquamish, WA 98392
http://www.suquamishmuseum.org/

Tamástslikt Cultural Institute
47106 Wildhorse Blvd., Pendleton, OR 97801
http://www.tamastslikt.org/

Tantaquidgeon Museum
1819 Norwich New London Tpke., Uncasville, CT
http://www.mohegan.nsn.us/

Three Affiliated Tribes Museum, Inc.
404 Frontage Rd., New Town, ND 58763
http://www.mhanation.com/

Tigua Indian Cultural Center
305 Yaya Ln., El Paso, Texas 79907
http://visitelpasomissiontrail.com/explore/tigua-indian-cultural-center.html

The Upper Missouri Dakota & Nakoda Cultural Lifeway Center and Museum

Fort Peck Assiniboine & Sioux Indian Reservation
Poplar, MT 59255
http://www.fortpecktribes.org/crd/museum.htm

Ute Indian Museum

17253 Chipeta Dr., Montrose, CO 81401
http://www.coloradohistory.org/hist_sites/UteIndian/Ute_indian.htm

Walatowa Cultural and Visitor Center

7413 NM-4, Jemez Pueblo, NM 87024
http://www.jemezpueblo.com/

Waponahki Museum & Resource Center

59 Passamaquoddy Rd., Sipayik, Pleasant Point, MN 04667
http://www.wabanaki.com/museum.htm

Yakama Nation Museum

100 Spiel-yi Loop, Toppenish, WA 98948
http://www.yakamamuseum.com/

Yupiit Piciryarait Cultural Center

420 Chief Eddie Hoffman Hwy., Bethel, AK 99559
http://bethelculturalcenter.com/

Ziibiwing Center of Anishinabe Culture & Lifeways

6650 E. Broadway, Mt. Pleasant, MI 48858
http://www.sagchip.org/ziibiwing

POWWOW ETIQUETTE

Each powwow begins with the Grand Entry in which participants enter the sacred dance circle (arbor), dancing their particular styles to a song by the drummers and singers. Leaders of the Grand Entry are the flag bearers, carrying the American Flag, POW Flag, Eagle Staff (Native Flag), and the flags of participating Native nations. The flags are usually carried by Native veterans, who, despite the horrible treatment they have received by the U.S. government, still honor the American flag.

Led by elders, the men dancers usually enter in the same order: men's traditional dancers in their double-feather bustles and performing their high step moves; men's grass dancers in stunning outfits sporting long and flowing fringes, their movements similar to wind-blown tall grasses; and men's fancy dancers decked out in a vast array of colors. Elder women then lead in the women dancers: women's traditional dancers who move elegantly and slowly as one in their beautiful intricate regalia; Jingle dress dancers with their cloth dresses adorned with handmade tin cones, which jingle to their rhythmic buoyant steps; and fancy shawl dancers, twirling and stepping rapidly as their graceful, fringed shawls twirl along with them. Next are the teen boys, followed by teen girls, younger children, and tiny tots. The emcee announces each category as they enter. Visitors are asked to stand for the Grand Entry. When all are in the arena, the powwow grounds are blessed with a prayer and the veterans are honored in song.

Although most powwows are intertribal, many feature culturally specific activities like games, foods, special dances, performances, and music. Powwows may be public festivals, but they are Indian indeed, with a certain code of ethics that spectators must respect:

- Dress modestly and refrain from wearing tee shirts with profanity or lewd graphics. For some dances, the public is invited to participate—women are usually required to cover their shoulders with shawls, so it is best to take one along.
- Listen and follow the instructions of the emcee.

- Stand for Grand Entry and any honorings or prayers.
- Do not call any Indian clothing "costumes"; the preferred word is "regalia." And never touch anyone's regalia without asking permission.
- Seating next to the arena is reserved for drummers, singers, and dancers; visitors may bring their own chairs and sit in the designated area.
- Ask permission before taking pictures or recordings and never photograph prayers or other ceremonies.
- The powwow circle has been blessed; it is sacred and needs to be revered in the same way as any religious gathering place.
- No drugs, alcohol, or weapons allowed.
- Refrain from making disruptive noise.
- Spectators should enjoy themselves, but remember that for many participants the powwow is a way of earning money. It is also a serious time when participants, who may be marginalized from their own cultures in their daily lives, have opportunity to connect with their friends, family, and heritage. Show respect.

INDEX

(ill.) indicates photos and illustrations.

Index

Index

Index

Index

Index

Smith, Jaune Quick-to-See, 177

Smith, John, 7

Smith, Joseph, 89

Smithsonian Institution, 27

Smoky, Lois, 145, 148

Snohomish, 304, 309

Snoqualmie, 304, 309

Snunéymuxw First Nation, 386

Sockalexis, Louis, 10

Sogobia, Newe, 168, 169

Sonoran, 192

Soto, Hernando de, 81, 82

Southeast Alaska Indian Cultural Center (Sitka, AK), 282

Southeast Alaskan Natives, 277–78

Southeast United States, 41–43

Southern Arapaho, 144

Southern Cheyenne, 144

Southern Paiute, 200, 266

Southern Plains Indian Museum (Anadarko, OK), 144, 144 (ill.)

Southern Ute, 226

Southern Ute Museum (Ignacio, CO), 226

Southwest Indians, 59, 102

Southwest United States, 186–87

Spalding, Henry, 172

Spang, Bently, 177

Speed Art Museum (Louisville, KY), 63

Spiro Mounds Archaeological Center (Spiro, OK), 153

Squamish, 391

Squamish Lil'wat Cultural Centre (Whistler, BC), 391

Squanto, 16

Squaxin Island, 307

Squaxin Island Tribe Museum Library and Research Center (Shelton, WA), 307

St. Anne's Church and Tulalip Reserve (Marysville, WA), 303–4

St. George Mi'kmaq, 335

St. Joseph's Indian School (Chamberlain, SD), 160

St. Louis Art Museum (St. Louis, MO), 114 (ill.), 114–15

St. Stephens Church, School, and Museum (St. Stephens, WY), 186

Standing Bear, Henry, 161

Standing Bear Museum and Education Center (Ponca City, OK), 151

Standing Bear Park (Ponca City, OK), 152

Standing Bear Sculpture (Ponca City, OK), 152

Steamboat, 196

Steve Witt Memorial Annual Gathering of the People Powwow (Terre Haute, IN), 98–99

Stewart, John, 124–25

Stewart Indian School (Carson City, NV), 179, 179 (ill.)

Stillaguamish, 309

Stockbridge-Munsee Community Band of Mohican Indians, 125, 126

Stockbridge-Munsee Historical Library/Museum (Bowler, WI), 126

Stone, Shirlee, 109

Stoney, 361

Stoney Nakoda, 362

Strikes the Iron, 177

Suiattle, 309

Su-Meg Village at Patrick's Point State Park (Trinidad, CA), 296

Sun Watch Indian Village/Archaeological Park (Dayton, OH), 117

Suquamish, 307–8

Suquamish Museum and Chief Sealth (Seattle) Gravesite (Suquamish, WA), 307–9, 308 (ill.)

Swampy Cree, 373

Swan Creek, 104

T

Taga, 326

Tagish, 381

Tahlonteeskee, Chief, 146

Tahlonteeskee (Cherokee Courthouse) (Gore, OK), 146–47

Tahquitz Canyon (Palm Springs, CA), 293

Talayumptewa, Lisa, 193

Tama Intertribal Powwow (Whigham, GA), 61–62

Tamátslikt Cultural Institute (Pendleton, OR), 299–300

Tamaya (Santa Ana Pueblo, NM), 249–51

Tamayame, 250

Tantaquidgeon, John, 6

Tantaquidgeon Indian Museum (Uncasville, CT), 6, 6 (ill.)

Taos Pueblo (Taos, NM), 258 (ill.), 258–59

Taylor, William S., 25

Tecumseh, 96, 116–17

Tecumseh Outdoor Drama (Chillicothe, OH), 116–17

Tekakwitha, Kateri, 22–23, 355

Tenskwatawa (the Prophet), 96

Teslin Tlingit, 380–81

Teslin Tlingit Heritage Centre (Teslin, YT), 380 (ill.), 380–81

Tewa, 208

Thanksgiving, 16

Thaw, Eugene and Clare, 21

Thomas, Jeffrey, 350

Thomas, Roy, 352

U

Index

X, Y

Z